David Bagot is Lecturer in History and Politics at Newcastle-under-Lyme College. Bagot wrote a doctoral thesis entitled 'State and Aristocracy in the Sasanian Empire' and completed his PhD at the University of St Andrews in 2015.

Margaux Whiskin is Senior Teaching Fellow in French at the University of Warwick. Her areas of interest are Cross-Cultural Studies and Comparative Literature during the long eighteenth century and World War I. She is the author of *Narrative Structure and Philosophical Debates in Tristram Shandy and Jacques le Fataliste* (2014) and 'Caricature of a British Gentleman, Portrait of a French Soldier: Humour and Nationality in André Maurois' *Les Silences du Colonel Bramble*', in Nicolas Bianchi and Toby Garfitt (eds), *Writing the Great War: Francophone and Anglophone Poetics* (2017).

'This is an important collection of essays which explores multiple expressions of cultural interaction between Iran and the West from Antiquity to the present. It introduces new perspectives on this complex relationship as well as reflecting current modes of thought and interpretation.'

Tim Greenwood, Senior Lecturer and
Director of the Institute of Iranian Studies,
University of St Andrews

IRAN AND THE WEST

Cultural Perceptions from the Sasanian Empire to the Islamic Republic

Edited by

David Bagot and Margaux Whiskin

I.B. TAURIS
LONDON · NEW YORK

Published in 2018 by
I.B.Tauris & Co. Ltd
London • New York
www.ibtauris.com

International Library of Iranian Studies 42

ISBN: 978 1 78453 856 9
eISBN: 978 1 78672 395 6
ePDF: 978 1 78673 395 5

A full CIP record for this book is available from the British Library
A full CIP record is available from the Library of Congress

Library of Congress Catalog Card Number: available

Typeset in Garamond Three by OKS Prepress Services, Chennai, India
Printed and bound by CPI Group (UK) Ltd, Croydon, CR0 4YY

FSC
www.fsc.org
MIX
Paper from
responsible sources
FSC® C013604

Dedicated to the memory of Gladys Davis and Léontine Moineau

CONTENTS

ACKNOWLEDGEMENTS

We are very much indebted to Professor Ali M. Ansari who has very kindly supported us throughout this project and has graced the present volume by writing its foreword. We would also like to thank Françoise Delignon from Radio France Internationale and Kate Courage from the University of Warwick for having directed us towards helpful media sources. Sue Dibben from the Humanities Research Centre has played a key role in helping us sow the seeds, of which this volume is the fruit. We owe much to Sylvia Howell and Marion Imber who have offered unwavering administrative and moral support. Our thanks also go to the team at I.B.Tauris who have very patiently helped and guided us through the editing process. Last but not least, we would like to thank our parents, Janet Bagot and Keith Whiskin who have kindly accepted to do some of the proofreading and, more importantly, have always been willing to listen to our ideas and to discuss them with us.

David Bagot (Newcastle-Under-Lyme College)
Margaux Whiskin (University of Warwick)

LIST OF FIGURES

CONTRIBUTORS

Ali M. Ansari is Professor of Iranian History and founding director of the Institute of Iranian Studies at the University of St Andrews. He is the author of *The Politics of Nationalism in Modern Iran*. In 2016 he was elected a Fellow of the Royal Society of Edinburgh.

Maryam Aras is a PhD candidate in Iranian/Islamic Studies at the University of Bonn. She received her MA in Oriental Studies, Political Science and North American Studies from the University of Cologne and has published and taught on modern Iranian history and politics, the Iranian diaspora, culture and gender studies. In her dissertation, Aras focuses on the Shi'i singing genre *madh* and its political dimension in contemporary Iran. Beside her academic interests, Aras works as a literary journalist for West German Public Radio and online media, covering especially diasporic literature and Iranian women's writing.

Amir Ahmadi Arian is Assistant Professor of Literature and Creative Writing at City College, New York. He completed his PhD in Comparative Literature at the University of Queensland (Australia), and an MFA in Creative Writing at New York University. He has published novels and short stories in Farsi, and academic articles and essays in English.

David Bagot is Lecturer in History and Politics at Newcastle-under-Lyme College. Bagot wrote a doctoral thesis entitled 'State and Aristocracy in the Sasanian Empire' and completed his PhD at the University of St Andrews in 2015.

Ali Beh-Pajooh gained his BA and MA in Sociology from the University of Tehran, and is a PhD candidate at the Graduate School of Economics and Social Sciences at the University of Hamburg. His main research interests include Iranian Studies, Sociology of Literature and Cultural Studies focused on popular film and literature. He is currently working on his PhD thesis entitled 'A Sociological Study of the Rise of the Novel in Iran'. He has been a professional journalist and a part-time book editor in Iran.

Roxanne Ellen Bibizadeh is a Research Assistant for the ESRC IAA-funded project 'Digital Wildfires: Mediation and Responsible Citizenship in the Digital Age'. Her personal research focuses on Literature of the Iranian and Arab Diaspora, for which she is currently completing her PhD. She won the Warwick Awards for Teaching Excellence in 2013–14 and was awarded an Academic Fellowship with the Institute for Advanced Teaching and Learning to create and convene an interdisciplinary module in 2015–16. For more information on her research or teaching, please visit her websites:
www.warwick.ac.uk/rebibizadeh and www.roxannebibizadeh.com.

Laleh Gomari-Luksch is a Friedrich-Ebert Foundation scholar researching Iran's foreign policy at the University of St Andrews in the UK and the University of Tübingen in Germany. She holds a master's degree in Peace Research and International Politics from the University of Tübingen and a bachelor's degree in International Studies major in European Studies from De La Salle University Manila, Philippines. She has co-authored a publication entitled 'An Eye for An Eye: Bargaining Theory, Mistrust and the Iranian Nuclear Crisis' in *Iran, die Bombe und das Streben nach Sicherheit (Iran, the Bomb and the Pursuit of Security)* (2014). She has recently completed her PhD thesis entitled 'Realism, Rationalism and Revolutionism in Iran's Foreign Policy: The West, the State and Islam'.

Leonardo Gregoratti was educated at the Universities of Udine (Italy) and Trier (Germany). He has conducted research in Udine, Trier, Kiel and Bergen. Since 2013 he collaborates with the University of Durham (UK). His research interests include Roman History and Epigraphy and the history of Western Asia, in particular the Roman Near East, Palmyra, the long-distance trade and the Parthian Kingdom.

Negar Habibi is an art historian and lecturer in Islamic Art History at the University of Geneva, Switzerland. Her research interests are Persian painting, the artists' careers and artistic patronage in pre-modern and modern Iran. She is also interested in gender issues in the artistic creations of the Iranian world. She has published several articles and a book, *ʿAli Qoli Jebādār et l'Occidentalisme Safavide, Une étude sur les peintures dites* farangi sāzi, *leurs milieux et commanditaires sous Shāh Soleimān (1666–94)* (2017).

Andrew Knapp is Emeritus Professor of French Politics and Contemporary History at the University of Reading. Having accompanied his father, a Middle East specialist at the University of Oxford, to Iran three times in his boyhood and youth, he became a British Council teacher of English in Isfahan in September 1976. He left Isfahan in summer 1978, six months before the Islamic Revolution.

Elham Malekzadeh has a PhD in contemporary history of Iran and is Assistant Professor at the Institute for Humanities & Cultural Studies (IHCS). Her field of research includes Social Studies, Women Studies and the correction of manuscripts and documents in contemporary Iran.

Her complete résumé is available at http://www.ihcs.ac.ir/Pages/Features/StaticPage.aspx?id=185.

Annie Pfeifer is Assistant Professor of German Studies at Tufts University in Boston, Massachusetts. Her research interests include nineteenth- and twentieth-century German and comparative literature, with a special interest in critical theory, political theory, aesthetics, and visual and material culture. She is currently completing her book manuscript on modernist practices of collecting. Her articles have appeared in the *New German Critique*, *German Life and Letters*, the collected volume *Que(e)rying Consent* as well as the opinion section of the *New York Times*.

Birgit Röder has researched widely into German Romanticism and the relationship between Islamic and German culture in the eighteenth and nineteenth centuries. She is the author of *E.T.A. Hoffmann. A Study of the Major Novellas* (2003).

Ali Sadidi Heris is a PhD student in Film at the University of Southampton. His research focuses on filmic cultures, national cinemas, minority and local filmmaking with a main interest in Iran. He has published articles in Turkish and English.

George Sanikidze is Professor at the Ilia State University, Georgia, and Director of the Institute of Oriental Studies at the same university. As a visiting scholar, he has worked at UC Berkeley, Paris–Sorbonne IV,

Hokkaido and Osaka universities. His research topics are: the history and politics of Middle Eastern countries (especially Iran), Iranian–Caucasian interactions, Islam and Islamic radicalism.

Giulia Valsecchi received her PhD in Intercultural Humanistic Studies at the University of Bergamo in 2017 and has been granted the printing dignity for her thesis, 'Identities in transit: quests of self-rewriting in Iranian–American women's memoirs and narratives'. Her research interests focus on literature by women of the Iranian Diaspora and, in particular, on the relationship between the concepts of dramatisation and in-betweenness. After graduating in Literature at the University of Milan (2004), she completed a three-year diploma in playwrighting at Civica Scuola di Teatro Paolo Grassi in Milan (2007), then worked as a playwright in several theatrical projects and performances. She has written a literary guide to the city of Istanbul, *Istanbul. Dalla finestra di Pamuk* (2010) and an essay on Middle Eastern women's culinary precepts, 'Cosa dicono le foglie del tè? Riti e ricette di madre in figlia dalla letteratura persiana alla poesia araba contemporanea' (2013).

Margaux Whiskin is Senior Teaching Fellow in French at the University of Warwick. Her areas of interest are Cross-Cultural Studies and Comparative Literature during the long eighteenth century and World War I. She is the author of *Narrative Structure and Philosophical Debates in Tristram Shandy and Jacques le Fataliste* (2014) and 'Caricature of a British Gentleman, Portrait of a French Soldier: Humour and Nationality in André Maurois' *Les Silences du Colonel Bramble*', in Nicolas Bianchi and Toby Garfitt (eds), *Writing the Great War: Francophone and Anglophone Poetics* (2017).

Lydia Wytenbroek is currently completing her doctorate degree in History at York University in Toronto, Canada. Her current research focuses on professional nursing and mission medicine in Iran. She is also a practising Registered Nurse.

Nina Zandjani is a doctoral research fellow and translator, writing her PhD thesis on 'Hidden meanings – Figurative language and paratexts in German translations of *Golestân (The Rose Garden)* by Sa'di' at the University of Oslo, where she has been teaching Persian language and literature at the Department of Culture Studies and Oriental Languages. Among her Norwegian translations from Persian are: Saadi's *Gulistan* and *Bustan*; novels by Simin Daneshvar, Mahmoud Dowlatabadi, Zoya Pirzad and Fariba Vafi; and poems by Abbas Kiarostami and Asieh Amini.

FOREWORD

Ali M. Ansari

Few relationships have been more systematically misunderstood than that of Iran's with the West. Indeed, the narrative has become so dominated by political myth from a range of ideological denominations that it can be a struggle to discover the 'history' behind the ideological headlines, and the subtleties of a relationship that has spanned centuries if not millennia remain shrouded behind the broad-brush strokes of ideological determination and simplicity. That is not to deny the very real difficulties of a relationship that in modern times at least, has been shaped by the vagaries and, one might add, inconsistencies, of Western imperialism, not least the coup against Dr Mohammad Mosaddeq in 1953 – an event which by all accounts flew in the face of Western protestations about the promotion of democracy. But it also remains problematic to see all Iran's relations with the West refracted through this single, albeit traumatic, event.

The fact that the Russians, for example, are largely exonerated of any guilt from their own imperial engagement with Iran in the last two centuries – an engagement which any objective historical assessment would likely conclude was more damaging to Iran's sovereign interests – is evidence of the reality that the relentless opprobrium heaped on the West has as much to do with ideological sentiment and political expediency as it does with historical objectivity. Project the frame of reference further back beyond 1953 for example and one can already detect the signs of a more sympathetic relationship, with both the United States and perhaps more surprisingly, Great Britain. Iranian statesmen projected strong pro-British sympathies for much of the nineteenth century, not only because they contrasted British ambitions favourably with those of Russia in the north, but perhaps more intriguingly, because they were attracted to British political ideals, even if they frequently complained at the British failure to live up to those ideals.

But the evidence clearly indicates a strong Anglophile strand among Iranian intellectuals which was practically realised during the Constitutional Revolution, when the revolutionaries refused any mediation with the Iranian government other than through the trusted intermediaries of the British Embassy.[1] Such a situation would no doubt astonish many Iranians today but an appreciation of the intimate nature of relations and Iranian aspirations and sympathies towards political ideals espoused by the British, go a long way in explaining both the affinity and the sense of betrayal that arose as a result of these ideals being sacrificed to interest and political expediency. The contradictions between the vagaries of policy and the attractions of political philosophy lie at the heart of the often-contradictory feelings held by Iranians towards the British and the West in general.

As for the Western appreciation of Iran or, more accurately, 'Persia', these too are riven with contradictions born perhaps of a deeper historical relationship drawn from the Greco–Roman encounter with the ancient Persian empires, that through the histories of Herodotus, places Persia and Persians very firmly within the foundation myth of the 'West'. Indeed it would not be an exaggeration to argue that the Persians were present at the birth of the West and, perhaps more evocatively, were an essential ingredient in the crystallisation of the *idea* of the West. The Greeks defined the perceived excellence of their civilisation against the failings of the Persians in part to explain their remarkable victories against their existential foes, in battles that are commemorated to this day (most obviously the Battle of Marathon), as defining moments in the emergence of a distinctive Western civilisation. But the antagonism they represent is of course but one aspect of a relationship that was far more respectful than subsequent narrators – and myth makers – would have us believe. Indeed as some have argued, it would not be remiss to view the Greeks as having operated within a broader *Pax Persica* from which they drew inspiration as well as in their own eyes, competitive advantage.[2] Indeed, as this volume admirably advances, Iran's relationship with the 'West', is as nuanced and interesting as that of the West with 'Persia'.

Men are disturbed, not by things, but by the principles and notions which they form concerning things.

Epictetus, *The Enchiridion*

INTRODUCTION

Margaux Whiskin

Misremembering Thermopylae

> The interest of the world's history hung trembling in the balance. Oriental despotism, a world united under one lord and sovereign, on the one side, and separate states, insignificant in extent and resources, but animated by free individuality, on the other side, stood front to front in array of battle. Never in history has the superiority of spiritual power over material bulk, and that of no contemptible amount, been made so gloriously manifested.[1]

On the one side Persia, on the other side the Hellenistic world, on the one side despotism, on the other side democracy. For Hegel, the Greco–Persian wars placed the world on the cusp between two opposite visions of man. The stakes were less about territorial dominion than a conception of the individual and his/her place within the State. Far from offering a new insight, the *Lectures on the Philosophy of History* carried on the tradition of mythologising the Greco–Persian wars, which has, as its founding narratives, Aeschylus' play *The Persians* and Herodotus' *Histories*.

Aeschylus' tragedy, *The Persians*, first performed in 472 BC, focuses on the defeat of Xerxes' navy at Salamis eight years earlier in 480 BC, a memory still raw in the minds of its first audience.[2] As for Hegel, the polarisation of Greeks and Persians structures the play. Democracy and despotism are not just two opposing modes of government, they are also two opposing identities. As Kantzios reminds us, this is less about historical accuracy as about perceptions of the Other and the Self.[3] The second founding text is Herodotus' *Histories*, which despite having been written slightly later (*c.*440 BC) is likely to have had a wider readership, with approximately 44 editions and translations in Europe between 1450 and 1700.[4] The *Histories* largely focus on the Greco–Persian wars and also play on the same polarisation as in *The Persians*.

Both Aeschylus and Herodotus are writing with an agenda. As Kantzios points out, Aeschylus is not so much showing how the Athenians behaved eight years ago, as how they should behave if another Persian invasion of Greece were to occur, which at the time seemed a distinct possibility.[5] The possibility of future Persian expansionist projects in the Mediterranean and the preservation of democracy were concerns Herodotus also shared.[6] The fact that Aeschylus and Herodotus had a point to make and were likely to have shared to a greater or lesser extent the prejudices of their own time, explains the starkness of the Greek–Persian polarisation, a starkness both authors temper by incorporating nuances in their approaches, which have often been ignored or overlooked.

In both texts, the dominant presence of Xerxes leads to a confusion between the character of the individual and that of his people or a model of government. As Kantzios puts it, 'is the behavior of Xerxes typical of absolute monarchy or simply a by-product of his own aberrant character?'[7] The presence of Darius in Aeschylus' play provides a clue to that question. Unlike his son Xerxes, Darius appears 'as a wise leader, respectful of the gods, and aware of human limitations.'[8] Yet, Kantzios doubts the Athenian audience of 472 BC would have been convinced, as they would have been aware of striking parallels between the conduct of the father and that of the son during the Greco–Persian wars. In the *Histories*, it is Cyrus the wise ruler who acts as Xerxes' opposite. Another nuance to the Greek–Persian polarisation is Aeschylus' treatment of the chorus representing the Persian people and queen, who have been portrayed sympathetically.[9] In the *Histories*, Xerxes, who is one of the most developed historical figures in the narrative, is depicted as cruel, full of hubris and lust, respecting neither the gods nor family ties. However, Flower argues that according to Herodotus, far from being representative of Persian behaviour, Xerxes blatantly goes against the Persian code of conduct and his behaviour is un-Persian. Even then, Xerxes' portrayal by Herodotus does not correspond to that of the pure villain, as exemplified by the tears he sheds when reflecting on the brevity of life of his soldiers.[10] As with Aeschylus, Herodotus offers a portrayal of the Persians more nuanced than might have been expected. Persian cruelty versus Greek humanity is disturbed on several occasions, one of these being instances of impalement and crucifixion, considered to be Persian practices and consequently not the Greek way of doing things.[11]

As Flower argues, the *Histories* challenge mono-dimensional representations of the Greeks and the Persians rather than entrenching them, which owed the author Plutarch's accusation of partiality in *On the Malignity of Herodotus*, not towards the Greeks, but towards the barbarians.[12] Herodotus' desire to bring forth a just account provides the opening of the *Histories*:

> This is the display of the inquiry of Herodotus of Halicarnassus, so that things done by man not be forgotten in time, and that great and marvellous deeds, some displayed by the Hellenes, some by the barbarians, not lose their glory, including among others what was the cause of their waging war on each other.[13]

Vasunia comments on the significance of Halicarnassus, a town on the frontier of the Persian Empire and the Greek world, a cultural crossroad where the two would have intermingled.[14] Thus, this 'powerful opening sentence, through a highly compressed use of language, opens out onto a tension that remains palpable and real, a tension between identity found on a plural understanding of culture and identity based on polarity'.[15]

An important caveat, however, is that, if the Greco–Persian wars along with the *Histories* and *The Persians* were perceived as fundamental by the West, this was not so for Iran where this memory seems to have been of lesser importance. The *Shahnameh*, Iran's national narrative, was 'seen as the repository of a quintessential "Iranian-ness" or "Persian-ness", which cannot be found elsewhere.'[16] Yet Bulliet remarks that in this text the Iranian gaze is turned towards Mesopotamia's lowlands instead of towards the Mediterranean.[17] Europe's attention was unreciprocated by Iran, more interested in its Muslim neighbours.

Despite the lack of perfect reciprocity, going back to these founding narratives is essential in a volume such as this, as they have arguably provided a frame through which to view the relationship between Iran and the West. They also lend a certain authority to anyone claiming them. Yet, more often than not, this authority has been usurped. This frame has led to a betrayal of the texts themselves as these have been reshaped according to the message to be conveyed. Snyder's film *300* (2006) is a case in point of the recycling of the founding narratives and their remodelling to fit a contemporary context. References to the classics have given a problematic legitimacy to this type of production which relies on the blurring between fact and fiction, education and entertainment. But as Tyma warns, what is also being blurred is what exactly is being taught:

> When these texts are presented, audiences are placed in the position of *learner* in addition to *consumer*. The movie becomes a pedagogical vehicle, not only entertaining the audience but also, because of the credence provided vis-à-vis the co-opted historical event, establishing new mythologies via the themes that are offered as *truths*.[18]

Under the entertaining instruction about the battle of Thermopylae lurks what is actually to be learnt, that is to say a set of hegemonic discourses to be adopted by the viewer. Snyder defended his film against accusations of ideological undertones:

> [W]hen I see someone use words like 'neocon[servative]', 'homophobic', 'homoerotic' or 'racist' in their review [of *300*], I kind of just think they don't get the film and don't understand. It's a graphic novel film about a bunch of guys that are stomping the snot out of each other. As soon as you start to frame it like that, it becomes clear that you've missed the point entirely.[19]

Murray supports Snyder's position by echoing his claim that the film is pure entertainment, yet there still seems to be a case of discrepancy between authorial intentionality and audience reception. Snyder has underestimated the function of the epimythium, in which the messenger delivers the message of the film. The ending of *300* functions in the same way as the ending of a fable in which the didactic purpose of its story is delivered. Through the mention of 'countless stories yet to be', the distance between past and present has been bridged and the audience is called upon to remember the Spartans and the day '[they] [rescued] a world from mysticism and tyranny and [ushered] in a future brighter than anything [they] [could] imagine.'[20] The spectator is encouraged to join the ranks and continue the fight.

Snyder's *300* illustrates how founding texts and events have been conveniently remembered, misremembered and forgotten so as to fit with the geopolitical context of the time and how they have infiltrated even the most popular levels of culture. From the fifth century BC to the present day, perceptions of Iran and the West have of course evolved, yet they rely on the same mechanisms of polarisation. The artificiality of this construct hides beneath the small fig leaf of history in an attempt to legitimise it whilst at the same time chiming with the essentialist notion that one has just to look back in history to see that nothing has changed. But whether we like it or not, tradition is an artificial construct:

> the traditions we inherit are not 'simply a permanent precondition,' one that would require us to devise proper methodologies to sift them out in the process of interpretation. Instead, we 'determine' tradition and contribute to its 'evolution,' in the act of interpreting and understanding.[21]

In periods of upheaval, the illusion of permanence is understandably comforting. In 1971, the Shah himself celebrated the 2,500 year-old Persian monarchy in the vain hope that it would live 2,500 years more.

Ultimately, perceptions of Self and Other is an attempt to pin identity down. This would explain why a plethora of other binary oppositions have been grafted to it: democratic–undemocratic, backward–progressive, modern–traditional, civilised–uncivilised, which are as many adjectives to qualify the Self and the Other, for, as Farneti signals, '[talk] of identity [. . .] bears an inherently polar structure'.[22] In order to capture this elusive identity, it has to be embodied so as to correspond to a concrete reality, specific sets of attributes and a tangible geography.

The East–West Dichotomy

The East–West dichotomy is today viewed with suspicion in academic circles, if not completely discredited. Its seemingly basic geographic divide is undermined by a vast array of other parameters just as vaguely defined and often contradictory.[23] As El Amine remarks, 'it is almost impossible to know where to draw the line between East and West in the first place'.[24] For the West, the Orient is a jumble of exoticism, despotism, spiritual roots, a land to be dominated, the hornets' nest of fundamentalism. For the East, perceptions of the West are just as conflicted. It is a model to follow, whether politically or scientifically, but also a colonialist and intolerant force.[25] The East–West dichotomy promises a clean and clear-cut categorisation, but this is one it simply cannot deliver. As Moaddel remarks, '[the] traditional perspective presumes that a belief system is a hierarchically organized set of values and normative rules of behaviour. In reality, citizens adhere to contradictory values.'[26] For Moaddel, far from being deplored, such contradictions are to be embraced as they help to ward off the type of 'monistic belief system' favoured by authoritarian states.[27]

The East–West dichotomy falls in the category of those traditional perspectives Moaddel describes. At first glance, its division appears reassuringly straightforward, but it does not take long before the contradictions with which it is riddled start surfacing. When viewed mainly as a Western construct, this dichotomy traces back its origin to the emergence of the West as the dominant world power and, on this basis, is dated back to European colonialism.[28] This dating would not undermine the pertinence of the present volume, for even though Iran was not actually under colonial rule, its twentieth-century history was written under the sign of British and American intervention. Yet, making the East–West dichotomy coincide with European empires in the late modern period is problematic. By using colonialism as the main frame, our understanding of the dichotomy has been both orientated and limited. Nor should the centrality of religion in current international relations mislead us into thinking that the relationship between Islam and Christianity started the East–West dichotomy. By not narrowing perceptions to a specific time frame, the editors of the present volume hope to show other ways in which these encounters were seen.

Using Iran and the West as the case study allows us to question the highly loaded East–West dichotomy. By focussing on Iran and opting for a diachronic approach, this volume arguably traces back the perceived genealogy of the East–West dichotomy and examines the recycling of its narratives and their adaptation to changing circumstances. What is important is how specific events and narratives were perceived as central to the founding of the East–West dichotomy and how they have shaped our way of understanding it, rather than actually being at its origin, a claim that would be very hard to make as we have reached the borderline between history and myth. As with all myths, the original event or narrative becomes less and less visible through the transmission process. Referring back to Baudrillard's *Simulations*, Tyma states that,

> [as] the stories are passed on, [. . .] the distancing between the discourse and the original source becomes greater and greater, developing layer upon layer of simulation-as-sediment until only the simulacra is accepted as original, subsuming the original discourse – the origin of the mythology – within itself.[29]

Our task now is to peel back the layers in order to compare the original narrative to its subsequent versions.

However problematic – even sometimes unsavoury – the East–West dichotomy may be, it remains a tool of thought still very much in use, including in the present volume. Despite its imperfections, it is an attempt to understand who we are and our place in the world. Recognising this dichotomy for what it is, instead of simply rejecting it completely, allows us to question it, to reveal its limits and hopefully to reach a fuller answer. In this, I very much follow Arnason's position: 'This ongoing deconstruction of a traditional problematic seems more fruitful than attempts to discard it *en bloc*, in the name of indiscriminate emphasis on cultural diversity and connectivity at the same time.'[30]

Methodology

The present volume deals with perceptions of Iran and Iranians by the West and perceptions of the West and Westerners by Iran from the Antiquity with the Parthians and the Sasanians to the present day with the Islamic Republic. Through an interdisciplinary approach and a broad timescale, the volume brings out patterns appearing throughout various disciplines and the evolution of these perceptions shifting according to the circumstances of the time. The study of perceptions is by definition subjective, yet is instrumental in understanding actual interactions, since perceptions shape our actions whether it be towards another person or another country. The volume looks at perceptions both at the level of the State and the individual. These may coincide, sometimes through a top-down manipulation, but they may also clash. The study of perceptions of Iran and the West has mainly been conducted through the lens of International Relations, with currently a focus on the impact of Iran's and the United States' image on the shaping of diplomatic relations between the two states, especially in the context of Iran's nuclear programme.[31] However, these works centre more on the impact of perceptions than on the way these perceptions have come into being.

If many studies focus on the West's perception of Iran, critics such as Ansari et al., Bakhshandeh and Amanat and Vejdani et al. have successfully redressed the imbalance. Bakhshandeh examines the negative perception of the West by Iran and its relation to the Iranian media and goes back to the Qajar period to explain the rise of Occidentalism in Iran.[32] Ansari et al. and Amanat and Vejdani et al., who focus on the construction of Iranian identity, take a much broader historical and disciplinary perspective.[33] Ansari et al. explore the impact of encounters with the West in the forging of Iranian national identity, whilst Amanat and Vejdani et al. examine the construction of Iranian identity through Iran's perceptions of the Other, whether this be a foreigner or a community within Iran, such as the Baha'i, perceived as outside this identity. National identity is a process constantly evolving and yet it claims some sort of permanence by anchoring its origins in a mythologised past. At its core is a narrative, presented as fixed but continuously being adjusted, which permeates all cultural areas, whether they be politics or literature, history or the arts, so as to be integrated by the individual. A multi-disciplinary approach combining a perspective both diachronic (to understand the evolution) and synchronic (to understand why the evolution has occurred) is thus necessary to examine national identity as a construct. This is also the approach adopted in the present volume. Like identity, perceptions of the Other are a construct claiming legitimacy through the past. As Davis remarks, 'the assumption is that we are what the past bestows upon us and constrains us to be, and the past is used to validate the ways in which we conceive of our identity vis-à-vis those who, we claim, do not share it.'[34] Often based on essentialist principles, perceptions claim a certain level of permanence whilst adapting to changing circumstances.

Perceptions of the Other play a fundamental role in the understanding of the Self and this is a recurring theme in many of the chapters. The direction of the present volume is not, however, to assess how perceptions of the Other have had an impact on the sense of Self in Iran and the West, especially as in the case of Iran this has already been done by Ansari et al. and Amanat and Vejdani et al. Instead, the focus of this book is to explore the way perceptions are shaped at both the level of the State and of the individual, the way they are legitimised, the way they adapt to changing geopolitical and cultural circumstances, the way they recycle recurring patterns and the way and reasons why they are used. Saying that current relations between Iran and the West are greatly suffering from negative perceptions of each other is merely stating the obvious. Nevertheless, objectively understanding the mechanism and origins of these very subjective perceptions is one step towards the possibility of a shift of position.

The methodological approach often adopted in works dealing with the issue is to focus on either Iranian perceptions of the West or Western perceptions of Iran.[35] The present volume takes on instead a cross-cultural approach. By looking at the reciprocity of these perceptions, it brings to light similarities in the way perceptions are constructed and used, whilst also showing that founding events are not necessarily shared. The resonance of the Greco–Persian wars is a case in point. Even if Iran and the West do not always share the same founding narratives, and despite differences existing between the West and Iran in the way perceptions of the Other are elaborated, there are also striking similarities as several of our contributors make clear. In these perceptions, the Other, whether Western or Iranian, becomes the mirror or counter-mirror reflecting the Self.[36] Cross-culturalism also provides a framework in which to make sense of the hybridity of those individuals (such as expatriates and those with dual nationalities) or states (in particular those who are geographically speaking on the borderline) who are in-between and escape categorisation.

The broad time scale of the volume participates in the questioning of the East–West dichotomy. Today seen as both a symptom and an extension of imperialism, the East–West dichotomy takes on a different significance when applied to periods preceding European colonialism. Bakhshandeh amalgamates the West with the United States and anti-Westernism with anti-Americanism, and this is justified by his focus on the twentieth and twenty-first century.[37] The broad chronology of the present volume makes a narrowing down of the West to a particular country seem an oversimplification, especially as the boundaries between East and West have themselves been subject to flux. Georgia and Romania are today perceived as Western countries, yet their relations with tsarist and Soviet Russia, the Ottoman Empire and Iran itself have placed them in the past in the other camp.

Perhaps inevitably because of the artificiality of such a frame, Iran itself sits uncomfortably in the East–West dichotomy. This is clearly expressed in the revolutionary slogan 'neither East nor West' through which Iran proclaimed its refusal to align with the American or Soviet model. For Iran, the East–West dichotomy inscribes itself into the broader Iran versus *Aniran* (non-Iran) dichotomy and the wider national narrative of invasion and struggle to preserve its own identity.[38] Far from being set on a constant hard-and-fast opposition between two sets of cultures and identities, the story of Iran and the West's relations has also been one of mutual self-recognition through the other. Under the Qajars and up to the Pahlavis, the elite and intellectuals turned to the European model to reinvigorate Iranian society, perceived as being in decline. They also echoed the problematic Orientalist notion that Iran's history had emerged from the rubble of the past and been saved from oblivion thanks to the works of Western historians.[39] Iranian intellectuals perceived that the threat to Iran's sense of self came less from the West than from the Arab heritage.[40] The emphasis on the distinctness of Iranian identity was not at this stage opposed to the Western model, it

> was essentially a construct forged against an Arab nemesis. It implied a sense of resentment not only towards the seventh century Arab conquest and imposition of Islam as an alien religion but toward the neighboring Arab countries of the region.[41]

After World War II and especially with the toppling of Mosaddeq, Iranians' perception of the West radically changed, as it now was synonymous with interference, manipulation and exploitation.[42] This shift in perceptions of the West corresponded to a shift in Iran's perception of itself. It focussed less on its past prior to the Arab conquest and instead re-embraced fully its Islamic heritage. As for the West, it sought itself in Iran, perceived as the origin of its own civilisation with Aryanism, however misguided this notion may be, as the umbilical cord linking the two.[43] Conversely, intellectuals in Iran recycled the idea of Aryanism for their own purpose as it placed on a racial level the distinction between Iranians (Aryans) and Arabs (Semites).[44]

Structure

The present volume has purposefully avoided perpetuating the problematic East–West antithetical frame by not opting for a structure pitching perceptions of the West by Iran against perceptions of Iran by the West. Instead, the chapters have been organised according to their discipline.

The first section of the present volume focuses on the recycling of classical sources. Gregoratti examines how the Romans reused Greek sources – Herodotus being unsurprisingly one of them – for their description of Persian kings, portrayed as cruel and weakened by a surfeit of wealth, a depiction later echoed by Fénelon. For the Romans, the stereotypical representation of the Persian king as impulsive, treacherous and fickle served as shorthand guidelines in how to act, for lack of more precise information. The recycling of sources leads to problems with reader expectations, an issue Bagot explores through the writings of Ammianus Marcellinus who preferred to his personal lived experience echoing descriptions of the Persians found in out-dated texts his readers would have been familiar with. Since Antiquity, the question of the function of these representations arises since writing within a tradition has superseded veracity, which contributes to the fixed narrative of a timeless Eastern Other. Such persistence can be understood as a sign of uncertainty, yet variations in these representations are also to be found. Gregoratti contrasts Josephus' description of Artabanus to that of other Roman historians and argues that this is due to Artabanus' support of the Jews, which Josephus approved of. Similarly, Bagot explains Ammianus' positive portrayal of Shapur II by his reaction to the fact that Rome was turning towards Christianity instead of staying faithful to its old gods, as the Persians had done. Bagot thus brings in the notion that representations of the Persians can be an indirect way of discussing concerns closer to home. The Other as mirror of the Self is the focus of my chapter where I examine how Fénelon, also heavily relying on classical sources, hides his criticism of Louis XIV behind that of Xerxes. Though strictly speaking a literary text, my analysis of Fénelon's dialogue centres on the reuse of classical sources to fit a modern context. Yet again, historical accuracy is of secondary importance; something else is at stake.

The second section on literary perceptions brings forward issues of identity constructed along binary lines. In her analysis of German translations of Saadi's *Gulistan* and on how these are not neutral in the perceptions of Iran they convey, Zandjani introduces the highly interesting idea of domestication and foreignisation, originally translation strategies concerning how the target culture is to be approached. The absence of a fixed and uniform perception is reflected in the different translation approaches favoured by Western countries. Germany and France favour a foreignising approach, where it is left to the reader to make the effort of meeting the author on his/her own ground, whereas Britain and the United States often opt for domestication, which is the reverse process. Thus Zandjani offers an example of how easily the notion of a unified Western perception of Iran can be undermined. The Shah retitling Eugène Sue's *The Mysteries of Paris* as *The Book of Rodolphe* in the style of Persian romances, as Beh-Pajooh mentions, is an example of how domestication and foreignisation can be applied outside Translation Studies. Beh-Pajooh argues that the novelist Kazemi looked to France to offer a new direction to Iranian literature, which had reached a standstill by continuously looking back to its classics. By breaking with the past and writing in a foreign tradition he made his own, Kazemi used the genre of the modern novel to reflect back to Iran an image of its contemporary self. In the texts Arian and Bibizadeh examine, the characters find themselves trapped in the identity emerging from the sometimes nonsensical polarisation of Iran and the West. Far from defending and promoting so-called Western values, more specifically democracy, Western powers are caught stifling them when they emerge elsewhere. As Bibizadeh remarks, in the eyes of the author Mandanipour, this contradictory, even hypocritical, attitude calls for a questioning of the categorisation of democracy as a Western value. Women are at the heart of this identity trap as the female body has been politicised and stands for the body of the nation. But for those Iranian women refusing to embody a polarised political identity, the only option is passive resistance. The veil of the Islamic Republic has now become a cloak of invisibility under which disappear Iranian women who resist the categorisation of their own identity. Arian provides another example of the untenability of an absolute Iran-versus-West polarisation. In *Reading Lolita in Tehran*, the author Nafisi conflagrates Iranian and Western spaces. The room where the book club is held signifies freedom attained through the reading of Western literature whilst replicating a harem in which the characters can withdraw from the outside world. Through the figure of the expatriate, Valsecchi brings forth another form of problematic identity. In the literary texts Valsecchi analyses, the Iranian characters living in Western countries are caught in an in-betweenness, a neither-here-nor-there, where alienation and nostalgia complicate their perception of the country they have left and the country they have adopted. The second section also discusses the politicisation of literature, an issue mentioned by Arian and examined in depth by Pfeifer in her chapter on how Iran became in 1968 a focus for German leftists who called for literature to take on a politically active role. Pfeifer shows that, despite not having been under direct rule, Iran became a focus for post-colonial discourse of which Farah, incarnating the Westernisation of Iran, infected by Occidentosis, became one of the targets.

The chapters in the third section focus on Iranian–Western perceptions based on actual encounters and on fantasy. Sanikidze depicts Georgia as a gateway where East and West meet and where Tbilisi, reminiscent of Herodotus' Halicarnassus, offers a symbiosis of both cultures. In turn under the control of the Ottoman Empire, the Iranian Safavid, Afsharid and Qajar dynasties and tsarist and Soviet Russia, Georgia offers a syncretism of Iranian–Western perceptions and illustrates the shifting of the East–West tectonic plates, revealing how perceptions shift accordingly. Malekzadeh offers another example of an in-between state. Romania and Iran's relation was forged through the struggle against a common enemy, the Ottoman Empire. This is an example of an East–West meeting in reaction to imperialism. Malekzadeh examines how the ties between Iran and Romania continued to grow despite the geopolitical changes in the region, in particular the Cold War and the Islamic Revolution. She shows the importance of soft power for influencing perceptions and explains how cultural ties led to economic ones. The fact that neither Georgia nor Romania carries on its shoulders the weight of being perpetrators of colonialism and imperialism brings forth a more complex and less ideologically orientated understanding of the East–West dichotomy. Unlike Sanikidze and Malekzadeh who look at cases where Iranian–Western encounters are mostly balanced, Wytenbroek discusses the perception of Iranians by American missionaries whose role evolved along with the conception of missionary work. The trope of disease appears regularly in Iranian–Western perceptions, in particular in the idea of *Gharbzadegi* or Occidentosis, but here this trope has been reversed through the pathologising of the Iranian body now cured instead of infected by the West. Providing an example to the consciousness industry Pfeifer discussed and introducing post-structuralism to understand how societies are shaped by discourse, Gomari-Luksch furthers the discussion on fact and fantasy by examining how the State manipulates its citizens' perceptions. Both Iran and the United States demonise each other whilst presenting themselves as victims. Fantasising the Other as an object of fear has become a political tool to legitimise foreign-policy objectives as made visible in the United States' war on terror and Iran's nuclear programme.

The final section centres on visual and media representations. Habibi, Röder and Aras examine the female embodiment of Iranian–Western perceptions. In the case of the Safavid paintings of European women, these embodiments have been decontextualised and principally focus on the exoticism of the Other. They also provide another example of domestication. Habibi suggests that some of the paintings inspired by European depictions of Susannah or Venus emerging from the sea could have been associated with Iranian representations of Shirin in the well-known episode when her husband Khosrow saw her for the first time whilst she was bathing. Through the example of Safavid paintings of exoticised and eroticised European women, Habibi points to similar principles on which work Orientalism and Occidentalism, though with arguably different aims since the Safavids' interest in European painting and dress seems to have been purely motivated by their exotic value rather than any desire to consolidate relations with Europe. Röder examines a similar process of foreignisation and domestication in the German press' treatment of Soraya, the Oriental fairytale princess reminiscent of the Austrian empress Sissi. However, contrary to the Safavid paintings, the representations of Soraya are heavily contextualised. Röder underlines how attractive and comforting the image of a timeless East was for Germany when trying to recover from World War II. Yet, this notion of timelessness does not preclude a considerable change in the way Germany perceived Iran. During her marriage, Soraya was made to fit in the patriarchal family model promoted by the Adenauer government. At her divorce, she became the female victim of Oriental backwardness. As Aras points out, the image of the Oriental princess is still current and has been reclaimed by a part of the Tehran elite who has turned away from the Islamic Republic's representation of the Iranian body. Instead of viewing this in terms of submission to Western orientalism, Aras suggests that the fashioning of the body to this type of beauty has been made extreme in order to outshine the Western version of the Oriental princess and demonstrate that the Iranian version is superior. Aras also shows that the embodiment of Iranian or Western values is not limited to the female body; she reminds us that under Reza Shah, the suited and clean-shaven Iranian male embodied Iran's westernisation. Heris and myself examine the importance of origins in representations of Iran, already briefly touched upon in Wytenbroek's discussion of the Assyrian Iranians viewed as primitive Christians by the American missionaries. In the 1925 film *Grass*, the linear directionality of civilisation follows the equally linear move from East to West. Iran is depicted as the cradle of Europe and through the Bakhtiari, presented as being of the same race as Europeans, the spectator has been transported into the past and is given to see his origins, his primitive self. During the 1971 Persepolis celebrations, the Shah put the origins of Iran centre stage and claimed that these were also the origins of the West, in an attempt to consolidate his rule and the position of Iran in the world.

The volume concludes not on an academic analysis, but on the personal experience of an Englishman's life in Isfahan in the 1970s, in search of a fantasised Orient in a country pressed to Westernise.

Notes

1. Georg Wilhelm Friedrich Hegel, *Philosophy of History*, tr. John Sibree (New York, 1902), p. 339, quoted by Richard W. Bulliet in 'Iran Between East and West', in *Journal of International Affairs*, 60 (2007), p. 5.
2. See Ippokratis Kantzios, 'The Politics of Fear in Aeschylus' "Persians", in *The Classical World*, 98 (2004), p. 4.
3. Ibid., pp. 4–5.
4. See Phiroze Vasunia, 'Between East and West: Mobility and Ethnography in Herodotus' Proem', in *History and Anthropology*, 23 (2012), p. 185.
5. See Kantzios, 'The Politics of Fear', p. 19.
6. See Michael Flower, 'Herodotus and Persia' in Carolyn Dewald and John Marincola (eds), *The Cambridge Companion to Herodotus* (Cambridge, 2006), p. 275.
7. Kantzios, 'The Politics of Fear', p. 13.
8. Ibid.
9. Ibid., p. 16.
10. See Flower, 'Herodotus and Persia', p. 283.
11. See ibid., p. 286.
12. See Vasunia, 'Between East and West', p. 185.
13. Quoted by Vasunia, 'Between East and West', p. 183.
14. Ibid., pp. 183–4.
15. Ibid., p. 197.
16. Dick Davis, 'Iran and Aniran: The Shaping of a Legend', in Amanat and Vejdani (eds), *Iran Facing Others*, p. 39.
17. See Bulliet, 'Iran Between East and West', p. 6. See also Davis, 'Iran and Aniran: The Shaping of a Legend', in Amanat and Vejdani (eds), *Iran Facing Others*, pp. 39–50.
18. Tyma, 'This is Sparta', p. 6.

19. J. Weiland, 14 March 2007, '*300* Post-Game: One-on-One With Zack Snyder', *Comic Book Resources*, <http://www.comicbookresources.com/news/newsitem.cgi?id=9982. > , quoted by G. N. Murray in 'Zack Snyder, Frank Miller and Herodotus: Three Takes on the 300 Spartans', in *Akroterion*, 52 (2007), p. 12.
20. Quotes for Dilios, *IMDb*, <http://www.imdb.com/character/ch0002517/quotes> [Accessed 13 June 2017].
21. El Amine, 'Beyond East and West', p. 113.
22. Roberto Farneti, 'Cleavage Lines in Global Politics: Left and Right, East and West, Earth and Heaven', in *Journal of Political Ideologies*, 17 (2012), p. 128.
23. See Bakhshandeh, 'The "Occidentalist West" vs "Orientalist East"', in *Occidentalism in Iran*, pp. 9–25.
24. Loubna El Amine, 'Beyond East and West: Reorienting Political Theory Through the Prism of Modernity', in *Perspectives on Politics*, 14 (2016), p. 102.
25. See for example Juan R. I. Cole, 'Invisible Occidentalism: Eighteenth-Century Indo–Persian Constructions of the West', in *Iranian Studies*, 25 (1992): pp. 3–16; Bakhshandeh, *Occidentalism in Iran*, pp. 2–7; and Eugenio Chahuan, 'An East–West Dichotomy: Islamophobia', in *Palestine–Israel Journal of Politics, Economics and Culture*, 12 (2005), pp. 48–9.
26. Mansoor Moaddel, 'Introduction: Theoretical and Methodological Issues in the Study of Values', in Mansoord Moaddel (ed.), *Values and Perceptions of the Islamic and Middle Eastern Publics* (New York, Basingstoke, 2010), p. 11.
27. Ibid., p. 12.
28. See El Amine, 'Beyond East and West', p. 111.
29. Adam W. Tyma, 'This is Sparta! Mediated Mythology as Pedagogy in *300*', in *Journal of Communication Inquiry*, 39 (2015), p. 7.
30. Johann P. Arnason, 'East and West: From Invidious Dichotomy to Incomplete Deconstruction', in Gerard Delanty and Engin F. Isin (eds), *Handbook of Historical Sociology* (London, 2003), p. 232.
31. See for example chapter 4 'Engagement with Iran: Shedding the Iranian 'myth' in Bernd Kaussler and Glenn P. Hastedt, *US Foreign Policy Towards the Middle East: The Realpolitik of Deceit* (London, New York, 2017), pp. 146–75 and Emily Landau, 'US counter-proliferation policy: The case of Iran' in Efraim Inbar and Jonathan Rynhold (eds), *US Foreign Policy and Global Standing in the 21st Century: Realities and Perceptions* (London, New York, 2016), pp. 198–212.
32. Ehsan Bakhshandeh, *Occidentalism in Iran: Representation of the West in the Iranian Media* (London, 2015).
33. See Ali Ansari (ed.), *Perceptions of Iran: History, Myths and Nationalism from Medieval Persia to the Islamic Republic* (London, 2013) and Abbas Amanat and Farzin Vejdani (eds), *Iran Facing Others: Identity Boundaries in a Historical Perspective* (Basingstoke, 2012).
34. Dick Davis, 'Iran and Aniran: The Shaping of a Legend', in Amanat and Vejdani (eds), *Iran Facing Others*, p. 39.
35. One notable exception is Abbas Maleki and John Tirman (eds), *U.S.-Iran Misperceptions: A Dialogue* (New York, 2014).
36. On the mirroring effect of the Self-Other discourse, see Bakhshandeh, *Occidentalism in Iran*, pp. 13–14.

37. See Bakhshandeh, *Occidentalism in Iran*, pp. 7, 9–10 and 21.
38. See Mohammd-Ja'far Mahjub, 'Goftar darbare-ye ba'zi farangan va mostafrangan,' in *Iran Nameh*, 12 (1994): 673–714, p. 697, quoted by Afshin Matin Asgari, 'The Academic Debate on Iranian Identity: Nation and Empire Entangled', in Amanat and Vejdani (eds), *Iran Facing Others*, p. 182.
39. See Ali M. Ansari, 'Myth, History and Narrative Displacement in Iranian Historiography', in Ansari (ed.), *Perceptions of Iran*, pp. 5–23 and Asgari, 'The Academic Debate on Iranian Identity: Nation and Empire Entangled', in Amanat and Vejdani (eds), *Iran Facing Others*, pp. 180–1.
40. See Amanat, 'Iranian Identity Boundaries: A Historical Overview', in Amanat and Vejdani (eds), *Iran Facing Others*, p. 18.
41. Ibid., p. 21.
42. See ibid., pp. 22–4.
43. See Asgari, 'The Academic Debate on Iranian Identity: Nation and Empire Entangled', in Amanat and Vejdani (eds), *Iran Facing Others*, p. 179.
44. See David Motadel, 'Iran and the Aryan Myth', in Ansari (ed.), *Perceptions of Iran*, pp. 119–45.

SECTION 1

CLASSICAL REPRESENTATIONS

CHAPTER 1

TACITUS AND THE GREAT KINGS

Leonardo Gregoratti

The Arsacid Parthian Empire was Rome's only serious political and military rival from the first century BC until the collapse of the Parthian dynasty in the third century AD. However, despite more than three centuries of coexistence, the representation of the Parthians in Roman literary sources remained one coloured heavily by stereotype or other cultural, literary or political concerns. Focussing on the work of Tacitus, this chapter will demonstrate his work shows us rather more of the author's own concerns than the reality of how the Romans perceived the Parthians, and hence even less of the reality of the situation. This chapter will argue that Tacitus systematically used his portrayal of Parthian monarchs to highlight the failings or strengths of the Roman emperors who populated his narrative. However, this political use of the portrayal of Parthian kings was built upon a seemingly deeply held perception of the Parthians by Tacitus' readership, a perception of 'eastern decadence' and barbarism which had been established by the works of the earlier seminal works of Herodotus and Xenophon.

The Parthian Empire entered the political horizon of Rome violently in the mid-first century BC, when Crassus' legions suffered a disastrous defeat on the steppes of northern Mesopotamia. From that time until the early decades of the third century AD, Rome's expansionist goals in the East had to deal with the Parthians. A few decades after Alexander the Great's death, Arsacid Parthian monarchs established their control over a considerable portion of territory on the remotest borders of the Seleucid Empire. The members of the Arsacid dynasty were able to gain the greatest advantage from the weakening and consequent disintegration of that huge Hellenistic state by spreading their control over large territories of southern Asia. When the struggle with Rome began, the Arsacid Empire stretched from the Euphrates to north-western India, including Mesopotamia, the whole Iranian plateau and all the territories lying between the Persian Gulf and the Indian Ocean to the south and the Caspian Sea and the Caucasus to the north.[1]

The Parthian Empire was thus a geographically imposing political entity, far longer lasting than many of the empires that preceded it, ruling over the same peoples and regions. Unfortunately, its role in the history of western Asia, as any scholar dealing with Parthian antiquities sadly knows, has for a long time been underestimated due to the scarcity of extant sources.[2] Modern researchers complain of the lack of work able to provide a more complete portrait of the Arsacid rule, such as Herodotus and Xenophon provide for the Achaemenids. The result is that what for a long time was known about history and state structure of the Parthian kingdom was mainly based on the incomplete and largely stereotyped accounts drawn up by Roman and Greek imperial writers. Since they wrote in a period during which the Parthians were often at odds with Rome, their interest in the Arsacids was restricted to the provinces of this vast domain lying closer to the Roman borders and to the historical episodes more closely connected with Roman policies.

In her fundamental book *L'Image des Parthes dans le Monde Gréco–Romain* Charlotte Lerouge showed that the Romans' conception of the Arsacid kingdom and its inhabitants, its organisation and culture was the result of a combination of the elements of Greek historiographic tradition, beginning with Herodotus, which had previously been attributed to the ancient people of Asia: the ancient Persians on one side and the Scythians on the other.[3]

Having to provide the Western public with a representation of the only state challenging Rome's supremacy in the east, Roman historians found that the best solution was to use the old stereotypes the Greeks had conceived, suggesting the potency of these representations and perceptions in the Roman imagination. Ethnographic *topoi* were amalgamated in order to create a mainly artificial representation of the Parthian people in order to describe to the Romans this new people Rome was not immediately able to subjugate. Thus, the Romans' perception of the Parthians was the result of a deliberate assemblage of stereotypes about Eastern people belonging to previous literary and historical traditions. Roman propaganda played a major role in moulding the way the Parthians were perceived in the West combined with a lack of genuine interest in most of the sources at the disposal to modern scholars, into understanding what the Parthian state really was like. That said, it is important to emphasise that only a few fragments survive from the works by the western authors explicitly dealing with the Parthians, such as like Arrian's *Parthika* and from those written by Greek authors living in the Arsacid empire, such as Apollodoros of Artemita or Isidoros of Charax, perhaps distorting our appreciation of Roman perceptions of the Arsacids.

Among the many examples, the words of Tacitus, who wrote a chronicle of first-century Roman history, appear significant concerning the Parthian attitude towards their kings.[4] After the death of the Great King Phraates (first half of the first century AD) Tacitus records that some Parthian nobles sent envoys to Rome in order to ask Augustus to send as new king Vonones, one of the Arsacid princes for many years living in Rome. Tacitus states: 'The barbarians welcomed him with rejoicing, as is usual with new rulers. Soon they felt shame at Parthians having become degenerate, at having sought a king from another world.'[5] Some time later Caius Cassius, governor of Syria, was commissioned to escort the young prince Meherdates to the bank of the Euphrates. Having encamped at Zeugma where the river was most easily fordable, they awaited the arrival of the chief men of Parthia, the Roman governor 'reminded Meherdates that the impulsive enthusiasm of barbarians soon flags from delay or even changes into treachery, and that therefore he should urge on his enterprise.'[6] In fact in the course of the campaign in the east, many Parthian vassal kings deserted with their troops, 'with their countrymen's characteristic fickleness,' writes Tacitus, 'confirming previous experience that barbarians prefer to seek a king from Rome than to keep him.'[7]

These passages taken from the work of an imperial author who more than others expressed some interest in the Parthians beyond the mere narration of the historical events, provide a vivid example of the stereotypical approach adopted by Roman writers. After the defeat Crassus suffered at Carrhae (53 BC), when the two states' political aspirations clashed, the Parthians began to be described by the Roman propaganda as a weak people, the barbarians of the east, characterised by a whimsical and inconstant nature. They were politically unstable because they were unfaithful, treacherous and unable to consolidate a kingdom always perceived as on the brink of collapse. Tacitus' narrations demonstrate that the Romans' explanation for the historical events, in the absence of a real historical investigation, was largely ascribed to the very nature of the 'barbarians.'

The Romans' point of view was based on well-known stereotypes regarding the oriental barbarians. Thus Arsacid rulers, like their Persian predecessors described by Herodotus, were cruel and despotic, weakened by luxury and wealth, and their decisions and policy were strongly influenced by palace intrigues and dynastic strife.[8]

Great King Phraates (37–2 BC),[9] according to Dio Cassius was the 'most impious of men' who committed many crimes, among which the most terrible was the murder of 'brothers and sons because they were his superiors in virtue'.[10] His son Phraataces (2 BC – AD 4) was by no means a better ruler according to Flavius Josephus:[11] a parricide, hated by his own people and expelled from the kingdoms due to a 'criminal conversation' he had with his mother Musa.[12] According to the Romans the reality could not be different: the Parthian kingdom was weak because the nature of its monarchs and subjects was weak.

Nonetheless Tacitus' *Annales*, the history of the Roman Empire from the later reign of Augustus to that of Nero (AD 6–68), composed at the beginning of the second century AD, in at least 16 books of which only a part are extant, constitute the richest and most important source of information about Parthian history in the first century AD.

Although Tacitus shares with other Roman historians the same stereotypical attitude towards the Parthians, the representations of the various Great Kings he provides differ from one another and, in some cases, tend to distance themselves from the stereotypical approach used for the anonymous masses. Each royal personality has some peculiar characteristics and these sometimes differ significantly from the traditional idea of the 'Persian' monarch. Tacitus elaborates his own particular and fictitious idea of the different Parthian monarchs, amalgamating each time in a different way traditional *topoi* and 'classical' virtues. This Tacitean representation of the Parthian kings was instrumental in conveying the political message that emerges in all his work.

Between AD 6 and 8, after the fall of Great King Phraataces, a diplomatic delegation sent '*a primoribus Parthis*' to ask the Roman emperor to appoint a new Great King to the vacant throne of the Parthian Empire from the many Arsacid princes who had been living in the *Urbs* or in its immediate surroundings since 10 BC when the Great King Phraates IV sent all his sons but one to the court of his ally and friend, the Emperor Augustus.[13]

The Roman *princeps* chose the old Vonones. According to Tacitus' report Vonones was enthusiastically welcomed in Parthia, but the enthusiasm of his subjects for their new 'master' soon gave way to indignation. Soon, states Tacitus, the Parthians began to see Vonones as a puppet king, a servant of Caesar, corrupted by foreign customs, *hostium artibus infecto.*[14] Vonones was perceived as a foreigner because he was *diversus a maioribus institutis*, reluctant to adopt the customs of his ancestors. Tacitus goes further making explicit reference to some of the habits most characteristic in the Roman mind of the Parthian people. Vonones was not in fact interested in hunting and horses, *raro venatu, segni equorum cura*, like his fellow countrymen, but he used a litter for his transport and rejected the lavish banquets of his predecessors, *fastu erga patrias epulas.* Furthermore, his Greek retinue and the abundant use he made of his seal provoked the derision of his subjects.

Vonones was a Romanised Parthian, chosen by Augustus, and therefore in some sense an emanation of the man who, in the Roman historiographical tradition, was the *princeps par excellence*, the first and most illustrious Roman ruler. He ideologically represented the attempt of putting at the head of a barbaric nation a 'minor Augustus', a man who would have ruled Parthia like a just and civilised Hellenised ruler. The Parthians in Tacitus' narration due to their nature and nationalistic pride, decided not to take that chance and rejected the 'generous' gift. They decided in other words to remain barbarians.

In opposition to Vonones the aristocratic factions immediately proposed Artabanus of Media Atropatenes, a member of a cadet branch of the royal family who, according to Tacitus, had strong links with the Dahae, the nomadic tribe living east of the Caspian Sea.[15] Finally Artabanus II in AD 12 gained the throne forcing Vonones to find shelter within the Roman borders.

By contrast Artabanus, the winner, is depicted as a sort of anti-Hellenised ruler. Probably giving voice to the anti-Arsacid propaganda spread within the population of Seleucia on the Tigris, the most important, wealthy and populous Greek metropolis outside Roman territory, Tacitus stresses Artabanus' connections with the Scythians, the central Asiatic nomads. The King was only half Arsacid, growing up with the Scythians, from whom he was descended.[16]

According to Tacitus, only after the death of Germanicus (AD 19), Emperor Tiberius' energetic heir presumptive and one of the positive characters in the *Annales*, Artabanus became more and more arrogant and ambitious towards Rome and cruel towards his subjects.[17] A number of military victories made him confident enough to show contempt for Tiberius' old age and 'insist on the ancient boundaries of Persia and Macedonia, and intimate, with a vainglorious threat, that he meant to seize the country possessed by Cyrus and afterwards by Alexander.'[18]

Around AD 35 a military setback in the West destabilised Artabanus' position at the head of the Parthian kingdom. A revolt of noblemen, supported by Rome, managed to overthrow him some time later. According to Tacitus, Artabanus was abandoned by nobles and courtesans and was accompanied only by his bodyguard formed from mercenary raiders, 'homeless and landless men, members of a class neither comprehending good nor regarding evil but fed as the agents of crime. Taking these with him, he hurriedly fled to the remote districts adjoining Scythia; where he hoped that his marriage connections with the Hyrcanians and Carmanians would find him allies.'[19] In the forests of Hyrcania he remained wandering in rags, providing food for himself with his bow. Artabanus went to the eastern satrapies looking for military support among the nomadic chiefs and the Hyrcanian aristocracy. He chose to present himself as a nomadic hunter king matching the idea of the leader typical of the Iranian tradition. Imitating the 'Scythian' Arsaces, the illustrious founder of the dynasty, he played the role of the nomadic warrior, able to survive in the wilderness far away from court leisure, relying only on his archery skills. The bow, the traditional weapon of Arsacid kings, which Arsaces, the founder of the dynasty, wields on all Parthian coins, had in fact an important symbolic and propagandistic value. Soon after that, at the head of an army of Sacae and Dahae he was able to regain the throne.[20]

Artabanus is just the opposite of a Hellenised king, he is a 'Scythian', the youngest and most cruel people of the Antiquity according to Herodotus, a cruel and arrogant ruler who could threaten the Roman supremacy in the area only because an old and weak Tiberius was leading at that time the empire. Tacitus establishes a vivid contrast between old Tiberius' policy, based on 'manipulating foreign affairs by policy and craft without a resort to arms,'[21] a policy destined to fail, and Artabanus' energetic and direct approach based on military intervention, rapid war manoeuvres and disdain for delay and hesitation.[22]

But Artabanus is not merely a cruel barbaric leader. In Tacitus' narration he is also a clever politician, a monarch who knows his people very well, as shown by the mentioned episode, and more importantly knows how to exploit his subjects' treacherous nature for his own advantage: found in distress in the forest and approached by a couple of Parthian noblemen who revolted against him 'the veteran monarch' as Tacitus defines him 'realised that, if they were false in love, they were not hypocritical in their hatreds.'[23] If their promises of friendship were not genuine, the hate they felt towards the leaders of the revolt was. By exploiting their rivalries, he managed to regain the throne.

The description of Artabanus as a cunning and cruel monarch contrasts sharply with the description of the same Great King provided by Flavius Josephus. According to the Jewish historian the Parthian king fell victim to the deceptive strategy of Tiberius and Vitellius, the Roman governor of Syria, who while pretending to seek peace through negotiations secretly and successfully managed to destabilise Artabanus' rule through bribery.[24]

Flavius Josephus describes Artabanus as a positive figure due to his support of the Jewish communities within the Parthian Empire. In the well-known episode of Asinaeus and Anilaeus, the Jewish brothers who revolted against local Parthian landlords gaining control of Babylonia, the Great King offered protection to the rebels from his generals who were eager to take revenge, granted them his trust and appointed them governors of the territories under their control.[25]

In contrast to Tacitus' description, Artabanus showed his humility when forced to leave the throne by appearing at the court of Izates, the recently converted Jewish king of Adiabene, to seek support. Izates helped him to regain the throne and was sumptuously rewarded by the grateful Great King.[26] Due to the power and autonomy gained, Izates entered into conflict with the kings of Parthia who succeeded Artabanus, Vardanes[27] and Vologases I,[28] both described as despotic rulers attempting to force Izates into submission. In Josephus' narration both failed because Izates enjoyed the favour of God.

Josephus was interested in narrating the history of Jewish communities across the world, thus he depicted the Great Kings like Artabanus who supported the Jews under a positive light and those who opposed them under a negative one. Tacitus' historiographical purposes were different. His intent was to investigate Roman history and express his ideas about Roman leadership and rulers. The Parthian kings, Rome's adversaries, were instrumental in this plan: their role in the events influenced the idea the historian was able to convey concerning Roman administration. In Tacitus' account, Vardanes is thus a glorious conqueror[29] in opposition to his rival, the cruel Gotarzes.[30]

Very different also is the description of the most significant Arsacid of the first century AD. In AD 51, Vologases I became the Great King. By associating to the throne his two brothers, monarchs in Armenia and Media Atropatenes he conferred stability to the top of the state structure, refunding and consolidating the whole empire.[31] Tacitus portrays him as an 'enlightened king.' The differences in the representation of this new Great King are evident from the first few lines: he was the son of a Greek concubine thus not entirely a barbarian.[32] Furthermore he ascended the throne 'with the acquiescence of his brothers'[33] and not like his predecessors through civic strife and family onslaughts. His reforms created a restricted council that shared the power once in the hands of the Great King alone.

He was Great King during the long war with Rome for the possession of Armenia (AD 58–63).[34] The cause of the conflict was again the control of the strategic kingdom of Armenia, whose throne a certain Rhadamistus, the son of the Iberian king, had usurped through assassinations and frauds, not without the connivance of the Roman officers in charge of overseeing the kingdom.[35]

Tacitus points out that Vologases decided to intervene in Armenia, a decision that violated Artabanus' agreements with Rome and finally caused the war, because an illegitimate ruler had criminally taken control of a kingdom historically considered part of the Parthian political sphere of influence. He then 'prepared to settle his brother Tiridates on the throne; so that no branch of his family should lack its kingdom'.[36] The contrast with the behaviour of his predecessors as described by Tacitus is immediately striking. Vologases is a just ruler, respectful of the agreements and ready to share his power with his brothers. He intervenes in Armenia to punish the crimes committed by another ruthless barbarian, similar in this respect to the other Great Kings in Tacitus' narration, and more relevantly by Roman officers, who could commit crimes undisturbed, thanks to the weakness of Claudius' administration.

The generous nature of Tiridates, Vologases' brother, pretender to the Armenian throne and the other protagonist of the events connected to the Armenian Wars, is made clear since his first apparition in the scene. Queen Zenobia, Rhadamistos' wife, mercilessly stabbed and thrown in the river by her fleeing husband is rescued and honoured by her enemy Tiridates, brought to the court and treated like a member of a royal house.[37]

The appointment of Corbulo as supreme commander in the east,[38] an extremely good Roman officer, highlights the moderate and wise nature of Vologases: both men prefer to conduct the confrontation through negotiations, seeking a more peaceful solution instead of bloodshed.[39]

After a quick and successful invasion of Armenia Nero put Tigranes, a hostage of Cappadocian origin on the Armenian throne. Tigranes invaded the prestigious Parthian client kingdom of Adiabene forcing Monobazos, the monarch, to seek refuge in Parthia proper. In collaboration with Tiridates, Vologases' brother and former king of Armenia, overthrown by the Romans, Monobazos denounced the situation in front of the Parthian court, accusing Vologases of not accomplishing his feudal duties and not doing enough to protect his subject king's throne.[40]

Having gathered all his dignitaries, vassal kings and officers in a council Vologases explains to them the decision of resuming the war, after praising his brother for his moderation and himself for having attempted on many occasions to avoid war through negotiations.[41]

Vologases was a wise and just ruler, ready to gather his subordinates to hear their voices. Always keen to look for peace, ready to depose arms in order to find a solution through negotiations, his figure, very similar to that of Corbulo, contrasts sharply, as it is clearly Tacitus' intention, with that of Nero who ruled during the war, the Roman emperor considered by the senatorial class to which the historian belonged, the most evident degeneration of the Julio–Claudian dynasty.

As a part of the peace negotiations the young Tiridates was requested to travel to Rome in order to receive the crown publicly from Nero's hands.[42] Unfortunately we do not know how Tacitus described the meeting between Nero and Tiridates. Tacitus' narration ends with the preparations for the journey. Probably the narration followed the lines of the later account by Dio Cassius.[43] Once in Rome Tiridates showed his skills in diplomacy and archery, while Nero made a fool of himself in front of the Arsacid prince. 'This made Tiridates disgusted with him; but he praised Corbulo, in whom he found only this one fault, that he would put up with such a master'.[44]

Gaius or Publius Conelius Tacitus was born in AD 56 and therefore he was only a child when the Roman–Parthian war began. Vespasian took Nero's place in 69 and founded a new dynasty. Tacitus advanced steadily through the *cursus honorum* under the Flavians, experiencing the tyranny of Domitian, Vespasian's second son and emperor. All his historical work is a warning against the dangers of despotism and the degeneration of the principate into tyranny. And all his portraits of Parthian Great Kings are more or less coherent with this concept.[45]

Augustus, the father of the empire, was a just king, but the Parthians, as barbarians, refused to accept Vonones, an equally just monarch. Artabanus, the cruel Scythian could rule and threaten Rome's supremacy only because in Rome the degeneration of power had already begun with the reign of the late Tiberius. Political instability both in Parthia and in Armenia was not properly exploited due to the weak policy of Claudius. Finally, Vologases' and Tiridates' (along with Corbulo's) righteousness rendered more despicable the amorality and arrogance of his Roman counterpart, Nero, despised even by barbarians.

It seems clear that for Tacitus, as for Flavius Josephus, the representation of the Parthian kings and the perception of their royal figure and historical role are not monolithic. In the case of Tacitus they vary from Great King to Great King according to how he and probably his readers perceived the Roman leadership that dealt with them. From a mere propagandistic or stereotyped description, he switches to a more 'classical monarch' portrait in order to convey a judgement on the Roman emperors. A 'barbaric' Parthian king could better highlight the righteousness of an Augustus, while on the contrary a righteous one could better emphasise Nero's inadequacy. Each Arsacid king's portrait was clearly tailored on his Roman counterpart. This circumstance poses of course some serious problems. Tacitus by distancing himself from the usual cliché of 'the Parthian', apparently provides the scholars with precious details and with what appears as a more serious historical investigation on the Arsacid kings. Nonetheless, by using his portraits for a specific purpose, he substitutes the usual stereotypical representation with a personal representation, but one probably no more objective.

The apparent selective use of well-known stereotypes on the Parthians to make political judgements on Roman emperors in Tacitus' narrative highlights the extent to which stereotyped views of the 'eastern barbarians' had seeped into the Roman perception of the world. The shocking civility of certain Arsacid monarchs, conflicting with the stereotypes proposed by Roman propaganda, highlighted the utter degradation to which rulers such as Nero had brought the Roman world. Though much of Tacitus' portrayal of the Arsacid kings might be a construct, it is a construct which is surely dependent upon, and therefore highly indicative of, a well established Roman perception of the Arsacid Empire.

Tacitus' description of Nero, a ruler more barbarian than a barbarian, indicates that the degeneration of Augustus' offspring was complete. The honest citizens of Rome had to get rid of an emperor who looked shameful even to the eyes of a Parthian king. And this is exactly what Vespasian, the political *patronus* of Tacitus, did by putting an end to the Julio–Claudian dynasty and founding his own.

Notes

1. For an introduction to the history of the Parthian kingdom see: N. C. Debevoise, *A Political History of Parthia* (Chicago, 1938); K. H. Ziegler, Die *Beziehungen zwischen Rom und dem Partherreich. Ein Beitrag zur Geschichte des Völkerrechts* (Wiesbaden, 1964); K. Schippmann, *Grundzüge der parthischen Geschichte* (Darmstadt, 1980); A. D. H. Bivar, 'The Political History of Iran under the Arsacids', in E. Yarshater, *The Cambridge History of Iran, The Seleucid, Parthian and Sasanian Periods*, vol. III (Cambridge, 1983); E. Dabrowa., *La politique de l'état parthe à l'égard de Rome – d'Artaban II à Vologèse I (ca 11 – ca 79 de n. è.) et les facteurs qui la conditionnaient* (Cracow, 1983); R. N. Frye, *The History of Ancient Iran* (Munich, 1983); J. Wolski, 'L'Empire des Arsacides', in *Acta Iranica* 32 (Leuven, 1993); A. Verstandig, *Histoire de l'Empire Parthe (-250/227)* (Brussels, 2001); L. Gregoratti., *'The Arsacid Empire'*, in T. Daryaee (ed.), *King of the Seven Climes A History of the Ancient Iran World (3000 BC – 651 CE)*, Jordan Center for Persian Studies at the University of California (Irvine, 2017), pp. 125–53.
2. For the sources of the history of the Parthian kingdom see U. Hack, B. Jacobs and D. Weber, Quellen zur Geschichte des Partherreiches (Göttingen, 2010).
3. Ch. Lerouge, 'L'image des Parthes dans le monde greco–romain. Du début du Ier siècle av. J.-C. jusqu'à la fin du Haut-Empire romain', in *Oriens et Occidens*, 17 (Stuttgart, 2007).
4. N. Ehrhardt, 'Parther und partische Geschichte bei Tacitus', in J. Wiesehöfer (ed.), *Das Partherreich und seine Zeugnisse, Beiträge des internationalen Colloquiums. Eutin (27.-30. Juni 1996)* (Stuttgart, 1998).
5. Tacitus, *Annals*, II.2.
6. Ibid., XII.12.
7. Ibid., XII.14.
8. L. Gregoratti, 'Parthian Women in Flavius Josephus' in M. Hirschberger (ed.), *Jüdisch-hellenistische Literatur in ihrem interkulturellen Kontext, Akten der Tagung, Düesseldorf, 10.–11. Februar 2011* (Frankfurt, 2012).
9. D.Sellwood, *An Introduction to the Coinage of Parthia* (London, 1980), 50–5, 159–79; M. Karras-Klapproth, *Prosopographische Studien zur Geschichte des*

Partherreiches auf der Grundlage antiker literarischer Überlieferung (Bonn, 1988), pp. 137–45; F. B. Shore, *Parthian Coins and History: Ten Dragons Against Rome* (Quarryville [PA], 1993), pp. 129–34.

10. Dio Cassius, *History*, XLIX. 23, 3–4.
11. Josephus, *Jewish Antiquities*, XVIII. 42–4.
12. Sellwood, *Coinage of Parthia*, pp. 58, 189–90; J. M. Bigwood, 'Queen Mousa, Mother and Wife (?) of King Phraatakes of Parthia: A Re-evaluation of the Evidence', in *Mouseion*, 4 (2004); E. Strugnell, 'Thea Musa, Roman Queen of Parthia', in *Iranica Antiqua*, 43 (2008); J. M. Bigwood, 'Some Parthian Queens in Greek and Babylonian Documents', in *Iranica Antiqua*, 43 (2008), p. 249.
13. Tacitus, *Annals*, II.1; E. Dabrowa 'Les premiers "otages" parthes à Rome', in *Folia Orientalia*, 24 (1987), pp. 64–5.
14. Tacitus, *Annals*, II.2–3; M. Pfordt, *Studien zu Darstellung der Außenpolitik in den Annalen des Tacitus* (Frankfurt, 1998), passim; J. Wiesehöfer, 'Augustus und die Parther', in R. Aßkamp and T. Esch (eds), *Imperium. Varus und seine Zeit* (Münster, 2010), pp. 190–1; M. J. Olbrycht, *Parthia et ulteriores gentes. Die politischen Beziehungen zwischen dem arsakidischen Iran und den Nomaden der eurasischen Steppen* (Munich, 1998), pp. 135–6.
15. Tacitus, *Annals*, II.3; VI.36, 41–2; U. Kahrstedt, *Artabanos III. und seine Erbe*, Dissertationes Bernenses I 2, Bern, A. Francke (1950), pp. 11, 14, 66; Frye, *Ancient Iran*, p. 237; Olbrycht, *Parthia et ulteriores gentes*, pp. 139–40; M. J. Olbrycht, 'Parthians, Greek Culture, and Beyond', in K. Twardowska, M. Salamon, S. Sprawski, M. Stachura, S. Turlej (eds), *Within the Circle of Ancient Ideas and Virtues. Studies in Honour of Professor Maria Dzielska* (Cracow, 2014), pp. 92–7.
16. Tacitus, *Annals*, VI.42.
17. Ibid., VI. 31.
18. Tacitus, *Annals*, VI.31; J. Wolski, 'Les Achéménides et les Arsacides, Contribution à l'histoire de la formation des traditions iraniennes', in *Syria*, 43 (1966), pp. 65–9; J. Wolski 'Arsakiden und Sasaniden', in R. Stiehl and H.E. Stier (eds), *Beiträge zur Alten Geschichte und deren Nachleben, Festschrift für Franz Altheim zum 6. 10. 1968* (Berlin, 1969), pp. 315–322; J. Wiesehöfer, Iranische Ansprüche an Rom auf ehemals achaimenidische Territorien', in *Archäologische Mitteilungen aus Iran*, 19 (1986), pp. 177–81; J. Wolski, 'L'heritage d'Alexandre le Grand et les Arsacides', in W. Will (ed.) *Zu Alexander d. Gr. Festschrift G. Wirth zum 60. Geburtstag am 9. 12. 86* (Amsterdam, 1988), p. 1004; J. Wolski, 'Alexandre le Grand: légende et réalité. De l'avènement des Séleucides à la chute des Arsacides', in J.M. Croisille (ed.), *Neronia IV. Alejandro Magno, modelo de los emperadores romanos. Actes du IVe Colloque international de la SIEN, Collection Latomus 209* (Brussels, 1990), pp. 108–9; R. Shayegan, *Arsacids and Sasanians: Political Ideology in Post-Hellenistic and Late Antique Persia* (Cambridge, 2011), pp. 293–5, 306–7. For a different opinion see L. Gregoratti, 'The Kings of Parthia and Persia, Some Considerations on the "Iranic" Identity in the Parthian Empire', in *Digital Archive of Brief Notes & Iranian Review 2015*, 1 (2015).
19. Tacitus, *Annals*, VI.43–4.

20. Tacitus, *Annals*., VI. 44. M. J. Olbrycht, 'The Political-Military Strategy of Artabanos/Ardawān II in 34–37', in *Anabasis: Studia Classica et Orientalia*, 3 (2012), pp. 225–7; L. Gregoratti, 'The Journey east of the Great King, East and West in the Parthian Kingdom', in *Parthica*, 15 (2013).
21. Tacitus, *Annals*, VI.32.
22. Ibid., VI.32.
23. Ibid., VI.44.
24. Tacitus, *Annals*, VI,36; Josephus, *Jewish Antiquities*, XVIII.100.
25. Josephus, *Jewish Antiquities*, XVIII.315–39. C. Colpe, 'Die Arsakiden bei Josephus', in O. Betz, K. Haacker and M. Hengel (eds), *Josephus – Studien, Untersuchungen zu Josephus, dem antiken Judentum und dem Neuen Testament, Otto Michel zum 70. Geburtstag gewidmet* (Göttingen, 1974), p. 101; N.G. Cohen, 'Asinaeus and Anilaeus, Additional Comments to Josephus' Antiquities of the Jews', in *Annual of the Swedish Theological Institute*, 10 (1976), pp. 30–7; J. Neusner, *A History of the Jews in Babylonia I: The Parthian Period* (Chico [CA], 1984), pp. 61–7; D. Goodblatt, 'Josephus on Parthian Babylonia (Antiquities XVIII)', in *Journal of the American Oriental Society*, 107 (1987) 1987, p. 605; G. Brizzi, 'Considerazioni di storia mesopotamica da un passo di Giuseppe Flavio (Ant. Jud. XVIII, 314–379)', in *Cahiers du Centre Gustave Glotz*, 6 (1995), pp. 70–1; T. Rajak, The Parthians in Josephus', in J. Wiesehöfer (ed.), *Das Partherreich und seine Zeugnisse, Beiträge des internationalen Colloquiums. Eutin (27.-30. Juni 1996)* (Stuttgart 1998), pp. 314–15.
26. Flavius Josephus, *Jewish Antiquities*, XX, 54–69. M. Marciak, 'Seleucid–Parthian Adiabene in the Light of Ancient Geographical and Ethnographical Texts', in *Anabasis. Studia Classica et Orientalia*, 2 (2011); M. Marciak, 'The cultural environment of Adiabene in the Hellenistic, Parthian, and Sasanian Periods', in *Parthica*, 16 (2014); M. Marciak 'Das Konigreich Adiabene in hellenistisch-parthischer Zeit', in *Gymnasium*, 122 (2015); L. Gregoratti, 'Sinews of the other Empire: Parthian Great King's rule over vassal Kingdoms' in H. Teigen and E. Seland (eds), *Sinews of Empire: Networks in the Roman Near East and Beyond* (Oxford, 2017), p. 100.
27. Josephus, *Jewish Antiquities*, XX,72.
28. Ibid., XX, 75–92.
29. Tacitus, *Annals*, XI.8–10.
30. Ibid., XI.8.
31. Sellwood, *Coinage of Parthia*, pp. 68–72, 223–4, 231–4; Shore, *Parthian Coins*, pp. 147–8; M. J. Olbrycht, 'Das Arsakidenreich zwischen der mediterranen Welt und Innerasien, Bemerkungen zur politischen Strategie der Arsakiden von Vologases I. bis zum Herrschaftsantritt des Vologases III. (50–147 n. Chr.)' in E. Dabrowa, *Ancient Iran and the Mediterranean World: Proceedings of an international conference in honour of Professor J. Wolski held at the Jagiellonian University, Cracow, in September 1996* (Cracow, 1998 [b]), p. 125; M. J. Olbrycht, 'Vologases I, Pacoros II and Artabanos III: Coins and Parthian History', *Iranica Antiqua*, 51 (2016), pp. 217– 8. On Artabanus and Vologases, see L. Gregoratti 'A Tale of two Great Kings: Artabanus and Vologaeses' in A. Krasnowolska and R. Rusek-Kowalska (eds), Studies on the Iranian World I, Before Islam (Cracow, 2015 [b]).

32. Tacitus, *Annals*, XII.44.
33. Ibid., XII. 44.
34. Pascal Asdourian, *Die politischen Beziehungen zwischen Armenien und Rom von 190 v. Chr. bis 428 n. Chr: ein Abriss der armenischen Geschichte in dieser Periode* (Venice, 1911), pp. 85–97; K. Gilmartin, 'Corbulo's campaigns in the East: an analysis of Tacitus' Account', in *Historia*, 22 (1973); M. L. Chaumont, *L'Arménie entre Rome et l'Iran I. De l'avènement d'Auguste à l'avènement de Dioclétien*, in H. Temporini and W. Hasse (eds), *Aufstieg und Niedergang der römischen Welt*, II, 9, 1 (Berlin and New York 1976) 1976, pp. 97–124; M. Sommer, 'La crisi romano–partica del 53–64 d.C.: la prospettiva "orientale"', in ὅρμος - *Ricerche di Storia Antica*, 1 (2009).
35. Tacitus, *Annals*, XII.44–9.
36. Ibid., XII.50.
37. Ibid., XII.51.
38. Ibid., XIII.8.
39. Ibid., XIII.9; 37; XV.2; 17.
40. Ibid., XV.1.
41. Ibid., XV.2.
42. Ibid., XV.29–31.
43. Dio Cassius, *History*, LXIII.1–7.
44. Ibid., LXIII. 6, 4.
45. R. Syme, *Tacitus* (Oxford, 1958); C. Questa, *Studi sulle fonti degli Annales di Tacito* (Rome, 1960).

CHAPTER 2

ROMAN AND IRANIAN PERCEPTIONS OF THE OTHER IN LATE ANTIQUITY

David Bagot

When considering the mutual perceptions of Iranians and Westerners (meaning, in this context, Romans) in Late Antiquity, we are immediately confronted by the same problem common to most discussions concerning Iran of this period – the problematic sources.[1] This does not necessarily mean a lack of sources. The late Roman literary tradition is relatively plentiful, with some major historians offering much of apparent interest. However, trying to extricate the truth of the Roman appraisal of the Iranians is a complex process. Also, it is significant that in general Roman historians only wrote about Iranians during times of war – there is very little Roman material for Sasanian history of the fifth century presumably due to the fact that relations between the powers were largely peaceable at this time. Therefore, any conclusions must be hedged with caveats.

On the Iranian side, the scarceness of evidence is nearly total. The few extant literary sources created during the Sasanian era tell us very little of how the Romans were perceived by contemporary Iranians. From the early Sasanian period there are a range of extant monumental reliefs and inscriptions, and from the post-Sasanian period there are works (most significantly Ferdowsi's *Shahnameh*) which reflect Sasanian-era sources to some extent (the precise extent is hotly debated).[2] For Sasanian cultural history, Ferdowsi's *Shahnameh* is a major source, given that Ferdowsi was relatively sympathetic to pre-Islamic Iran and does not seem to have wilfully misinterpreted or misremembered the Zoroastrian-flavoured sources with which he worked. By way of comparison, though himself Iranian, the tenth century historian Tabari showed little sympathy for or attachment to pre-Islamic Iranian culture, for instance fusing the Iranian mythic–historical past with his Qur'anic understanding of history.[3] This is not the case for Ferdowsi. Despite writing over three centuries after the Arab Conquest, Ferdowsi's life seems almost identical to that of a Sasanian nobleman. He came from the *dehqan* (gentry) class, the lifestyle of which is assumed to have been similar to that of Sasanian antecedents,[4] and he seems to have faithfully reported pre-Islamic Iranian myths, rather than hammer them into conformity with Islamic belief, as Tabari seems to have done. In terms of understanding the cultural outlook of the late antique Iranian elite, the *Shahnameh* of Ferdowsi is difficult to better.

Despite the limitations of our literary sources and how they give a warped or partial view (whether deliberately or not) of the 'other' people, one does feel it is possible to get some sort of idea of mutual perceptions of the Other in Late Antiquity. Though it can only be provisional and cautiously offered, based as it is on highly fragmentary evidence, one would contend that it is also both credible and reasonable.

Roman Perceptions of the Iranians

We believe that it is possible to construct a reasonably coherent impression of how the Romans perceived the Iranians in Late Antiquity. However, in general there appears to be something of a disconnect between the relatively nuanced governmental views on the one hand and popular prejudice and stereotype on the other. The Roman popular perception of Iranians, seemingly only loosely based on reality, does appear to have clouded the perceptions (or at least the published perceptions) of people who one would expect to have been better informed. This in itself is instructive – the imagined Iranian appears to have been a very powerful image in the Roman mind, so much so it seems to have to some extent crowded out reality. Schneider has discussed in detail Late Antique Roman 'orientalism' with regards the depictions of 'easterners' in Roman art and imagery.[5] One would contend that we get a similar sense from Roman literature, too.

Let us first consider in some detail the account of Ammianus Marcellinus, which in many ways offers the fullest impression of Iran of all the Roman writers. Ammianus was a staff officer in the Roman army and fought in two major campaigns against the Persians, in 359–60 and 363, this latter advancing deep into Sasanian Mesopotamia. He was seemingly an acquaintance of Prince Hormizd, Shapur II's elder brother or half-brother. Prince Hormizd had fled the Sasanian Empire following the power struggles after the death of their father Hormizd II, but now sought refuge in the Roman court.[6] This meant that Ammianus not only saw the Sasanian Empire firsthand, but he almost certainly knew at least one high-ranking Iranian, meaning that Ammianus was potentially far better versed in Iranian affairs than most of his contemporaries – certainly it is hard to think of a Late Antique Roman historian who might be better informed. Finally, Ammianus publicly performed his account in Rome in the early 380s,[7] and as such we might assume that his treatment of the Iranians had some resonance for his audience, making him a very useful source for our purposes.

Ammianus' account has two main points of interest for us – his ethnographic and geographical descriptions of the Persians and their lands, and his descriptions of contemporary Persians, in particular King Shapur II, and the Persian army. Let us first consider Ammianus' lengthy description of the Persian Empire, which appears in his narrative immediately before Julian's invasion in 363 (Book XXIII, Chapter 6). Ammianus offers a very brief overview of Iranian history, showing his awareness of the Achaemenids and Alexander.[8] Then, he gives a descriptive summary of the Sasanian domains and their organisation, offering comments on points of interest.[9] He then describes the Iranians themselves, their habits and military systems,[10] before concluding with a curious commentary on pearls.[11]

How valuable is Ammianus' testimony? Some of it is likely very accurate, for instance Ammianus' assessment of the Sasanian army is in accordance with the other evidence available, one which is largely accepted by military historians today.[12] In general, however, the historical value of Ammianus' account is reduced by the fact that it was largely drawn from outdated literary sources, rather than Ammianus' own experiences,[13] despite these apparently being extensive and detailed. Ammianus' main source seems to have been Ptolemy's *Geography*, then over two centuries old, supplemented with the work of Strabo (active in the Augustan period) and that of Pliny the Elder (working in the later first century AD).[14] He also seems to have been influenced by Herodotus' venerable account, then over 700 years old.[15] Ammianus may not have even read these works in full, instead relying on popularising facsimiles and glosses,[16] with Sabbah suggesting that Ammianus' scientific, geographic and ethnographic digressions were a means to demonstrate his learning and all-round reliability as a source,[17] which seems reasonable given Ammianus' likely, though admittedly disputed, status as a propagandist for conservative, pagan values.[18]

His reliance on dated literary sources caused Ammianus to make egregious errors. He states that the Arsacids were still ruling Iran, despite them having been deposed 150 years earlier.[19] He glosses over the Sasanian capital Ctesiphon in this description, but lavishes praise on the Hellenistic city of Seleucia (which would have had resonance with his audience),[20] but which by the Sasanian period was in terminal decline.[21]

Ultimately, Ammianus' portrayal of the Sasanian Empire appears to be one deliberately constructed to conform with Roman stereotypes of the Iranians, stereotypes heavily informed by respected, if venerable, literary accounts and therefore quite valuable in ascertaining how the Romans perceived the Iranians. Clearly, Ammianus' audience, which we might assume to be made up of relatively educated people, was not well acquainted with even the fundamentals of recent Iranian political history, if Ammianus could present the Arsacid dynasty as still ruling Iran without making himself look painfully ill informed. Such a representation perhaps implies a Roman belief of a timeless Eastern Other, where neither the passage of centuries nor changes of dynasty (and, arguably, the fundamental political reorganisation of the Iranian domains which went with that)[22] significantly alter the perceptions of Iranians in the minds of the Romans.

This Roman desire to link the Sasanians into the distant antique past is echoed, albeit in a different form, with the treatment of the wars between the early Sasanians and the Romans in the mid-third century, which were presented by Roman writers as an attempt by the Sasanians to recreate the Achaemenid Empire.[23] Given that the understanding of the Achaemenids by the Sasanians was imprecise at best,[24] and the impression given by Roman historians is much at variance with that which appears in the early Sasanian royal inscriptions,[25] one has to concur with Canepa's observation that '[s]cholarship is largely in agreement that although the early Sasanians counted the Achaemenids as ancestors, they had imperfect knowledge of them and did not set out to recreate the Achaemenid empire.'[26] Given earlier comments concerning Ammianus' use of outdated sources to inform his narrative, in preference to his own personal experiences, one is inclined to argue that portraying Sasanian war aims in an Achaemenid light owed rather more to the desire of Roman historians to use the timeless past as a prism through which to perceive the present rather than any sort of objective appraisal of reality in Late Antiquity and that the core of Western perceptions of Iranians were informed more by Herodotus et al. than contemporary reality.

Let us return to Ammianus' narrative. Ammianus seemingly constructed his narrative with his audience's expectations in mind. For instance, his descriptions of Persian heavy cavalry are nearly identical to those in Heliodorus' third-century novel *Ethiopica*.[27] Heliodorus' fictional representation of cavalry suggests that the image of the fully armoured eastern cavalryman was compelling to the Roman imagination. Clearly, Ammianus' descriptions were not wholly fictitious. There is indisputable pictorial and archaeological evidence that some Persian cavalry were equipped as he recorded (including the monumental reliefs of Sasanian kings). However, it is exceedingly likely that the *clibinarius* cavalryman formed only a small minority of Sasanian cavalry forces.[28] However, Ammianus implies that the *clibinarius* archetype was the norm, in apparent accordance with popular perceptions.

Similarly, Ammianus portrays Sasanian infantry as of very low quality, a portrayal he shares with other Roman commentators.[29] The low quality of Persian infantry, though doubtless with some basis in reality, also has a very ancient pedigree in Greek writing.[30] However, in the battles Ammianus describes, most notably the Siege of Amida, Iranian infantry (or more likely dismounted cavalry – he records them as being organised into *turmae* – that is, cavalry squadrons)[31] were more than capable of threatening Roman legionaries holding defensive positions.

Elephants, though certainly present in Persian armies were doubtless something of a rarity, with the Armenian writer Elishe recording in the fifth century that for each elephant which attacked the Armenians, there were 3,000 other soldiers – whether we accept Elishe's figures or not, the elephants were hardly the mainstay of the army.[32] Romans writing in more dispassionate circumstances, such as the diplomatic historian Menander, recognised elephants were more for show than actual use.[33] Certainly in the late Sasanian period, elephants appear to be used by commanders more as a mobile command centre than as actual weapons.[34] Indeed, this rather less dramatic use of elephants is somewhat implied by Ammianus, who does put the elephants at the back of the Persian army in 363.[35] However, the impression one gets from Ammianus' narrative is one of Iranian armies liberally populated with bellicose pachyderms,[36] presumably indicating that this was something his audience expected to be recounted.

Therefore, Ammianus was probably guilty of perpetuating popular perceptions of the Persians, regardless of their accuracy, and preferring well-regarded, if dated, literary sources to his own experiences, significantly reducing the value of the unique strength of his account – his personal experience of the Persian Empire. Ammianus apparently preferred to have been perceived as a scholarly author, this seemingly conferring greater status than that of being a reliable eyewitness, who would challenge the popular, but erroneous, perceptions of his audience. However, the manner in which Ammianus constructed his narrative does give us an understanding of how the Roman public (or at least the intelligentsia who were exposed to Ammianus' work) perceived the Iranians – with perceptions dominated by the well-established tropes of armoured cavalry, elephants and slave-like infantry, an impression which had been largely established for centuries.

However, a rather less cliché-ridden impression comes from Ammianus' description of the Persian king, Shapur II. Though Shapur was endowed with features of the stock barbarian king (such as irrational anger and avarice),[37] Shapur is also portrayed as a king whose courage, piety and respect for the aristocracy far outstripped that of the contemporary Christian Roman rulers.[38] Indeed, one might see Shapur II as the second hero of the text, behind the emperor Julian who Ammianus particularly celebrates.

Should we see this as evidence of Ammianus' respect for the Persians and for their systems of governance? It is doubtful. One would rather posit that it tells us more about how Ammianus viewed the Roman Empire of his day. Ammianus was a conservative pagan author, who seems to have viewed Christianity as a profound threat to the Roman way of life. He depicts a Roman government and elite, now increasingly Christianised, which has lost touch with traditional Roman values of piety to the established gods, honour and courage, and that, relatively speaking, the Iranians represent good governance, courageous leadership and proper piety. This is highly significant for us. Unpicking the detail of Ammianus' portrayal of the Sasanians, which appears a complex mishmash of fabrication, fair reporting and pandering to popular stereotypes, goes beyond the scope of this present work. What is important for us is not so much the veracity (or lack thereof) of Ammianus' account, but rather that it surely indicates that if a Sasanian king can be presented as a moral exemplar, then Ammianus' portrayal of Shapur must be underpinned by at least some Roman positive appreciation of the Iranians as a people. Certainly, Roman historiography has a long tradition of using 'noble savages' to expose the flaws in Roman society (such as with Tacitus' portrayal of the Caledonians and Germans) and as such, arguably, Ammianus' account tells us more about how some Romans viewed other Romans than how they viewed the Iranians. However, it is still worth emphasising that the portrayal of Iranians in general, and Shapur II in particular, is perhaps more positive in Ammianus' narrative than we might expect.

This does contrast considerably with Roman historians working later. For Procopius, the most significant of the Roman writers of the sixth century, the most important figure of his account of the Persians Wars is not a Roman, but the Sasanian king, Khusrau I. Khusrau is treated as a study in royal tyranny – he is cruel, avaricious, vindictive and rules with scant regard for tradition and persecutes the established elite wilfully and needlessly,[39] clearly playing upon the 'oriental despot' caricature. We concur with Kaldellis' argument that the greater part of Procopius' treatment of Khusrau illustrates Procopius' desire to demonstrate to his Roman audience how terrible arbitrary royal power was and to let them apply this to their estimation of their own government, which Procopius clearly disdained, as evidenced through his *Secret History*.[40] However, despite the political undertones, Procopius' portrayal of Khusrau remains significant for us. For Procopius' demonisation of Khusrau to not devalue his main narrative, his audience must have assumed that Persian rulers were tyrannical, cruel, avaricious, etcetera – the portrayal of Khusrau I must have rested upon implicit assumptions. Procopius offers no indication of where he got his tales of Persian court life and intrigue from. One tends to believe they were drawn from a mixture of hearsay, speculation and fabrication and therefore must have played upon popular perceptions to be believable.

Such a perception of Iranian cruelty is supported by Agathias' account of the Sasanians. Agathias has a prominent place in Sasanian Studies thanks to his lengthy description of Persian religion and the purported inclusion (via translations made by a friend working in the Roman diplomatic service) of Persian chronicles.[41] It is because of this that Howard-Johnston considered Agathias '[t]he only Roman historian to have made a serious attempt to understand the Sasanian world.'[42] Regardless of from where Agathias might have sourced his information, perhaps counterintuitively, it is helpful that Agathias was not well read (and did not pretend to be well read) in the classics of Latin and Greek literature. His work is free of allusions to notable classical authors, probably increasing the usefulness of his account on the Sasanians. He seems to have based his account more on the contemporary information he gathered (of whatever provenance) than classical texts centuries out of date.[43] Agathias was deeply anti-Persian.[44] Though compromising the reliability of his analysis, especially regarding Zoroastrianism and Persian culture (which are unremittingly and exaggeratedly negative), it does give us what is probably the nearest thing to a 'genuine' Roman perception of Iranians. Though hardly a 'man in the street' – he was still a relatively well-to-do professional – Agathias offers us a view of the Persians closer to that of the Roman masses.

Agathias lets his anti-Persian prejudices run riot. In his discussion of Zoroastrian religion, he associates all manner of eccentricities to the faith, repeatedly associating it with incest.[45] He includes scurrilous accounts of the ancestry of the Sasanian royal house, stating that Ardashir I, the founder of the Sasanian dynasty, was the illegitimate offspring of a liaison between the wife of Pabak the tanner and a travelling soldier named Sasan.[46] He accuses the Persians of extreme cruelties to the Romans, for instance accusing the third-century king Shapur I of flaying the captive Roman Emperor Valerian alive.[47] Roman accounts from the third to fifth centuries state that Valerian died in servitude in Persia (presumably of natural causes), with some accounts stating Shapur used Valerian as a mounting block.[48] The tenth-century Persian historian Tabari offers three fates – either being used as a labourer for a dam, being released after paying a large indemnity and having his nose cut off or that he was simply killed.[49] It is impossible to tell what the fate of Valerian was in Shapur's captivity, but Agathias' gruesome account of his end, given the less bloody earlier ones, seems to be fabrication, but all the more telling of sixth-century Roman perceptions of the Persians for it. By way of comparison, Ammianus (though a far from ideal source, as previously discussed) does accuse the

Iranians of occasionally flaying their enemies and accuses them of promiscuity, but not incest.[50] As a side point, it is worth mentioning that what appears to be the declining perception of Iranians in Roman literature between the fourth and sixth centuries does indicate that though much of the Roman understanding of the Iranians appears in accordance with long-established norms, there also appears a degree of mutability.

How should Agathias' anti-Persian prejudice be interpreted? Certainly, it suggests that lurid anti-Persian tales circulated amongst some sections of the Roman public. It is our suggestion that Agathias' straightforward account, lacking the added layers of literary complexity of Ammianus' or Procopius' works, gives us a better idea of how more-or-less normal Romans perceived the Persians – as cruel, sexually deviant and – to Roman eyes – holding bizarre cultural practices.

On a diplomatic and governmental level, there appears considerable mutual respect between Iranians and Romans. For instance, Procopius records that the Roman emperor Arcadius appointed the Persian king Yazdgird I as guardian for his infant son Theodosius,[51] which, even if only a diplomatic formality, does suggest a deep sense of trust and respect between them. Embassies between Rome and Iran in Late Antiquity were clearly carefully choreographed events and doubtless underpinned by considerable mutual respect. However, even in the driest of Roman literary accounts, one does get a sense of assumed Roman superiority. Though it is very possible that certain Roman diplomats and statesmen might well have been witty and charming and that their Iranian counterparts were arrogant and boorish, one does feel that Menander's neat characterisation on national lines of the moral qualities of the assorted diplomats and princes in his account implies an assumption of Roman moral superiority.[52] For a diplomatic historian to describe the Sasanian king as having sent a 'juvenile letter' and to 'have boasted and acted the vulgar braggart'[53] is in itself highly illustrative of Roman perceptions of Iranian behaviour. Significantly, when Menander reports on Roman diplomatic failings, he puts it down to John, the Roman emissary, being incompetent rather than arrogant or tactless, which (from a moral standpoint) was presumably preferable.[54]

Therefore, how might we sum up our understanding of Roman perceptions of Iranians? Of course, any conclusion must be provisional, but the literary evidence clearly suggests two main interwoven strands colouring Roman thought – that there was (to some extent) an unchanging Orient which had remained largely static for centuries, and an assumption of Roman cultural superiority, which, if perhaps not all encompassing (such as Ammianus' portrayal of Shapur II), was still potent.

Iranian Perceptions of Romans

It is difficult to offer any impression of Iranian perceptions of Romans in Late Antiquity given the limitations of the sources. From the third century, there are monumental reliefs and inscriptions, most significantly those of Shapur I commemorating his victories over the Romans. The reliefs show his triumph over the Roman emperors Gordian, Philip and Valerian, with near-identical versions of the reliefs at Naqsh–e Rustam, Bishapur and Darabgird, and complement his triumphal inscription at Naqsh-e Rostam (also known as the *Res Gestae Divi Saporis*).[55] Shapur's victories are celebrated in other media, such as the famous cameo showing the capture of Valerian in 260. Perhaps significantly, this piece of artwork seems to have been made by an Iranian craftsman copying Western styles.[56] This probably indicates a degree of appreciation for Roman culture on the part of Shapur I, though as we lack a firm understanding of the circumstances of the creation of this cameo (such as for whom it was intended) interpretations of it can only be tentative. Indeed, the monumental sources of the early Sasanian period tell us remarkably little as to how the Sasanians (much less the Iranians generally) perceived the Romans. Rubin is surely correct in his interpretation of certain sections of the *Res Gestae Divi Saporis* as 'serv [ing] to intensify the impression that the Roman Empire enjoyed a special position in the eyes of the early Sasanians' and that, though the inscription was doubtless a grandiose piece of Sasanian propaganda, it still conveys 'an attitude of respect towards the Roman Empire'.[57] Beyond showing us that the early Sasanians saw the Romans as 'worthy' foes and that victory over the Romans helped burnish their reputation – neither inference which might be viewed as revelatory – the various triumphal and monumental media of the early Sasanian period only marginally advance our understanding of how the Sasanians perceived the Romans.

Similarly, the other extant third-century inscriptions, such as those at Paikuli or those of Kirdir, tell us nothing of relevance. Nerses records at Paikuli that he made peace with the Romans (using the phrase

'Caesar and the Romans were in gratitude and peace and friendship with me' – a rather positive interpretation of the recent disasters suffered by Sasanian arms),[58] whilst Kirdir offers us nothing at all on how he saw the Romans.[59] The other extant literary sources from the Sasanian period do not offer us anything of particular significance either.

Ferdowsi's epic poem offers us relatively little directly, but what it does offer is instructive, given his utility as a source for Late Antique Iranian cultural history. Perhaps the most significant direct intervention of the Romans is during the reign of the fourth-century king Shapur II, when Ferdowsi offers a fanciful account of Shapur disguising himself as a merchant to spy on the Romans, being recognised, captured and trussed up in an ass' skin, whilst the Romans cause havoc in Iran, until, through the intervention of a Persian maiden in service to the Roman empress, he is able to escape and wreak his revenge on the Romans.[60]

Ferdowsi's account of the reign of Shapur II and the Romans seemingly conflates the Roman wars of the reigns of Shapur I (whose own Roman campaigns are treated very briefly),[61] Narses and Shapur II, along with a large amount of fantasy, which play on similar motifs to some of the mythic tales of Rostam, such as the disguised hero and the helpful maiden. In furthering our understanding of how the Iranians perceived the Romans, Ferdowsi's narrative does suggest that Roman successes over the Persians are down to trickery and that a Roman emperor in open battle is no match for a Persian shah. This plays upon the motif established early in the *Shahnameh* with the relationship between Iraj, Salm and Tur, the sons of the legendary hero Ferydun where the rulers of the west (Salm) and the lands to the east of Iran (Tur) are portrayed as killing the upstanding Iraj, ruler of Iran, through deceit, who then suffer their comeuppance at the hand of Manucher, the next true shah of Iran.[62] In that sense, the portrayal of Romans (or 'Westerners' generally) in these episodes of the *Shahnameh* serves to confirm the moral and martial superiority of Iranians.

Finally, Ferdowsi offers us a detailed physical and moral description of a particularly malevolent 'Westerner' (in reality a curious and highly illustrative portrayal of the Armenian prince Smbat Bagratuni – someone from the western fringe of the Iranian world, rather than a Westerner as such). Ferdowsi describes how Khusrau II looked for a particularly wicked governor to punish the rebellious city of Rayy after his vizier convinced him not to just have the city destroyed:

> The king replied [to his vizier] 'Then the place needs an ill-natured governor, an incompetent fool, someone who is ignorant and foul mouthed.' A courtier called Bahman said, 'If the king wishes, we will look for such an incompetent, but we need some kind of guide.' Khosrow said, 'He should have red hair, a crooked nose, and an ugly face; he must be an infamous man, with a sallow complexion, someone who's malevolent, short in stature, his heart filled with anguish, base in his nature, vengeful and with a lying tongue; his eyes should be green and squinting, he should have big teeth, and he should lope along the road like a wolf.'[63]

Here Ferdowsi could be said to draw a caricature of a Westerner, quite possibly someone of Celtic extraction (perhaps in reference to the Galatian Celts of central Anatolia, who might have remained a distinct group in Late Antiquity). Ferdowsi's treatment of this individual suggests that a pale-skinned individual with, among other features, ginger hair and green eyes, was a figure of fun in some early-medieval Iranian circles and such a physical appearance was associated with limited intellect and moral turpitude. Significantly, Ferdowsi's description depends upon an assumed moral and physical superiority of Iranians over 'Westerners' – by the man's physical description, it is clear that Khusrau has to look outside the Iranian world to the west to find a governor sufficiently degenerate to be a fitting punishment for the city of Reyy.

In the *Shahameh*, there are indications of similarities between the way Iranians are portrayed in Roman literature – i.e. an assumption of superior moral qualities. However, given the primary function of the *Shahnameh* was to entertain, we should not exaggerate the reality of the picture it paints – it very probably shows us what Iranian noblemen wanted to believe about the Romans or Westerners in general, which may not have been what they actually did believe. Given the lateness of the composition of the *Shahnameh*, nearly four hundred years after the fall of the Sasanian Empire, it certainly must be treated with caution, though the assumption of Iranian superiority seems credible.

Conclusion

In conclusion, then, what can we say about Roman and Persian perceptions of the other in Late Antiquity and how these perceptions may or may not have converged? I fear that the conclusion I offer can hardly be considered revolutionary. Both Romans and Iranians seem to have perceived the other in terms of cultural and moral inferiority. Though perhaps an oversimplification, the only conclusion one might offer is that the notion that one's own ethnic, religious or national grouping was inherently superior was alive and well in Late Antiquity.

Notes

1. By way of introduction, see G. Widengren, 'Sources for Parthian and Sasanian History', in Ehsan Yarshater (ed.), *The Cambridge History of Iran 3 (2): The Seleucid, Parthian and Sasanian Periods* (Cambridge, 1983), pp. 1261–83.
2. By way of introduction, see Ehsan Yarshatar, 'Iranian National History', in Yarshater, Ehsan (ed.), *The Cambridge History of Iran: Volume 3 (I): The Seleucid, Parthian and Sasanian Periods* (Cambridge, 1983), p. 359f; see pp. 370–83 for a summary of the contents of the *Khwaday Namag* from post-Conquest sources.
3. Dick Davis, *Epic and Sedition: The Case of Ferdowsi's Shahnameh* (Washington, DC, 1992), p. 14.
4. A. Shapur Shahbazi, *Ferdowsi: A Critical Biography* (Costa Mesa, 1991), pp. 20–1. 33–4.
5. Rolf Michael Schneider, 'Orientalism in Late Antiquity: The Oriental in Imperial and Christian Imagery', in Josef Wisehöfer and Philip Huyse (eds), *Eran ud Aneran: Studienzu den Beziehungen zwischen dem Sasanidenreich und der Mittelmeerwelt* (Stuttgart, 2006).
6. For some references to Hormizd see Ammianus Marcellinus, *History*, XVI.10.16, XXIV.1.8, XXIV.2.11.
7. John C. Rolfe, 'Introduction' in Ammianus Marcellinus, *History* (in three volumes), tr. John C. Rolfe (Cambridge, MA, 1935), p. xvi.
8. Ammianus, *History*, XXIII.6.1–9.
9. Ibid., XXIII.6.10–74.
10. Ibid., XXIII.6.75–84.
11. Ibid., XXIII.6.85–7.
12. Ammianus, *History*, XXIII.6.83; David Nicolle, *Sasanian Armies: The Iranian Empire, early 3rd to mid-7th centuries AD* (Stockport, 1996); Kaveh Farokh, *Shadows in the Desert: Ancient Persia at War* (Oxford, 2004), part 3; Peter Wilcox, *Rome's Enemies (3): Parthians & Sassanid Persians* (Oxford, 1986).
13. J. den Boeft, J. W. Drijvers, D. den Hengst and H. C. Teitler, *Philological and Historical Commentary on Ammianus Marcellinus XXIII* (Groningen, 1998), pp. 129–31.
14. Ibid., pp. 130–1.
15. See the notes in Ch. XXIII.6 of Rolfe's edition for the allusions to Herodotus' account.
16. Charles W. Fornara., 'Studies in Ammianus Marcellinus: II: Ammianus' Knowledge and Use of Greek and Latin Literature', in *Historia: Zeitschrift für Alte Geschichte*, vol. 41. No. 4 (1992), p. 421.

17. Guy Sabbah, *La Méthode d'Ammien Marcellin: Recherches sur la Construction du Discours Historique sur les Histoires* (Paris, 1978), pp. 525–8.
18. See T. G. Elliott, *Ammianus Marcellinus and Fourth Century History* (Toronto, 1983); Gavin Kelly, *Ammianus Marcellinus: The Allusive Historian* (Cambridge, 2008). Warrington makes us aware of how (in books now lost, but surviving in the eleventh-century work of Cedrenus) Ammianus ascribed the outbreak of war between Constantine and Shapur II in 330 to fanciful causes which show the Roman emperor in the worst light; B. H. Warmington, 'Ammianus Marcellinus and the Lies of Metrodorus', in *The Classical Quarterly Review, New Series*, vol. 31, No. 2 (Cambridge, 1981), pp. 464, 468; see Cedrenus, *Chronicle*, tr. Michael H. Dodgeon, in Michael Dodgeon and Samuel Lieu, *The Roman Eastern Frontier and the Persian Wars: A.D. 226–363* (London, 1991), p. 153. However, Seager, Thomson and Camus have in different ways articulated a more positive view of the historical merits of Ammianus' narrative. See Robin Seager, *Ammianus Marcellinus: Seven Studies in His Language and Thought* (Columbia, 1986), pp. 131–3; E. A. Thompson, *The Historical Work of Ammianus Marcellinus* (Cambridge, 1947), pp. 121–4, 131–3; Pierre-Marie Camus, *Ammien Marcellin: Témoin des Courants Culturels et Religieux à la fin du IVe Siècle* (Paris, 1967), pp. 106f, 113–4, 256f. We should note in particular Seager's argument that Ammianus in particular was interested in the threat 'barbarism' (not Christianity) played to the Roman way of life.
19. Ammianus, *History*, XXIII.6.5–6.
20. Ibid., XXIII.6.23–4.
21. St John Simpson, 'Mesopotamia in the Sasanian Period: Settlement Patterns, Arts and Crafts', in J. Curtis (ed.), *Mesopotamia and Iran in the Parthian and Sasanian Periods: Rejection and Revival: c.238 BC–AD 642* (London, 2000), p. 61.
22. This is a highly disputed issue; for the two extremes of the debate, see Arthur Christensen, *L'Iran sous les sassanides* (Copenhagen, 1944) and Parvaneh Pourshariati, *Decline and Fall of the Sasanian Empire: The Sasanian–Parthian Confederacy and the Arab Conquest of Iran* (New York, 2008).
23. Herodian, *History of the Empire*, 6.2.2; Dio Cassius, *History*, 80.3.4; Zonaras, *Extracts of History*, 12.15.
24. E. Yarshater, 'Were the Sasanians Heirs to the Achaemenids?' in *La Persia nel Medioevo* (Rome, 1971), pp. 517ff.
25. Touraj Daryaee, 'Ethnic and Territorial Boundaries in Late Antique and Early Medieval Persia (Third to Tenth Century)' in Florin Curta (ed.), *Borders, Barriers and Ethnogenesis: Frontiers in Late Antiquity and the Middle Ages* (Turnhout, 2005), p. 128.
26. Matthew Canepa, 'Technologies of Memory in Early Sasanian Iran: Achaemenid Sites and Sasanian Identity', in *American Journal of Archaeology*, vol. 114, No. 4 (2010), p. 563 and *passim*.
27. Ammianus, *History*, XIX.7.4, XXIV.6.8, XXV.1.1, 12–13; Heliodorus, *An Ethiopian Romance*, tr. Moses Hadas (Philadelphia, 1957), pp. 229–31.
28. See esp. J. C. Coulston, 'Roman, Parthian and Sassanid Tactical Developments', in Philip Freeman and David Kennedy (eds), *The Defence of the Roman and Byzantine East: Part I* (Oxford, 1986), pp. 60–1, 66–8; Nicolle, *Sassanian*

Armies, p. 20; Simon James, 'Evidence from Dura Europos for the Origins of Late Roman Helmets' in Syria, T. 63, Fasc. 1/2 (1986), p. 15.

29. Ammianus, *History*, XXIII.6.8, Procopius, *Wars*, I.xxiv.24–6, Menander, *The History of Menander the Guardsman*, tr. R. C. Blockley (Liverpool, 1985), Fragment 20.3 (p. 191).
30. A. R. Burn, 'Persia and the Greeks', in Ilya Gershevitch (ed.), *The Cambridge History of Iran: Volume 2: The Median and Achaemenian Periods* (Cambridge, 1985), p. 355.
31. Ammianus, *History*, XIX.2.2–3. Furthermore, we have some archaeological evidence of Sasanian dismounted cavalry. The well-equipped dead Persian in the Dura Europos siege mine was presumably a horseman, as he wore a mail coat cut to facilitate horse riding; Simon James, *Excavations at Dura-Europos 1928–1937: Final Report VII: The Arms and Armour and other Military Equipment* (Oxford, 2004), p. 116.
32. Elishe, *History of Vardan and the Armenian War*, tr. Roberts W. Thomson (Cambridge, MA, 1982), p. 114.
33. Menander, Fragment 20.3 (p. 191).
34. Touraj Daryaee, 'From Terror to Tactical Usage: Elephants in the Partho–Sasanian Period', in Vesta Curtis, Elizabeth Pendleton, Michael Alram and Touraj Daryaee (eds), *The Parthian and Early Sasanian Empires: Adaptations and Expansion* (Oxford, 2016), p. 39.
35. Ammianus, *History*, XXIV.6.8.
36. See e.g. Ibid., XXIV.6.8, XXV.1.14–5, 3.4.
37. Barbara Sidwell, *The Portrayal and Role of Anger in the Res Gestae of Ammianus Marcellinus* (Adelaide, 2008), see esp. ch.2; see e.g. Ammianus, *History*, XVIII.4.16, 6.18, XIX.1.4–6.
38. Ammianus, *History*. XVIII.5.6 which refers to the Persian king taking advice from his nobles; regarding piety, Shapur made sacrifices before his invasion of 359 (XVIII.7.1) and according to Ammianus, Shapur refrained from attacking the Romans in 361 '*dum moveri permitterunt sacra*' – 'until the *sacra* (divine/ holy) [force/power] would permit a move.' Shapur's personal courage is demonstrated by leading from the front during the siege of Amida; XIX.7.8.
39. Procopius, *Wars*, I.xxiii.1–25, II.i.1, 12–14, II.ix.8–12, II.xi.37–8.
40. Anthony Kaldellis, *Procopius of Caesarea: Tyranny, History, and Philosophy at the End of Antiquity* (Philadelphia, 2004), *passim*, esp. p. 49; for evidence to support *The Secret History* to be simultaneously or near simultaneously, with *Wars*, see Geoffrey Greatrex, 'The Dates of Procopius' Works', in *Byzantine and Modern Greek Studies* 18 (1994), pp. 113–14.
41. McDonough sees Agathias as 'traditionally' the most important Roman source on the Sasanians because of this; Scott McDonough, 'Were the Sasanians Barbarians? Roman Writers on the "Empire of the Persians"', in Ralph W. Mathiesen and Danuta Shanzar (eds), *Romans, Barbarians and the Transformation of the Roman World: Cultural Interaction and the Creation of Identity in Late Antiquity* (Farnham, 2011), p. 55. See Averil Cameron, 'Agathias on the Sasanians', in *Dumbarton Oaks Papers*, vol. 23/24 (1969/1970), pp. 113ff; there are strong arguments against the veracity of Agathias' claims to use genuine Sasanian documents, see Tim Greenwood, 'Sasanian Echoes and

Apocalyptic Expectations: A Re-Evaluation of the Armenian History Attributed to Sebeos', in Alice Rio (ed.), *Law, Custom and Justice in Late Antiquity and the early Middle Ages. Proceedings of the 2008 Byzantine Colloquium* (London, 2011), p. 332.

42. James Howard-Johnston, 'The Two Great Powers in Late Antiquity: A Comparison', in Averil Cameron (ed.), *The Byzantine and Early Islamic Near East: III: States, Resources and Armies* (Princeton, 1995), p. 177.
43. Averil Cameron, 'Herodotus and Thucydides in Agathias', in *Byzantinische Zeitschrift*, 57, Issue 1 (1964), pp. 33ff. See too Cameron, 'Agathias on the Sasanians', pp. 75, 91, 99.
44. Cameron, 'Agathias on the Sasanians', pp. 59–60; Drijvers, 'Roman Image', pp. 74–5.
45. Agathias, *History*, in Averil Cameron, 'Agathias on the Sasanians', 116.4 (p. 81); though it seems clear that Late Antique Zoroastrians did practice incest to some extent, Daryaee argues convincingly that 'while such a law [incestuous marriage] was on the books, it seems to have taken place on a practical function in its reaction to the Islamization of the Iranian Plateau' – that is, it was not the norm in Sasanian times; Touraj Daryaee, 'Marriage, Property and Conversion among the Zoroastrians: From Late Sasanian to Islamic Iran', in *Journal of Persianate Studies*, 6 (2013), p. 92. Sasanian law did explicitly state that adoptive brothers were more suitable for *stur*-ships (marriages whose purpose was to provide an estate with heirs) than biological brothers, showing that though incest for keeping assets within the family did happen, the law preferred for it to be avoided; see *The Book of a Thousand Judgements*, tr. into Russian by Anahit Perikhanian, tr. from Russian into English by Nina Garsoïan (Costa Mesa, 1997), 42, 15–17 (p. 115).
46. Agathias, *History*, 123.18 (p. 87).
47. Ibid., 256–8 (p. 121).
48. See Cameron, 'Agathias on the Sasanians', pp. 138–9 for a discussion of the sources.
49. Tabari, *The History of al-Tabari: Volume V: The Sasanids, the Byzanties, the Lakmids, and Yemen*, tr. C.E. Bosworth (New York, 1999), 827 (pp. 30–1).
50. Ammianus, *History*, XXIII.6.76, 80.
51. Procopius, *Wars*, I.ii.1–8.
52. Menander, *History*, Fragments 6.1.203–11 (p. 65), 9.3.33–4 (p. 107), 18.1.18–25 (p. 159), 18.4.18–27 (p. 163), 20.2.93–94 (p. 187), 23.1.10–40 (p. 197–9), 23.9.2–3 (p. 209), 26.107–10 (p. 233).
53. Ibid., Fragment 18.1.18–25 (p. 159).
54. Ibid., Fragment 9.2.1–14 (pp. 103–5). It should be mentioned that Menander does record the Emperor Justin as acting unreasonably at one juncture; Fragment 16.1.51–6.
55. For the translation of this text see André Maricq, 'Res Gestae Divi Saporis', in *Syria*, T. 35, Fasc. 3/4 (1958), pp. 295–360.
56. Dorothy Shepherd, 'Sasanian Art', in Ehsan Yarshater (ed.), *The Cambridge History of Iran 3 (2): The Seleucid, Parthian and Sasanian Periods* (Cambridge, 1983), pp. 1100–1.

57. Zeev Rubin, 'The Roman Empire in the *Res Gestae Divi Saporis*', in Edward Dabrowa (ed.), *Ancient Iran and the Mediterraean World: Studies in Ancient History* (Cracow, 1998), p. 184.
58. *The Paikuli Inscription*, tr. Prods Skærvø (Munich, 1983), l. 91; on the war between Nerses and Diocletian see Beate Dignas and Engelbert Winter, *Rome and Persia in Late Antiquity: Neighbours and Rivals* (Cambridge, 2007), pp. 28–32.
59. See Philippe Gignoux, *Les Quatre Inscriptions du Mage Kirdīr: Textes et Concordances* (Paris, 1991); see too Philippe Gignoux, 'Etude des variants textuelles des inscriptions de Kirdīr, Genèse et datation', in *Le Muséon* 86 (1973).
60. Ferdowsi, *Shahnameh*, tr. Dick Davis (London, 2006), pp. 582–97.
61. Ibid., pp. 574–6.
62. Ibid., pp. 38ff.
63. Ibid., p. 807.

CHAPTER 3

XERXES AND LEONIDAS: CONVERSATIONS BETWEEN ANCIENT PERSIA AND SEVENTEENTH-CENTURY FRANCE IN FÉNELON'S DIALOGUE OF THE DEAD

Margaux Whiskin

The year 1715 witnessed the death of Archbishop Fénelon, the entry of the Persian embassy to the French royal court at Versailles in February and the death of the Sun King, Louis XIV, in September. The year 1715 marked a political transition with Louis XV now on the throne, but also a cultural transition with Enlightenment thinkers increasingly interested in contemporary accounts of other peoples and less inclined to rely principally on classical sources. Yet within these shifts remains a continuity of purpose. Fénelon mainly relied on classical sources in his depiction of a historic Persian figure, but his motives were fundamentally the same as those used later by Enlightenment philosophers, such as Montesquieu. Beyond the historical and anthropological interest, the Other is a projection of the Self, be it on an individual, social or political level, as exemplified in the dialogue between Xerxes and Leonidas from Fénelon's *Dialogues des Morts Anciens et Modernes*.

The souls of Xerxes I of Persia, king of the Achaemenid Empire from 486 to 465 BC, and Leonidas I who was king of Sparta from

489 to 480 BC, meet in the afterlife in Hades' underworld and continue to settle a few scores about the Second Persian War. Xerxes and Leonidas, whose armies clashed at the Battle of Thermopylae, but who never met in person, transcended their own individual importance and ended standing for two civilisations, respectively Persia and Greece. Fénelon exploited this double opposition developed in classical sources and made it relevant to his own time. The dichotomy of Persia versus Greece was altered, but in a subtler way than expected. Fénelon shifts the reader's perspective from Xerxes as a foreign and classical figure to one more resembling Louis XIV and his grandson, the Duke of Burgundy.

Fénelon's dialogues of the dead were written at the very close of the seventeenth century, a period when contact between France and Persia, under the rule of the weakening Safavid dynasty, was limited to a handful of missionaries and merchants. As Williamson points out, France was behind England and the Netherlands in its trading connections with Persia, as the French East India Company was only founded in 1664. The English had founded theirs in 1600 and the Dutch in 1602.[1] As for diplomatic relations with Persia, they were impeded by Franco–Ottoman alliances. Yet, the trading relation between France and Persia, however limited it may have been, grew into a textual one, as merchants wrote and published their travelling accounts. The three most famous instances of such accounts are *Les Six Voyages de Jean-Baptiste Tavernier... qu'il a fait en Turquie, en Perse et aux Indes*, the *Journal du Voyage du Chevalier Chardin en Perse et aux Indes Orientales* and the *Voyages de Monsieur le Chevalier Chardin en Perse et Autres Lieux de l'Orient*, respectively published in 1676, 1686 and 1711.[2] Travellers' accounts were a source of information for eighteenth-century authors, amongst them Montesquieu who used Tavernier's and Chardin's texts for his *Lettres Persanes* (1721) and *Esprit des Lois* (1748), in particular to draw attention to the dangers of despotism.[3] Fénelon, who was writing his *Dialogues des Morts Anciens et Modernes* at the time some of these accounts were published, did not incorporate such up-to-date representations of Persians. Instead, Fénelon relied on classical sources for the dialogue between Xerxes and Leonidas, a perfectly sensible choice when considering the two characters. Yet, as shall be demonstrated, the purpose of the dialogue goes beyond the historical commentary on the Second Persian War (480–479 BC). Fénelon's true purpose was to discuss two different models of government; but, unlike Montesquieu who turns to modern sources, Fénelon chose to use classical texts.

François de Salignac de la Mothe-Fénelon (1651–1715) was from 1689 to 1697 in charge of the education of the young Duke of Burgundy, Louis XIV's grandson and son of the Dauphin, the second in line to the throne. Fénelon had been chosen for his innovative pedagogy, consisting in indirect teaching.[4] Instead of being presented as a chore, learning was to take the guise of pleasure, so that the pupil would not realise that he/she was being taught. The *Dialogues des Morts Anciens et Modernes* were written between 1689 and 1699. Fénelon used these as teaching material for the education of the young prince and did not intend to have them published.[5] As in the better-known *Les Aventures de Télémaque*, published in 1699, Fénelon puts into practice his pedagogical principles, that is to say instruction disguised as entertainment. The preface of the 1718 edition informs the reader of Fénelon's method and intentions in the dialogues:

> He wrote them very quickly, according to what was needed, either to redress in a soft and gentle way the defects in the Duke of Burgundy's nature, either to strengthen his natural virtues, or, through teaching suited to his age, to instil in the Duke the most sublime maxims on good politics and ethics. Whilst he thus shaped his pupil's tastes, heart and mind, he would also teach him fiction and history, along with great men's characters of Antiquity and of times closer to us. Thus he would combine precepts and examples, depict virtue in the most interesting and delicate colours, and he would show the Duke that virtue is not only beautiful and worthy of love when considered in the abstract, but also that its practice is not beyond man's strength and that there lies the only path for a king to true glory and happiness. [. . .] Wisdom appears in all its guises: but it is always accompanied by insinuating graces.[6]

The programme has been set out: through indirect teaching and by adapting his subject to his pupil's level, Fénelon combined lessons in history, politics and ethics, whilst at the same time guiding the Duke of Burgundy to become a good person and a good king.

Use of Classical Sources

Classical studies would have constituted the core education of any well-read seventeenth-century French gentleman and it is no surprise that it should appear in educational material designed for the Duke of Burgundy. In the dialogues, Fénelon proceeds by allusions, probably to prompt further explanations from his pupil and/or to refresh his memory on previous lessons. The dialogue between Xerxes and Leonidas is a good example of this method. At the very beginning, Xerxes, the 'grand Roi' distances himself from Leonidas, 'a beggar who never had anything but the name of a king without the authority', insisting later by describing Leonidas as 'poor, and [having lived] without state, and without authority'.[7] The stark opposition between the absolute monarchy of the Achaemenids and the more constrained dual monarchy of Sparta has been alluded to, thus creating the opportunity for an exchange between teacher and pupil.

Far from offering an original representation of Xerxes, Leonidas and their deeds, Fénelon substantially drew his information from classical sources.[8] Caution must be taken when attempting to identify exactly what sources Fénelon used. As mentioned, Fénelon is not precise in his description, which makes it harder to locate the exact source. Another factor to take into consideration is the borrowings classical authors make, one example being that of Xenophon possibly making use of Herodotus' *Histories* in his own writings.[9] This being said, clear similarities can be found between Fénelon's dialogue and *The Histories* in the depiction of Xerxes and Leonidas. Herodotus extensively discusses the vast numbers constituting the Persian fleet and army in Book 7, which Fénelon has Xerxes refer to: 'I covered the earth with my army, and the seas with my fleet'.[10] The size of the Persian army takes on mythical proportions when Xerxes boasts that 'my soldiers could not quench their thirst without draining rivers'.[11] This anecdote appears several times in Herodotus to dramatise Greece's position as it faced the army from what seemed to be a whole continent: 'After all, was there any Asian people [Xerxes] did not lead against Greece? And was there any source of water, apart from huge rivers, they did not drink dry?'[12]

The difference in manpower between the two characters is again referred to by Leonidas who admits 'Tis true, that like you, I could not have pierced Mount Athos', a feat Herodotus describes and sees as a sign of Xerxes' 'grandiosity and arrogance'.[13] Fénelon's depiction of Xerxes as a man filled with hubris, thinking he can bend both men and nature to his will, is very much in line with Herodotus. Leonidas does not hesitate to upbraid Xerxes for his hubris, both in life and in death:

> [B]ut still thy shade is haughty and proud; thou wert not more arrogant when thou hadst the sea lashed: indeed you richly deserved to be lashed yourself for that extravagant action. Do you remember those golden chains which you threw into the Hellespont, pretending thereby to enslave the winds? A pretty sort of a fellow truly, to subdue the seas![14]

The sea receiving lashes and golden shackles offers a vivid and dramatic image, but Fénelon offers very little in terms of context. Leonidas' question to Xerxes, 't'en souviens-tu' ('do you remember'), has an extradiegetic application as the teacher redirects it to his pupil to check his historical knowledge. Herodotus mentions that Xerxes 'ordered his men to give the Hellespont three hundred lashes and to sink a pair of shackles into the sea', but, unlike Fénelon, he explains that the bridge Xerxes had just finished building over the Hellespont for his army to cross, crumbled 'when a violent storm erupted which completely smashed and destroyed everything'.[15]

So far, similarities between Fénelon and Herodotus have been remarkable. Fénelon, however, does not hesitate to depart from *The Histories* to strengthen his moral commentary. Herodotus mentions a variant in the story of the Persian retreat from Athens according to which Xerxes fled on a Phoenician ship (8.118). Herodotus expresses his doubts about this variant and concludes that Xerxes returned home by road (8.119). Fénelon's own version departs from that of Herodotus. The Phoenician ship is now but a humble boat:

> But soon after you were glad to return hastily to Asia, in a boat like a fisherman. This is what the intolerable vanity of that man will come to, who endeavours to force the laws of nature, and forgets his own weakness.[16]

Fénelon's depiction of Xerxes' humiliating flight in a fishing-boat bears strong similarities with the account Justin gives in his *Epitome of the Philippic History of Pompeius Trogus*:

> Here he found his bridge broken by the winter storms, and he crossed in a panic in a fishing boat. That was a turn of events worth contemplating for the light it sheds on the human condition: by an amazing reversal of fortune, to see the man whom recently the entire ocean could barely contain, and whose armies had burdened the earth by their numbers, now hiding in a tiny boat and completely deprived of the assistance of even his slaves![17]

Justin's version plays on Xerxes' dramatic reversal of fortune, a key element to Fénelon's moralistic intentions, but also very much in keeping with the dialogues of the dead genre.

Dialogues of the Dead

Fénelon resorted to classical sources for content, but also for form. Lucian of Samosata wrote the first dialogues of the dead in the second century AD, a type of dialogue in which the dead engage in conversation whilst in Hades. Dialogues of the dead became a popular sub-genre, especially in France, Great Britain and Germany in the seventeenth and eighteenth centuries, with famous and anonymous authors alike trying their hand at it.[18] Fénelon and before him Fontenelle who published in 1683 his *Nouveaux Dialogues des Morts*, would be the two great names attached to the genre in its early modern form.[19] The Second Persian War constitutes a fitting subject for a dialogue of the dead. Hades is the logical place from which to pick up the story as, on the last day of the Battle of Thermopylae, Leonidas 'passed the word to his soldiers to eat breakfast in the expectation that they would be having dinner in Hades'.[20] As for Charon the ferryman, wars are a cause for rejoicing, since they send him more travellers, each paying an obol for the crossing of the Styx.[21] In the dialogue, Fénelon makes a reference to the increased population in Hades after war, when Leonidas points to the thousands of Persian casualties killed by the Spartans, now wandering by the shores of the Styx: 'Do you not see around you those wandering shades that cover the whole shore? These are the twenty thousand Persians whom we have slain'.[22]

As with the content of classical sources, Fénelon adapted Lucian's genre to mould it to his own intentions.[23] Besides from being a genre in tune with the subject, dialogues of the dead nicely served Fénelon's pedagogical aim. Dialogues of the dead are most commonly between historical and mythical figures and, amongst Fénelon's other dialogues, we find Hercules, Theseus, Achilles, Homer, Ulysses, Romulus, Remus, Socrates, Plato, Aristotle and Alexander, to name but a few. Knowledge of these figures would have been important for a well-rounded education and is here reached through a playful 'what if' scenario. What would Leonidas and Xerxes say to each other if they were to meet? Who would win the argument? Dialogues of the dead also constitute a short format: the dialogue between Xerxes and Leonidas, which is representative of Fénelon's other dialogues in terms of length, is approximately 1050 words long. The brevity of the dialogues means that there is no time to set up a narrative frame, allowing Fénelon to keep his pupil's attention and to remain focussed on the subject matter rather than being distracted by peripheral details.

Dialogues of the dead rely on colourful contrasts, on binary oppositions, which create the dynamic within the conversations, making them lively and engaging, but also forcing out truth. In Fénelon's dialogue, the absolute king is opposed to shared monarchy, Europe is opposed to the East, but the opposition is also a human one. Keener remarks that, in Lucian's dialogues, 'a central device [...] is the confrontation of *alazon* and *eiron*, of the boastful, self-deceiving man and the self-deprecating, intelligent man given to questioning and understatement'.[24] Fénelon carries on that model with opposing the boastful and stormy Xerxes with the calm and righteous Leonidas. It is important to remember that the shades in Hades are waiting to receive judgment from Minos on their past life. Though he is alluded to, Minos rarely intervenes in person and judgment is left to the reader. The Duke of Burgundy would have taken on this role and would have insensibly been led to adopt the very position Fénelon would have wanted him to.

Decontextualisation

Classical knowledge should not, however, be perceived as the limit to Fénelon's pedagogical intentions. As Haillant remarks, Fénelon is less interested in offering a comprehensive history lesson as in making a point, as can be seen in the absence of references to Xerxes' glorious deeds in the dialogue.[25] Fénelon is responsible for the education of the heir to the French throne, consequently his teaching, going beyond general knowledge, contains a strong political dimension. At a closer look, the dialogue between Xerxes and Leonidas is less about Antiquity as about kingship in seventeenth-century France. One of the common features of dialogues of the dead is the obsession the dead have with the world of the living, often asking new comers about the state of the world.[26] Fénelon's dialogue offers no such scenario, but the fact that the genre focuses so heavily not so much on the world of the dead as that of the living should alert us to the fact that Fénelon's intentions are going further than just giving the Duke of Burgundy a lesson in classical history. In the same way as Fénelon disguised learning as a pleasurable activity, Xerxes is but a disguise for Louis XIV and his model of kingship. Turning to the past was a way to understand the present:

> It was not simply pedantry, a scholarly passion for history, nostalgia, or a taste for learned embellishment that made many eighteenth-century authors look backward before advancing. Contemporaries of Clarendon, Burnet, Hume, Robertson, and Gibbon depended heavily upon history for norms and ideals of human conduct, thought the past a laboratory for the present.[27]

Fénelon should be included to the list, as he moved beyond the historical anecdote to isolate universal principles. The dialogue between Xerxes and Leonidas opens on the following maxim, ''Tis wisdom and valour that makes a state invincible, and not the number of subjects, or the unlimited authority of princes'.[28] The truth of this maxim is proven in the course of the dialogue opposing the vast numbers of the Persians to the bravery of the few Spartans, Xerxes' excessive power to Leonidas' bravery and discipline. The maxim is by essence timeless and the dialogue acts as a warning for the present.

The transition from the classical world to that of early modern France necessitates decontextualisation and this is brought about by the genre itself. Decontextualisation is necessary for the dialogue to happen in the first place. Xerxes and Leonidas are able to converse because they are on the same plane. Cultural, social, linguistic differences are abolished in the Elysean Fields. Michel Henrichot talks of an 'ecumenical universe' where:

> [T]he splits dividing the society of the living no longer apply. The Republic of the Underworld unites the dead and abolishes the illusory frontiers which had divided them. Even those frontiers we consider natural, such as those of space, time and language,

> disappear. As a result, the author's perspective places the debates *sub specie aeternitatis*. Of course, the dead persevere in their being (this is the very condition of the dialogue of the dead), but the universe in which they evolve is that of Ideas and Truth, which inevitably surfaces in the debates.[29]

Death is the great leveller. Kings are reminded that their pomp and magnificence will not follow them in the afterlife, they will be stripped of all such trappings and will walk in Hades as naked as the other shades. Every individual has been reduced to his core self. Dialogues of the dead take particular pleasure in putting low those who were once high and Leonidas' rebuke is illustrative of this:

> This is not a fit time either to flatter, or to offer affronts, we are in the region of truth. Do you still imagine yourself a potent monarch? Thy treasures are far off, thou hast no guards, no army, no pomp, no pleasure; your ears no longer will be soothed with praise; you are naked, alone, and just about to appear before Minos' judgment-seat.[30]

Decontextualisation acts as a form of decluttering to unearth universal principles – in this case the opening maxim – for the reader to ponder on and apply to his own time.

Educating a Future King

Fénelon was highly critical of Louis XIV's reign and hoped the Duke of Burgundy, once king, would not follow the path of his illustrious grandfather. In *Les Aventures de Télémaque*, Fénelon had criticised the military expansion and mercantilism of Louis XIV. When it was published in 1699, most likely without Fénelon's consent, contemporaries were quick to spot its thinly veiled criticism. Fénelon, already embroiled in a matter of religious orthodoxy, had been removed in 1697 from his position as royal tutor and exiled from court. The publication of *Les Aventures de Télémaque* did nothing to help Fénelon's position.[31] In his dialogues of the dead and in this dialogue in particular, the same criticisms as those made in *Télémaque* appear, though less thoroughly developed due to the brevity of the genre.[32] Fénelon was against warfare waged for glory; war was justified only when purely defensive. Louis XIV's aggressive military expansion in Europe is mirrored by that of Xerxes in Greece: 'Oh, how grieved I am, that I did not enter into Peloponnesus, after having ravaged Attica; I would have reduced thy Lacedaemon, as I did Athens, to ashes'.[33] An army had to be kept in case of enemy attack, but Fénelon advocated that it should be reduced to the size of a simple militia, with soldiers properly trained and receiving a decent wage, following Fénelon's view of the Spartan model. Louis XIV's army, numbering up to 420,000 soldiers, many of them through conscription, was much closer to that of Xerxes than Leonidas'.

As Schuurman demonstrates, warfare and luxury were complementary evils according to Fénelon. The richer a country and the more luxury goods it possesses, the more it will be an object of envy for other countries and the more likely it will be attacked. Luxury also corrupted men by making them effeminate, soft and idle. At the beginning of the dialogue, Leonidas sends Xerxes back to his women, eunuchs, slaves and flatterers, implying that Xerxes has been so softened that he is no longer fit for the company of true men. Later, Leonidas refers to the Persians as 'those soft and effeminate men' and says that Xerxes has been corrupted by softness.[34] For Fénelon, a king should avoid excessive pomp, show restraint, not be pleasure seeking, but instead devote himself to the happiness of his people. Fénelon's alternative model was in stark contrast to Louis XIV's reign with costly warfare, a court perceived as decadent, a focus on glory and an economy encouraging the production of luxury goods. References to the golden shackles Xerxes threw into the sea point to an excessive luxury so abundant that it can be thus wasted.

Educating a Future Man

One would expect a future king to be well versed in the military arts, yet Fénelon, as Henrichot remarks, appears more eager to temper than excite his pupil's pugnacious ardour. The young Duke of Burgundy was known for his tantrums and fits of anger.[35] Fénelon wished to correct his pupil's temper, not through punishment but through calm and reasoned recognition, and he used the dialogues of the dead to this end. The introductory dialogue between Mercury and Charon sets out the aims and objectives of the text: 'In what manner those who are entrusted with the education of Princes, ought to correct their growing vices, and fill them with virtues suitable to their quality'.[36] Fénelon thus clearly laid out the tutor–pupil relationship, but also indirectly criticised his pupil's temper through the description of Prince Pierochole whilst at the same time showing what a great king he could become if he could only curb his emotions:

> Charon: How will he wage war?
>
> Mercury: As he does now, without pain or trouble – war at chess; he has already fought above a hundred battles.
>
> Charon: Fatal war! Which sends us no subjects.
>
> Mercury: Notwithstanding this, if we can but throw aside his wantonness and effeminacy, I hope he will one day make a great figure. He can rage and weep like Achilles, why then should he not be as courageous too? In his forwardness he resembles him. They say that he loves the muses, and that he has a Chiron, a Phoenix.
>
> Charon: But all this makes nothing for us; we want a young, rash, ignorant, unpolished prince, who, despising learning, should love nothing but arms; who always ready to glut himself in blood, should place his happiness in the misfortunes of mankind. Such a one would fill my boat once a day.
>
> Mercury: So, so, you want one of those princes, or rather one of those monsters, who are greedy of slaughter. This is one of a milder disposition; I believe he will love peace, yet know how to wage war. In him you may discover the principles of a good prince, as in the bud of a rose you may perceive how beautiful the flower will be.[37]

In *Les Aventures de Télémaque*, Fénelon took the guise of Mentor guiding his pupil Telemachus, the Duke of Burgundy's fictional double.[38] Fénelon resorted to a similar device in his dialogues of the dead by opposing impetuous youths to older and wiser men, examples of this being the three dialogues between Alcibiades and Socrates. The pairing of tutor and pupil reappears with Xerxes being upbraided by Fénelon's mouthpiece, the wise Leonidas. Whereas Pierochole has his life in front of him and can still mend his ways, Xerxes, who is now a shade, has lost the opportunity to reform and become a better man and king. The story of Xerxes thus acts as a warning to the Duke of Burgundy, urging him to change before it is too late.

In Fénelon's dialogue, no description of either Xerxes or Leonidas is given and references to past actions are the only way to identify them. These two shades no longer embody themselves; they embody a type. Characterisation has shifted from action to behaviour and ultimately this is the criterion on which Xerxes will be judged. Xerxes' actions in the dialogue all bear the stamp of hubris and excess, but at the end of the text one element has been placed in the scales in his favour. After having heard Leonidas' damning indictment, Xerxes puts forward what would seem at first a rather weak defence: 'But I was neither cowardly nor mischievous, as you imagined'.[39] Surprisingly, Leonidas acknowledges Xerxes' more humane qualities:

> You naturally had a share of courage and good-nature; the tears which you shed at the sight of so many thousand men, of whom not one was to see another age, are a sufficient proof of your humanity; this was the finest action of your life: had you not been too powerful, and too happy, you might have been an honest man.[40]

The fact that the dialogue closes on these lines forces the reader to make a dramatic shift in his judgment from antipathy to pity. Xerxes' climactic moment was not a military victory, but instead a very simple human feeling.

The fiery Duke of Burgundy shared a similar temper to Xerxes, but also found himself in a similar situation of absolute power which encourages a king's faults, instead of checking them, as Xerxes laments:

> Alas! I see (but too late) that those kings who think that everything is in their power, are slaves to their own passions. How can a man resist his own power, and the flattery of those by whom he is surrounded? What a misfortune it is to be born amidst so many dangers?[41]

Through the pathetic image of Xerxes lamenting the lost possibility to redeem himself, Fénelon urged the Duke of Burgundy to reform his behaviour before ascending the throne, since the power he would then have wielded would have exacerbated his fiery and mercurial temper.

The decontextualisation which the genre has operated, thus serves a dual purpose in the dialogue. As recipient, the Duke of Burgundy was invited to think about what lessons could be taken from Xerxes and

Leonidas and how they could be applied to his own time. The dialogue between Xerxes and Leonidas offers a perfect example of Fénelon's method of indirect teaching. The Duke of Burgundy would have thought that he was receiving a lesson on classical history, when in reality the true focus is a criticism of Louis XIV's reign. As any good pedagogue would do, Fénelon follows his criticism by a positive alternative model for kingship through the example of Leonidas:

> I was king, upon condition that I should lead a hard, sober, and laborious life, like my people. I was a king only to defend my country, and to put the laws in force: my sovereignty gave me the power of doing good, without permitting me to do what was evil.[42]

That this description of Leonidas' kingship is historically inadequate does not matter here. Its purpose is to show that there is an alternative model to that of Louis XIV. Decontextualisation reinforces this alternative by redirecting the focus on humane qualities: greatness as a man lays the foundation for greatness as a king.

Conclusion

The 1715 reception of the Persian embassy at the court of Louis XIV triggered Montesquieu's *Persian Letters*, an epistolary novel published in 1721 constituted of the letters between two Persian travellers, Usbek and Rica, to their acquaintances back home and containing their impressions of Europe, more specifically of France. One of the main strengths of the novel is that the French are now the Other and France has been transformed into an exotic trope viewed by the Persian characters. The purpose of this shift of perspective is to offer a critical examination of eighteenth-century France, made more acceptable and amusing because it is seen through foreign eyes. However, the tactic of using the other to think about the self was not new.

Fénelon used classical sources, such as Herodotus, Justin and Plutarch for the content and Lucian's dialogues of the dead for the structure. Another type of text should also be mentioned: mirrors for princes. The identity of the intended reader, the Duke of Burgundy, is essential to understand Fénelon's purpose. He was writing for the heir to the throne and, by steering the education of his pupil, Fénelon hoped he would also be steering the future of France.[43] The mirror Fénelon held to the Duke of Burgundy did not reflect an ideal model of kingship. The dialogue focuses far more on Xerxes than on Leonidas whose main purpose is to bring out and develop the character of his interlocutor. It is the Persian, not the Spartan, who acts as mirror and this at two levels. Xerxes, with all his hubris, desire for glory, love of warfare and luxury, is a reflection of Louis XIV, whereas his temper is a reflection of the Duke of Burgundy himself. As a doubly negative reflection, the Persian Xerxes is thus more familiar than had been at first expected. In truth, this is not a dialogue between classical Sparta and Persia; this is a dialogue between seventeenth-century and eighteenth-century France.

Notes

1. See Clare Williamson, 'Safavid Persia Through the Eyes of French Travellers' in John Arnold and Susan Scollay (eds), *Persian Cultural Crossroads* (Melbourne, 2013), p. 65.
2. On Tavernier and Chardin, see Williamson in *op.cit.*, pp. 65–75; specifically on Chardin, see Ronald W. Ferrier, *A Journey to Persia: Jean Chardin's Portrait of a Seventeenth-Century Empire* (London & New York, 1996).
3. See David Young, 'Montesquieu's View of Despotism and His Use of Travel Literature', in *The Review of Politics*, 40 (1978), 392–405.
4. I have borrowed this term from Marguerite Haillant who talks of 'instructions indirectes' in *Culture et Imagination dans les Œuvres de Fénelon "Ad Usum Delphini"* (Paris, 1983), p. 14.
5. This information is given by Frederick M. Keener, who also mentions, on the same page that '[f]our were published in 1700, an edition of forty-five in 1712, all not until 1823', in *English Dialogues of the Dead, A Critical History, An Anthology, and A Check List* (London & New York, 1973), p. 22.
6. My translation. 'Il les lui (the Duke of Burgundy) composait sur-le-champ, selon ses divers besoins, tantôt pour corriger d'une manière douce et aimable ce que son naturel avait de défectueux, tantôt pour confirmer en lui ce qu'il y avait de bon et de grand, tantôt enfin pour lui insinuer, par des instructions familières à la portée de son âge, les plus sublimes maximes de la bonne politique et de la morale. Tandis qu'il formait ainsi son goût, son cœur, et son esprit, il lui apprenait en même temps la fable et l'histoire, avec les caractères des grands hommes de l'antiquité et des temps plus proches de nous. Par là il unissait les préceptes et les exemples, lui peignait la vertu d'une manière sensible et intéressante, et lui montrait qu'elle n'était pas seulement belle et aimable dans la spéculation, mais encore que la pratique n'en était point au-dessus des forces de l'homme, et que c'était par elle seule qu'un roi pouvait arriver à la véritable gloire et au vrai Bonheur. [...] La sagesse prend ici toutes les formes: mais elle est toujours accompagnée de grâces insinuantes.' François de Salignac de la

Mothe-Fénelon, *Dialogues des morts anciens et modernes, avec quelques fables, composez pour l'éducation d'un prince*, vol. I (Paris, 1718), preface.

7. Unless mentioned otherwise, all translations are from *Dialogues of the Dead* (London: printed for D. Browne, at the Black Swan, without Temple-Bar; J. Jackson in St. James's Street; and A. and C Corbette in Fleet-Street, 1760), p. 36 & 38. '[u]n gueux qui n'eut jamais que le nom de Roi sans autorité', 'pauvre, sans éclat, sans autorité' Fénelon, *Dialogues des morts*, pp. 65, 69.
8. On the use of classical sources in Fénelon's dialogues of the dead, see Haillant, *Culture et Imagination*, pp. 48–79 and pp. 57–8 specifically for the dialogue between Xerxes and Leonidas.
9. See William J. Keller, 'Xenophon's Acquaintance with the History of Herodotus', in *The Classical Journal*, 6 (1911), pp. 252–9.
10. p. 36. 'je couvrais la terre de Soldats et la mer de navires' Fénelon, *Dialogues des morts*, p. 65. For more information on Herodotus' representation of Xerxes, see Robert Rollinger, 'Xerxes according to Herodotus', in *Encyclopaedia Iranica*, XII/3, pp. 270–6; available online at http://www.iranicaonline.org/articles/herodotus-vii [Accessed on 18 September 2015] and Heleen Sancisi-Weerdenburg, 'The Personality of Xerxes, King of Kings', in Egbert J. Bakker, Irene J. F. Jong and Hans van Wees (eds), *Brill's Companion to Herodotus* (Leiden, 2002), pp. 579–90.
11. p. 36. 'mon armée ne pouvait en un repas se désaltérer sans faire tarir des rivières', Fénelon, *Dialogues des morts*, p. 65.
12. Herodotus, *The Histories*, tr. Robin Waterfield (Oxford, 1998), p. 416. This anecdote is repeated in 7.187.
13. p. 38. 'Je n'aurais pas eu de quoi percer le Mont Athos comme toi', Fénelon, *Dialogues des morts,* 69; Herodotus, p. 417, see also 7.22–4, 37, 122.
14. p. 37. 'Mais ton ombre est encore bien colère et bien superbe. Tu n'étais pas plus emporté quand tu faisais fouetter la mer. En vérité, tu méritais bien d'être fouetté toi-même pour cette extravagance. Et ces fers dorés, t'en souviens-tu, que tu fis jeter dans l'Hellespont, pour tenir les tempêtes dans ton esclavage? Plaisant homme pour dompter la mer !', Fénelon, *Dialogues des morts*, pp. 67–8.
15. Herodotus, p. 420, see 7.34–6. Rollinger mentions similarities between Herodotus and Aeschylus' *Persae* in their representation of Xerxes, including the interpretation of this particular event.
16. p. 37. 'Tu fus contraint bientôt après de repasser à la hâte en Asie dans une barque comme un pêcheur. Voilà à quoi aboutit la folle vanité des hommes, qui veulent forcer les lois de la nature, et oublier leur propre faiblesse.' Fénelon, *Dialogues des morts*, p. 68.
17. Justin, *Epitome of the Philippic History of Pompeius Trogus*, tr. J. C. Yardley (Atlanta, 1994), II, 13, p. 42.
18. See Johan Egilsrud, *Le Dialogue des Morts dans les Littératures Françaises, Allemande et Anglaise (1644–1789)* (Paris, 1934). Though old, this volume remains a reference.
19. In his preface to his own *Dialogues of the Dead*, Lyttelton acknowledges Fénelon's mark on the genre: 'Lucian among the Ancients, and among the Moderns Fénelon, Archbishop of Cambray, and Monsieur Fontenelle, have written

Dialogues of the Dead with a general Applause'; quoted by Keener, *English Dialogues of the Dead*, p. 3.

20. Plutarch, *Plutarch on Sparta*, tr. Richard J. A. Talbert (London, 1988), *Sayings of Spartans*, 225ff, p. 147.
21. Charon's enthusiasm for war appears in Lucian's dialogues of the dead.
22. p. 36. 'Ne vois-tu pas encore ici près ces ombres errantes en foule qui couvrent le rivage? Ce sont les vingt mille Perses que nous avons tués', Fénelon, *Dialogues des morts*, pp. 65–6.
23. Fénelon openly departed from Lucian's satirical tone in the dialogue between Herodotus and Lucian, who delighted in exposing the hypocrisy of men. See Stéphane Pujol, *Le Dialogue d'Idées au Dix-Huitième Siècle* (Oxford, 2005), pp. 231–2.
24. Keener, *English Dialogues of the Dead*, p. 19.
25. Haillant, *Culture et Imagination*, p. 58.
26. Discussing the serio-comical genres, in which he includes dialogues of the dead, Bakhtin remarks on 'their new relationship to reality: their subject, or – what is more important – their starting point for understanding, evaluating, and shaping reality, is the living *present*, often even the very day. For the first time in ancient literature the subject of *serious* (to be sure, at the same time comical) representation is presented without any epic or tragic distance, presented not in the absolute past of myth and legend but on the plane of the present day, in a zone of immediate and even crudely familiar contact with living contemporaries. In these genres, the heroes of myth and the historical figures of the past are deliberately and emphatically contemporised; they act and speak in a zone of familiar contact with the open-ended present.' Mikhail Bakhtin, *Problems of Dostoevsky's Poetics*, ed. and tr. Caryl Emerson (London, 1984), p. 108.
27. Keener, *English Dialogues of the Dead*, p. 7.
28. p. 35. 'La sagesse et la valeur rendent les Etats invincibles, et non pas le grand nombre des sujets, ni l'autorité sans bornes des princes', Fénelon, *Dialogues des morts*, p. 64. Fénelon could have been using one of Leonidas' laconic phrase from Plutarch's *Sayings of Spartans*, p. 225: 'When someone said, "Leonidas, are you here like this, to run such a risk with a few men against many?" he replied, "If you think that I should rely on numbers, then not even the whole of Greece is enough, since it is a small fraction of their horde; but if I am to rely on courage, then even this number is quite adequate"', p. 146. This exchange is also echoed in Fénelon's dialogue: 'Xerxes: Ton action est un coup de fureur et de désespoir. / Léonidas: C'était une action sage et généreuse', p. 66.
29. My translation. '[L]es clivages qui divisent la société des vivants ne sont plus de mise. La République des Enfers réunit les morts et abolit les frontières factices qui les divisaient. Même les frontières que l'on pourrait qualifier de naturelles, comme les frontières géographiques, temporelles et linguistiques disparaissent. Il en résulte que le point de vue de l'auteur place les débats *sub specie aeternitatis*. Certes ces morts persévèrent dans leur être (c'est la condition même du dialogue des morts) mais l'univers où ils se meuvent est celui des Idées et de la Vérité en sorte que celle-ci perce inévitablement des débats.' Michel Henrichot, 'Mars aux

Enfers: la Guerre Vue des Dialogues des Morts', in Jean Garapon (ed.), *Armées, Guerre et Société dans la France du XVIIe Siècle* (Tübingen, 2006), p. 146.

30. p. 37. 'Ce n'est plus ici le temps ni des injures ni des flatteries. Nous sommes au pays de la vérité. T'imagines-tu donc être encore le grand Roi ? Tes trésors sont bien loin. Tu n'as plus de Gardes ni d'Armées, plus de faste, ni de délices. La louange ne vient plus chatouiller tes oreilles. Te voilà nu, seul, prêt à être jugé par Minos', Fénelon, *Dialogues des morts*, p. 67. Fénelon was not alone in using the trope of Xerxes' might and riches and in taking pleasure in operating a dramatic reversal of fortune. In book 2 of Rabelais' *Pantagruel*, Xerxes ends up selling salt in the Elysean Fields. On the connection between war and dialogues of the dead, see Henrichot, 'Mars aux Enfers', 139–50.
31. On Fénelon's criticism of warfare mercantilism, see Paul Schuurman, 'Fénelon on Luxury, War and Trade in the Telemachus', in *History of European Ideas* 38 (2012), 179–99.
32. Similarities between *Les Aventures de Télémaque* concern not just objects of criticism but also the way in which it was made as Fénelon also resorts to the image of past kings now in Hades and being punished for their preference for a life of luxury and indulgence instead of service to the people and State. See Schuurman, 'Fénelon on Luxury', p. 181.
33. p. 37. 'Ho! Que je suis fâché de n'être point entré dans le Péloponèse, après avoir ravagé l'Attique: j'aurais mis en cendres ta Lacédémone, comme j'y mis Athènes', Fénelon, *Dialogues des morts*, p. 67.
34. p. 38. 'hommes lâches et effeminés', Fénelon, *Dialogues des morts*, pp. 70–1. This depiction of the Persians as soft and effeminate can be traced back to Herodotus. In *The Histories*, the only Persian female naval commander, Artemisia, advises against a battle between the Greek and Persian navy: 'do not commit the fleet to a battle, because at sea your men will be as far inferior to the Greeks as women are to men' (8.68), p. 510. Later, witnessing Artemisia's naval victories, Xerxes supposedly exclaimed: 'My men have turned into women and my women into men!' (8.88), p. 517.
35. See Henrichot, 'Mars aux Enfers', pp. 144–6 and Haillant, *Culture et Imagination*, pp. 9–12.
36. p. 1. 'L'on voit ici comment ceux qui sont préposés pour l'éducation des Princes, doivent travailler à corriger leurs vices naissants, et à leur inspirer les vertus de leur Etat', Fénelon, *Dialogues des morts*, p. 1.
37. pp. 2–3. 'CHARON - Comment ira-t-il à la guerre?

    MERCURE - Il la fait avec des échecs, sans mal et sans douleur. Il a déjà donné plus de cent batailles.CHARON - Triste guerre. Il ne nous en revient aucun mort.

    MERCURE - J'espère pourtant que s'il peut se défaire du badinage et de la mollesse, il fera grand fracas un jour. Il a la colère et les pleurs d'Achille. Il pourrait bien en avoir le courage. Il est assez mutin pour lui ressembler. On dit qu'il aime les Muses, qu'il a un Chiron, un Phénix.

    CHARON - Mais tout cela ne fait pas notre compte. Il nous faudrait plutôt un jeune prince brutal, ignorant, grossier, qui méprisât les lettres, qui n'aimât que

les armes, toujours prêt à s'enivrer de sang, qui mît sa gloire dans les malheurs des hommes. Il remplirait ma barque une fois par jour.
MERCURE - Ho! ho! Il t'en faut donner de ces princes, ou plutôt de ces monstres affamés de carnage! Celui-ci est plus doux. Je crois qu'il aimera la paix, et qu'il saura faire la guerre. On voit en lui les commencements d'un grand prince, comme on remarque dans un bouton de rose naissante ce qui promet une belle fleur.' Fénelon, *Dialogues des morts*, pp. 3–4; quoted by Henrichot, 'Mars aux Enfers' pp. 144–5.

38. See Schuurman, 'Fénelon on Luxury', p. 180.
39. p. 39. 'Mais je n'étais ni lâche ni méchant comme tu l'imaginais', Fénelon, *Dialogues des morts*, p. 71.
40. p. 39. 'Tu avais naturellement du courage et de la bonté de cœur. Les larmes que tu répandis à la vue de tant de milliers d'hommes, dont il n'en devait rester aucun sur la terre avant la fin du siècle, marquent assez ton humanité. C'est le plus bel endroit de ta vie. Si tu n'avais pas été un Roi trop puissant et trop heureux, tu aurais été un assez honnête homme.' Fénelon, *Dialogues des morts*, p. 72. In *The Histories*, Xerxes, who has been caught weeping, thus explains his feelings: 'I was reflecting on things and it occurred to me how short the sum total of human life is, which made me feel compassion. Look at all these people – but not one of them will still be alive in a hundred years' time' (7.46), p. 424.
41. pp. 37–8. 'Ah! les Rois qui peuvent tout, (je le vois bien, mais hélas ! je le vois trop tard) sont livrés à toutes leurs passions. Hé! quel moyen quand on est homme de résister à sa propre puissance et à la flatterie de tous ceux dont on est entouré. O quel malheur de naître dans de si grands périls!', Fénelon, *Dialogues des morts*, p. 68.
42. p. 38. 'J'étais Roi à condition de mener une vie dure, sobre et laborieuse comme mon peuple. Je n'étais Roi que pour défendre ma patrie, et pour faire régner les lois; ma Royauté me donnait le pouvoir de faire du bien, sans me permettre de faire du mal', Fénelon, *Dialogues des morts*, p. 69. By encouraging the Duke of Burgundy to recognise his faults and the necessity to address them, but also by showing how through the example of Leonidas, Fénelon is putting into practice his own pedagogical theory: 'Ne dites point à l'enfant son défaut, sans ajouter quelque moyen de le surmonter, qui l'encourage à le faire', 'Never tell a child his fault without adding some way to overcome it, which will encourage him to do so' (my translation), in *De l'Education des Filles* (Paris, 1687), pp. 54–5.
43. This was not to be as Fénelon predeceased his pupil, and Louis XIV his grandson who died in 1712.

SECTION 2

LITERARY REPRESENTATIONS

CHAPTER 4

SAADI'S PERCEPTION OF THE WEST AND GERMAN TRANSLATORS' PERCEPTION OF IRAN IN SAADI'S *GULISTAN* (*THE ROSE GARDEN*)

Nina Zandjani

Introduction

The aim of this chapter is to explore Saadi's perception of the West and Westerners in the thirteenth century as shown in *Gulistan* (گلستان), and Western perceptions of Iran and the Iranians as shown in the paratexts of three German translations of this work (*Der Rosengarten*) from the nineteenth and twentieth centuries. The translators use paratexts to convey the references of the culture-specific elements in Saadi's *Gulistan* to German readers. The selected target texts are *Der Rosengarten*, by Karl Heinrich Graf,[1] Dieter Bellmann[2] and Kathleen Göpel.[3] The Persian edition of Yusofi[4] is used as the assumed source text and Rehatsek's English translation[5] used mainly for comparison for non-German readers.

The Persian classical work *Gulistan* (*The Rose Garden*) by the poet Saadi from Shiraz (*c.*1210–90) was first published in 1258. The book maintains a central position in Persian literature and is considered an important work within world literature. David Damrosch defines world literature as 'all literary works that circulate beyond their culture of origin, either in translation or in their original language'.[6] For centuries, *Gulistan* has been used as a textbook within philosophy of life and morals in the Persian cultural area, stretching from India in the East to the Balkans in the West, as pointed out by Browne,[7] Yohannan,[8] Dashti,[9] Katouzian[10] and Thackston.[11] *Gulistan* consists of a number of anecdotes written in prose, with short verses in-between, where the well-travelled author narrates his experiences from numerous journeys across the Middle East and Northern Africa. It has been translated into many languages within various cultural areas, first into Turkish in 1391, later followed by French, German, Latin and Dutch in the seventeenth century and English in the eighteenth century.[12] Numerous German translations, rewritings, renderings and imitations of *Gulistan* have been published, including Johann Wolfgang von Goethe's *West–Eastern Diwan*[13] and Johann Gottfried Herder's *The Rose Valley* (*Rosenthal*). Some German and English translations have been re-translated and revised several times. My own Norwegian translation of *Gulistan* (*Rosenhagen*), published in 2006, was the first complete and direct Norwegian translation from a Persian classical work.

Paratexts and the Translator's Visibility

The German theologian and philosopher Friedrich Schleiermacher in 1813 identified two possible translation methods: 'either the translator leaves the author in peace as much as possible and moves the reader towards him; or he leaves the reader in peace as much as possible and moves the author towards him'.[14] The first approach has later been called foreignisation (*Verfremdung*) being possible only when the reader is acquainted with that culture, the other approach domestication (*Einbürgerung*) or Germanising (*Verdeutschung*) being necessary when the reader is not familiar with the source text culture. Schleiermacher clearly preferred the first strategy. Goethe expressed almost the same idea at the same time. Graf in his foreword[15] refers to Goethe's three epochs of translation,[16] and seems to have been inspired by this when translating *Gulistan*. Both Schleiermacher and Goethe seem then to have influenced Venuti, who differentiates between the two translation strategies of domestication and foreignisation and argues against what he calls the translator's invisibility, through domesticating strategies. Venuti claims that foreignising is more common in the German and French translation cultures, while British and American cultures have long been dominated by domesticating theories recommending fluent translations.[17] By foreignising strategies, however, the reader is sent abroad instead of bringing the author home. The translator is made more visible by bringing out the foreign identity in the source text and protecting it against the ideological dominance of the target culture.

From a great number of German translations of *Gulistan*, published over a period of 150 years, I have selected three for this study: the first by Karl Heinrich Graf published in Leipzig (1846), because it is the first complete and direct translation of the book from Persian into German. The second, by Dieter Bellmanns, is a revision of it, published in Leipzig during the GDR period (1982) and in Munich (1998) after the German reunification, and is the edition currently used in academia. The third translation in this comparative study, Göpel's indirect translation, is based on an English translation and published in Berlin (1997). These three different kinds of translations have different purposes and intended readership, which guide the choice of translation strategies, in regard to the linguistic expressions, cultural filtration and the use of paratexts. In this respect, the paratexts also may give an answer to the translator's or publisher's intention with the translations.

The term paratext was first elaborated by Genette, as an 'undefined zone' between the inside and the outside, an edge, 'a fringe of the printed text which in reality controls one's whole reading of the text'.[18] The paratexts examined here are the translators' own foreword/afterword, glossaries, notes, lists of names of persons and places, references to other pieces of literary works and to the Qur'an, as well as acknowledgements. All of these mediate the work to the reader. Paratexts have rapidly caught the interest of translation scholars who wish to focus on elements connecting translated texts with their readers, shaping their reception, according to Tahir Gürçağlar,[19] who was one of the first scholars to discuss paratexts and translation.

This paratextual analysis of the German translations of Saadi's *Gulistan*, through close reading of the paratexts, focuses on the occurrence and presentation of certain textual elements that constitute the threshold of interpretations as defined by Genette.[20] Such elements have various terms and expressions within Translation Studies. Pedersen, among others, introduces the term 'extralinguistic cultural references' and defines them as 'references to people, places, customs, institutions, food etc. that are specific to a certain culture, and which you may not know even if you know the language in question'.[21]

Paratexts guide the reading and reception of the German translations of *Gulistan* and the hidden meanings of the references and thus give important insight into the translators' cultural view and their perception of the Iranians.

The Persian Poet Saadi's Perception of the West

Sheikh Muslih al-din Saadi lived for about 90 years (*c.*1200–90). Although there is uncertainty about his exact years of birth and death, we know that he was born and buried in his hometown Shiraz, in Fars in southern Iran. His grave has become a popular place of pilgrimage and a tourist attraction. Saadi's life can be divided into three parts. The first 30 years he acquired knowledge, mainly through studies at the Nezamiyeh School in Baghdad. Then he travelled for 30 years, to India, North Africa and through the Middle East, as an ascetic dervish. He devoted the last 30 years of his life to writing poems and recording his own travels and life experiences as well as those of others, mainly in *Bustan* (1257) and *Gulistan* (1258), as explained by Bellmann[22] and Zandjani.[23]

The following examples have been chosen to illustrate Saadi's perception of the West, as it can be derived from some of the anecdotes of *Gulistan*. As part of the concept of the West I have included Christians, Jews, Greeks and Rum (the Byzantine Empire), in contrast to Arabs and Muslims.

In chapter 2, 'On the Morals of Dervishes' (در اخلاق درویشان), Saadi narrates his negative encounter with the Franks (فرنگ, *farang*), the western crusaders. He became their prisoner and was put to work, digging in the earth in Tripoli together with Jews, which he considered a great humiliation. Complaining about his situation, Saadi calls the Jews non-humans (نامردم, *nâmardom*):

که در طویلهٔ نامردمم بباید ساخت

That I must be satisfied in the stable of non-humans

In the above example, Graf uses the German word 'non-humans' (*Nichtmenschen*)[24] for *nâ-mardom* (non-humans). Although this could be regarded as a foreignising translation strategy, the concept 'Nicht-Mensch', as a bad, godless person, had been introduced and discussed before Graf used it here.[25] Bellmann's 'barbarians' (*Barbaren*)[26] and Göpel's 'brute' (*Unmensch*)[27] both tend towards a more domesticating solution, as these are more common German terms.

In the same story, Saadi expresses that being a prisoner together with friends, the non-foreigners, is preferable to staying with strangers in a garden, although the latter is considered one of the most pleasant places in Persian literature, as pointed out by Riccardo Zipoli.[28] Here Saadi makes a clear difference between the positive 'us' (Persians) and the negative 'them' (Westerners):

پای در زنجیر پیش دوستان / به که با بیگانگان در بوستان

The foot in chain with friends / is better than with strangers in a garden.

Both Bellmann and Graf call strangers 'unknown' (*Unnbekannte*),[29] while Göpel uses 'strangers' (*Fremde*)[30] as translations of the Persian *bigâgegân* (strangers).

Saadi is more admiring towards the Westerners when he meets a tradesman in chapter 3, 'On the Excellence of Content' (در فضیلت قناعت) who lists Greek brocade among other precious trade goods:

گوگرد پارسی خواهم بردن به چین که شنیدم عظیم قیمتی دارد و از آنجا کاسهٔ چینی به روم آرم و دیبای رومی به هند و فولاد هندی به حلب

I shall carry Persian brimstone to China because I heard that it fetched a high price. I shall also carry Chinese porcelain to Rum and Rumi brocade to India and Indian steel to Aleppo.[31]

Saadi also refers to the prominent Greek physician, surgeon and philosopher, Galen in chapter 4, 'On the Advantages of Silence' (در فوائد خاموشی). Witnessing a fool fighting with a scholar and cursing him, Galen states these wise words:

اگر این دانا بودی، کار او با نادان بدین جایگاه نرسیدی

If this man were wise, he wouldn't have tangled thus with the ignorant.[32]

Two of the German translators, Bellmann and Göpel,[33] have added paratextual explanations about Galen, stating his role as a Roman royal physician. Bellmann adds that he had a high reputation among the Arabs and Persians because of his knowledge within various branches of medicine.

In chapter 6, 'On Weakness and Old Age' (در ضعف و پیری), when in the mosque in Damascus, he is asked by a young man to help him understand the last words of a dying Persian old man. This time Saadi again quotes the wisdom of Greek philosophers:

که فیلسوفان یونان گفته‌اند: مزاج ارچه مستقیم بود، اعتماد بقا را نشاید

> Ionian philosophers have said that although the constitution may be good no reliance is to be placed on its permanence[34]

When Saadi comments on Christians and Christianity, he calls the Christians unclean and states that Jesus' donkey will always stay a donkey, even if taken to Mecca, as in chapter 7, 'On the Effects of Education' (در تأثیر تربیت):

خر عیسی گرش به مکه برند / چون بیاید هنوز خر باشد

> If the ass of Jesus be taken to Mecca / He will on his return still be an ass.[35]

This means that even though Jesus is considered a prophet in Islam, his donkey remains one of the less noble animals in the bestiary of Persian poetry, as Zipoli explains.[36] Here the German translator Bellmann adds a note, explaining Jesus' position in Islam and that the story refers to the young Jesus arriving in Egypt on a donkey.[37] He thus assumes that his German readers know their Bible story.

In chapter 3, 'On the Excellence of Content' (در فضیلت قناعت), Saadi calls both Christians and Jews so unclean that it would even not matter if a dead Jew was washed in a Christian's well:

گر آب چاه نصرانی نه پاک است / جهود مرده می شویی چه باک است؟

> If the water of a Christian's well is impure / what matters it if thou washest a dead Jew therein?[38]

Yet again the German translator Bellmann adds a note, explaining the necessity of the body and clothes to be clean before prayer and that the ritual washing therefore is an obligation (for Muslims).[39]

Though Saadi has a partly negative and critical view towards the Franks and other foreigners in the first two examples and towards Christians in the last two examples, he clearly values positively the wisdom of Greek philosophers and physicians and the precious Greek textiles. This dislike and admiration might have been a typical Persian perception of the West and Westerners in the thirteenth century, especially as Sufism, the mystical trend within Islam, included elements from Greek philosophy.[40]

German Translators' Perception of the Persians

Translation of literature into German experienced a tremendous activity from about 1820, resulting in the creation of what Norbert Bachleitner calls translation factories.[41] The production reached its peak around 1845, when translated novels amounted to 48 per cent of the total novel publication in German. Of the 261 translations that year, 43 were from languages other than English and French.[42] The earliest translation in this study, the one by Graf, was published in 1846. Goethe in the early decades of the nineteenth century called for World Literature (*Weltliteratur*), the international circulation and reception of literary works in Europe, including works of non-western origin. According to Bachleitner, Goethe's famous words 'National literature is now a rather unmeaning term; the epoch of world literature is at hand, and everyone must strive to hasten its approach', can be seen as the spark which increased German translation activity. Through translations the German language was revived, enriched and developed, as Bernhard Zeller among others claims.[43] Goethe's own *West–östlicher Divan*, a collection of lyrical poems inspired by Hafez and other Persian poets, was published in this period (1819–27). In his *Notes*,[44] Goethe characterises Saadi as the Persian poet with a need to collect stories and a desire to teach, and whose works are thus useful to Westerners. Helge Jordheim[45] points out that Goethe's *West–östlicher Divan* was written during a time when Europe was in full disintegration during the Napoleonic Wars and may have been an escape from the European chaos.

The translators use their paratexts (i.e. foreword, afterword, glossaries, notes) to explain to the new readership, the German readers, facts that are known to the Persian language user. This includes explanations about how to understand the figurative language, references to events and other implied, hidden messages. Such paratexts are useful when analysing the translator's perception of Iran (Persia) and the Iranians (Persians), because it gives us an impression of the target culture, the society and readers whom they are writing for.

In Graf's German translation of *Gulistan*, the paratexts consist of acknowledgements,[46] a foreword,[47] notes, an alphabetical list of themes in his notes and references to other literary works.[48] In his foreword, Graf compares his own translation and method with those of his predecessor Olearius, placing the latter into a German sociopolitical context. He comments on his own method of translating and his fidelity towards Saadi,[49] attempting to provide the German reader with the same associations as the Persian reader receives when reading the original.[50] Among the translation challenges were themes such as pious people and homosexuality.[51] Graf was a scholar and a theologian, illustrating Edward Said's claim in his controversial *Orientalism*, that by and large, until the mid-eighteenth century Orientalists were mainly Biblical scholars and Islamic specialists, while the nineteenth-century Orientalist was either a scholar, a gifted enthusiast or both.[52] His translation was based on a comparison of three Persian editions of *Gulistan* printed in Paris and London.

In the second German translation examined, Bellmann (1982/1998), wrote an afterword rather than a foreword, putting the writer in a less visible position according to Genette.[53] In this afterword, Bellmann explains that the present translation is a revision and retranslation of Graf's from 1846. Bellmann has in addition taken the Persian edition by Soviet–Russian Rustam Alijew (1959) into consideration,[54] this may show that Bellmann does not rely only on Graf's interpretation and that he knows Persian. He might also have had contact with the Iranian Communists who were in exile in East Germany, such as the Iranian leftist writer, novelist and translator Bozorg Alavi (1904–97), one of the founders and leaders of Iran's communist Tudeh Party,[55] who was at the Humboldt University in East Berlin for years.[56] In his afterword, Bellmann gives details about Saadi's life, the sociopolitical situation in Persia in Saadi's time, Sufism, the use of figurative language, other language translations, including also Goethe's comments about Saadi.[57] Further, there is an overview of early Persian printed editions in Europe,[58] and explanations about Islam, its belief and rules. In addition to the afterword, Bellmann has included 172 notes[59] and details about persons referred to.[60] He evidently wants to enlighten his readers and has extensive knowledge about the field.

In the third translation examined, Göpel (1997) has a foreword,[61] signed by the translator of the English edition, Sayed Omar Ali-Shah. The foreword shows an emphasis on Sufism, as Ali-Shah was a teacher of this religious direction within Islam. There are 123 notes,[62] considerably fewer in number and with less content and also less didactic, than in Graf's and Bellmann's translations.

The following examples illustrate how the translators have presented the Iranians (Persians) to their readers of various social, economic and cultural backgrounds, assuming certain knowledge of Middle Eastern philosophy and literature among them or lack thereof, and what the translators therefore have considered necessary to explain.

The Persian expressions for 'pious people' (*abed* عابد and *zahed* زاهد) is translated into '*Werkheilig*' by Graf, who states in his foreword that he found it difficult to find a German equivalent. As the French are more pious than the Germans, he claims, they have the word *devot.*[63] Here Graf uses his paratext to criticise his fellow German Christians. Bellmann writes 'those who pretend to be pious' (*die sich fromm stellen*),[64] 'a believing servant of Allah' (*gläubiger Diener Allahs*)[65] and 'a hypocritical believer' (*ein scheinheiliger Gläubiger*),[66] while Göpel uses more domesticating solutions, such as 'a man' (*ein Mann*)[67] and 'another traveller' (*ein anderer Reisender*)[68] and 'blasphemer' (*Spötter*).[69]

Saadi frequently refers to names of persons who would be familiar to most Persian speaking people, names which would involve memories and knowledge from mythology, history, politics or religious traditions. These names are explained as part of the notes by Graf and Göpel, but given in a separate list of proper names by Bellmann. An example is King Fereidun, about whom Graf gives detailed explanations over several pages,[70] while Bellmann has a short note[71] and Göpel only refers to an assumed date of reign.[72]

Certain animals, such as the owl and the bird Huma, would give the Persian reader associations regarding their character and nature, positive or negative. In chapter 5, Saadi writes about the shadow of the owl and the bird Huma:

کس نیاید به زیر سایهٔ بوم / ور همای از جهان شود معدوم

No one would stand in the shadow of the owl, even if the Huma should disappear from the world.

The associations have to be explained to the German reader. Graf explains only the mythological bird Huma,[73] which he translates into phoenix (*Phönix*)[74] but calls *Humai* in a note.[75] Bellmann adopts Graf's translation solution, without any explanatory notes here, but he explains Huma elsewhere in his notes.[76] Göpel explains two birds, the owl and what she calls the Simurgh,[77] though the latter bird is not mentioned in *Gulistan*, but occurs in Attar's *The Conference of the Birds*. Göpel uses a domesticating solution by adding the characteristics 'distastrous' (*unheilvoll*) to the shadow of the owl and 'auspicious' (*glückverheißend*) to the Simurgh.[78]

To illustrate that something which is regarded as inferior by most people, can be valuable to others, Saadi uses barley bread as an example in chapter 1:

ای سیر تو را نان جوین خوش ننماید / معشوق من است آن که به نزدیک تو زشت است

O you full man, barley bread pleases you not,
she is my beloved who appears ugly to you.

Most Persian speaking readers would associate this with the legendary couple Leily and Majnun, the Arab and Middle Eastern counterpart to Romeo and Juliet. She, Leily, small and of dark complexion, is passionately loved by Majnun. None of the translators mentions this reference, but Bellmann explains that barley is known to be of less value.[79]

Also in chapter 1, Saadi speaks about the water of life, which has its source in darkness:

که آب چشمهٔ حیوان درون تاریکی است

Because the spring of life is in darkness

Graf gives an explanation over several pages,[80] referring to Alexander the Great and the Qur'an. Bellman and Göpel have short notes, stating that the source of the immortalising water of life is surrounded by darkness.[81] Bellmann adds that its place is unknown.

Still in chapter 1, we hear about a man who steals firewood from the poor and gives to the rich. As his storage of wood ignites, he wonders how this could happen and a pious man tells him that what he sees is actually the 'smoke from the heart' (*dud-e del* دود دل) of the poor people, meaning a sigh:

ندانم که این آتش از کجا در انبار هیزم من افتاد. گفت: از دود دل درویشان

'I do not know whence this fire has fallen into my house.' He replied: 'From the smoke of the hearts of dervishes.'

Graf enlightens his readers about the popular Persian image of heart smoke in a note,[82] while Bellmann just keeps Graf's foreignised translation without any paratextual explanation.[83] Göpel adopts Graf's explanation in her translation, 'sigh from the heart' (*Seufzer des Herzen*),[84] again using a domesticating solution.

In chapter 4, Saadi writes about an astrologer who finds his wife at home, together with a stranger. Furious, he wants to shout it out, but is stopped by a pious man, maybe Saadi himself, claiming that shouting would only bring disgrace upon himself. He, who has detailed knowledge of astrology and the stars, a field of study from ancient times in Iran,[85] is blamed for not knowing what is going on closest to him.

تو بر اوج فلک چه دانی چیست؟ / که ندانی که در سرای تو کیست

How do you know what is in the zenith of the sky,
If you are not aware who is in your house?

Graf has a note, but instead of explaining the story, he quotes another similar anecdote.[86] Bellmann and Göpel have no paratexts, the disgrace is not explained as it is universal and thus understandable for Western readers.

The donkey has various qualities and properties in Persian culture. It is said to be stupid, but also useful as a loadbearing animal. In chapter 4, Saadi uses a quote from the Qur'an when he compares the voice of a person with that of a donkey. All three translators have notes referring to the sura and verse of the Qur'an (31:18), stating that the donkey has the ugliest voice of all.

Conclusion

These examples and discussions have given us insight into Saadi's perception of the West and likewise insight into the translation solutions used by Graf, Bellmann and Göpel, indicating their view of the Persians. Saadi writes negatively about the Westerners. He considers Christian and Jewish people unclean and that Jesus' donkey remains stupid even if brought to the most holy place for Muslims, Mecca, and he states that staying together with friends in prison is preferable to being with strangers in pleasant gardens. But Saadi – and presumably his Persian contemporaries – also values Western, i.e. Greek, brocade, wisdom and philosophy highly.

Through the German translations and the paratexts, i.e. forewords/afterwords, notes and glossaries we get some insight into how Western translators may have perceived the Persian source culture and how they chose to convey, through paratexts, the reference system of the figurative language in the source text to the contemporary German language readers in the nineteenth and twentieth centuries. Two opposite translation strategies have been applied, foreignising which closely follows the source text and brings the reader towards the text and domesticating where unfamiliar concepts are replaced by domestic variants to enhance the reader's understanding and the text thereby is brought closer to the reader.[87]

As Graf writes for colleagues and educated scholars, he does not necessarily give explanations. He chooses a more foreignising translation solution than Bellmann and Göpel, by using unfamiliar figurative expressions such as 'smoke of the heart' for a sigh. He shows that he has knowledge beyond this work and sees connections to other works of Saadi and other poets. Graf even uses paratexts to express his critique against his own fellow Christians when demonstrating the challenges in translating 'pious people' into German (section 4). As more than 130 years passed between Graf's and Bellmann's editions, language and stylistic ideals have changed. Bellmann more clearly wants to enlighten his educated/interested readers and expand their knowledge, as in the translation of barley bread (section 4). He explains and connects the text to the readers' world and, in this way, narrows the cultural gap. Göpel's paratexts are both shorter, fewer and not as scholarly as those of the other two, clearly meant for a broader public.[88]

Saadi's *Gulistan* belongs to the world literature and, as David Damrosch points out, world literature can be seen in one or more ways: 'as an established body of *classics*, as an evolving canon of *masterpieces*, or as multiple *windows on the world*'.[89] For the three German translators, Graf, Bellmann and Göpel, *Gulistan* was undoubtedly a window on the world, regardless of which translation strategy they have used. Narratives shape and reflect society and, as Sir Malcolm in *Sketches of Persia*, comments on the role of Saadi's work: 'Were I to judge from my own observations, I should say, that these stories and maxims, which are known to all, from the king to the peasant, have fully as great an effect, in restraining the arbitrary and unjust exercise of power as the law of the Prophet'.[90] Saadi's stories and maxims still are part of every Persian's vocabulary and memory.

I have shown that the above-mentioned German paratexts not only guide the reading and reception of the three translations of *Gulistan*, but also give us an insight into the translators' and the target cultures' perception of the source culture, Iran (Persia) and Iranians (Persians). Graf's use of a mostly foreignising translation strategy was possible because his German readers in the nineteenth century would, to a large degree, be acquainted with Persian culture. He can keep close to the source text. The other approach, a more domesticating translation, was necessary for Bellmann and Göpel, because their readers presumably would not be that familiar with the Persian source text culture.

Notes

1. Saadi, *Moslicheddin Saadis Rosengarten*, tr. K. H. Graf from Persian, with notes and additions (Leipzig, 1846).
2. Saadi, *Der Rosengarten*, tr. D. Bellmann, based on tr. K. H. Graf, revised (Leipzig, 1982); Saadi *Der Rosengarten*, tr. D. Bellmann, based on tr. K. H. Graf, 3rd corrected edition (Munich, 1998).
3. Saadi, *Gulistan – Der Rosengarten*, tr. K. Göpel, based on tr. S. O. Ali-Shah (Berlin, 1997). Today her name is Göbel.
4. Saadi, *Golestan-e Sa'di*, گلستان سعدی, commented by Gholam-Hossein Yusofi (Tehran, 1368H/1989).
5. Saadi, *Gulistan*, tr. E. Rehatsek. Bilingual series (Tehran, reprint 2004 [1888]). Where no reference is given, the English translations are mine.
6. David Damrosch, *What is World Literature?* (Princeton, 2003), p. 4.

7. Edward G. Browne, *A Literary History of Persia*, vol. II (Maryland, 1997), pp. 525–39.
8. John D. Yohannan, *The Poet Sa'di – A Persian Humanist* (Lanham, 1987).
9. Ali Dashti, *The Realm of Sa'di*, tr. S. Dashti (Costa Mesa, 2013).
10. Homa Katouzian, *Sa'di: The Poet of Life, Love and Compassion* (Oxford, 2006).
11. Wheeler M. Thackston, 'Translator's Preface', in *The Gulistan of Sa'di* (Maryland, 2008), pp. iv–xi.
12. Wheeler M. Thackson, 'Bibliography of Sa'di's Gulistan', in *The Gulistan of Sa'di* (Maryland, 2008), pp. 182–9.
13. *West-östlicher Divan*.
14. Friedrich Schleiermacher, *Kritische Gesamtausgabe: 1. Abt. 11: Schriften und Entwürfe Akademievorträge* (Berlin, 2012), p. 74.
15. Karl H. Graf, 'Vorrede', in Saadi, *Rosengarten* (Leipzig, 1846), p. xiv.
16. Johann W. Goethe, 'Translations', tr. Sh. Sloan, in L. Venuti (ed.) *The Translation Studies Reader*, pp. 64–5.
17. Lawrence Venuti, *The Translator's Invisibility – A History of Translation* (London, 2008), pp. 15–20.
18. Genette, *Paratexts*, p. 2.
19. Ş. Tahir-Gürçağlar, 'Paratexts', in Y. Gambier and L. van Doorslaer (eds): *Handbook of Translation Studies*, vol. 2 (Amsterdam, 2011), p. 113.
20. Genette, *Paratexts*.
21. Jan Pedersen, *Subtitling Norms for Television* (Amsterdam, 2011), pp. 2–3.
22. Dieter Bellmann, 'Nachwort', in *Der Rosengarten* (Leipzig, 1998), p. 349.
23. Nina Zandjani, 'Translator's foreword', in Saadi, *Rosenhagen* (Oslo, 2006), p. 7.
24. Saadi, *Der Rosengarten*, tr. Graf, p. 84.
25. Though the concept of *Nicht-Mensch* is not very common in German, Graf may have known the following work: Gillis Gerleman, 'Der Nicht-Mensch. Erwägungen zur hebräischen Wurzel N B L' in *Vetus Testamentum*, vol. 24, Fasc. 2 (1974), pp. 147–58.
26. Saadi, *Der Rosengarten*, tr. Bellmann (1989), p. 124.
27. Saadi, *Gulistan – Der Rosengarten*, tr. Göpel, p. 118.
28. Riccardo Zipoli, 'Poetic Imagery', in Bruijn (ed.) *A History of Persian Literature*, vol. I (London, 2009), p. 187.
29. Saadi, *Der Rosengarten*, tr. Graf, p. 84; Saadi, tr. Bellmann (1998), p. 124.
30. Saadi, *Gulistan – Der Rosengarten*, tr. Göpel, p. 118.
31. Saadi, *Gulistan*, tr. Rehatsek, p. 391.
32. Saadi, *The Gulistan of Sa'di*, tr. W.M. Thackston, p. 99.
33. Saadi, *Der Rosengarten*, tr. Bellmann (1998), pp. 393–4, Göpel, *Gulistan – Der Rosengarten*, p. 317.
34. Saadi, *Gulistan*, tr. Rehatsek, pp. 529–31.
35. Ibid., p. 557.
36. Zipoli, Poetic Imagery', pp. 182–3.
37. Saadi, *Der Rosengarten*, tr. Bellmann (1989), p. 387.
38. Ibid., p. 389.
39. Saadi, *Der Rosengarten*, tr. Bellmann (1998), p. 380.
40. Ibid., p. 358.

41. Norbert Bachleitner, '"Übersetzungsfabriken". Das deutsche Übersetzungswesen in der esten Hälfte des 19. Jahrhunderts', in *Internationales Archiv für Sozialgeschichte der deutschen Literatur (IASL)*, 14 (1989), pp. 1–49.
42. Ibid., p. 5.
43. Bernhard Zeller, 'Vorwort', in *Weltliterarur – Die Lust am Übersetzen im Jahrhundert Goethes* (1982), p. 5.
44. Johann W. Goethe, *Noten und Abhandlungen zu besserem Verständnis des West-östlichen Divans* (1819). Available at http://www.wissen-im-netz.info/literatur/goethe/diwan/14.htm [Accessed 24 September 2015].
45. Helge Jordheim, 'Verdenslitteratur og litteraturforskningens kairós: Goethe, Auerbach, Said – og vi', in *Norsk Litteraturvitenskapelig Tidsskrift*, vol. 9 (1) (2006), p. 15.
46. Saadi, *Der Rosengarten*, tr. Graf, p. v.
47. Ibid., pp. ix–xxii.
48. Ibid., pp. 299–302.
49. Ibid., p. xv.
50. Ibid., p. xvi.
51. Ibid., pp. xx–xxi.
52. Edward Said, *Orientalism* (London, 2003), p. 51.
53. Gennette, *Paratexts*, pp. 238, 172, 239.
54. Saadi, tr. Bellmann, *Der Rosengarten* (1998), p. 368.
55. Ervand Abrahamian, *Iran Between Two Revolutions* (Princeton, 1982), p. 158.
56. For further reading, see: http://www.iranicaonline.org/articles/alavi-bozorg-novelist.
57. Saadi, *Der Rosengarten*, tr. Bellmann (1998), pp. 349–70.
58. Ibid., p. 368.
59. Ibid., pp. 375–90.
60. Ibid., pp. 391–8.
61. Saadi, *Gulistan – Der Rosengarten*, tr. Göpel, pp. 9–14.
62. Ibid., pp. 315–8.
63. Saadi, *Der Rosengarten*, tr. Graf, p. xx.
64. Saadi, *Der Rosengarten*, tr. Bellmann (1998), p. 93.
65. Ibid., p. 114.
66. Ibid., p. 118.
67. Saadi, *Gulistan – Der Rosengarten*, tr. Göpel, p. 109.
68. Ibid., p. 113.
69. Ibid., p. 113.
70. Saadi, *Der Rosengarten*, tr. Graf, pp. 247; 252–3.
71. Saadi, *Der Rosengarten*, tr. Bellmann (1998), p. 393.
72. Saadi, *Gulistan – Der Rosengarten*, tr. Göpel, p. 315
73. Saadi, *Der Rosengarten*, tr. Graf, p. 128.
74. Ibid., p. 21.
75. Ibid., p. 248.
76. Saadi, *Der Rosengarten*, tr. Bellmann (1998), p. 378.
77. Saadi, *Gulistan – Der Rosengarten*, tr. Göpel, p. 315.
78. Ibid., p. 36.

79. Saadi, *Der Rosengarten*, tr. Bellmann (1998), p. 378.
80. Saadi, *Der Rosengarten*, tr. Graf, pp. 263–7.
81. Saadi, *Der Rosengarten*, tr. Bellmann (1998), p. 379; Saadi, *Gulistan – Der Rosengarten*, tr. Göpel, p. 315.
82. Saadi, *Gulistan – Der Rosengarten*, tr. Göpel, p. 260.
83. Saadi, *Der Rosengarten*, tr. Graf, p. 50; Saadi, *Der Rosengarten*, tr. Bellmann (1998), p. 75.
84. Saadi, *Gulistan – Der Rosengarten*, tr. Göpel, p. 70.
85. For further reading, see: http://www.iranicaonline.org/articles/astrology-and-astronomy-in-iran-#pt1.
86. Saadi, *Der Rosengarten*, tr. Graf, p. 283.
87. Schleiermacher, *Kritische Gesamtausgabe*, p. 74.
88. Nina Zandjani, 'German Translations of Medieval Persian – The Rose Garden of Sa'di', in *Norm-Focused and Culture-related Inquiries in Translation Research*, *Gdansk Studies in Languages series* (Frankfurt am Main, 2016).
89. Damrosch, *What is World Literature*, p. 15.
90. John Malcolm, *Sketches of Persia* (London, 1861), p. 69.

CHAPTER 5

'PARISIAN OR PERSIAN?': AN INTRODUCTION ON THE FRENCH ROOTS OF THE FIRST IRANIAN SOCIAL NOVELS

Ali Beh-Pajooh

Introduction

For many centuries, Iran has been a land of poetry and great poets. However, the Qajar dynasty was a period of gradual transition to newer aesthetic and artistic forms of expression. One of the most controversial literary debates of Iran's post-constitutional revolution, the 1917 debate between Mohammad-Taqi Bahar, poet laureate, and Taqi Rafat, poet and critic, was dedicated to revising Iran's most established literary form, traditional poetry. Rafat radically believed that the abstract works of Persian poets (Saadi, Hafez and Ferdowsi) were no longer relevant for interpreting 'the meaning of life' in the context of Iran's then-transitional society. In fact, Rafat was in search of 'Saadis of his own time', competent literary figures who could relay modernist messages to the Iranian society. Addressing Bahar as the main defender of Classic poetry, he wrote in the newspaper *Zaban-e Azad* (*Liberated Language*):

> Our challenge is to find out whether the thoughts and teachings of the poets, literary figures, and philosophers of old times can provide adequate answers to contemporary problems of a modern

> and innovative nation. In other words, do the poems and prose compositions of our classics produce in us new thoughts, new impressions, new awareness, new sensations, new whatever, or no?[1]

Not long after such debates, the first widely read Iranian novel, *Tehran-e Makhuf* (*The Dreadful Tehran*),[2] was published in sequential instalments in the Tehran-based newspaper *Setareh-ye Iran* (*The Star of Iran*) in the course of summer and autumn of 1922. The author, Morteza Moshfeq Kazemi (1902–77), focused on depicting contemporary issues in Iran's capital as it was poised on the threshold of modernisation. The novel aimed at revealing evils of urban life, most notably prostitution and the corruption of ruling class. In doing so, it took a great step beyond traditional Persian poetry in objectifying social contemporary dilemmas in a realistic and detailed way. *The Dreadful Tehran* gained extraordinary popularity in a short time and was published in book format in Tehran (1924, two volumes) and subsequently translated into four languages (Azeri Turkish, Russian, Uyghur and Uzbek).

However prominent, *The Dreadful Tehran* was not the first Iranian novel. At least four major historical novels had been written by that time, including *Love and Kingship, or The Victories of Cyrus the Great* (1919, Musa Nasri, Hamadan) and *An Ancient Story, or The Life of Cyrus* (1920, Hasan Badi, Tehran) which overall meant to glorify and idealise ancient Persia. These novels could not compete with *The Dreadful Tehran* thematically, hence these novels were not 'a suitable medium for animated description and discussion of contemporary social, political and economic problems. In their search for the forgotten beauty of the past, the writers failed to illuminate the face of the present. [. . .] Readers wanted literature concerned with present reality rather than with a vague romantic past'.[3] That is, literature just like *The Dreadful Tehran*.

It seems that Kazemi himself was vaguely conscious of going against the grain in literary fashion and making an innovative movement in the context of Persian literature. The first lines of the book provide a telling example on this account, whereas the writer cynically portrays the Tehran of 1912, first as a 'dusty and stormy city which is hard to pass in its streets' and then promptly, locates this gloomy city as 'the capital of Iran: a country which is proud of its ancient civilization and its great and glorious poets.'[4]

But was Kazemi's success only because he was a pioneer ahead of his time or was his debut novel a worthwhile representation of his society's issues?

There are some doubts about this (discussed further below). Perhaps the answer lies in a key sentence in the very first pages of the novel, where the author tries to contextualise the location of his story and depicts a suburb in Tehran, in the following sentences: 'In the south of Tehran, there is a suburb named Chaleh Meydan, which, to a great deal, resembles the Cour des Miracles in Paris [...].'[5] What is notable about this sentence is the way Kazemi illustrates Chaleh Meydan, the oldest neighbourhood in Tehran, by comparing it to the Cour des Miracles. The Cour des Miracles was a slum famous in Paris before the French revolution and featured prominently in Victor Hugo's *Notre-Dame de Paris* (*Hunchback of Notre-Dame*, 1832). Why does the writer rely on an exotic object to introduce a familiar object, a locality that his readers of the time already know? In fact, this sentence has a symbolic significance throughout the novel and also reveals the orientation of the author in the work as a whole. Like many of his contemporaries, Kazemi does not necessarily draw from his own culture and the existing realities of his society, but provides a frame of reference from translated French novels.

This chapter first of all attempts to demonstrate how the Iranian literature during the mid-nineteenth and early-twentieth century was under the hegemonic influence of French literature. I will then focus on how a specific French novel, *Les Mystères de Paris* (*The Mysteries of Paris*, 1842), written by Eugène Sue, had an undeniable and formative role on *The Dreadful Tehran*, as the first Iranian popular novel in its true meaning. Finally, I will discuss the reactions of contemporary critics and explore the contributions of Kazemi's novel to the development of Iranian fiction.

French Connection

Even though Iran had a long and brilliant tradition of storytelling,[6] at the time *The Dreadful Tehran* was published it had no background in novels in the modern sense. Franco Moretti describes such countries which lack any tradition in novel writing as 'periphery' in the context of the global 'narrative market' of the nineteenth century: a very large group that imported a lot and exported almost nothing, with very little freedom and creativity.[7] He asserts that as a

> *law of literary evolution* [...] in cultures that belong to the periphery of the literary system (which means: almost all cultures, inside and outside Europe), the modern novel first arises

> not as an autonomous development but as a compromise between a Western formal influence (usually French or English) and local materials.[8]

Interestingly, Kazemi's reading list in his teenage years (in the 1910s) serves as a model for Moretti's 'literary evolution': a hybrid of French materials, such as *Triboulet*, a French popular novel written by Michel Zévaco (a novel under the influence of Hugo's *Notre-Dame de Paris*, with Cour des Miracles as its main setting), and Persian heroic romances such as *Amir Arsalan* and *Hosein Kord-e Shabestari*.[9] In a similar way, one generation later, Ebrahim Golestan (1922–), an Iranian modernist writer, recalls reading *The Dreadful Tehran* alongside Alexandre Dumas' works in his adolescence in Shiraz in the 1930s.[10]

The above examples properly show Iran's tendency toward the French side of this prevailing Anglo–French narrative model. It became a French-oriented periphery throughout the long nineteenth century: 'Many French novels, and very few British ones.'[11] The prime reason that facilitated the development of French novelistic paradigm in the country was strategic: Iran was seeking an independent policy to counterbalance British and Russian colonialist intervention: 'With the Great Game, the fight for supremacy between the United Kingdom and Russia over Central Asian territories between 1813's Treaty of Gulistan and World War II, Iranians suffered the effects of both British and Russian imperialism [. . .].'[12] France appeared as the ideal choice: a major power that had no direct interests in the region and no visible colonialist ambition in terms of political and economic issues and therefore, Iran could strengthen ties with it in the cultural and educational domain.[13]

But what do we mean when we speak of a French-oriented market? There were several trends in Iranian literature consumption that indicated the nation's preference for French narrative. Educated people started using the French term *roman* for recognising the new literary discourse, i.e. the novel,[14] a term which has remained relevant in Iranian culture through to the present day. If anyone was totally ignorant of the phenomenon of the novel, he was advised to read translations from French novels. Mohammad Taher Mirza's translations from Dumas' *Les Trois Mousquetaires* (*Three Musketeers*) and *Le Comte de Monte-Cristo* were considered particularly great reads for beginners. Ebrahim Zanjani, an influential figure of the era, became as well acquainted generally with novels by reading those books in 1895 or 1896.[15]

Furthermore, a considerable number of citizens had the ability to read French sources directly. 'Most Iranians who had been and/or studied abroad had been to France and thus French was the lingua franca for cultural matters. According to Etemad al-Saltaneh, in 1887, there were 4,000 to 5,000 people in Tehran who knew French.'[16] At the turn of the century, these citizens could find a large selection of original French books in the well-known bookshops of Tehran (including the famous bookshop Tarbiyat). Literary books, which provided related material for the curriculum of foreign schools in Tehran, were especially common.[17] People could also reach a wide range of French novels in the library of French books at Dar al-Fonun (polytechnic college), which opened in January 1908.[18] Therefore, it was not surprising that Iranians read and translated world literature (including English novels) from French sources at that time. As Anvar Khamei (1917–), a famous political activist, remembers, in his early childhood his father read the French translation of *Robinson Crusoe* to him and orally translated it to Persia[19]. In some cases, the translation of non-French literary canons such as *The Adventures of Hajji Baba of Isfahan* (1824) and the abridged edition of *Don Quixote* were based on French versions.

Another trend in Iran's narrative market was the massive interest towards French *roman feuilleton* (the serial novel running in regular episodes in French newspaper columns between 1836 and the early years of the twentieth century).[20] However, Persian readers were rarely aware of the process of its publication and consumed it in their final format as a book. Many of the widely favoured novels in the Iranian market actually were the masterpieces of *roman feuilleton*, most notably works of Eugène Sue (*The Mysteries of Paris*, 1842–3 and *The Wandering Jew*, 1844–5), Pierre Alexis Ponson du Terrail (*Rocambole* Series, 1857–71), Michel Zévaco (*Pardaillan* Series, 1907–26), Maurice Leblanc (*Arsène Lupin* series, 1905–39). The character of Arsène Lupin (a gentleman thief who enjoys solving riddles) was originally created in reaction to the success of the *Sherlock Holmes* detective stories. But ironically, the Iranian readers of the era selected Lupin over Holmes: another sign for the centrality of French literature in the Iranian narrative market.

Reception of *The Mysteries of Paris* in Iran

The fate of Sue's *The Mysteries* in the history of novel reading is similar to the fortune of a typical character in a popular fiction, with all his/her highs and lows and twists of fate: once considered as the first really popular novel and the most widely read novel of the nineteenth century (the novel was published initially as a serial in the *Journal des Débats* from 9 June 1842 to 15 October 1843), it served as inspiration for *Les Misérables*,[21] influenced the development of *Le Comte de Monte-Cristo*[22] and then became an altogether neglected work by public readers through the twentieth century, only considered as an absorbing work for a few academicians and literary critics in 1990s and 2000s.

Mirza Fatali Akhundzade (1812–78), playwright and critic, was the first Persian literary figure who acknowledged Eugène Sue's place amongst important contemporary European authors. Akhundzade, 'a turkophone resident of Russian Caucasia who considered himself Iranian',[23] put Sue's name alongside Alexandre Dumas and Voltaire in a letter dated 29 March 1871.[24] In Akhundzade's opinion, these authors' fictional writings paved the way for progress in European nations through their critique of social issues. Akhundzade's literary criticism centred on social aspects of Iranian society in his time, including social problems such as injustice, ignorance and superstition.[25] By highlighting socially engaged literature such as Sue's novels in his critiques, Akhundzade was emphasising that reading and creating such works of literature in Iran would push the nation to take further steps towards development.

However, just two decades later *The Mysteries of Paris* was no longer regarded as a serious and reformative text containing social criticism. Instead, it became a popular pastime in the court of Naser al-Din Shah Qajar. At that time, it was one of the more exclusively translated novels and out of reach of the public.[26] By the Shah's direct command, the skilful translator Mohammad Taher Mirza undertook the translation of *The Mysteries of Paris* into Persian, which was divided in two distinct parts: the first part in 1892 and the second followed one year later (both were in manuscript format).

Fortunately, there are two reports from private gatherings of Naser al-Din Shah's court between 1892 and 1894 that indicate the special interest in *The Mysteries of Paris*. In one report, Naser al-Din Shah Qajar explains that the book was read aloud every night in the Dooshan-Tappe Palace by his professional storyteller (*Ketabkhan*) in the presence of a few members of his inner circle.[27] *The Mysteries of Paris* was so significant to the Shah that within his inner circle, he had changed its title to 'The Book of Rodolphe' after the protagonist Prince Rodolphe (the Prince of Gerolstein, an imaginary state in Germany). The new title was in the style of Persian traditional romances, such as *Amir Arsalan*, *Samak-e Ayyar* and *Hamzeh-Nameh*. This suggests that the Shah did not recognise the book as a whole new literary genre, but rather engaged with it as another variation on Persian traditional romances.

In the second report (1954), which has not been published to date, Dustali Khan-e Moayyer-ol-Mamalek, Naser al-Din Shah's grandchild, vividly remembers listening to *The Mysteries of Paris* as a child in the Qajar court:

> In 1892, I was 9 years old and my father, Dust-Mohammad Khan-e Moayyer-ol-Mamalek, had traveled to Farang {Europe} and his journey took three whole years. My mother, Esmat al-Dowleh, the most noble daughter of Naser al-Din Shah, had an insatiable desire to read tales {*qasas*} and narratives {*hikayat*}. At that time, Farangi novels were not translated and published in Tehran. Mohammad-Hasan Khan-e Etemad al-Saltaneh, the minister of press and publication {*wazir-e enteba'at*}, was the director of the Government Translation House {*Dar al-Tarjomeh*} and in Shah's order, he was translating Farangi {European} histories and tales; one of these translations was 'The Book of Rodolphe'. Hence Etemad al-Saltaneh's wife, Ashraf al-Saltaneh, was aware of my mother's inclination to such books, she had sent my mother the unbound manuscript of the book. It was a lengthy one and reading it would take a long time, therefore my mother divided the pages of the book into several parts and delivered each part to a different scribe to copy it. There were always 10 to 15 people in my mother's company, including princesses, other honourable women and old ladies, agreeable in conversation. In winter, they used to gather around a large *korsi* {heated low table} in the mirror room and spent their time with cosy chats and reading books; at the time, my mother or one of her companions would read aloud 'The Book of Rodolphe' and whenever one became exhausted by reading, the other one kept reading it. Meanwhile, they talked about what was going on in the story in a very pleasant manner.[28]

Among the many topics provoked by this memory (Iranian women as the first readers of novels, the hierarchy in the court's Translation House), that which is the most salient is the revolutionary shift in reading materials of the Iranian people in the final decades of the nineteenth century. Before this time, Iranians spent their leisure time together around the *korsi*,[29] reading Persian traditional narratives such as *Amir Arsalan* and *Hosein Kord* and sometimes narratives with a Persian origin such as *A Thousand and One Nights*. They also read from samples from classic poetry such as Ferdowsi's *Shahnameh*, Saadi, Hafez, *Khamseh* of Nizami.[30] However, the final decades of the nineteenth century brought a new source of stories: French novels. Same mise en scène (*korsi*), different stories.

It is not yet known at what point *The Mysteries of Paris* became accessible to the public. The earliest evidence of public access dates back to 20 August 1907,[31] in the heyday of Iran's Constitutional Revolution. According to a report, written by Ali Dashti, a leading writer and critic of the time, the book was still a favourite in November 1925, nearly two decades later. Dashti captures his experience in a bookshop in Tehran, as follows:

> Three or four respectable ladies entered the bookstore and one of them asked for a copy of the sixth volume of *The Pardaillan*. They did not have it. Therefore, she requested 'another good book which could amuse us at least for two or three days'. The head of the bookstore gave her a short book entitled *Henry IV* [but] she found it too short and requested for a lengthier book for more amusement. The bookseller gave her the first volume of *The Mysteries of Paris*. A youth who was also standing there – seemingly a pupil – praised the book.[32]

The Relationship Between *The Mysteries of Paris* and *The Dreadful Tehran*

Kazemi's *The Dreadful Tehran* owes a considerable debt to *The Mysteries of Paris*. This debt varies from the exact imitation (or strictly speaking signs of plagiarism) in the opening scene to the general inspiration related to mood and atmosphere. The prime influence of *The Mysteries of Paris* on *The Dreadful Tehran* is the setting of the novel. Sue shaped nineteenth-century popular imagination by representing the city as a sinister world with secret networks: '*The Mysteries of Paris* exposes a dark, disturbing world of urban poverty, social injustice, criminality and corruption. Almost no other novel before had focused to such an extent on the grimmer realities of urban life.'[33] In a similar manner, *The Dreadful Tehran* focused on the seedier sides of city life (most controversially, the dilemma of prostitution) in the context of an urban romance with a gothic sensibility. In the middle of the first volume of his book, Kazemi digresses from the plot and allocates four whole chapters to narrate the life stories of four innocent young women who have been involved in prostitution.

The Mysteries of Paris launched a large number of imitators referred to as 'city mysteries' or, in Laura Hapke's terms, 'wicked city' warning novels in Europe and America in the 1840s.[34] The most famous among them were W. M. Reynolds's *The Mysteries of London* (1844), José Nicasio Milà de Roca's *The Mysteries of Barcelona* (1844) and Ned Buntline's *The Mysteries and Miseries of New York* (1849). *The Dreadful Tehran* (1922) was as an exception: a late imitation of Sue's novel in a non-European and non-American context. It would not have been surprising if Kazemi had titled his novel *The Mysteries of Tehran*, as even Kazemi's novel is described in one advertising catalogue as 'a romantic, moralistic, social novel that reveals the secrets of living in Tehran'.[35]

Richard Maxwell, a contemporary critic, considers *The Mysteries of Paris* as an intrigue story and argues that in Sue's work, 'Paris becomes a giant conspiratorial mechanism, describable on the assumption that everyone is scheming against someone else'.[36] Similarly, *The Dreadful Tehran* evokes mystery and adventure. This is apparent even in titles for each chapter of the novel, e.g. chapter 3 (Who is the unknown youth?), chapter 24 (How was the lover's nest found out?) or chapter 38 (A meeting of four wretches).[37]

The first chapter of Kazemi's novel provides a good entry for understanding how deeply *The Dreadful Tehran* is structured around *The Mysteries of Paris* right from the beginning. In both works, 'mysteries' lie in the criminal and poor quarters of the nation's capital. Sue and Kazemi paint a romantic underworld hiding in the shadows of the modern urban metropolis. Sue makes reference to the barbaric world of James Fenimore Cooper's novels (in the beginning of his career, he was known as 'French Cooper') and writes:

> We are going to attempt to depict some episodes from the lives of *French* who are as far removed from civilization as the Indians Cooper so vividly depicts. We will spend time with them in the dens in which they get together to plan murders and robberies, in the holes where they divvy up their victims' spoils among themselves.[38]

In a different vein, Kazemi reflexively regards French novels as his point of reference (the case of Cour des Miracles). In describing the slum dwellers, he follows much of the pattern adopted by Sue in *The Mysteries* and emphasises the unpleasant conditions in which the poor are forced to live. In this regard, Kazemi makes a sharp contrast between inhabitants of the south and north of Tehran:

> However, Tehran is a rather large city, but only in its northern section do droshkies [an open four-wheeled carriage] and wagons cross. The southern sector, which is where the dwellings of the third class [poor people] are, has very narrow and cavernous alleys. In this sector, i.e. the south of Tehran, there is a slum named Chaleh Meydan, which, to a great deal, resembles the Cour des Miracles in Paris; just as in the Cour des Miracles, since olden times many people have lived there whom, due to the lack of social upbringing, have lost their humanity and appear ready to kill for money or for most trivial incidents [. . .], they kill them on the spot and rob their properties [. . .].
>
> The people of this part of the city are entirely cut off from politics. They lead their own lives without any restrictions; and more often than not, they are unaware of the important events that occur in 'northern Tehran', or in the world. Events like the change of government remain unknown to them for a long time.[39]
>
> Any time a thief or criminal successfully escapes from *nazmiyyeh* [city's police]'s prison, the police search this slum and are able to arrest them there. One can see special coffee houses in different sectors of this slum, each one a hangout for a band of these people. The day that our story begins, in one such coffee house, a number of people were gathered and talking to each other. The entire coffee house was filled with the smoke of clay pipes, opium and samovar, so that if an ordinary man entered there, he would feel sick and repulsed [. . .] If one noticed, he could see the vilest people of every trade in that place.[40]

What seems controversial about these first paragraphs of *The Dreadful Tehran* is that apparently, Kazemi has copied a few sentences of Sue's depiction of *tapis-franc* [tavern]. Thus Sue writes:

> Whenever a crime has been committed, the police first cast their nets in this mire, so to speak. And here they almost always find their man. This opening should alert readers to the sinister scenes that await them. If they proceed, they will find themselves in strange places, foul urban abscesses that teem with criminals as terrifying and revolting as swamp creatures.[41]

By a cursory glance, one might be tempted to simply call this similarity a case of plagiarism, but a more thorough study results in another conclusion. After a state of high dependence in the few pages, Kazemi pushes his limits and more or less succeeds to establish his own voice. However, *The Mysteries* (notably Book I of the work, the novel consists of ten books) is always present in the fictitious world of *The Dreadful Tehran* and functions as a compass in the whole work.

The Dreadful Tehran and its Discontents

The Dreadful Tehran was published alongside the wave of literary translations and initiated the literary genre of social novels, which would become extremely popular in the later decades in Iran. But it was not an easy success: the majority of writers and intellectuals of that time did not embrace it. On one hand, the cultural elites of the late Qajar and the first Pahlavi dynasty assumed that the main duty of the novelist was to represent Iran's splendid distant past, according to Ebrahim Zanjani:

> The best novels are those which cover the history of an era: celebrate the heads of nation, make the nation to be proud of positive points of their history, and raise the national pride in the hearts of youth. Involving romantic relations in such novels encourages the readers to read these types of novels.[42]

On the other hand, the Iranian writers of that period did not consider Iranian contemporary issues interesting enough, as Nasrollah Falsafi, translator of *Arsène Lupin* series, once said: 'The incidents that take place in Iran are worthless for inspiration to write a work of fiction, while it is sufficient for a writer to wander in Paris and gain a lot of ideas for writing.'[43]

The publication of the first samples of social novels sheds light on the everyday lives of contemporary Iranian men and women for the first time. Apparently, by representing Iran's contemporary society, the social novelists had broken a taboo and following the birth of social novels, gradually a large body of criticisms appeared in the press of that time. Almost all of the critics began to blame these writers and speak about whether their work was original or not and on the whole, they were unanimous in their criticism of the inauthenticity of these novels. Critics such as Saeed Nafisi, one of the prominent scholars of the era, expressed his contempt for *The Dreadful Tehran*, due to its imitative nature:

> The whole new literature of Iran is limited to Cloak and dagger drama. *Amir Arsalan* and *Hosein Kord-e Shabestari* have been Westernised and replaced by *Sherlock Holmes* and *Arsène Lupin*. Thousands of literary canons have not still entered Iran, but several thousand copies of *The Count of Monte Cristo* and *The Mysteries of Paris* are published and benefit booksellers. The strange thing is when an Iranian wants to compose a novel, he writes *The Dreadful Tehran* which is wholly the same style as Western novels.[44]

Some critics, including novelist Ali-Asghar Sharif, in a different manner thought that *The Dreadful Tehran* portrays a distorted image of Iranian society:

> Iranian contemporary novelists depict Tehran and Iran as 'Dreadful' and hard to live, and instead of praising and celebrating Iran's milieu and Iranian lifestyle, present it as bad and frightening. I once heard a girl fascinated by European novels, was interested in traveling to Europe. It is obvious that such a false interest was created by French novelists and in contrast, the opposing feeling, i.e. hatred for Iranian lifestyle, was created by Iranian novelists.[45]

It seems both Nafisi and Sharif had misled the readers of the period and had provided a narrow view. The issue was not how original *The Dreadful Tehran* is, in terms of aesthetic achievement (referring to Nafisi's point of view). The Persian novel was in its infancy at that time and imitating Western novels and modelling writings on them was a practical solution. And in the terms of social criticisms, the originality of *The Dreadful Tehran* was not actually the bone of contention. Sharif in an inaccurate way, criticised the novel for its distorted portrayal of Iranian society, completely neglecting that it is one of the first samples of Iranian narrative prose ever written which deals with contemporary social issues. The publication of *The Dreadful Tehran* was the realisation of one of the post-Constitutional Revolution's dreams to represent social issues and the leading critics of the period missed the chance of recognising it. Writing *The Dreadful Tehran* was an extraordinary and exceptional chance for Iranian writer Kazemi to create an image of his own society on the basis of a French novel, *The Mysteries of Paris*.

Notes

1. Ahmad Karimi-Hakkak, *Recasting Persian poetry: Scenarios of Poetic Modernity in Iran* (Salt Lake City, 1995), p. 128.
2. It is difficult to give a satisfactory translation of the title in English. If one translates the word *makhuf* in the title to 'Horrible', as many scholars have in the past, it leads to an exaggeration of being unpleasant, and the other connotations of *makhuf*, relating to something strange and mysterious, will be missed. I am indebted to Professor Franklin Lewis on this point.
3. A. R. Navabpour, *A Study of Recent Persian Prose Fiction with Special Reference to the Social Background*. PhD diss., Durham University, 1981, pp. 119–20. Available at http://etheses.dur.ac.uk/1101 [Accessed 27 November 2016].
4. Morteza Moshfeq Kazemi, *Tehran-e Makhuf* (Tehran, 1924), p. 2.
5. Ibid., p. 3.
6. William L. Hanaway's works provide useful further reading on this subject, for instance: William L. Hanaway, *Persian Popular Romances before the Safavid period*. PhD diss, Columbia University, 1970. See also: Steven Moore, '[The Eastern Novel:] Persian', in *The Novel: An Alternative History: Beginnings to 1600* (New York & London, 2011), pp. 499–527 and Steven Moore, 'Persian Fiction', in *The Novel: An Alternative History, 1600–1800* (New York & London, 2013), pp. 527–32.
7. Franco Moretti, *Atlas of European Novel 1800–1900* (London & New York, 1998), pp. 173–4.
8. Franco Moretti, *Distant Reading* (London & New York, 2013), p. 50.
9. Morteza Moshfeq Kazemi, *Ruzegar va andisheh-ha* (Tehran, 1971), p. 58.
10. Vahid Davar, Nahang va Sayeh-hash: Sar-sokhan-e Goftegu ba Ibrahim Golestan, *Tuti Mag*, 2016. Available at http://www.tootimag.com/%D9%85%D8%B7%D9%84%D8%A8/2069/%DA%AF%D9%8F%D9%84%D9%90%D8%B3%D8%B3%D9%88%D9%86 [Accessed 27 November 2016].
11. Moretti, *Atlas of European Novel 1800–1900*, p. 181 (The way Moretti concludes the Spanish 'narrative market').
12. Laetitia Nanquette, 'Cultural and Translation Exchanges Between Iran and the West (France, Germany, Great Britain, the United States)', in *Publishing in Persian language in Iran, Afghanistan, Tajikistan, Uzbekistan, Europe and the United States* (International Alliance of Independent Publishers, 2015), p. 114.

Available at http://www.alliance-editeurs.org/IMG/pdf/publishing_in_persian_language-9.pdf [Accessed 28 November 2016].

13. Laetitia Nanquette, *Orientalism Versus Occidentalism: Literary and Cultural Imaging Between France and Iran Since the Islamic Revolution* (London, 2013), pp. 11–2.
14. Hashem Ahmadzadeh, *Nation and Novel: A Study of Persian and Kurdish Narrative Discourse* (Uppsala, 2003), p. 65.
15. Gholam-hosein Mirza-Saleh (ed.), *Khaterat-e Shaykh Ebrahim-e Zanjani* (Tehran, 2000), p. 149.
16. Willem Floor, *The History of Theater in Iran* (Washington, DC, 2005), p. 220.
17. Homa Nateq, *Karnameh-ye Farhangi-ye Farangi dar Iran* (Paris, 1996), pp. 53–4. (Also useful for information on the list of these books).
18. Masoud Kouhestani-nejad, *Akhbar va E'lan-e Ketab va ketabkhaneh be Revayat-e Matbu'at* (Tehran, 2016), p. 363.
19. Anvar Khamei, *Khaterat-e Ruznameh-negar* (Tehran, 2001), p. 14.
20. Paolo Tortonese, 'The Mysteries of Paris' in Franco Moretti (ed.), *The Novel, Volume 2: Forms and Themes* (Princeton, 2006), pp. 182–3.
21. John Cruickshank (ed.), *French Literature and Its Background: The Early Nineteenth Century*, vol. 4 (London, 1969), pp. 66–8, 177.
22. Umberto Eco, *Mouse or Rat? Translation as Negotiation* (London, 2003), p. 52.
23. Ali Miransari, 'The Constitutional Revolution and Persian Dramatic Works: An Observation on Social Relations Criticism in the Plays of the Constitutional Era' in H. E. Chehabi and Vanessa Martin (ed.), *Iran's Constitutional Revolution: Popular Politics, Cultural Transformations and Transnational connections* (London, 2010), p. 239.
24. Mirza Fatali Akhundzade, *Alefba-ye Jadid va maktubat* (Baku, 1963), p. 213.
25. Iraj Parsinejad, *Mirza Fath Ali Akhundzadeh and Literary Criticism* (Tokyo, 1988), pp. 20–1.
26. In the final decades of the nineteenth century, Naser al-Din Shah had employed a group of translators in his court, who were exclusively translating for his personal use. A wide range of subjects, from European history, world geography, biographies of political figures to French novels, was covered. These translations were shelved in the royal library and only the royal family and courtiers had limited access to them; see Abbas Amanat, *Pivot of the Universe: Nasir Al-Din Shah Qajar and the Iranian Monarchy, 1831–1896* (London, 1997), p. 430. It should come as no surprise that as a result of such a procedure, for a while in the second half of the nineteenth century, certain novels (among them some erotic novels) were regarded as a luxury and were out of the reach of the public.
27. Abdollah Anvar, *Fehrest-e No'sakh-e Khatti ketabkhaneh-ye melli-e Iran*, vol. 4 (Tehran, 1992), p. 319.
28. Unpublished manuscript, Document No. IR 2148 (Tehran: Kitabkhaneh-ye Majles-e Shora-ye Eslami [Iran parliament]). My translation.
29. Korsi is one of the traditional Iranian furniture-heater ensembles, used during cold weather by the members of the families to keep warm. Korsi consists of three parts: a low four-legged wooden table or large stool; a heater, traditionally

a brazier filled with charcoal or coal, placed under the table; a blanket or quilt covering the table overhanging the sides of the table. The people sit on cushions around the korsi, covering their laps with the overhanging parts of the blanket covering the korsi. H. Dizadji, *Journey from Tehran to Chicago: My Life in Iran and the United States, and a Brief History of Iran* (Bloomington, 2010), p. 90.

30. Shirin Mahdavi, 'Amusements in Qajar Iran' in *Iranian Studies*, vol. 40, No. 4 (2007), p. 490.
31. Kouhestani-nejad, *Akhbar va E'lan*, p. 53.
32. Kamran Sepehran, *Rad-de Pa-ye Ta'zal'zol: Roman-e Tarikhi-e Iran 1300–1320* (Tehran, 2002), p. 38.
33. Berry Chevasco, 'Lost in Translation: The Relationship between Eugene Sue's Les Mysteres de Paris and G.W.M. Reynolds's The Mysteries of London' in Anne Humpherys and Louis James (ed.), *G. W. M. Reynolds: Nineteenth-century Fiction, Politics, and the Press* (Aldershot, 2008), p. 137.
34. Laura Hapke, *Girls Who Went Wrong: Prostitutes in American Fiction*, 1885–1917 (Bowling Green, 1989), p. 24.
35. Farid Ghasemi, *Kitab* (Tehran, 2001), not numbered.
36. Richard Maxwell, *The Mysteries of Paris and London* (Charlottesville, 1992), p. 197.
37. Kamil Banak, 'Mushfiq Kazimi's Novel The Horrible Tehran: Romantic Fiction or Social Criticism' in *Asian and African Studies*, 13 (1977), p. 151.
38. Eugène Sue, *Mysteries of Paris* (New York, 2015), p. 3.
39. Abdelwahab M. Aloob, *The Persian Social Novel from 1900 to 1941*. PhD diss, University of Michigan (1988), p. 119.
40. Moshfeq Kazemi, *Tehran-e Makhuf*, pp. 2–4. My translation except the paragraph referenced in no. 39.
41. Sue, *Mysteries of Paris*, p. 3.
42. Ebrahim Zanjani, Moghad'dameh [Preface] in Sanatizadeh Kermani, *Salahshur* (Tehran, 1933), p. Aleph.
43. M. F. Farzaneh, *Ashna'ee ba Sadegh Hedayat, Ghes'mat-e av'val: An'cheh Sadegh Hedayat be Man Goft* (Paris, 1988), p. 32.
44. Sepehran, *Rad-de Pa*, pp. 55–6.
45. Ali-Asghar Sharif, *Khun-baha-ye Iran* (Tehran, 1925), pp. 4–5.

CHAPTER 6

'OUR WHITE HANDS,' IRAN AND GERMANY'S 1968

Annie Pfeifer

In May 1967, Ulrike Meinhof, the German leftwing militant and co-founder of the Red Army Faction (RAF) wrote an 'Open Letter to Farah Diba'. She warned the Shah's beautiful and famously glamourous third wife, 'in Hamburg, a book was recently published by your countryman, who, like you, is interested in German knowledge and culture, and like you, has read Kant, Hegel, the Brothers Grimm, and the Brothers Mann. He is named Bahman Nirumand and the title of his book is *Iran: Model of a Developing Country*.' Concluding with a provocative afterword written by the notable leftist author and intellectual, Hans Magnus Enzensberger, Nirumand's ironically-titled book was released only weeks prior to Mohammad Reza Shah Pahlavi's controversial visit to Berlin in June 1967 and went on to become one of the most influential, canonical texts of the 1968 Movement. His book is widely regarded as a major catalyst of the Third World activism of leftist students in West Germany in the 1960s, helping to spur the anti-Shah protests which ultimately radicalised the student movement.[1] The question remains: with the Vietnam War claiming so much public air time in the United States and Europe, how did Iran become the rhetorical centrepiece of a German political movement?

My chapter analyses the symbolism of Iran in Germany's 1968 leftist discourse through a literary, rhetorical angle. I suggest that it is not coincidental that references to German literature and philosophy surface in Meinhof's aforementioned statement. As I will argue, Meinhof's polemical letter, like Enzensberger's afterword, moves away from a canon of established German authors to propose a new hybrid multicultural literary tradition steeped in anti-colonial and anti-capitalist discourse. By launching a strong cultural as well as political critique, Nirumand, Enzensberger and Meinhof use the German–Iranian cultural nexus to globalise and radicalise the role of the writer and literature more broadly. Examining the relationship between Meinhof's letter, Nirumand's book and the '68 Movement, I aim to disentangle the complex political and intellectual exchange between Germany and Iran in the 1960s to understand how Iran came to occupy a central role in the rhetoric of the European left.

For Nirumand, Enzensberger and Meinhof, the Shah was not only a reviled puppet of western imperialism but also a threatening despot whose tactics hearkened back to Nazi Germany. Present-day Iran reflected Germany's own fascist past – a past which the '68 Movement was desperately trying to come to terms with. It is for this reason, I argue, that Iran more than Vietnam, becomes a fitting symbol of oppression for West Germany's 1968 generation.[2] By taking the correct ethical stance on Iran, German leftwing activists believed they had a chance to avoid the catastrophic mistakes of the Auschwitz generation. For this reason, I will conclude, both Enzensberger and Meinhof employ the rhetorical tool of shaming the reader in hopes of prompting self-critique and political action. While the historical details surrounding the Shah's visit to Germany are well known, the central rhetorical role Iran occupied in the 1968 Movement has been largely ignored by scholars. Rarely analysed from a literary and rhetorical perspective, this historical encounter also highlights the way dissident Iranian émigrés like Nirumand helped inform the German student movement and the ensuing political discourse.

Nirumand's Critique

Born in 1936 to educated civil servants in Tehran, Nirumand moved to West Germany in his early teens, where he did most of his schooling. After finishing his studies, he returned to Iran, where he taught at the University of Tehran and co-founded a Marxist–Leninist organisation which sought to promote revolution by employing urban guerilla warfare. He returned to West Germany in 1965 when he began to face state persecution during the Shah's crackdown on leftist political activity. It was in Iran where Nirumand met Enzensberger, who encouraged him to write a book about the political situation in Iran.[3]

A reaction against the perceived authoritarianism and hypocrisy of Germany and other Western governments as well as the poor living conditions of students, West Germany's '68 Movement arose from a complex constellation of factors: denazification and the legacy of World War II, the recession of 1966, the worldwide growth of student participation in universities and the struggles for decolonisation in Cuba, China and Vietnam. In popular memory, 2 June 1967 marks the beginning of Germany's 1968.[4] The conflict escalated as students demonstrated against the Shah's official state visit, organised by Heinrich Lübke, the president of West Germany. Between 3,000 to 6,000 demonstrators protested outside the German Opera while the Shah was attending a performance of the *Magic Flute*. During the ensuing confrontation, Berlin Police and Iranian pro-Shah demonstrators attacked protestors. Benno Ohnesorg, an unarmed 26-year-old student was shot in the head from behind and killed by the plainclothed officer Karl-Heinz Kurras, who was later revealed to be an informant for the Stasi, the East German secret service. Ohnesorg's death, in turn, motivated even previously apathetic students to join forces.[5] This notorious event arose out of overlapping fields of engagement: West German students protesting against the Shah as a symbol of neo-colonial oppression and members of the Iranian diaspora, concerned with issues facing Iran, Germany and the world.

According to the anti-Shah protestors, the German government was condoning the actions of an authoritarian government that was suppressing and torturing its own people. Moreover, in the eyes of the protestors, the Shah's Iran came to symbolise the same problematic conditions which had resulted in German fascism 30 years earlier. Provocative signs linked Iran's contemporary situation to Germany's political past: 'Iran – KZ in the Orient'.[6] Protestors wore *Schah-Tüte*, paper bags printed with caricatures of the Shah of Iran and Farah Diba, originally designed to conceal the identity of Iranian dissidents from the West German state and the SAVAK, the Iranian secret police which was known to be active in Germany.[7] This cooperation between the governments of West Germany and Iran was not new, dating back to the early 1960s, when German authorities strictly policed the content of Iranian protesters' messages and suppressed their public impact.[8]

Less well known than the events of 2 June is the pivotal role dissident Iranian students and activists played in publicising the Shah's abuses. As of 1961, there were approximately 2,500 Iranian students studying in West German universities, one of the highest contingents of foreign students at the time.[9] It was thus unsurprising that Germany became one of the centres of anti-regime activity by Iranian students in the 1960s. For several years, the Iranian student organisation Confederation of Iranian Students, National Union (CISNU) had been lobbying the SDS (Students for Democratic Society) and other student activist groups to take up the cause of Iran. As Nirumand reports, 'Abroad, the Confederation of Iranian Students endeavors to correct the image that the Shah wants to impress on world public opinion by staging demonstrations, distributing leaflets, going on hunger strikes, etc., in order to deprive the Shah of the foreign support and benevolence he has won by trickery and guile'.[10] Ultimately, it was the Confederation together with the SDS who mobilised the several thousand people to demonstrate during the Shah's visit.[11]

The bloody denouement of the events of 2 June has eerie historical parallels with Iran's Student Day, which designates an incident that occurred in Iran nearly 15 years earlier. During the state visit of the then-American vice-president Richard Nixon to Iran in December 1953, students from the University of Tehran organised protests. In the chaotic aftermath of the demonstrations which erupted into larger protests, Iranian security forces killed three Iranian students on 7 December. One can see the anti-Shah protests in Berlin as a continuation of the longstanding struggle among Iranian students against government surveillance and repression.

As Nirumand suggests in the penultimate chapter of his book, he seeks to unveil the complicity of West German authorities in the repression of Iranian university students:

> Let us depict a few scenes from the daily life of Teheran University, in order to identify the persons with whom German authorities cooperate so willingly. Conversations among more than three students are forbidden on the entire campus. Groups contravening

> this regulation are dispersed, by force if necessary. Spies everywhere, scattered through all the lecture halls, endeavor to overhear students' conversations, informing on them if they are in the slightest degree suspect. The Shah does not hesitate to send troops into the university.[12]

Nirumand's book played a formative role in several anti-Shah protests in Germany, as leaflets citing Nirumand's text were declared illegal by the police force in Bonn and other cities.[13] The most prominent casualty of police brutality on 2 June, Benno Ohnesorg himself joined the anti-Shah protests after reportedly reading Nirumand's book and being 'enraged by it'.[14] In keeping with the centrality of literary and cultural metaphors in the anti-Shah polemics, Nirumand's book became an oft-invoked symbol for the movement. Yet the question of how such a modest book became *Pflichtlektüre* or mandatory reading for leftwing intellectuals of the time merits closer consideration.

Iran: The New Imperialism in Action, the English title of Nirumand's book curiously belies the satirical, biting tone of his critique. Mocking the Western governments' designation of Iran as an 'exemplary nation' which had modernised without the Soviet orientation and economic nationalism of Egypt, Nirumand argues that foreign aid merely enriched the upper class and furthered Iran's dependency on Western aid. Writing, 'every Cadillac sits next to a broken-down donkey cart, every villa next to dozens of mud huts, and in Hilton hotels and nightclubs, people walk on carpets woven by children working 14-hour days,' Nirumand paints a vivid picture of the disparity modernisation had created in Iran.[15] His book begins with an account of Iran's modern history, which outlines the country's quasi-colonial status under British and Russian influence, the discovery of oil and the Shah's disastrous concession to the British businessman William D'Arcy for exclusive rights to drill and prospect for oil. The solution, sketchily outlined by Nirumand in his book, was a nationalist revolution that would transition into an international 'solidarity of poor peoples.'[16] Apart from his vitriolic criticism of capitalism's role in Iran's subjugation and exploitation, Nirumand remains vague about the role socialism should play in this revolution.

With a section entitled 'Europe as Illness,' Nirumand taps into the discourse of Westernisation as infection or disease already established in Jalal Al-e Ahmad's well-known book, *Occidentosis* or *Gharbzadegi*, published in the early 1960s. Although Nirumand never cites Al-e Ahmad, this trope of disease as well as the overall tenor of Nirumand's book seems to be greatly influenced by its predecessor. In *Occidentosis*, Al-e Ahmad chronicles and diagnoses the disease of occidentosis – an obsession with the West that had stricken contemporary Iranian society. Medical illness becomes a useful trope for Al-e-Ahmad to conceptualise the pernicious influence of the West, while contemplating the factors within Iranian society that make it susceptible to infection. The first chapter of *Occidentosis* is entitled, 'Diagnosing an Illness,' is followed by 'Earliest Signs of the Illness,' and 'The First Infections.' After describing the decay of Iranian culture and values under Western influence, Al-e-Ahmad calls for a radical reassessment of the Iranian intellectual milieu and resistance to the hegemony of a foreign, neo-colonial culture.

Similarly, illness as metaphor allows Nirumand to criticise the all-pervasive cultural and political effect of hegemonic Western culture on Iran:

> The transformation already begins in Kindergarten [...] fairy tales, songs, clothing, behaviour are all European. In school, history means primarily European history, European geography [...] the citation of European authority and everything European is authoritative, it means a priori evidence, even in the few areas of unrivalled Persian achievements, such as in the interpretation of Persian literature.[17]

Nirumand seems to anticipate what Enzensberger would later call the *Bewusstseinsindustrie*, the consciousness industry, namely the institutions and agencies involved in the cultural reproduction of human consciousness as a social product in the interests of economic and political elites. According to this perspective, the ruling class seeks to control the content and output of the media in order to naturalise the status quo in the consciousness of subordinate classes. The end result of this process in Iran, according to Nirumand, is simply the mimicry of European methods rather than the independent thought or indigenous production of knowledge. Like for Enzensberger and Meinhof, literature is not only a vehicle for national pride but also an indicator of cultural influence. When describing Iran's infatuation with the West, Nirumand again invokes literature: 'Some indication of his absolutely uncritical admiration of Europe is conveyed by the titles of the first European books to be translated into Persian: popular novels like *The Three Musketeers,*

The Count of Monte Cristo.'[18] This list of canonical European novels once again helps to set the stage for the new multicultural literary tradition steeped in anti-colonial and anti-capitalist discourse.

Nirumand's diagnosis of Iranian *Selbstentfremdung* or 'Self-Estrangement' and the latent cultural schizophrenia hearkens back to Frantz Fanon's seminal text, *The Wretched of the Earth* (1961), cited by Enzensberger in his afterword. 'A new person is born,' writes Nirumand, 'The occidentized Oriental, a mass product from a synthetically imported culture'.[19] Claiming, 'this book doesn't philosophise. It delivers facts, where the opposition philosophises with good reason,' Nirumand aims to present evidence to counter the philosophical arguments used by Western powers to support colonialism and neo-colonialism.[20] Enzensberger picks up on this rhetoric, writing in his afterword, 'This book doesn't scold, doesn't preach, supplies no consolation, waves no banners, furnishes no prescriptions'.[21] Rhetorically, Nirumand also tries to counter the 'a priori evidence of European authority' with his own presentation of incontrovertible facts.[22] Yet, in spite of his trenchant anti-colonial rhetoric, Nirumand often taps into the same Orientalist stereotypes that helped justify colonisation. Writing about the destructive effect of technology on this 'land of Roses and Nightingales,' he juxtaposes Western science with Iranian traditionalism, Western bankers with Iranian farmers.[23]

Nirumand, like Enzensberger and Meinhof, launches an implicit critique of the affinity between elite Iranian and European culture. In his 1968 introduction to the English translation, he notes that 'while this homicidal action was going on [the crackdown on protestors and killing of Ohnesorg] the Shah and the Lord Mayor of Berlin were listening to Mozart's *Magic Flute* at the Opera'.[24] The fact that the Shah was attending an opera seems to underscore precisely the way European high culture was implicated in the Shah's repressive tactics. The hypocrisy of this German–Iranian cultural alliance was amply demonstrated by Germany's complicity with the Iranian government's crackdown on universities. The kind of shared cultural *Bildung* or formation that the Shah, his wife and their German counterparts were advocating was not a universal one which supported freedom of thought and expression.

Completely Empty and Strangely White

Unsere weißen Hände (*Our White Hands*), the title of Enzensberger's afterword foregrounds Europe's guilt and complicity in Iran's problems.

Following Nirumand, he juxtaposes the public image of Iran as a model 'developing country' with the dire economic and political conditions for most Iranians. Unlike the more visible conflicts in Vietnam, Guatemala and Indonesia, Iran becomes a poignant symbol for the '68 Movement precisely because it foregrounds the great disparity between the glossy external perception and the basic ugly reality. 'Iran is a model for big lies,' Enzensberger writes.[25] In contrast to Vietnam, Indonesia and Algeria which waged bloody struggles for decolonisation and independence, Iran was never explicitly colonised although frequently the subject of intervention and manipulation by British, Russian, French and American governments for centuries. Thus, according to Enzensberger, neo-colonialism avant la lettre reigned in Iran from the very beginning and preempted any impetus for popular revolt or revolution.[26] The result was a society that seemed free, democratic and open but in reality was underpinned by the same repressive forces that existed in more openly authoritarian regimes.

For Enzensberger as well as his German readers, the myth of Iran as an exemplary model of development is part of a greater cover-up scheme which plagued the European media: 'for years the entire European press has been lying to us about poor countries and our connections to them,' he writes. In a similar vein, a column written by Meinhof in 1968 compared the 'dishonest journalistic practices' of *Der Spiegel* with the authoritarian, repressive tactics of the Shah's police state.[27] For Enzensberger, Meinhof, as well as Nirumand, the orderly appearance of the Shah's regime is precisely what makes it an uncanny reminder of Nazi Germany. In a section tellingly entitled 'Order through Torture' (Ordnung durch Folter), Nirumand describes not only the torture tactics routinely used by the regime but also the politics of surveillance whereby an estimated 60,000 state guardians, supported by the military and police force, 'monitor every action in the country'.[28] Highlighting the illusion of harmony and order which concealed the suppression of free speech, Enzensberger posits, 'No bearded revolutionaries but rather clean-shaven civil servants, no state control, but rather the free sale of Mercedes and Coca-Cola, no coup or guerrillas but rather order, order, order, order.'[29] Unlike war-torn Vietnam or Guatemala, Iran seemed to be a parallel society which embodied the anxieties of West German activists about the surveillance, repression and brutality of their own government. In short, Iran was a more dramatic case of what leftwing Germans had feared their own postwar society had become.

In all three accounts, books are treated ambiguously as both a valuable medium of dissent as well as a problematic deterrent to action. Enzensberger's afterword ends on a chilling note:

> Now we place the book on the bookshelf next to *Eichmann in Jerusalem*, *The Crisis of India*, *The Politics of Apartheid*, *The Wretched of the Earth, A Vietnam Reader*. The bookshelf fills itself. We are informed. And our representatives which we have elected democratically in Bonn, London, and most of all in Washington, will do it right. They have counted the hairs on the Shah's head and no sparrow can fall from the roof of Persia without them knowing it. They are informed. Now we can place the book next to the other books on the shelf. Then we carefully observe our hands. They are completely empty and strangely white.[30]

The books he lists are a deliberate choice, linking Hannah Arendt's exploration of fascism to Frantz Fanon's critique of colonialism and the Vietnam War. In the community of the other books on the shelf, Nirumand's text is physically connected to the anti-colonial struggles in Vietnam, India and Africa as well as Germany's own attempt to confront its Nazi past. Even at his most radical, Enzensberger seems keen to embed Nirumand's work within a larger anti-colonial discourse in order to create a new canon of literature steeped in third-world political activism. Building on the existing cultural affinity between Iran and Germany, Enzensberger, like Meinhof sought to replace Kant, Hegel, the Brothers Grimm and the Brothers Mann with a new, politicised, multicultural canon. In short, Enzensberger offers a redefinition of literature and the role of the writer to transform consciousness.[31] In later writings, Enzensberger even uses Nirumand as an example of a new intellectual who was practically oriented toward action and offered more than simply petitions and critiques.[32]

The titular 'white hands' both reinforce the economic privilege and the racial prerogative of his educated, mostly white, European readers. Yet, here, the adjective 'white' functions as a signifier for privilege, race, as well as complicity and guilt. Neither have Nirumand's readers dirtied their hands while reading in their ivory towers, nor have they become personally involved in the conflicts of their third-world counterparts, Enzensberger seems to imply. This memorable performative gesture at the end of Enzensberger's text serves as a call to action through the tactic of shaming the reader by pointing to the limitations of its own medium. As part of the 'consciousness industry', books are merely useful insofar as they are a catalyst for action. Which reader could contendedly place Nirumand's book back onto the shelf and rest easy, simply knowing he or she was 'fully informed'?

The act of looking at one's own hands is a fundamentally self-reflexive gesture that prompts introspection. Unlike in English, to feel shame (*sich schämen*) in German is expressed as a reflexive verb that draws the individual back to him or herself, as the philosopher Max Scheler has pointed out.[33] In other words, according to Scheler, shame is always a self-reflexive feeling whereby an individual feels ashamed of 'oneself in front of oneself'.[34] For Enzensberger's readers, the shame of complicity lies not in having a hidden aspect of oneself revealed to others, but in being ashamed of oneself in front of oneself. At the same time, in the postwar German context, private shame cannot be extricated from the collective shame about the recent past. Thus, shame for Enzensberger becomes a critical introspective force that prompts readers to re-evaluate not only their personal convictions but also their relationship with society more broadly. This rhetorical technique of shaming the reader is also a device which Meinhof similarly deploys in her letter to Farah Diba, as I will argue shortly.

Is Farah Happy?

Perhaps nobody symbolically embodied the Shah's excess more than Farah, the Shah's glamourous third wife. Anticipating Meinhof's personal critique of Farah, Enzensberger describes the gaping contradictions of Iranian society, writing, 'All questions are silenced except one: is Farah happy?'[35] Her vanity is also criticised by Nirumand, who points out, 'Abroad it is well known which clothes Farah Diba wears and the name of her hairdresser. But does the world also know that the Iranian army has been waging a brutal campaign against the population of the southern province of Fars?'[36] As a Westernised woman who sported the latest European fashions and hairstyles, Farah was both a prototype of the westoxified Iranian whom Nirumand critiqued as well as a symbol of the cultural premium placed on appearance and illusion. Like Meinhof, Nirumand undercuts general knowledge of Iran's glittering, cosmopolitan, progressive exterior by revealing facts about the harsh reality of everyday life in the provinces. Although not particularly rhetorically sophisticated, such statements take on the appearance of revelations, which perhaps helps to explain the widespread attraction of Nirumand's book among leftwing activists.

Meinhof's letter is structured as a rebuttal to Farah's recent description of her life in the German publication, *The New Review* (*Die Neue Revue*). Each point begins with a direct quotation from Farah's account, which is then polemically used by Meinhof to foreground her ignorance, incompetence and complicity in her husband's actions. Emphasising the primacy of evidence, Meinhof's text, like Nirumand's, is peppered with numbers and statistics, ranging from the alarmingly high rates of illiteracy, infant mortality and drug addiction in Iran to the exorbitant prices of Farah's high-end jewellery. Chronicling scenes of torture carried out by the Shah's agents, Meinhof concludes:

> Don't you wonder why the President of Germany invited you and your husband in spite of his awareness of all these dreadful events? We don't. Why don't you ask him about his proficiency in the area of concentration camps? He is an expert in this area.[37]

Beyond her combative, irreverent tone, Meinhof again taps into the oft-invoked rhetoric linking the Shah's regime with Germany's Nazi past. Not only is the Shah, for Meinhof, a latent reminder of recent German history, but the ongoing cooperation between the Iranian and West German governments suggests that the spectre of fascism persists. Noting the similarities between the ascent of Hitler and Reza Shah in Iran, Nirumand also draws a parallel between fascism in Europe and authoritarianism in Iran.[38] By opposing the Shah's fascist tendencies, the '68 generation hoped it could help avoid the calamitous mistakes of their parents and grandparents.

Citing Farah's account, Meinhof's letter continues in a rebuttal form, 'You write, "In art and scholarship, Germany, like France, England, Italy, and other great civilisations [*Kulturvölker*] takes a leading role, which will continue for the future."'[39] More than merely a sycophantic attempt to flatter her German readers, Farah's original quotation builds on the central role Germany historically occupied for Iranian *Bildung*. Already a century before Mohammad Reza Shah Pahlavi's professed political and cultural affinity with Germany, Iran had looked to Germany as a viable cultural alternative to the ongoing interventions of British, Russian and French forces.[40] But this affinity too is subverted by Meinhof in her pedantic way, 'As for what pertains to West Germany, why not leave these predictions to German cultural politicians who are more knowledgeable? But why not state that 85 per cent of the Iranian population is illiterate?'[41] Not only is the veracity of Farah's claims questioned by Meinhof, but her attention to traditional means of cultural production such as literature and art is swiftly undercut by Meinhof's factual focus on illiteracy rates in Iran.

This rhetorical tactic also helps to explain why Meinhof's otherwise politically motivated letter ends with these curious literary references mentioned in the opening lines of my chapter. She supplements the Kant, Hegel, Mann cited and celebrated by Farah with a new multicultural canon that includes Farah's own countrymen. Literature and philosophy become not only a site of intellectual and artistic exchange, as they had been for many years between Germany and Iran, but also the beginning of a new form of shared activism which connected West German leftists with Iranian dissidents and other third-world activists throughout the world. Meinhof, like Enzensberger, aims to redefine literature by gesturing toward the new activist role of the intellectual who boldly acts and intervenes. Yet, this alliance could only be accomplished through a new kind of shared *Bildung* which used non-canonical texts to think beyond the printed page.

Ultimately, like Enzensberger, Meinhof signs off with a reader-shaming gesture. Citing Nirumand's book, she claims, 'I don't know if there are people who, after reading this book, can sleep well at night without feeling ashamed [*ohne sich zu schämen*].'[42] Although she clearly also hopes to elicit shame with her rhetoric, Meinhof explicitly uses it reflexively (*sich schämen*), as the reader ought to experience shame 'of oneself in front of oneself' rather than in front of others.[43] Like for Enzensberger, the private shame of her reader prompts self-reflection and self-critique and ultimately serves as an impetus to action.

Like Enzensberger, Meinhof suggests that Nirumand's book cannot simply be shelved and forgotten. By foregrounding its emotional impact on the reader, she draws attention to the affective dimension of the text while, like Enzensberger, hinting at its shortcomings as an effective tool of political action. What is the use of reading, if one merely goes back to sleep, she seems to ask. At the same time, as with Enzensberger's afterword, this gesture seems slightly disingenuous particularly by appearing in the same medium that it critiques. By focusing on German complicity in Iranian social repression, these '68 writers were also implicating their own readers for merely reading instead of acting and inciting. Complicity is extended to all those who read and write, who cannot help but feel a certain sense of shame in the act of reading itself, especially when confronted with the descriptions of the impoverished, illiterate masses of Iran.

Notes

1. The historian Quinn Slobodian notes '[p]erhaps most crucial for the success of Nirumand's argument in more radical student circles was his outline of the global context that linked the struggles in Iran, Vietnam, and the rest of the Third World'. Quinn Slobodian, *Foreign Front: Third World Politics in Sixties West Germany* (Durham, 2012), p. 108. Quinn Slobodian, *Foreign Front: Third World Politics in Sixties West Germany* (Durham, 2012), p. 108.
2. Jamie Trnka notes the overwhelming number of references to Latin America in German intellectual writings in the 1960s and 1970s, stating: 'Latin American anti-imperialism and revolution, particularly in Cuba and Chile, had an emotional valence that even Vietnam in the early 1970s could not ... where in the German popular imagination Vietnam marked embattlement, injustice, anger, and retribution, revolutionary violence in Latin America signified hope'; Jamie Trnka, *Revolutionary Subjects: German Literatures and the Limits of Aesthetic Solidarity with Latin America* (Berlin, 2015), p. 22.
3. Slobodian, *Foreign Front*, p. 106.
4. Ibid., p. 101.
5. Beyond West Germany, Iranian activists placed Ohnesorg's death into a succession of martyrs in the campaign for democratic rights in Iran. As a testament to the ongoing significance of the German protests within Iranian culture, a Tehran street was renamed after Ohnesorg shortly after the 1979 Revolution. See Ibid., p. 128.
6. Ibid., p. 116.
7. Ibid., p. 102.
8. Ibid., p. 40.
9. Heinrich Pfeiffer, *Ausländische Studenten an den wissenschaftlichen Hochschulen in der Bundesrepublik und West-Berlin, 1951–1961* (Wiesbaden, 1962), p. 9.
10. Bahman Nirumand, *The New Imperialism in Action* (New York, 1969), p. 155.
11. See Afshin Matin-Asgari, 'Confederation of Iranian Students, National Union,' *Encyclopedia Iranica* (2011). As Slobodian has shown, the CISNU was initially unsuccessful in lobbying the SDS about collaborating on the 2 June demonstration: 'focused on Vietnam, the socialist students were concerned that working on Iranian issues would divide and dissipate the energies of the anti-imperialist movement' (p. 103). Ultimately, Slobodian notes, the personal connections of West German students to Iranian dissidents were a 'crucial spur to activism', *Foreign Front*, p. 104.
12. Bahman Nirumand, *Persien, Modell eines Entwicklunglandes oder Die Diktatur der Freien Welt* (Hamburg, Reinbek, 1967), p. 156.

13. Slobodian, *Foreign Front*, p. 110.
14. Uwe Soukup, *Wie starb Benno Ohnesorg: Der 2. Juni 1967* (Berlin 2007), p. 143.
15. Nirumand, *Persien*, p. 10.
16. Ibid., p. 144: 'Mit dem Nationalismus werden die Kräfte freigesetzt und in Gang gebracht, die die Unterdrückung gewaltsam und zwangsläufig beseitigen. Nach der Revolution tritt an die Stelle des Nationalismus die Solidarität der armen Völker.'
17. Ibid., p. 137.
18. Ibid., p. 21.
19. Ibid., p. 136.
20. Ibid., p. 142.
21. Hans Magnus Enzensberger, 'Unsere weißen Hände' in Nirumand, Bahman, *Persien, Modell eines Etnwicklunglandes oder Die Diktatur der Freien Welt* (Hamburg, 1967), p. 149: 'Dieses Buch schimpft nicht, predigt nicht, spendet keinen Zuspruch, schwenkt keine Spruchbänder, liefert kein Rezept. Es stellt fest und tritt Beweise an.'
22. Nirumand, *Persien*, p. 22.
23. Ibid., p. 136
24. Nirumand, *New Imperialism*, p. 7.
25. Enzensberger, 'Unsere weißen Hände', p. 150.
26. Ibid., p. 152.
27. 'In this way, the Spiegel represents the interests of the rich here like the Shah represents them in his country, the Spiegel – consciously or otherwise – with the means of misrepresentation, suppression, obfuscation (one can of course think of other words for it) the Shah with the means of a police state' (translation by Passmore, 23). In a 1969 column, Meinhof wrote: 'the realization that West German capital and the Iranian terror regime are closely allied was pounded into the students by the police. The same goes for the awareness that the opposition here – in the metropolitan centres – and the opposition in the Third World countries must work together' (Slobodian, *Foreign Front*, p. 127).
28. Nirumand, *Persien*, p. 128.
29. Enzensberger, 'Unsere weißen Hände', p. 149; 'Keine bärtigen Revolutionäre, sondern glattrasierte Beamte, kein Staats–Dirigismus, sondern freier Verkauf von Mercedes und Coca-Cola, keine Staatsreiche, Putsche, Geurillas: sondern Ordnung, Ordnung, Ordnung, Ordnung'.
30. Ibid., p. 150.
31. Henning Marmulla, 'Re-Thinking the Writer's Role: Hans Magnus Enzensberger and Cuba or A Story of Self-Censorship,' in Ingrid Gilcher-Holtey (ed.) *A Revolution of Perception?: Consequences and Echoes of 1968* (New York, 2014), p. 22.
32. In his November 1968 article 'Gemeinplätze die Neue Literatur betreffend' [Commonplaces on the Newest Literature], Enzensberger outlines the activist role of the intellectual: 'The writer should set political alphabetization as his aim. In doing so, he should follow the examples of Günter Wallraff's reports from German factories, Bahman Nirumand's book on Persia, Ulrike Meinhof's

columns, Georg Alsheimer's Vietnam report'; Hans Magnus Enzensberger, 'Gemeinplätze die Neue Literatur betreffend', in *Kursbuch* 11 (1968), p. 194. I am indebted to Henning Marmulla for citing this article ('Re-Thinking the Writer's Role', pp. 22–3).

33. James Hart, *Who One Is: Existenz and Transcendental Phenomenology* (New York, 2009), p. 345.
34. Ibid., p. 345.
35. Enzensberger, 'Unsere weißen Hände', p. 149: 'Da schweigen alle Fragen, außer der einzigen: "Ist Farah glücklich?"'
36. Nirumand, *Persien*, p. 129.
37. Ulrike Meinhof, 'Offener Brief an Farah Diba,' in *Konkret* 6 (1967), pp. 21–2: 'Sie wundern sich, daß der Präsident der Bundesrepublik Sie und Ihren Mann, in Kenntnis all diesen Grauens, hierher eingeladen hat? Wir nicht. Fragen Sie ihn doch einmal nach seinen Kenntnissen auf dem Gebiet von KZ - Anlagen und Bauten. Er ist ein Fachmann auf diesem Gebiet.'
38. Nirumand, *Persien*, p. 25.
39. Meinhof, 'Offener Brief an Farah Diba', p. 22. 'Sie schreiben: "In Kunst und Wissenschaft nimmt Deutschland - ebenso wie Frankreich, England, Italien und die anderen großen Kulturvölker - eine führende Stellung ein, und das wird auch in Zukunft so bleiben."'
40. Firoozeh Kashani-Sabet, 'The Evolving Problem of Iranian Nationalism,' in Nikki Keddie and Rudi Matthee (eds), *Iran and the Surrounding World* (Seattle, 2002), p. 176.
41. Meinhof, 'Offener Brief an Farah Diba', p. 22: 'Was die Bundesrepublik angeht, so sollten Sie solche Prognosen vielleicht lieber den deutschen Kulturpolitikern überlassen, die verstehen mehr davon. Aber warum nicht rundheraus gesagt, daß 85 Prozent der persischen Bevölkerung Analphabeten sind.'
42. Ibid., p. 22. 'Ich weiß nicht, ob es Menschen gibt, die nach der Lektüre dieses Buches nachts gut schlafen können, ohne sich zu schämen.'
43. Hart, *Who One Is*, p. 345.

CHAPTER 7

ENTRAPPED IN A CARVED-UP LAND: REVISITING *READING LOLITA IN TEHRAN*

Amir Ahmadi Arian

In July 2015, the drawn-out negotiation process over Iran's nuclear programme came to a conclusion and a deal between Iran and six world powers was finally struck. It seemed that the frost between Iran and America had begun to thaw. Simultaneously, we witnessed a rise in the number of Iran-focused cultural products in America, produced by celebrities such as Ben Affleck (*Argo*) and Jon Stewart (*Rosewater*). It appeared that, in the aftermath of the nuclear deal, a desire emerged in the American cultural industry towards putting a different spin on popular perceptions of Iran. The 2016 presidential election in America turned the tide, and Donald Trump came to office with an agenda that was practically the diametrical opposite of what Barack Obama propagated. Iran is back in headlines again, this time for different reasons. As these developments take place, it seems timely to re-examine a text that was by far the most widely read and probably the most controversial book of the new millennium with respect to the complicated story of Iran–America relations.

Reading Lolita in Tehran, the memoir of Azar Nafisi, an Iranian–American literary scholar, begins shortly before the 1979 Revolution, while Nafisi is in the US. She moves to Iran after the revolution to participate in the enthusiastic movement to build a new Iran. She lands a job as a professor of English literature at the University of Allameh

Tabatabai and starts teaching, but things begin to take a frightening turn. She loses her job thanks to her refusal to wear the compulsory hijab, then selects a handful of her favourite students and forms a study group at her house to discuss modern literary masterpieces. The main body of the book consists of the explorations of this study group into Western novels, along with intermittent allusions to the lives of their readers in post-revolutionary Iran. The book is divided into four parts, each dedicated to the study of a Western literary figure, beginning with Vladimir Nabokov, from there to F. Scott Fitzgerald, Henry James and Jane Austen.

As this summary suggests, this book does not strike one as an immediate bestseller in turn-of-the-millennium America. The subject matter and the setting are both alien to the average American reader and the book contains fairly long, somewhat technical passages about highbrow literature. To explain this unexpected popularity, many have underlined the timing of its publication: the book appeared in the politically heated period between the collapse of the Twin Towers in New York and the Iraq War, when Iran reappeared on the radar of Western media. The sensitivity over Iran increased dramatically when, in May 2002, it was labelled an 'axis of evil' along with North Korea and Iraq by President George W. Bush, which implied the possibility of military engagement.

Reading Lolita went off to a flying start: it became the number one bestseller on the *New York Times* list and remained on the list for 18 months. 'By April 2004 it ranked second on the list of most-read books on college campuses' and became 'the fifth-most-borrowed nonfiction book in US libraries.'[1] Most of the early reviews of the book were overwhelmingly positive. Later editions are packed with blurbs by big names on the first pages of the book, praising the book for reasons such as its 'celebration of the power of the novel' according to Geraldine Brooks, its 'properly complex reflections about the ravages of theocracy' in Susan Sontag's opinion and being 'a literary life raft on Iran's fundamentalist sea' as Margaret Atwood suggested. The academic analyses of the book appeared later, their opinions often in sharp contrast with those of reviewers. The largely negative assessments considered *Reading Lolita* as 'an excellent example of how neoliberal rhetoric is now being deployed by neoconservatives',[2] 'one-sided and extreme, in fact as extreme as the views of the revolutionaries it criticises'[3] and 'blatantly advancing the presumed cultural foregrounding of a predatory empire.'[4]

The debate around *Reading Lolita* has been strikingly polarised. Amy DePaul suggests that such a contrast relates to the dramatic political shift in American politics over a short period of time. Under Mohammad Khatami's presidency in Iran, blunt expressions of anti-Americanism reduced dramatically, so much so that in the wake of 9/11 almost all the people in high positions of power condemned the attacks. Such an atmosphere continued until the end of Khatami's presidency. From 2003 the Iraq War increased the level of anti-Americanism dramatically across the Middle East and Mahmoud Ahmadinejad took power in 2004 in Iran. Iranian–American relations entered another precarious phase as the rhetoric of hardliners on both sides gained the upper hand. This turning point marks two different kinds of response to *Reading Lolita* in the US. Before the Iraq War, the US was still considered a victim by many, but the Iraq War turned many scholars and intellectuals against the new incarnation of American imperialism. Therefore, given that *Reading Lolita* is highly complimentary towards American culture, it predictably received such contrary receptions. DePaul is right that 'Nafisi's book [was] operating in a different America than the one in which it first appeared.'[5] One might add to this a different Iran as well.

This is not the whole story. *Reading Lolita* itself has the potential to polarise its readers, largely for its way of presenting memories and facts. That is an understudied aspect of the book: the politics of the time was so heated that the spotlight remained fixed on the political, sometimes ideological function of the book, rather than what it actually has to offer. Now that *Reading Lolita* has moved into the second decade of its life and the charged political atmosphere in the wake of 9/11 has slightly abated, one can reexamine it with a certain critical distance.

The Truth and the Whole Truth

The Western legal system demands that witnesses in court give the truth, the whole truth and nothing but the truth. This trinity of conditions suggests that telling the truth does not amount to telling the whole truth, as the partial truth can easily obfuscate the whole truth and cause a miscarriage of justice. In other words, telling a partial truth can easily be the equivalent of fabrication. The third condition suggests that even telling the whole truth can be misleading if delivered together with non-truth.

A preponderance of criticism directed at *Reading Lolita* revolves around the confusion that the subtle distinction between the truth and the whole truth causes. Nafisi has been frequently accused of leaving certain facts and truths out of the picture to make it consistent with a certain political ideology. Fatemeh Kesharvz shows how not only is an entire group of characters, Muslim men in particular, rendered 'faceless' in Nafisi's account, but how 'entire groups of Iranians who lived and produced significant work before, during and after the revolution are totally erased from the image of Iran in RLT.'[6] She provides a detailed list of prominent authors and intellectuals in contemporary Iran to rebut Nafisi's sweeping assertion that 'we live in a culture that denies any merit to literary works.'[7] Another controversial point is the way in which Iranian women are portrayed in *Reading Lolita*. Nafisi tends to be suspicious of anything that carries the name of Islam, even when a group of Muslims engage in equal rights for women: 'It was then that the myth of Islamic feminism – a contradictory notion, attempting to reconcile the concept of women's rights with the tenets of Islam – took root.'[8] When it comes to politics, the book is uninterested in all the Western interventions that disrupted nascent democracies in Iran throughout the twentieth century and blames the troubles of the country on Iranians in general and Muslim men in particular. This lopsidedness is such that to some the book seemed like a political conspiracy. Hamid Dabashi argues that this narrative, driven by an 'unfailing hatred of everything Iranian',[9] might have been written as a collaboration with hawkish American neo-conservatives. Negar Mottahedeh sees *Reading Lolita* as an element of a larger cultural project which uses the memoirs of Iranian women for sinister purposes and questions their financial success 'at a time when Washington hawks would like these authors' country of birth to be the next battleground in the total war of the twenty-first century.'[10]

Nafisi has been evasive about this flurry of criticism: 'debate that is polarised isn't worth my time'[11] is her remark on Dabashi's scathing attack. On rare occasions when she fights back, she takes a simple line of argument: 'Some people criticised me and said, "Why didn't you talk about Persian literature?" I tell them that I was an English professor, this is what I studied.'[12] She has a point: to provide a list of the facts we would like to see in a memoir will fail to undermine its reliability. Moreover, at the beginning of the book, she admits that her memory is prone to skewing the facts: 'the facts in this story are true insofar as any memory is ever truthful.'[13]

However, the impossibility of delivering the 'whole truth', if it existed at all, should not be used to exempt selective memory from scrutiny. It is true that memory is selective by nature and by no means comprehensive, but precisely because of this selective nature, no memory is innocent, especially when a memoir plays such a significant role in shaping a perception of Iran in the West.

Here I will not focus on the left-out facts, they have been extensively discussed before. I am pursuing an analysis of what the book puts forth, rather than what it conceals, by studying the ways in which the facts are organised to construct a compelling narrative and, through that, a certain perception of Iran.

The Carved-Up Space: Tehran Through the Window Frame

Reading Lolita revolves around a room. The study group of Nafisi and her students considers the room as the only safe zone, the sacrosanct space of liberty, where each can 'become her own inimitable self.'[14] There they do everything the world outside has denied them. They discuss novels and thereby turn the room into a 'place of transgression,' a 'wonderland.'[15] One cannot help but be reminded of Virginia Woolf's *A Room of One's Own*, as is alluded to in the book by Mana, who describes Nafisi's living room as 'a sort of communal version of Virginia Woolf's room of her own.'[16]

Indeed, Woolf's motivation for writing her groundbreaking essay resembles Nafisi's: one day she is barred from the library, because: 'The ladies are only admitted to the library if accompanied by a fellow of the college or furnished with a letter of introduction.'[17] Both women, one in the England of the early twentieth century and the other in the Iran of the late twentieth century, are banned from the public domain on the grounds of their gender, which makes them devote their intellectual careers to fighting the system that deprives them of their basic rights. Like Nafisi, facing this outrageous discrimination, Woolf resorts to literature, but does not stop there. She digs into her family history and castigates the women of previous generations who, rather than 'powdering their noses,' should have 'learnt the great art of making money.'[18] She reads through the archives and unearths documents about the poverty of women and their enslavement to men's desire.

Nafisi's room, however, is a rather different place. She calls the living room 'our world', whose only connection to the outside is a window that frames the Alborz Mountains to the north. Nafisi herself would sit on a chair before an oval mirror, which reframes the already confined sight of her beloved mountains. The streets and people between the building and the mountain are censored from her view. She takes relief in this sight:

> That censored view intensified my impression that the noise came not from the street below but from some far-off place, a place whose persistent hum was our only link to the world we refused, for those few hours, to acknowledge.[19]

The room is set up to minimise the contact of its inhabitants with the world outside and replace that world with that of the English literary canon, uncontaminated by the ravages of Iranian society. While throughout the book Western literature is promoted as a free world of beauty and perfection, the path to it passes through a circumscribed, harem-like, detached space of security and forgetfulness. Nafisi's attitude, therefore, contrasts Woolf's: Woolf thinks herself out of the room, reads herself out of social confinement in order to change it to her advantage. She calls on other women to bring about a real change in the distribution of power, to face the injustice wreaked on them and do something about it. Nafisi sets up the space in a way that eliminates the world outside: 'we were in that room to protect ourselves from the reality outside.'[20]

However, since *Lolita* is being read in Tehran, Nafisi has to leave the comfort of her room and talk about the reality outside. Because of her suspicions, she designs a mechanism that enables her to deal with the city more easily. It comes through a mutilation or carving-up: employing narrative devices, she reduces the complexity of the space down to detached pieces by removing grey areas and drawing sharp lines that divide people along political and ethical lines. The result is a simplified, fragmented societal space, which pretends to be representative of the whole, but is in fact a reaction to its enormity.

Her portrait of the university is a good example of this mechanism. In her classroom, the front rows are occupied by devout Muslims, the main culprits of the book. Then there are 'the most radical students,' who 'sit in the very back rows.'[21] There is no devout Muslim in that back row, just as no secular person sits among the Muslims. The second group of culprits are the leftists, who form another 'immutable river' in parallel with the Muslims, yet do not sit among them. In the area between reside the non-political students, the ultimate victims of extremists on both sides. In Nafisi's representation of the space of the classroom, all the students are neatly divided along political lines. There is no overlap, no common ground, no shift from one space to another. This pattern can be extended to the rest of the book. This division of the space is played out at Gatsby's trial: the students in the front row, made up entirely of Muslim men, make many stupid comments about the book and the students in the back row, predominantly secular women, giggle them off and come out with witty comments. Everybody plays in the space assigned to them, trapped in all the foreseeable clichés of Muslim men and secular women.

Iran in *Reading Lolita* is a set of segments with isolated spaces at one end and the State at the other and no space of manoeuvre in between. The forces that could complicate this spatiality in post-revolutionary Iran are named in the book, only to be demonised (leftists) or disdained (Islamic feminism).

People without Backgrounds

Nafisi's first reminiscence in the book is prompted by two pictures she has brought over to the US: in the first one the women in the study group are veiled, in the second unveiled; in both they are 'standing against a white wall.'[22] She begins with the latter and introduces the students one by one. They are dubbed names such as 'my lady', 'comedian', 'the wild one' and apart from that we learn little about them. After the initial introduction, over the course of the book information is incrementally revealed. Mahshid has spent some time in jail, which cost her a kidney and caused a slew of recurrent nightmares. Mana's father has died of a heart attack and their house has been confiscated by the government. Sanaz's life is a series of mishaps and abuses, from warnings by street patrols to 'being harassed by bearded and god-fearing men.'[23] The 'girls' are 'never free of the regime's definition of them as Muslim women.'[24] They have been humiliated throughout their lives: 'most of these girls have never had anyone praise them for anything.'[25] They are particularly alien to their bodies: 'we know nothing, *nothing*, about the relation between a man and a woman, about what it means to go out with a man.'[26] Overall, the young women of the book are despondent, trapped between the rock of religious totalitarianism and the hard place of a backward conservative society and, except for the time they spend with their teacher to delve into Western masterpieces, they experience no moment of delight.

In Nafisi's memoir, the male characters are numerous. They range from ultra-conservatives to established intellectuals, from misogynist religious devotees to liberals sympathetic to feminism. Despite this variety, it is hard to find good men in this book. The list of the terrible men begins with Nafisi's first husband: a man 'so sure of himself', 'insanely jealous' and 'success-oriented' who abused and restricted her. Her students' partners and relatives seem like replicas of the author's first husband. Azin's first husband is 'jealous of her books, her computer and her Thursday mornings.'[27] Sanaz's brother is violent and possessive. So is Nassrin's father. Yassi has three aunts, all quite intelligent and hard-working, yet have to 'put up with spoiled, nagging husbands, inferior to them intellectually and in every other way.' The main cast of male villains appears at the university as her Muslim students: Mr Ghomi has dodged the war but now enjoys 'undeserved privileges.'[28] Mr Nahvi is slightly more intelligent, but fixated on 'Western decadence' and is calmer because 'there were no doubts in him.'[29] Mr Forsati is a pure opportunist obsessed with getting ahead and when he shows any interest in culture, 'it is only to be a Roman in Rome.'[30] The lack of literary taste is the most egregious flaw they share. Mr Nyazi reads *The Great Gatsby* as a pamphlet for a certain kind of lifestyle and in the trial sympathises with Gatsby's killer with a funny remark: 'He is the only victim. He is the genuine symbol of the oppressed, in the land of, of, of the Great Satan!'[31] The list of illogical, irascible Iranian men in the book is quite long. Misogyny, sexual abuse and bigotry are commonplace.

There do exist, however, a few good men in the book, if one cares to look hard. Two of them are crucial to the author's life: Nafisi's second husband, Bijan and the magician, Nafisi's mysterious guru. Bijan makes surprisingly few appearances in the book. He is described as a rather calm and withdrawn man, glued to the sofa, drinking and watching the BBC or reading. His presence becomes more significant towards the end of the book, particularly when they debate staying in Iran or leaving for the US. His point of view is represented now and then, but he is 'most articulate in his silences.'[32]

The magician's presence is dominant, his life uncanny. Nafisi's description of his lifestyle makes him look more like an apparition than a human being. To begin with, he does not bear a name and remains 'the magician' throughout. He resembles sectarian gurus: 'he saw only a select few, [. . .] at night if the light in one of his rooms facing the street was on, it was a sign that he would see visitors; otherwise they should not bother him.'[33] It is implied several times that he holds a beyond-earthly knowledge of things: 'He talked as if he knew me, as if he knew not only the known facts but also the unknown mysteries,'[34] 'photographs can be deceptive, unless, like my magician, one has the gift of discovering something from the curve of a person's nose.'[35] He has read everything, knows answers to all the dilemmas of the world. This is how he sums up his own existence in Iran: 'I don't lose, I don't win. In fact, I don't exist. You see, I have withdrawn not just from the Islamic Republic but from life as such.'[36] Bijan and the magician have one thing in common: they are strikingly quiet, aloof to the point of invisibility. In this way, they represent the other side of the coin of 'bad' men: just as the coarseness and crudity of other men is clear-cut and unquestionable, the goodness of the acceptable ones amounts to their near absolute detachment and disengagement. In Nafisi's characterisation, men are one-dimensional and uncomplicated.

We have, therefore, a group of miserable students who barely experience a moment of happiness, a bunch of annoying men who know nothing about the modern world, a few modern men who stay far away from reality and a narrator who stands above them all. This is in keeping with Nafisi's logic of compartmentalisation: just as public spaces are divided into clear-cut spaces with little common ground, characters are also divided into separate, often hostile camps.

The Politics of Resignation: An Avenue Towards Disappearance

The author of *Reading Lolita* consistently reminds the reader that she is against political activities and prefers an escape into literary masterpieces when times are hard. However, Nafisi's stance in the book is quite political, since non-interventionism is indeed a political position. She articulates her stance in conspicuously political terms:

> I understood then that this resignation was perhaps, under the circumstances, the only form of dignified resistance to tyranny. We could not openly articulate what we wished, but we could by our silence show our indifference to the regime's demands.[37]

Nafisi's refusal of involvement is ultimately directed toward change and is meant to be a form of 'resistance to tyranny', hence innately political. She calls her political strategy 'resignation' or 'active withdrawal from a reality that had turned hostile.'[38]

Nafisi enacts this idea in a game she invents to soothe herself after being searched outrageously by a female guard. She decides to find a way to make her body invisible and comes up with a peculiar chador game:

> My constant obsession with the veil had made me buy a very wide black robe that covered me down to my ankles, with kimono-like sleeves, wide and long. I had gotten into the habit of withdrawing my hands into the sleeves and pretending that I had no hands. Gradually, I pretended that when I wore the robe, my whole body disappeared.[39]

The game is a practice in invisibility, to the extent that it affects the very materiality of her body. The game goes beyond political disengagement and suggests the ideal state of living under the Islamic Republic as lack of bodily presence. She resists the tyranny by vanishing.

Putting this message in the context of its time gives us more insight into the popularity of the book. This political stance, woven intricately into the fabric of the book, reiterated the message that the most powerful book club of the time, run by Oprah Winfrey, was propagating. *Reading Lolita* is the story of a book club published at the advent of book clubs in the US. One cannot help but take note of this simultaneity, especially given that *Reading Lolita* 'has been heavily marketed by its publisher, Random House, to women's book groups.'[40] Georgiana Banita argues that the success of the book relates partly to 'the timely publication of the memoir which coincides with a proliferation of female book clubs and book groups under the lasting impact of Oprah Winfrey's groundbreaking achievements in the field.'[41] The cover of *Reading Lolita* is embossed with a quotation from Geraldine Brooks' review: 'anyone who has ever belonged to a book group must read this book.' Nafisi herself has lauded Oprah's book club: 'For a while it seemed like the only one who was talking about classics in America was Oprah, and I'm happy she did so.'[42]

Like Winfrey, Nafisi also believes in the practical benefits of reading literature, albeit in a different way. She chooses books for her reading group unilaterally, but her criteria are different: 'their author's faith in the critical and almost magical power of literature',[43] as opposed to the Winfrey-inspired search for something tangible readers ought to utilise in their everyday life. Nafisi seeks the ostensible absolute freedom that novels offer, so that readers can travel to them from their confines. She tends to attribute marvellous qualities to her selected novels and reads them as flawless objects that a genuine reader could only admire. She understands those novels to be so detached from the mundane that they are 'an escape from reality',[44] 'golden emissaries from that other world'.[45] Thus the impact these novels make on the reader is seen as one of ecstatic disengagement, having to do more with magic than with practical matters. Unlike Winfrey's insistence on taking novels as blueprints for engineering a certain form of self, Nafisi sees them running in parallel with reality, a safe haven for the damaged soul, a distant resort for the fatigued.

Therefore, although both Nafisi and Winfrey believe in the use of literature as panacea for the self, their versions of this 'self' differ. Winfrey subscribes to the idea of the 'strong self', one capable of standing up and moving on in the face of all problems, one who blames herself for the miseries she suffers. Winfrey propagates a certain kind of change whereby one leaves the system intact and lays the problem at one's own door. Nafisi also rejects any effort to change the system. Instead, she believes in the sacrosanct superiority of individuals and argues that novels nurture this notion with their sublime beauty and perfection. Winfrey and Nafisi agree on staying away from society as a whole and forgoing any attempt toward large-scale changes.

Conclusion

To finish this chapter, I would like to draw a comparison between *Reading Lolita* and another canonical American novel, although from a strand of the canon Nafisi never teaches in her classes. In Ralph Ellison's *Invisible Man*, the relationship between the protagonist and early twentieth-century American society resembles that of Nafisi and Iranian society: the narrator, a black man from the south, is rendered invisible, because white Americans refuse to see him.[46] When Nafisi points out her 'irrelevancy' she suggests a fairly similar idea of exclusion. Ellison's character goes through a painful and dangerous process to make himself and, by extension his community, visible. He becomes a street orator and community organiser to give voice to the excluded and make them visible. In *Reading Lolita*, however, reading literature functions as the engine of invisibility. In that sense, the act of reading, ironically enough, complies with the line of the authorities: one reads novels in order to disappear, which helps fulfil the project the Islamic regime or any other totalitarian state has for its people.

In *Reading Lolita*, the portrait of Iran bolsters the necessity of disappearance: a minority of 'good' people (secular, cultural, Westernised) is faced with a majority of 'bad' people (Muslims, leftists, the closed-minded), with virtually no ground in between. In keeping with this static population, the space is also compartmentalised into various sections, each allocated to a certain part of the society. Just as no conversation takes place among people, invisible yet insurmountable barriers separate spaces and no possibility of linking up indoors and outdoors, public and private, seems to exist. In such a context, reading literature represents a means of forgetting, an entirely separate universe in which one can delve deep and leave behind all the ugliness of the world outside.

Notes

1. Anne Donadey and Huma Ahmed-Ghosh, 'Why Americans Love Azar Nafisi's Reading Lolita in Tehran' in *Signs* 33.3 (2008), p. 626.
2. John Carlos Rowe, 'Reading Reading Lolita in Tehran in Idaho', *American Quarterly* 59.2 (2007), p. 253.
3. Fatemeh Keshavarz, *Jasmine and Stars: Reading More than Lolita in Tehran* (Wilmington, 2007), p. 110.
4. Hamid Dabashi, 'Native Informers and the Making of the American Empire', Al-Ahram Weekly Online, 2007. Available at: http://weekly.ahram.org.eg/Archive/2006/797/special.htm [Accessed 27 June 2017].
5. Amy DePaul, 'Re-Reading Reading Lolita in Tehran', in *MELUS*, 33 (2008), p. 77.
6. Keshavarz, *Reading More than Lolita*, p. 123.
7. Azar Nafisi, *Reading Lolita in Tehran: A Memoir in Books* (New York, 2008), p. 25.
8. Ibid., p. 315.
9. Dabashi, 'Native Informers'.
10. Negar Mottahedeh, 'Off the Grid: Reading Iranian Memoirs in Our Time of Total War', in *Middle East Research and Information Project* (2004). Available at: http://www.merip.org/mero/interventions/grid [Accessed 27 June 2017], p. 9.
11. Robert Fulford, 'Reading Lolita at Columbia', *National Post*, 1 November 2006. Available at: https://www.pressreader.com/canada/national-post-latest-edition/20061101/281913063609343 [Accessed 27 June 2017].
12. Azar Nafisi, 'Fiction: Open Space in a Closed Society', in *New Perspectives Quarterly* 22.3 (2005): 12–4.
13. Nafisi, *Reading Lolita*, p. 1.

14. Ibid., p. 6.
15. Ibid., p. 10.
16. Ibid., p. 14.
17. Virginia Woolf, *A Room of One's Own/Three Guineas* (London, 2000), p. 9.
18. Ibid., p. 22.
19. Ibid., p. 16.
20. Ibid., p. 72.
21. Ibid., p. 114.
22. Nafisi, *Reading Lolita*, p. 4.
23. Ibid., p. 32.
24. Ibid., p. 33.
25. Ibid., p. 267.
26. Ibid., p. 359.
27. Ibid., p. 327.
28. Ibid., p. 234.
29. Ibid., p. 233.
30. Ibid., p. 248.
31. Ibid., p. 153.
32. Ibid., p. 397.
33. Ibid., p. 209.
34. Ibid., p. 210.
35. Ibid., p. 327.
36. Ibid., p. 219.
37. Ibid., p. 183.
38. Ibid., p. 13.
39. Ibid., p. 202.
40. Catherine Burwell, 'Reading Lolita in Times of War: Women's Book Clubs and the Politics of Reception', in *Intercultural Education* 18.4 (2007), pp. 281–96.
41. Georgine Banita, 'Affect, Kitsch and Transnational Literature: Azar Nafisi's Portable Worlds' in Sarah Sackel *et al.* (eds), *Semiotic Encounters: Text, Image and Transnation* (Amsterdam, 2009), p. 88.
42. Azar Nafisi, 'Fiction: Open Space in a Closed Society' in *New Perspectives Quarterly*, 22 (2005).
43. Nafisi, *Reading Lolita*, p. 22.
44. Ibid., p. 45.
45. Ibid., p. 265.
46. Ralph Ellison, *Invisible Man* (New York, 2010), p. 1.

CHAPTER 8

'DEATH TO FREEDOM, DEATH TO CAPTIVITY': BEYOND SHAHRIAR MANDANIPOUR'S 'ISLAMIC' LOVE STORY

Roxanne Ellen Bibizadeh

The quest for sexual and political freedom is central to Shahriar Mandanipour's *Censoring an Iranian Love Story* (2011). Within neo-liberal political rhetoric and popular culture, Western freedom is often set in opposition to the un-freedom of Islam, Mandanipour's text complicates the meaning of freedom and oppression. He blurs the boundaries between what has been freely chosen, coercion and force, to suggest that proposals of freedom and un-freedom are an inherently global problem and oppression is not exclusive to Islamic societies.[1] Mandanipour compares challenging censorship with the struggle for gender equality and in doing so he equates the relationship between the censor and writer with that of male–female relationships. He highlights the limited social space available to demonstrate dissent and he shows how sexual morality is influenced by social and cultural issues.[2] The conflict inequality creates for women (both internally and externally) is similar to the political conditions challenging writers who struggle to continue their work. Both are made to bear the burden of cultural national values. When Mandanipour puts down his pen and leaves the text unfinished, he opens up the possibility of exploring the different ways in which censorship and gender inequality interact to inform a narrative of resistance.

Mandanipour introduces his protagonist Sara amid the turbulence of student protests in contemporary Iran, 'she is timidly holding a sign that reads DEATH TO FREEDOM, DEATH TO CAPTIVITY.'[3] Both the demonstrators and the anti-riot police are perplexed by her message, they dismiss her as 'one of those Communists who have recently come back to life,' who must be watched 'with extreme vigilance and caution.'[4] For Mandanipour, this sign embodies the dilemma he finds himself in and one that he shares with his protagonist Sara. The phrase is repeated at the end of the novel to emphasise the impermanence associated with finding your voice and the cost of this dissent. Neither Mandanipour nor Sara can escape surveillance, if they achieve freedom they will remain captive because censorship can become an internalised norm. Equally, even if they resist and find their voice, it could cost them their freedom, country, home, loved ones and possibly their lives. Thus, they become imprisoned by their own voice. Mandanipour (the narrator), eventually concedes, 'I no longer have any energy or passion to write.'[5] He refuses to continue to speak on behalf of Sara or allow anyone to dictate his story, instead Sara is finally given a chance to speak, but she uses this voice to describe the paradoxical feeling of captive freedom. 'To allow a plant freedom to spread throughout the garden is beautiful. [...] Now I realize that it seemed as if a pair of terrifying eyes were looking at me from inside the bush.'[6] Mandanipour reveals they are both stunted with fear and their identities and voices are being erased. Their resignation ultimately results in their metaphorical and literal disappearance from the text.

Censoring an Iranian Love Story was written in Farsi and translated by Sara Khalili, the text has been published in at least ten other languages, but Mandanipour has never achieved his dream of publishing his love story in Iran, his 'homeland'.[7] The conclusion of Mandanipour's text seems to concur with the position outlined by J. M. Coetzee in *Giving Offence: Essays on Censorship* (1996), in which Coetzee explains, '[c]ensorship looks forward to the day when writers will censor themselves and the censor himself can retire. [...] Writing does not flourish under censorship.'[8] Coetzee acknowledges that censors tend to brand the 'undesirable' 'uneasily and even haphazardly assimilat[ing] the subversive (the politically undesirable) and the repugnant (the morally undesirable).'[9] Mandanipour demonstrates the censorship he experiences is based on both political and moral grounds, to show us that writers and 'freedom-loving women'[10] are equally 'undesirable'.

Mandanipour attempts to self-censor his own work and write an Islamic love story, but in the end he laments, '[l]ook at what has become of my hopes and dreams. Every single bone in this story is broken. Every single one of its chapters has gone to a wasteland around Tehran, those same places where they burn rubbish.'[11] Although Mandanipour does not succeed in publishing his love story in his native home, perhaps rather ironically, he did win the Novel of the Year at the Muslim Writers' Awards in 2011, which complicates the notion of 'Islamic' undesirability. Irfan Akram, the director of the awards explained in an interview that he hoped the organisation would 'give Muslim writers confidence in their abilities and offer a platform to communicate their experiences and creativity through the power of the pen.'[12] Mandanipour's refusal to write the love story that Mr Petrovich, 'an official of the holy government of the Islamic Republic'[13] would approve of, results in his declaration that 'writing a love story with a happy ending is not in the destiny of writers of my generation [. . .] and my work on this story is done. I no longer have any control over it or its characters.'[14]

Coetzee described the relationship between the censor and writer:

> Working under censorship is like being intimate with someone who does not love you, with whom you want no intimacy, but who presses himself in upon you. The censor is an intrusive reader, a reader who forces his way into the intimacy of the writing transaction, forces out the figure of the loved or courted reader, reads your words in a disapproving and censorious fashion.[15]

Mandanipour connects the censorship of his text with Sara, she becomes the collateral cost he must forfeit in order to gain approval for publication. Sara, like the text, becomes raw material that Mr Petrovich can mould according to his desires. Mandanipour refuses to oblige Mr Petrovich's fancy and objectify Sara into a helpless victim whose value and destiny is determined by a man, in so doing, putting down his pen becomes a protest, a refusal to accept all that is oppressing him and Sara.

After 9/11 and the 'War on Terror' there has been a growing interest in Iranian writers, considerable scholarship has focused on Iranian writing about the diaspora, in particular the genre of Iranian women's memoirs.[16] Most notably in 2007 Gillian Whitlock's *Soft Weapons* discussed this genre of writing as a 'serious and emerging discourse', consequently the interest and field of scholarship expanded.[17] However, there is limited scholarship on Mandanipour's writing, but Marie Ostby in her essay 'Decensoring an Iranian–American "Memoir"' compares his autofiction to the diasporic Iranian memoir genre. She argues that Mandanipour successfully 'elude[s] what Gillian Whitlock terms the transnational "economy of affect" that publicizes, protects and ultimately drives the reception of memoir across borders.'[18] Ostby concludes that Mandanipour might be attempting to complicate the 'contemporary Iranian novel–memoir hybrid as a literary space [...] [that serves] as acts of resistance against the circumscribed powers of states.'[19] Ostby's comparison between Mandanipour's autofiction and the diasporic Iranian memoir genre is problematic. To conclude that Mandanipour succeeds where many of these memoirists fail in escaping the 'economy of effect' and labels such as 'enlightened escapee'[20] and 'native informer',[21] results in the homogenisation of the experiences of these writers.

Mandanipour left Iran after securing a fellowship to travel to the United States for the International Writers project at Brown University in 2006 and is currently a visiting professor at the same university. His experience in academia in America, places him within a privileged minority of diasporic Iranians who would have quite a different experience of the diaspora compared with those exiled into a harsh socioeconomic position. Although Ostby is careful to acknowledge Mandanipour's position, she focuses on the threats and intimidation, which have forced him to remain in exile.[22] The memoir genre referred to by Ostby is largely populated by diasporic Iranian women and, as Therese Saliba and Jeanne Kattan argue the complexity of 'the roles of power, economics, literacy, and the marketing of the so-called Third World authors, *particularly women*, in the global economy,'[23] [my emphasis] can easily be ignored or obscured when they are read within a transnational context. Ostby fails to factor in the socioeconomic and gendered differences between Mandanipour and the memoirists she refers to.

Rather than comparing the nuanced differences between the genres of memoir writing with autofiction, this chapter will focus on the symbolism of the love story that Mandanipour is so desperate to tell, which contrasts with the Islamic love story that he is permitted to write. The love story becomes an emblem for a crucial site of struggle, not just for Mandanipour, but also Sara's suitors, who fight to claim her and the love story as their own. Sara, the object of desirability, becomes synonymous with the nation, a vision for Iran that is being fought for.

The construction of Sara as the idealised feminine woman binds her virginal body to 'sovereign nationhood',[24] whereby she must erase her sexuality in the world outside the home to ensure the 'integrity of the nation' is protected.[25] The policing of women's bodies normalises the alliance between gender and the nation.[26]

Mandanipour tells his story using three typographical layers, which emphasise the differences between Sara's three suitors. Each suitor depicts a different section of Iranian society. Dara represents the disenfranchised youth of Iran, a subversive underclass who are paradoxically revolting against a revolutionary government, thus they have no place and remain lost amid the lack of opportunities not just for those that challenge the State, but those that are born into lower socioeconomic positions. His education and hope of bettering himself are quite literally beaten out of him and he resorts to floating through life, aware of all that he cannot have, including his love, Sara. Dara's love story is for the most part in bold font but is often crossed out.

Sinbad, Sara's second suitor, has her parents' approval; he is a bureaucrat turned businessman whose wealth enables him to escape the wrath of the censor:

> People like Sinbad who belong to the nouveau riche class of Iranian society and, because of their government-granted import monopolies, have amassed wealth that no Western industrialist could ever dream of have no fear of the patrols from the Campaign Against Social Corruption. Even if they commit murder and are arrested, with a single telephone call to a government official their record will be cleared.[27]

Sinbad's narrative remains in bold and is never crossed out. Sara's final suitor is the censor himself Mr Petrovich, who is based on a character from Fyodor Dostoevsky's *Crime and Punishment*. Mr Petrovich wants to claim Sara as his own, '[e]ver since I read segments of your story, she has attracted my attention. Don't think I have wicked intentions. I want to ask for her hand in marriage. Rest assured that I can make her happy [...] delinquent boys like Dara will have ruined Sara.'[28] As a representative for the Ministry of Culture and Islamic Guidance, obtaining Sara's hand in marriage equates to safeguarding Sara and in turn Iran, from being corrupted and penetrated by 'that house of sin.'[29] Rebecca Gould elucidates the significance of the connection between women and the nation. She contends the 'nation could be regarded as politically fortified only so long as the women who upheld its domestic foundations had never been penetrated by their husbands.'[30] Mandanipour refuses to turn Sara into a token sacrifice for a national identity that subordinates women's freedom and identity for the sake of the nation. Instead, she remains independent and unnarratable, Mandanipour cannot represent her voice any more than Dara, Sinbad or Mr Petrovich.

Gender is at the heart of the struggle for both power and freedom in Mandanipour's text. He blurs the lines between prohibitions on the grounds of religion and gender. This brings out a failure Karima Bennoune has pointed out in international law in the language used in the drafting of the International Covenant on Civil and Political Rights. Bennoune argues that whilst 'Freedom of thought, conscience and religion is a fundamental human right [. . .] the language displays an exclusionary dimension often found in considerations of religious freedom which frequently ignores the lives of women and the reality of their pervasive subordination, including by and in religion.'[31] Mandanipour articulates this silent space of subordination inhabited by women, because it is one he is familiar with as a writer. In this way his self-imposed silence could be read as a form of solidarity confronting the consequences of denying fundamental human rights and freedoms.

In the inaugural issue of the journal *Feminist Dissent*, Dhaliwal et al. contextualised the struggle to find a 'genuine space for dissent and analysis' within 'a new global capitalist order where gender is increasingly instrumentalised to sustain power.'[32] Mandanipour's text could be seen to call for a simultaneous deconstruction of censorship alongside a feminist critique of gender inequality. Mandanipour explains:

> [I]n Iran there is a politico–religious presumption that any proximity and discourse between a man and a woman who are neither married nor related is a prologue to deadly sin. Those who commit such prologues to text, and such texts to sin, in addition to retributions that await them in the afterworld, will in this world too be sentenced by Islamic courts to such punishments as imprisonment, the lash and even death.[33]

Crucially, the responsibility to preserve modesty lies with women, as Bennoune confirms 'women of Muslim heritage are under pressure to cover more and more of their skin, their hair, their very beings.

To disappear. The mere physical manifestation of their existence is now a provocation.'[34] Furthermore, it has long been acknowledged that female chastity is often fused with national integrity, with discourses of nationalism inevitably gendered and the preservation of the home embodied in the physical person of the woman.

Chatterjee within the context of the contradiction of nativist anti-colonial nationalism, explains how indigenous traditions are set in opposition to Western society:

> The home was the principle site for expressing the spiritual quality of the national culture, and women must take the main responsibility for protecting and nurturing this quality. No matter what the changes in the external conditions of life for women, they must not lose their essentially spiritual (that is, feminine) virtues; they must not, in other words, become essentially Westernized.[35]

Mandanipour articulates this double bind through Sara, who like many women, is given the responsibility of preserving the spiritual quality of the national culture. The home becomes the space where traditional values must remain intact, to ensure the space remains unconquered and uncompromised. This legitimates a woman's confinement to the home, because it is assumed by nationalists that if Western values and norms are adopted within this space then the integrity of the nation comes under threat and one's very identity and autonomy is annihilated.[36] Mahnaz Afkhami, the first-ever minister of women's affairs in Iran, explains 'women's participation in society was an even greater threat, since it struck at the heart of hierarchal, patriarchal family and community structures.'[37] At the centre of this conflict for Muslim women's human rights is often the dilemma between the demands of modernity and tradition.

Mandanipour anticipates the standard anti-national charge against diasporic authors associated with neo-colonial powers, by enunciating the way in which women are used as a battleground on which the fight against an oppressive nativist government is being waged. This problem is embodied in Sara's choice between Dara and Sinbad:

> She knows with all her being that she is not willing to repeat her mother's life, to let her youth and dreams be frittered away in the

> kitchen for the ideal ambition of how best to feed the family, with only hardship on the kitcheny horizon. [...] Each time she thinks of marrying Dara, all the financial and political difficulties that await her flash before her eyes, and consequently she thinks of Sinbad [...] She sees herself with him in the capital cities of Europe, drunk on the beauties and joys that await her there, with all the things that she knows can only be attained with money and Western freedom.[38]

Mandanipour exposes the limited opportunities for Sara, she can choose to become a housewife to a man of limited means or be an 'unchained Eastern beauty' fetishised into the exotic Other in exchange for 'Western freedom'.[39] Similar to the '*new* patriarchy'[40] Chatterjee describes, with both men, Mandanipour emphasises Sara would be swapping one form of patriarchy and subordination for another.

Traditional indigenous culture is often set in opposition to the perceived cultural modernity of the West,[41] but Mandanipour is not suggesting that liberation lies in westernisation of social, economic, cultural processes and modes of governance. From the very first page we are informed that, '[t]he anti-riot police, armed with the most sophisticated paraphernalia, including stun batons purchased from the West, stand facing the students.'[42] Throughout the text Mandanipour emphasises that he is not subscribing to the notion that Iranians or Muslims are unable to understand Western notions of freedom of expression. In fact, he alludes to the culpability of Western powers in aiding authoritarian political culture, 'they have input their findings into special software that we purchased from a Western country.'[43] Bennoune would concur with this accountability, as she contends:

> Many wanted the United States to take a long look at its own policies that had promoted fundamentalism – whether collaborating with the Saudi government, financing fundamentalist groups in Afghanistan, or violating international law in our own treatment of Muslim majority populations in places like Iraq. [...] Empowering civil society is not a strategy that has really been tried in combating Muslim extremism. The West has mostly empowered autocrats [...] [who] have often constrained liberal civil society any way they could because they are more afraid of its democratic spirit than of fundamentalism.[44]

Anti-fundamentalist and progressive Muslim voices are rarely heard or transmitted and they receive little international attention. For these reasons, Mandanipour's decision to write in Farsi, his native language becomes quite pertinent.

Many diasporic Iranian writers describe exchanging their national language for an international one as both necessary and liberating. Although Mandanipour shares this diasporic status writing and teaching within America, he refuses to cater to a Euro–American audience by making himself more globally accessible to achieve the financially lucrative advantages of a wider international audience. 'The word *vessāl*, in the age-old Iranian literature, has many explicit and implicit religious, mystic, amorous and sexual connotations and hence is not really translatable.'[45] Mandanipour attempts to alienate and displace both the reader and censor using language; neither is left feeling entirely comfortable because he deliberately complicates the translation of the text and his intended meaning. As a consequence he avoids being labeled as Westernised or accused of cultural betrayal. It is possible to conclude that his strategy seems to be to foreignise his resistance, rather than homogenise the unfamiliar for the benefit of Western readership.

Mandanipour's text maintains a perpetual state of conflict throughout to replicate the emotions felt by a writer who is negotiating governmental structures and anticipating censorship. The text conveys a sense of hopelessness; when we first meet Sara she is protesting, but we are informed:

> [I]n precisely seven minutes and seven seconds, at the height of the clash between the students, the police, and the members of the Party of God, in the chaos of attacks and escapes, she will be knocked into with great force, she will fall back, her head will hit against a cement edge, and her sad Oriental eyes will forever close.[46]

At the end of the text, when Sara speaks 'the wisest and most ironic response that can come from the lips of an Iranian woman,' Mandanipour crosses out '~~She opens her eyes that had been closed to the fantasy of a kiss~~'.[47] Proving that every attempt to resist is futile, Sara will remain objectified, destined to passively accept the exclusionism that constrains her opportunities and life prospects. Her death, in the opening of the novel, might signify that her story, much like Mandanipour's, is not easily translated, neither can it be passed on.

The conflict between life and death is fused with the struggle between truth and fiction. In this autofictional text, Mr Petrovich is a character of Mandanipour's creation, but to what extent he represents an interaction in real life with a censor is unclear. When Mandanipour describes Dara's attempted murder it is ambiguous who is threatening his life, 'with a stab of his knife renders the Achilles tendon in the assassin's right foot useless. [. . .] Stunned, I look at this Dara who is walking out of the dead-end alley, and I feel the blade of a knife against my Achilles tendon.'[48] Initially we are led to believe that Mandanipour himself could be responsible, until he accuses Mr Petrovich, thus alluding to the possibility of the writer's subjectivity fusing with that of the censor. Crucially, the distinction between Mr Petrovich and Mandanipour, like the line between truth and fiction, has become so unclear that the story is indecipherable.

Mandanipour seems intent on preventing his struggle and that of his protagonist Sara, becoming a globalised commodity, in order to avoid '[t]he most frightening thing about imperialism, its long-term toxic effect, what secures it, what cements it, is the benevolent self-representation of the imperialist as savior.'[49] Mandanipour identifies the barriers that prevent women and writers (both male and female) from fulfilling their potential within their native home. The desire for the abolition of socially institutionalised gender roles and the sociopolitical and religious pressures on writers, are never realised in the course of his text, which is perhaps the most autobiographical point. Mandanipour's text articulates the 'precarious position' that Gayatri Spivak identifies and which results in 'divided loyalty':

> [B]eing a woman and being in the nation, without allowing the West to save them. [. . .] Women can be ventriloquists, but they have an immense historical potential of not being (allowed to remain) nationalists; of knowing, in their gendering, that nation and identity are commodities in the strictest sense: something made for exchange. And that they are the medium of that exchange.[50]

Women are instruments of power in Mandanipour's text, in the same way that a writer is expected to reinforce state ideologies. The closing image Mandanipour presents us with is Sara's desire to return home and 'lock the door from the inside.'[51] Venturing out into the world to defy the restrictions placed upon her, might signify her desire to preserve what Chatterjee defines as 'one's inner spiritual self, one's true identity.'[52] Her withdrawal implies that her womanhood and identity cannot be determined by or found in a union with Dara, Sinbad or Mr Petrovich. Neither Mandanipour nor Sara has a viable route to emancipation, thus they both retreat.

Mandanipour frees himself from imitating a Western construction of freedom. Which, as Sadia Abbas points out, is incredibly difficult in the current climate, 'in the wake of September 11, 2001, it is virtually impossible to hear the word "freedom" without an entire colonial history, and the consequences of the encounter between Muslim societies and the West, being summoned.'[53] In the process of writing, Mandanipour concludes that he is not prepared to forgo his integrity as a writer or to commodify his characters and text in order to be published in his native home. Although Mandanipour abandons his love story, his refusal to become an instrument helping to maintain state control or justify Western colonialism is a significant political protest, placing him in a 'precarious position'[54] and one which he shares with Sara. By merging the struggle against censorship with gender inequalities, Mandanipour's text could be seen to demonstrate that freedom and agency are often considered the sole property of Western modernity and these notions tend to be set in opposition to the Muslim woman. Mandanipour and Sara's joint refusal to surrender to someone else, results in the desertion becoming a form of self-assertion.

Notes

1. The question of how we define choice and what it means to assert freedom is widely contested in writing on Muslim women's lives. For a few examples, see Sadia Abbas, *At Freedom's Limit: Islam and the Postcolonial Predicament* (New York, 2014); Lila Abu-Lughod, *Do Muslim Women Need Saving?* (Cambridge, MA, 2013); and Mona Eltahawy, *Headscarves and Hymens: Why the Middle East needs a sexual revolution* (London, 2015). Simplistic ideas about freedom are challenged by scholars such as Wendy Brown, who asserts, 'the idea that Western women choose while Islamic women are coerced ignores the extent to which all choice is conditioned by as well as imbricated with power, and the extent to which choice itself is an impoverished account of freedom, especially political freedom.' Wendy Brown, 'Civilizational Delusions: Secularism, Tolerance, Equality', in *Theory and Event*, 15 (2012), p. 10.

2. 'Strictly speaking, the law [in Iran] forbids social contact between the sexes and regulates sexual conduct.'; Kamran Talattof, *The Politics of Writing in Iran: A History of Modern Persian Literature* (Syracuse, 2000), p. 135.
3. Shahriar Mandanipour, *Censoring An Iranian Love Story* (London, 2011), p. 2.
4. Ibid., p. 3.
5. Ibid., p. 292.
6. Ibid.
7. Ibid., p. 6.
8. J. M. Coetzee, *Giving Offence: Essays on Censorship* (Chicago and London, 1996), pp. 10–11.
9. Ibid., p. vii.
10. Mandanipour, *Censoring An Iranian Love Story*, p. 289.
11. Ibid., p. 291.
12. Shelina Zahra Janmohamad, 'A platform emerges for British Muslim Writers', *Common Ground News Service: Constructive articles that foster dialogue*, 19 July (2011). Online at: http://www.commongroundnews.org/article.php?id=30086&lan=en&sp=0 [Accessed 4 August 2016].
13. Mandanipour, *Censoring An Iranian Love Story*, p. 291.
14. Ibid., p. 292.
15. J. M. Coetzee, *Giving Offence: Essays on Censorship*, p. 38.
16. Sanaz Fotouhi, *The Literature of the Iranian Diaspora: Meaning and Identity since the Islamic Revolution* (London, 2015), p. 5.
17. Ibid., p. 5.
18. Marie Ostby, 'De-censoring an Iranian–American "Memoir": Authorship and Synchronicity in Shahriar Mandanipour's Censoring an Iranian Love Story', in *Iranian Studies*, vol. 46, no. 1 (2013), p. 73.
19. Ibid., p. 93.
20. Rehana Ahmed, *Writing British Muslims: Religion, Class and Multiculturalism* (Manchester, 2015), p. 189.
21. Hamid Dabashi, *Brown Skins, White Masks* (London, 2011), p. 15.
22. Marie Ostby, 'De-censoring an Iranian–American "Memoir"', pp. 74–5.
23. Therese Saliba and Jeanne Kattan, 'Palestinian Women and the Politics of Reception', in Amal Amireh and Lisa Suhair Majaj (eds), *Going Global: The Transnational Reception of Third World Women Writers* (New York, 2000), p. 84.
24. Partha Chatterjee, *The Nation and its Fragments: Colonial and Postcolonial Histories* (Princeton, 1993), p. 130.
25. Rebecca Gould, 'Engendering Critique: Postnational Feminism in Postcolonial Syria', in *Women Studies Quarterly* 42.3/4 (2014), p. 220.
26. Ibid., p. 224.
27. Mandanipour, *Censoring An Iranian Love Story*, p. 159.
28. Ibid., p. 290.
29. Ibid., p. 292.
30. Rebecca Gould, 'Engendering Critique: Postnational Feminism in Postcolonial Syria', p. 220.
31. Karima Bennoune, 'Secularism and Human Rights: A Contextual Analysis of Headscarves, Religious Expression, and Women's Equality Under International

Law', in *Columbia Journal of Transnational Law*, vol. 45, Number 2 (2007), pp. 398–9.

32. Sukhwant Dhaliwal, Chitra Nagarajan and Rashmi Varma, 'Editorial', in *Feminist Dissent*, Number 1 (2016), p. i.
33. Mandanipour, *Censoring An Iranian Love Story*, p. 8.
34. Karima Bennoune, *Your Fatwa Does Not Apply Here: Untold Stories from the Fight Against Muslim Fundamentalism* (New York, London, 2015), p. 8.
35. Chatterjee, *The Nation and its Fragments*, pp. 126–7.
36. Ibid., p. 121.
37. Mahnaz Afkhami, '"Sunlight, Open Windows, and Fresh Air": The Struggle for Women's Rights in Iran', in *Shirin Neshat: Facing History, a major exhibit on the Iranian artist-in-exile's work*, The Hirshhorn Museum (Washington, DC, 2015). Online at: http://www.mahnazafkhami.net/wp-content/uploads/Proof.Afkhami.Essay_.2.5.15.pdf [Accessed 5 August 2016], p. 42.
38. Mandanipour, *Censoring An Iranian Love Story*, p. 195.
39. Ibid.
40. Chatterjee, *The Nation and its Fragments*, p. 127.
41. Ibid., p. 117.
42. Mandanipour, *Censoring An Iranian Love Story*, p. 1.
43. Ibid., p. 141.
44. Bennoune, *Your Fatwa Does Not Apply Here*, pp. 332–3.
45. Mandanipour, *Censoring An Iranian Love Story*, p. 57.
46. Ibid., p. 7.
47. Ibid., p. 289.
48. Ibid., p. 264.
49. Gayatri Chakravorty Spivak, 'Acting Bits/Identity Talk', in *Critical Inquiry*, 18 (1992), p. 781.
50. Ibid., p. 803.
51. Mandanipour, *Censoring An Iranian Love Story*, p. 293.
52. Chatterjee, *The Nation and its Fragments*, p. 120.
53. Abbas, *At Freedom's Limit*, p. 44.
54. Spivak, 'Acting Bits/Identity Talk', p. 803.

CHAPTER 9

HOMELAND DRAMATISATIONS AND NATIVE GAZE DEMOLITIONS IN NAHID RACHLIN'S *FOREIGNER* AND POROCHISTA KHAKPOUR'S *SONS AND OTHER FLAMMABLE OBJECTS*

Giulia Valsecchi

In *Reflections on Exile* Edward Said shows how, in modern cultures, narrations of exile spring from a rift between the self and its true home: 'Because exile, unlike nationalism, is a discontinuous state of being',[1] it passes through continuous efforts to defeat a loss of roots. The same loss – which Said depicts as to be cut from one's past and native land – entails primary conflicts among the viewpoints of the I, of the family and of the homeland.

The ambivalent I of the exile takes part in narrations of estrangement at home, where the constitution of identity is always changing. Moreover, the doubleness connected with the definition of home between the exilic and diasporic labels – in a more general tension that involves the issues of isolation and negotiation – allows us to see home as a vulnerable gap among the categories of the I, of the family and of homeland. In other words, for an exile or a 'diasporean',[2] home could be seen as a fragile border between the I, as a subjective condition of solitude and loss, and the varying perspectives on family and the homeland.

According to Stuart Hall 'the diaspora experience' is never unified and 'is defined, not by essence or purity, but by the recognition of a necessary heterogeneity and diversity; by a conception of identity which lives with and through, not despite, difference'.[3] This can be closely related to the diasporic awareness of uncertainty and scattering and so to the mixed poles of home and host culture. Hence, together with the growing divide between national ideals of belonging and the effects of globalisation, the deterritorialised subject of diaspora has to deal with confused borders, but also with a kind of nostalgia which is shared by different communities of people striving to rebuild or to reinvent a collective memory.

If we look at nostalgia and memory as means for cultural exchanges between host societies and diasporic communities, they disclose fractures within the valencies of home and homeland, as much as within those of language and identity. The so-called mythical return to the roots is replaced by more interstitial and transient poetics coming from new cultural geographies:[4] the increase of the migratory movement brings about narratives where the writer plays the role of a global subject, who needs to restore the hybrid outcome of migration through a literary process of self-assertion. It means to rethink the diasporic dispersion both as a state and a legacy to investigate and dramatise through fiction.

When considering contemporary Iranian women writers who have moved to the West before and after the Revolution (1979), Iranian–American literature seems mostly concerned with matters of veils and gender confinement, as well as with misunderstandings or misidentifications spread by a common stereotyped 'Arabic appearance'. These topics also refer to post-9/11 events and to the most conventional concerns about Iran: the oppressed country of Islamic censorship and capital punishment. This occlusive portrait keeps out a thick Iranian diasporic writing crossed by an inner longing for a lost life in the homeland and a simultaneous feeling of dislocation and foreignness in Western societies, where to write means also to relocate the shifty notions of nostalgia, memory and identity as tools for a dramatisation.

As Daniel Grassian writes, recalling in turn Persis Karim and Nasrin Rahimieh's words: 'For the generation of Iranian–Americans coming of age in the post-exile, post-revolution period, literature becomes a vehicle by which to wrestle with their origins and the landscape of their American identity.'[5] That is to say that, from the outbreak of instrumental memoirs on gloomy days under the Islamic Republic to George W. Bush's inclusion of Iran within the 'Axis of Evil' and so on, the uncomfortable literary explorations by a large group of Iranian–American women writers reveal helpful and multifaceted traces of counter-narrations centred on the I, on the family and on the homeland.

We could add that, apart from widespread captivity chronicles inspired by the repressive drifts of the Iranian Revolution, other narratives by women of the Iranian diaspora grew before and after Khomeinism. Currently, they go on preserving both an ancient tradition of Persian lyrical symbolisms and the more contemporary achievements of in-depth studies on identity and gender.

This women's writing includes various generations of authors who differently explore the diasporic bewilderment as a space of re-creation, as to prevent the female voice from being limited to the subaltern role promoted by several anti-Iranian portraits. It is a progressive shift in self-representation, as the author passes through the contradictions and connections between fiction and reality, in order to create a plot where estrangement appears as a living and a literary circumstance to re-territorialise the subjective and the collective self.

Among the writers who started dramatising the diasporic tensions, Nahid Rachlin was the first Iranian–American to publish a novel in English – *Foreigner*, in 1978 – based on the trip from America to Iran made by an Iranian–American woman. More recently, in 2007, Porochista Khakpour with her novel *Sons and Other Flammable Objects* tells of the limited ability to adjust to the new situation of an Iranian family that migrated to the USA after the Revolution.

So, if *Foreigner* takes us from America to Iran through the eyes of just one character, *Sons and Other Flammable Objects* plunges the reader into the conflict of a family staying in the USA. These are two contrary vectors, even though they stem from a common search for the self and from the dual relationship between memories and the need to redraft them into the fictional time–space line of new characters.

More specifically, Rachlin's and Khakpour's strategies of rewriting could be seen as the results of the splintering of archetypes, the mixing of linguistic codes and the exchange of clichés between Iran and America. All this implies a first demolition of the native gaze followed by the dramatisation of homeland perceptions, to reconfigure cultural differences and turn roles upside down. But it means, above all, considering estrangement as a narrative device to look into the sense of displacement that makes both Rachlin and Khakpour responsible for the reshaping of the I, family, homeland polarisations.

The writer's hybrid gaze – as if behind a Brechtian observation,[6] focused on the confrontation between a suspicious Iranian past and a motionless American present, flowing into each other as in a cinematic reverse shot – answers to that dramatic responsibility to destroy and then reconstruct. Yet, to be responsible reminds us also of what Christa Wolf describes in *Cassandra*,[7] with reference to the death of words before images: in Rachlin's and Khakpour's novels, images go by flashbacks full of conflicting atmospheres, yet they remind us of the essential role of a witness going on 'biting memories', as Wolf puts it.

Indeed, in *Foreigner* the I is an intimate storyteller and literally an 'eye', a sort of camera witness. But between the I who tells and the homeland, introduced as a menacing community, there is a family that epitomises a longstanding feeling of alienation. The same alienation – a condition that Rachlin primarily experienced as an immigrant – changes into the evanescent life and consciousness of a protagonist, who repeatedly copes with the fight between a kind of Iranian remoteness and an impersonal but comforting American settlement. Actually, from the first pages, the author lingers on the details of a return to the mother country characterised by obscure past recalls and present pictures of mystery.

On the other hand, in *Sons and Other Flammable Objects*, the I grows into a more choral perspective to show how the family acts rather as a primordial enemy. Not by chance, in Khakpour's novel, the idea of homeland is erased by a portrait of tragic memories and paradoxes aimed at overthrowing the positions of father and son. Also, the recurring theme of a never-fixed staying transforms the introspective and solitary insight drawn by Rachlin into a more open and shared situation: Khakpour shows how the family's role collapses into the doubts and obsessions deployed by the struggle between Persian mythologisation and American demonisation. At the same time, the reader is led into the opposite clash between Persian demonisation and the American dream, so that he can explore the family's divisions from a reversed standpoint.

In summary, the initial partition of roles in the novels considered might be as follows:

Nahid Rachlin, *Foreigner*

– I as an intimate witness

– **family** as an old stranger
– **homeland** as a menacing community

Porochista Khakpour, *Sons and Other Flammable Objects*
– **I** as a choral perspective
– **family** as a primordial enemy
– **homeland** as a collected, tragic memory

As mentioned above, *Foreigner* was published one year before the outbreak of the Iranian Revolution. For this historical reason, Nahid Rachlin is considered a pioneer of novel writing in English. Born and partly brought up in Iran under the Shah's regime, she migrated to the USA to attend college and to continue writing, 'what was considered dangerous with all the Shah's censorship'.[8] In an interview published in the journal *Melus* in 2008, Rachlin declares:

> I always felt like a foreigner in my own country and then I felt that way in the small, provincial, all-women's college I attended. That feeling of being an outsider led to my desire to write, the process that ultimately helped me. [. . .] I feel I am an Iranian–American writer in that most of my short stories and novels include both Iranian and American characters and also I have absorbed some of both cultures in my own conduct and attitudes and outlook on things.[9]

The confessed splitting of the I, between Iran and America, is a declaration of estrangement made clear from the very beginning of *Foreigner*. The protagonist, Feri, travels from Boston to Tehran: she is going to Iran to catch up with her native family and to look for her mother, with whom she has not been in touch for many years. But the first sketch of her homeland goes through a light and dark impression: the American airport, a non-place of beating light, contrasts with the Iranian airport, a non-place of disorientation, with women under dark chadors. Even the first harsh conversation between Feri and a taxi driver, about the best way to get home, takes place among descriptions of crowded streets, 'tall western buildings' and cars 'passing each other recklessly'.[10]

This contrast carries out a very traditional Iranian landscape oriented by a Western mistrust: it tells of beggars and of a transitory discomfort that hinders any attempt to recover a homogeneous past by the subject or rather by the I. The author outlines the episode with a sense of debris at home, but also with a past and present loneliness made heavier by all the fears about an imagined, backward homeland:

> We passed through quieter, older sections. The driver slowed down on a narrow street with a mosque at its center, then stopped in front of a large, squalid house. This was the street I had lived on for so many years; here I had played hide-and-seek in alleys and hallways. I had a fleeting sensation that I had never left this street [. . .]. The doors of the house across the street were open. I had played with two little girls, sisters, who lived there. I could almost hear their voices, laughter. The April air was mild and velvety against my skin but I shivered at the proximity to my childhood.[11]

Then, recurring expressions like 'You look different' and 'You look Western'[12] draw attention to the broken relationship between the I and the family, represented by a difficult father–daughter bond and by the protagonist's confession: 'I *was* a stranger, with people I had not seen for so long and hardly knew any more.'[13] A background of enduring suspicion seems to permeate the native suburb, which is isolated from the capital Tehran. The same mistrust creeps into Feri's mind to turn her vision of the Iranian home into that of a suspended space of missing discourses and sudden departures.

A cyclical suspicion characterises the family as well: it implies Feri embodies the worst 'vices about being 'Americanised', because she has gone back to Iran without her American husband. In the meantime, the protagonist looks with caution at every Iranian woman wearing a black chador or Iranian man with a 'sleazy smile hovering on his face'.[14]

Thus, both Iranian and American preconceptions collide particularly when, in the attempt to recall her life in the USA, Feri converts the landscape into a various and slippery inscape. On the one hand, there is the soothing stillness of 'the grass-covered backyard' in Lexington; on the other hand, the Persian 'sun-choked, dust-swept courtyard, the melancholy sunsets and hazy noons. The hum of prayers pouring out of mosques, a child climbing an ancient tree. Uncertainty, a mystery in the air'.[15] All this could resemble an exotic depiction, but it better underlines the disjunction between a 'peaceful' life in the USA and a 'menacing'[16] one in Iran, although both are joined by the possessive 'our' to implicitly reassert the fluctuating assimilation of the two worlds.

Furthermore, Feri's native gaze is corrupted by the tales of nightmares and vague words used to share Iranian smells and sounds with the reader, as if behind a broken mirror. Her search for the true self is once again upset by the question of an impossible exit visa at the passport bureau, another condition of foreignness concerning the fragile notion of national identity produced by the return to the mother country. In general terms, it could be attributed to restrictions after the Shah's regime, but the protagonist's will to escape back to America could also be a narrative device to introduce a digression about Feri's mother, the woman who left her child to follow another man.

Hence, since in the plot no one knows where the woman is, Rachlin portrays her as someone who has 'gradually become a dark memory'.[17] She is an illusion or, at worst, a whore as Feri's stepmother asserts. As a result, the portrayal the reader can get is that of a threat and the mother who abandoned her child corresponds to an unsettling profile filtered through her daughter's remembrances and visions, as through her challenged sense of the I, of the family and of the homeland belonging.

As such, the maternal figure emanates from a more inner and imaginative world of rosewater scents and dreamlike appearances: Feri looks at these flashes as if they were all scraps of a mask or as an unreal refuge that seems to her more authentic than reality. In particular, the protagonist associates the absence of her mother to the rag doll the woman gave her before escaping: the doll is another fetish that reinforces Feri's difficulty of recognising herself as native. From now on, the narration emphasises sensations of helplessness, confirmed by other flashbacks and subplots about old pains, on which Rachlin builds up a dialectic criticism. The intention to understand Feri's mother's voluntary exile develops into a tragic myth nurtured by fancies on the encounter between two foreigners:

> How would she react to me, a stranger, suddenly turning up and claiming to be her daughter? A sense of the absurdity of the trip struck me. But the next instant I pictured my mother squatting in the shade of a tree, washing clothes in abundant suds or walking around with a broom sweeping dry leaves and twigs from rose bushes. Seeing me she pauses and we look at each other, first like

> strangers and then our faces form into familiar shapes, shining over the expanse of years.[18]

Words like 'absurdity', 'stranger', 'pictured' and 'shade' drive to a climax where the issues of the I, of the family and of the homeland become even more elusive points. Through the same climax, a recurring theme can be identified in Rachlin's novel: the mutual relationship between remembrances and questions of identity as if, according to Maria Wagenknecht, 'memory tends to change as identity changes'.[19] As a result, each time Feri's remembrances merge with fantasies, her attempt to get away from the patriarchal rule is reinforced. The sense of interruption the woman confesses is reaffirmed as a 'double-estrangement', that is a double-edged positioning Feri can discern both as an immigrant and a stranger in the homeland.

The insistent use of evasive descriptions – as well as of words in a climax like 'dangerous', 'wrong', 'conspiracy', 'fights' and 'nightmares' – also marks Porochista Khakpour's *Sons and Other Flammable Objects*. Linguistic features dominate the narrative doubling from the first line of the novel: 'Darius Adam began with kindness, kindness and some deception.'[20] The novel refers to the tricks adopted by one of the protagonists, Darius Adam, to lure a few wild cats and keep them far from the blue jays in the green American suburb where he started living with his family after moving from Iran. It is the first anecdote of a more figurative use of the language, which is clear also in the chapters' titles and in their metaphorical sequence: from 'The Birds and the Birds', 'Heavens', 'Hells' to 'The Missing', 'Homelands' and 'Departures'.

The same figurative mark springs from Khakpour's focus on divided Persian cultural heritages – with all the references to words such as *gorbeh* for 'cats' or to honored kings like Darius – when it bumps into a more globalised and imperialist viewpoint, where a new diasporic consciousness was born and now lives in the midst of the limbo before and after 11 September 2001.

Born in Tehran in 1978, Khakpour moved to the West during the Iran–Iraq war and grew up in California, studying and majoring in creative writing. Her way to conceive stories refers to an ancestral battle between past and present and to a sort of declared mimic state:

> I never really felt comfortable claiming the 'child of the Revolution' tag. For the first two and a half decades of my life,

> my inner life was devoted to rehearsing for American Girl roles. [. . .] Like many immigrants, I focused adamantly on looking forward and never back; like many 'hyphenates', I felt the existential confusion of a two-pronged identity. [. . .] I focused on all the pretty things of ol' Persia: Kings, Cyrus and Darius and the Persian Empire; Persepolis (the ruins! the Satrapi graphic novel!); saffron-and-pistachio Persian ice cream!; rugs!; mystical Avesta chants mashed-up against hokey, hooky Googoosh lyrics back to back and backward even. . . . did I mention Persian cats?![21]

Thus, for Khakpour, to identify herself with second-generation immigrants is not an oversimplified matter of longing for Persian roots, but a living circumstance to take advantage of the rift between the archetypes of a father – Darius – and of his son – Xerxes – as to sound out with the reader the more complex splitting between native and host languages.

Not accidentally, as observed before, *Sons and Other Flammable Objects* narrates the struggle of a family to adjust to a new American homeland: words like 'history', 'misunderstanding' and 'father–son bond' mark the first flash backward into bad memories. The young Xerxes, his father Darius and his mother Laleh (then called Lala) come to Los Angeles after the Revolution with names difficult to pronounce in a 'near-perfect' English or 'bastard tongue'.[22]

So, the reader participates in the disoriented accommodation of this Iranian family in the West, while the task given to the choral I is to show the homeland as a country of tragic boundaries: 'The Iranians [. . .] it's like they were made for tragedy, always trapped in some sad dramatic past, generational pain, familial anguish, personal turmoil, a collective tragic disposition, an almost genetic mass pessimism. Tragedy everywhere; blood always in the air.'[23] Memories are consequently developed by Khakpour as if they were unspoken confessions, while generational incomprehensions reflect the tragi-comic impossibility of living together because of the debts to a shared and painful recollection of past events.

In this way, the first lines of the novel could offer the two main sides of an archetypical diasporic society: on the one hand, there is an immigrant Iranian family with traditional Persian names, on the other hand, an American immigrant suburb is described as an Eden-like scenery with oaks and palms. This could remind us of an Orientalist frame full of 'all the pretty things of ol' Persia',[24] as Khakpour writes. But soon memories clash against one another, giving rise to the need to retrace them within linguistic traps and the sense that the primordial hierarchy between father and son must be overturned.

Moreover, this family unsettlement goes beyond 'typical' portraits: the dramatic crash of the I points to a loss of identity within the family–homeland framework and it coincides with the rule not to pronounce bad words. Indeed, in the so-called 'house of swallowed discontentment',[25] no one can express unpleasant opinions nor raise upsetting memories, so that a silent veil will prevent the risk of the mixing of the two worlds: 'an unusual past'[26] for Xerxes and a 'suffocating cultureless California life'[27] for Darius. So, the final act of this generational and diasporic estrangement is the break in the silence between father and son: 'The past had come full circle [. . .] history had become theirs, just theirs. [. . .] It was as if their entire lives they had waited for the power of a single story to split them forever.'[28]

Among native nightmares, Darius' favourite word to condemn American life is 'enough': to repeat 'enough' means for him to go against Western life, but it is also an attack against Xerxes and his favourite American foods or television series, as the boy is the imperfect son with whom Darius only shares the fact of being named after kings. The family's last name, Adam, is not accidental either: 'Adam', like the first man, comes from 'Odd-damn' in the adjustment of 'odd' plus 'damn'; it could be an allusion to 'Goddamn' or to 'A-dumb', in other words, a combination of damned oddity and foolishness.

In these ways, Khakpour's plot flows into a verbal labyrinth to concentrate upon disconnections and the aphasiac nature of the links inside the I, family, homeland hierarchy. What is primordial, such as the Persian homeland, brings a dark force that cannot be easily identified and that separates the I from national history. The family is once again ruined and, in its inner ruins, it pollutes any historical inheritance so that Xerxes and Darius often look like Beckett's well-known characters, Vladimir and Estragon: they both wait for a Persian past to forgive or to be proud of.

In this stillness, made for Xerxes out of an empty hate for history, all the family is overwhelmed by the explosion of preconceptions after 9/11. However, Xerxes chooses to live in New York where he meets his girlfriend, while Darius and Lala stay in Los Angeles. Each of them embodies a way of living in the USA not oriented towards renovation, but towards an anonymous, flat condition of normality. And if Lala embodies a one-way direction that goes forward, her naiveté stands opposed to Xerxes' fixation with death and tragedy: as a consequence, we could say that the son best embodies Khakpour's 'two-pronged identity'.[29]

Moreover, if Xerxes is at ease with the American common sayings, he also tries to hide himself behind the television icons: it is by identifying with these 'partial presences' that he can temporarily silence the permanent conflict between Iranianness and Americanness. By contrast, Darius strives to enhance his bonds with a Persian world full of scents and words he has lost after migrating. It follows that father and son become two masks of the same collective self deprived of roots. When Darius looks at himself in the mirror he can recognise only a mirage standing for an incomplete identity:

> the themes, the worries, the dilemmas, they were all the same, had been there for a while now, too long, all the unsolvables, unreachable but nameable, the thing in his life that was missing, the one that he'd admit was missing only at that hour, when his figure would appear before him, like a mirror whose reflection had been missing for all too long. . . . In the end, it came only in mirage form – he would never make it as a character – only in essence, the corresponding reality less personal but always infinitely worse, his child mixed in with men he didn't know, anonymous wars, ambiguous history, eternal bloodshed, consistent violence and overall hopelessness, adding up to vacuums, uncharitable expanses, hot desolate deserts that were his own, sadly, all he and his kind had for landscape within their most secret nocturnal selves. . . .[30]

What is more, the everlasting match between ethnicity and nationality, between inside and outside means Xerxes looks at Iran as an anti-home, the birthplace of his nightmares, where Darius represents the messenger of all the ghosts. But when the son feels similar to his father, the wall of silence is nearly overthrown. Only at this point, after trying to reconcile with his hard memories of the Iranian Revolution and with a missed return to the homeland, Xerxes can declare to an airport officer that he was born in Iran, because he has definitely realised that: 'Leaving, escaping, exiling, always running off and away – it was natural. It was in his blood [. . .].'[31]

Khakpour follows the discontinuity of the Adams to fight for the utopian geography of a family that, like the homeland for a refugee, is always questioned and separated. In the end, the two consumed archetypes of father and son represent tradition and modernity and confront each other 'like positive and negative ends of a magnet'.[32] So, the first and the last word ever spoken by Xerxes – 'Dad' – seals the prologue and the final act of a family relationship where, however, only Darius tries to look forward again:

> in the highly flammable chambers of his old mind, Xerxes lit the sentence like the wick of a dynamite stick and let the words combust into shattered particles of forever-rejected memories refuse. . . . There was nowhere to go [. . .] and so he chose his oldest word, the best one, his first word.[33]

Also in *Foreigner*, Feri's new life in Iran does not correspond to finding roots, but to a new unsolved comfort next to the rediscovered mother and far from a bland American marriage. After facing her 'Western disease'[34] – an ulcer, at the Iranian hospital, where she runs into Dr Majid and his emphasis on the need to break with an anti-Iranian propaganda, as with all the distresses of emotions become 'dull and colorless as if they had been bleached'[35] – Feri can do without facing her memories too. She looks at herself in a mirror and can grasp the physical evidence of a hurt at the point of contact between past threads and vague self-representations:

> I took out a mirror from my pocketbook and looked at my face, studying it for signs of unhappiness. [. . .] A haunted look, what might be expected from a person who had lain in bed for so long in fear and uncertainty. But beneath those signs I saw scars. Scars of pain brushed aside. Dissatisfactions not coped with. Memories rolled before me like a rug, worn and faded in some spots and vivid in others.[36]

So, if in both the novels examined every act of demolition and dramatisation might be seen in the transition from a light and dark prologue to a suspended epilogue – from the return to a restless staying – truly, each writer, like a playwright, directs rehearsals for changing roles in the double map between Iran and America. We could understand it in terms of a diasporic detachment, but in the cases of both Rachlin and Khakpour the role exchange compels the reader to investigate estrangement as a shifting narrative, which finally rebuilds the I, the family and the homeland, and which functions as follows:

Nahid Rachlin, *Foreigner*
- **I** as 'an immense shell, emptying from one side and filling from the other'[37]
- **family** as a rediscovered stranger
- **homeland** as a reversed, undefined community

Porochista Khakpour, *Sons and Other Flammable Objects*
- **I** as an identity outside
- **family** as an overturning archetype
- **homeland** as a collected photograph

In *Foreigner*, Feri chooses to stay in Iran with her mother probably until she can feel a somewhat similar bond with her invisible roots in America. The USA is the host homeland where she married a man, Tony, who feeds himself with fixed Persian icons and Orientalist tags that now Feri can hardly share,[38] plunged as she is into her native life, even though she had at first demolished them as 'primitive'. In the same way, in *Sons and Other Flammable Objects*, the transition from the helplessness to recollect a Persian identity to the hard work of 'getting the sides of himself straight'[39] drives Xerxes to finally declare his nationality and look at himself through his father's eyes.

Therefore, to rewrite means above all to watch, to overthrow and to recreate, adding a dramatic distance. In Rachlin's novel, this tension made its way from an empty national pride of 'to be like' to a depiction of the I 'as an immense shell, emptying from one side and filling from the other'.[40] And if Khakpour condenses the act of overthrowing in a word, 'Dad', Rachlin explores her protagonist's soul using a kind of interior monologue. That is why the two novels stage the dramatic doubling of a search for the self that probably will go on until, as we read in Xerxes' thoughts, 'the pieces of anger and misery'[41] will be put together in a single photograph.

In several poems by contemporary Iranian–American women writers,[42] the mixing traditions of ancient Persia and modern America flow into ghostly spaces, made of insecure words and code-switching techniques. They lyrically show that the nexus among the I, family, homeland generates another unstable positioning, what identifies with the well-discussed notions of in-between boundaries.

In *Sons and Other Flammable Objects*, these interstitial borders are better unveiled when the son confesses to his father: 'I'm trying to find myself, an identity outside yours, outside nationality, outside ethnicity, outside family, outside history, foreign to them and to you and to everything, wholly my own lone person.'[43] The need to break with prejudices and discomfort due to displacement is the foundation upon which the I can refashion cultural differences inside family–homeland bonds.

Rachlin's and Khakpour's ways of seeing diaspora provide a dramatic scene for going beyond exoticism and misidentification and open up possibilities for the rewriting of subjective stories and diasporic roles. In *Nation and Narration*, Homi Bhabha makes a similar point remarking the inward birth of narrations from hybridity: 'Content becomes the alien *mise en scène* that reveals the signifying structure of linguistic difference which is never seen for itself, but only glimpsed in the gap or the gaping of the garment.'[44]

Finally, from menacing Iranian airports to false American self-confidence, from a challenging racial consciousness to identity-producing through dramatisation, the vulnerable eye of the Iranian–American writer seems to record: 'I am Iranian until I open my mouth. Then I am American [. . .] Will you understand when it gets hard for me to breathe easy and I become American again?'[45]

Notes

1. Edward W. Said, *Reflections on Exile and Other Essays* (Cambridge, 2001), p. 177.
2. For the historical differences between the exile and 'the diasporean or immigrant' see Kobena Mercer (ed.), *Exiles, Diasporas & Strangers* (Cambridge & London, 2008), p. 8.
3. Stuart Hall, 'Cultural Identity and Diaspora', in Jonathan Rutherford (ed.), *Identity. Community, Culture, Difference* (London, 1990), p. 235.
4. For the concept of cultural geographies marked by flexible boundaries see Anderson: 'Nations have no clear identifiable births, and their deaths, if they even happen, are never natural', in Benedict Anderson, *Imagined Communities. Reflections on the Origins and Spread of Nationalism* (London & New York, 2006), p. 205.
5. Daniel Grassian, *Iranian and Diasporic Literature in the 21st Century. A Critical Study* (North Carolina, 2013), p. 5.

6. For the idea of Brechtian observation see Bertolt Brecht, *Schriften zum Theater. Über eine nicht-aristotelische Dramatik* (Frankfurt, 1957).
7. Christa Wolf, *Cassandra. A Novel and Four Essays* (New York, 1988).
8. 'Interview with Nahid Rachlin', *Červená Barva Press* (2005–6), Available at http://www.cervenabarvapress.com/rachlininterview.htm [Accessed 27 June 2017].
9. Persis M. Karim, 'Talking with a Pioneer of Iranian American Literature: An Interview with Nahid Rachlin', in *MELUS*, xxxiii/2 (2008), pp. 154–6.
10. Nahid Rachlin, *Foreigner* (New York & London, 1978), p. 11.
11. Ibid.
12. Ibid., p. 15.
13. Ibid., p. 14.
14. Ibid., p. 21.
15. Ibid., p. 37.
16. Ibid., p. 38.
17. Ibid., p. 40.
18. Ibid., p. 72.
19. Maria D. Wagenknecht, *Constructing Identity in Iranian-American Self-Narrative* (New York, 2015), p. 68.
20. Porochista Khakpour, *Sons and Other Flammable Objects* (New York, 2007), p. 1.
21. Porochista Khakpour, 'What I saw at the Revolution', *The Daily Beast*, 2 November 2009. Available at www.thedailybeast.com/articles/2009/02/11/what-i-saw-at-the-revolution.html. [Accessed 27 June 2017].
22. Khakpour, *Sons and Other Flammable Objects*, p. 4.
23. Ibid., pp. 59–60.
24. Khakpour, 'What I saw at the Revolution'.
25. Khakpour, *Sons and Other Flammable Objects*, p. 4.
26. Ibid., p. 34.
27. Ibid., p. 18.
28. Ibid., pp. 34–5.
29. Khakpour, 'What I saw at the Revolution'.
30. Khakpour, *Sons and Other Flammable Objects*, p. 167.
31. Ibid., p. 351.
32. Ibid., p. 280.
33. Ibid., p. 395.
34. Rachlin, *Foreigner*, p. 102.
35. Ibid., p. 100.
36. Ibid., p. 103.
37. Ibid., p. 191.
38. 'It used to be called Persia.' Tony says at the first close encounter with Feri: 'I liked that name better. It fits with my image of the place. [...] Gardens springing up in the midst of deserts, magic carpets, caravans jingling in the night, and dark-eyed girls behind veils.' Ibid., p. 141.
39. Khakpour, *Sons and Other Flammable Objects*, p. 137.
40. Rachlin, *Foreigner*, p. 191.
41. Khakpour, *Sons and Other Flammable Objects*, p. 210.

42. See, for example, *Disassociation* by Laleh Khalili in P. M. Karim and M. M. Khorrami (eds), *A World Between. Poems, Short Stories, and Essays by Iranian-Americans* (New York, 1999), pp. 52–4.
43. Khakpour, *Sons and Other Flammable Objects*, p. 211.
44. Homi K. Bhabha, *Nation and Narration* (London, 1990), p. 314.
45. See Parissa Milani, *American Again*, in P. M. Karim (ed.), *Let Me Tell You Where I've Been. New Writing by Women of The Iranian Diaspora* (Chicago, 2006), p. 220.

SECTION 3

IMAGINING THE OTHER: FACT AND FANTASY IN CULTURAL AND POLITICAL INFLUENCES

CHAPTER 10

TBILISI AS A BRIDGE BETWEEN IRAN AND EUROPE, FROM THE NINETEENTH TO THE EARLY TWENTIETH CENTURIES

George Sanikidze

The nineteenth century was a period of crucial transformations in Iran. Defeats during the Russo–Persian Wars brought home to Iran that it was lagging behind on the road towards progress. Russia forced Iran to turn its attention westward by threatening its territories in the Caucasus, but the Qajars also looked west for a model for modernisation to try to reverse Iranian decline. Contacts with Europe and the processes of modernisation became the moving force for changes in the perception of history, of identity and culture. Georgia, wedged between Russia and Iran, the Black and the Caspian Seas, became a hotly disputed territory. Against the backdrop of the Russo–Persian Wars, this chapter argues that Georgia's geopolitical in-betweenness made it a place of syncretism, a touchpoint between Iran and Europe. Using both Persian and European written sources and focussing on Tbilisi, capital of the Georgian kingdom of Kartli–Kakheti which moved from Iranian to Russian hands, the present chapter examines how this city became a place of convergence for European–Iranian trade and also inevitably for European–Iranian perceptions. It analyses the evolution of these perceptions which echo the changes Iran underwent under the Qajar dynasty.

It must be stressed that there existed fundamental differences between European and Iranian perceptions of Georgia and of Tbilisi. For Europeans it was considered as 'a window, gateway to the Orient' and its most attractive aspect was 'the oriental image' of the city (from the second half of the nineteenth century – a kind of mixture of East and West), whilst for Iranians Georgia gradually became 'a window to Europe', the most interesting for them being the European image of the city ('strange' at the beginning and 'attractive' from the second half of the century) – museums, clubs, printing houses, different European-style establishments. Interest in Georgia for Iranian travellers was also conditioned by an important factor – it was considered as a part of the so-called Persianate world. Incorporation of Georgia (and the whole South Caucasus) into the Russian Empire and the political and cultural consequences that ensued, were considered by Iranians as an error of history, as an illegal violation of Iranian territorial integrity.

Georgia appears in several books written by Iranian travellers in the nineteenth and early twentieth centuries. The overwhelming majority of them visited Georgia on their way to other countries. Two major routes – to Mecca and to Western Europe – went through Georgia. A small number of Iranian authors either settled or lived for some years in Tbilisi (especially political refugees from the end of the nineteenth century). During the Middle Ages and early modern period Iranian authors of travelogues were, in general, pilgrims to Mecca or other holy places, emissaries of Iranian rulers and merchants, but from the nineteenth century the aims of travellers became wider – Iranians were travelling to foreign countries for education, for entertainment and simply, for new adventures and curiosity.

In general, Iranian travelogues of this period were based on the dichotomy of Self and Other (Iranian and European). In this regard, Georgia represented a unique case. Despite being peripheral and non-Muslim it was considered a 'part' of the Iranian world, though in the nineteenth century the situation changed due to the Russian expansion to the south and its victories in the Russo–Persian Wars of 1804–13 and 1826–8.

Concerning the European sources, the nineteenth-century memoirs and records on Georgia can be divided into three basic groups. These groups reflect changes in the political and economic situation in the East–West relations which had immediate implications for Georgia. The first period coincides with the 'Great Game' during the

Napoleonic Wars when Georgia inadvertently became part of France's Eastern policy. The second period was a time of increasing economic interest in Georgia and its capital Tbilisi, which by then (especially under the so-called preferential tariff policy) had become a transit trade route for European and above all French goods going East and to Iran in particular. The third period focused less on supporting European states' political and economic interests, as by then Russia had consolidated its position in the Caucasus. Three main dates in the process of the consolidation of Russian authority in Georgia during the first third of the nineteenth century can be cited. Firstly, the annexation of the eastern Georgian kingdom by the Russian Empire in 1801. Secondly, the Treaty of Culistan after the 1804–13 Russo–Persian War, whereby Iran surrendered its claims to eastern Georgia and to the important part of the eastern Transcaucasia, which signalled the end of Iran's interference with political affairs of Georgia. Thirdly, the Treaty of Turkmanchai after the 1826–8 Russo–Persian War, through which Iran was obliged to finally concede eastern Transcaucasian territories to the Russian Empire.

Russo–Persian Wars and Georgia

By virtue of its location between Asia and Europe and its traditional and original culture Georgia represented something of a bridge between East and West since Antiquity.[1] Historically, Tbilisi was perceived by Iranians as one of the most distinguished and beautiful cities in the 'Persianate' world. In medieval Iranian sources Tbilisi is even called *Dar as-sorur* (city of joy, paradise).[2]

At the end of the eighteenth century, when the Russian advance to the south became extremely sensitive for Iran, Agha Muhammad Khan attacked eastern Georgia and in 1795 a Persian army plundered Tbilisi. 'The conquest was an attempt by the emerging dynasty to stake its claim to the heritage of the Safavid dynasty and their territory,'[3] but it did not succeed in stopping the Russian advance.

The incorporation of the eastern Georgian kingdom of Kartli and Kakheti into the Russian Empire (1801) was followed by the annexation of western Georgia by Russia in 1812. Two Russo–Persian wars ensued, ending with the defeat of Iran and with Iran being obliged to recognise Russian supremacy in the south Caucasus. It is worth noting that one of the principal Iranian aims in these wars was the restoration of its domination of eastern Georgia. Iranian historian Naser Najem explains: 'The incorporation of Georgia into Russia was unbearable for Iran whose prestige had been severely damaged; this country had been considered tributary of Iran for centuries and it could not just be allowed to join such an alliance. That is why Iran was extremely frustrated and ready to put up strong resistance.'[4] The true state of affairs about the early Russian–Iranian conflict over Georgia is probably best captured by the French diplomat Amadée Jaubert,[5] who quotes the words of a ruler of an Azeri province, Ahmad Khan, regarding the Crown Prince Abbas Mirza: 'our current ruler [...] with his mighty hand has united everything, except Georgia, a province that in reality hasn't been part of the empire for a long time now.'[6] Thereby, the annexation of the eastern Georgian kingdom by the Russian Empire proved especially poignant for Persia.

During the first Russo–Persian War the Georgian political elite were divided. Some supported accession to the Russian Empire, while others hoped to regain the country's independence by using their connections with Iran. Some Georgian princes, initially Prince Alexander (who died in Iran in 1844), expected that in the event of an Iranian victory in the war, Georgia would be much more independent and the kingdom would be restored. These expectations had no real basis due to the weakness of Iran, which was defeated twice by Russia. Prince Teimuraz initially supported the Iranians, but from 1810 he settled in St Petersburg and achieved great success in scientific activities. Prince Teimuraz is known to have compiled an Italian–Persian–Turkish dictionary for General Gardane, the French ambassador in Iran. It was printed as a supplement to a book published in 1809 in Paris and Marseille.[7]

During the Napoleonic Wars, the Treaty of Finkenstein (April 1807) was signed between Iran and France. Iran had cancelled contacts with Britain and allied itself with France over the central issue of the south Caucasus generally and of Georgia in particular.[8] France supported Iranian claims on eastern Georgia but in an equivocal manner – in the case of Iran's success in expelling Russians from Tbilisi. However, only one month later, as a result of the Peace Treaty of Tilzit, France recognised Russian domination in the east, which amounted to the abrogation of the Treaty of Finkenstein. Under the circumstances, Iran redirected its diplomatic efforts back to Britain. Georgia still remained a vital issue for the Qajars in the negotiations between Persia and Britain, although Britain did not undertake any effective measures in favour of Iran either.[9]

This long-lasting war between Russia and Iran ended with the signing of a peace treaty in Gulistan on 12 October 1813. Iran recognised Kartli and Kakheti and Azerbaijan Khanates as the property of Russia and the Caspian Sea came under Russian control. After the second war, in 1828, the Nakhichevan and Yerevan Khanates also became Russian possessions.

Later one of the Iranian travellers stressed the undesirable consequences of the incorporation of this territory into the Russian Empire for the Georgian nobility:

> Russian authorities ordered the Viceroy of the Caucasus to grant the title of *kniaz* (noble) to all who used to be *begs*. This action was conditioned by two circumstances: first, that Georgian nobility would receive Russian citizenship with great pleasure and enthusiasm, and second, that Russian authorities during the period of domination in Caucasus opened The Land Bank. *Begs* who were transformed into *kniazs* and abandoned agriculture and cattle-herding, mortgaged their lands in this bank and received money. Thus, the lands of Georgian nobles became the property of Russia.[10]

Economic Interactions

It is during this period that Georgia attracted, practically for the first time, the attention of Europeans as a transit road to Iran. In 1807 the French general Gardane returned from Iran to Europe via Tbilisi. 'It was this journey of the French mission that first marked Tbilisi as a transit town between Persia and Europe.'[11]

As was stressed, by the beginning of the nineteenth century Georgia had become part of global geopolitical games. For some time to come Georgia would become a bargaining chip in the Great Game, but the country retained political significance of this kind for only a short while. Nonetheless, it was the first time Europe had a clear perception of Georgia from political and military points of view as a crossroads between Europe and Asia. Set as it was halfway between the Caspian and the Black Sea, Tbilisi was a natural transit point for visitors of every nationality and for economic transactions.

Even before the annexation of the Georgian kingdom, European travellers emphasised the favourable geographical position of Georgia for trade with the East. For example, in the 1760s, the French traveller, Peyssonel, wrote: 'Tbilisi indeed is the most convenient place for establishing trade with Persia.' The same author went on to say: 'at times there is a possibility in Tbilisi of purchasing Iranian goods of any kind. These goods are delivered from Ganja, Shemakh, Tavriz, Erivan and Erzurum.'[12]

Following a gradual conquest of the south Caucasus by Russia, the idea of linking the trade routes of the Black Sea and those of the Caspian was again revived. The south Caucasus was seen as a bridge between Europe and Asia as it was a convenient route for transit trade. Russia wanted to revive this transit route and, by the decree of 8 October 1821, temporary (for ten years) preferential tariffs were introduced. Customs-duties imposed on goods imported from Europe were set at only 5 per cent of the price of goods and transit of European goods bound for Iran via Transcaucasia was made toll-free. Thanks to this decree, Tbilisi soon turned into a specific transit point of European and Asian commodities.

France was especially interested in the economic importance of Georgia as a transit road to Iran and to the East more generally. The French consulate opened in Tbilisi specifically for the purpose of making use of Georgian territory for trade with the East. The French consul in Tbilisi during 1820s, Jacques–François Gamba, wrote about the Black Sea and therefore the significance of the Georgian territory: 'an adequate measure to contain England's monopoly and excessive might, and free Europe from her influence, would be the reunification of Europe and Asia, interconnecting the two through the Black Sea.'[13]

Europeans were also interested in developing industries in Georgia and in importing goods produced here to Iran. In 1827, a Frenchman named Castella built a silk-spinning mill in Georgia. Several skilled workers came from France to work for Castella, but most of the workers – usually 15 to 20 but sometimes as many as 50 – were local. Most of the machinery, of course, was imported. This factory attracted the attention of an Iranian traveller in 1829, who wrote: 'Among the enterprises in Tbilisi should be noted the silk factory which was built by one Frenchman, but he couldn't complete this work because he died.'[14]

However, in 1831 the Russian government cancelled the toll-free regime and consequently for Europeans the significance of Georgia's territory for trade with Iran was diminished.[15] Later, in 1885, the Iranian traveller Farahani wrote: 'Commerce in this city is controlled by

Russia so far because goods basically arrive from there. There used to be a transit road for European countries' goods entered in Iranian *vilayets* and Rum via Tbilisi. Now this road is closed and the profits of merchants are diminished. Though there is another sort of commerce in Tbilisi, for example silk, other goods are imported from Rasht and Khorasan.'[16]

Europeans Visiting Tbilisi

The French consul, Gamba, was primarily interested in economic aspects, but travellers in subsequent years not only paid attention to economic aspects, they also took notice of other features, such as the multi-ethnic and multi-confessional character of Tbilisi. These included everyday life of Tbilisi citizens, changes in the city's architecture, the effects of exposure to European culture and, at the same time, the close cultural ties with Persia. It should be noted that, according to the French traveller Bélanger, Persian language even in the late 1820s was popular in Georgia, especially among the nobility, and knowledge of this language was considered as *de bon ton*, so too was imitating Persian manners.[17] Simultaneously, a European-style public school started to educate Europeanised young citizens of Tbilisi.[18] If the parents spoke Persian, their children began to study European languages. This process continued throughout the first third of the nineteenth century.

European travellers were particularly impressed by the transformation of Tbilisi from a small Asian town into a European city. Alexandre Dumas, who visited Tbilisi in 1859, wrote in his *Caucasus*:

> [T]hose who know Tbilisi only by Klaproth and Gamba's accounts would not guess it was the same city, which the two travellers described, should they arrive in the city today [...] I admit that when I was coming to Tbilisi I thought I would see a half-savage town. But it seems I was wrong. Thanks to the French colony, which is primarily made up of Parisian tailors and milliners, Georgian ladies are only two weeks late in keeping up with the fashion trends of the Italian theatre and the Grand Boulevard.[19]

On the other hand, Dumas was also charmed by the Asian side of the city, especially by the famous Persian baths of Tbilisi. During his stay in Tbilisi Dumas visited these baths several times and he even thought to invite masseurs of Tbilisi to France.[20]

The account of the French traveller E. Orsolle, who visited Georgia in the 1880s, centres on a description of the ethnic and confessional diversity of Tbilisi's population. Orsolle provides valuable information on Persian nationals of the Russian Empire:

> [A]s for the Persians of Yerevan province, who have been the Tsar's subjects since 1828, they have joined the Russian army and administration voluntarily; knowledge of eastern languages makes them very useful in the Asian provinces; being adroit and intelligent the majority of them have become completely European in their habits and ideas, and have sometimes achieved high posts; above all they are remarkable gentlemen; many of them speak French fluently.[21]

From a social point of view the most advanced stratum among the subjects of Iran were merchants, followed by artisans, other workers and hired labourers. Orsolle writes on the Iranians of Tbilisi: 'the majority of these Iranians are businessmen and they are distinguished by their intelligence. We should trust the saying: "it takes two Jews to rob one Armenian, and it takes two Armenians to rob one Persian".'[22]

The Dutch traveller Chevalier Lyclama à Nijeholt devoted his attention to describing Tbilisi neighbourhoods: 'The Sololaki district is almost entirely Russian and most houses here are private. There is also the palace of a prince, a descendant of the last king of Georgia. Here are the residences of the French and Persian consuls.'[23] It is worth noting that the French and the Persian consulates are located side by side.

Another French traveller Le Baron de Baye stresses the great authority of the Shi'i leader Akhund-Zadeh with the city population and also his links with Iran:

> A visit to the Shi'i spiritual leader of the Transcaucasian Sheikh ol-Eslam was very interesting. His name is Akhund-Zadeh. He is from the Tartar Azerbaijan and about sixty years old. He was born in Elizabetpol which adopted the Persian language and he comes from the mullah's family. He must be grateful to the Caucasus administrators for his appointment; therefore he can be regarded as a functionary, although he makes use of his strong influence over his coreligionists.[24]

Iranians in Tbilisi

In the nineteenth century, Persians comprised the largest Muslim community of Tbilisi. For the most part, the Persian population retained their Iranian nationality and remained subjects of the Iranian shah. There were two Muslim educational institutions in Tbilisi: one for Shi'i Muslims (opened in 1847) and another for Sunnis, where in addition to Persian and Arabic Languages, Russian Language, World History and Literature, Geography, Arithmetic and Physics were taught. Both schools were under the patronage of the Sheikh ul-Islam of the Caucasus. Several prominent Iranians taught in these schools, for example Fazel Khan Garusi.[25] There were also Iranian charity organisations: the Caucasus Muslim Women's Charity Organisation and the Iranian Charity Organisation.[26] At the beginning of the twentieth century, through the efforts of the Charity Organisation of Iranians (founded in 1905) and the Iranian consul in Tbilisi Mofammakh as-Soltaneh, two other schools were opened: firstly *Ettefaq-e Iranian* (Union of Iranian) and secondly *Nejjat* (Liberation). The first was situated in the Muslim district of Tbilisi – Shaitan-Bazaar – and sometimes was called the School of Shaitan-Bazar. Though initially it was a school for boys, it was latterly transformed into a co-educational school. It is in Tbilisi that Iranians encountered, for the first time, European theatre which was fundamentally different from the traditional Iranian theatrical performances, which comprised of religious mysteries and impromptu comic performances.

Despite extensive Europeanisation during the second half of the nineteenth century, which also affected the town's Muslim population (especially the privileged classes), clothes retained specific ethnic characteristics. For instance, a tradition of dyeing the hair and beard with henna was maintained for a long time and the frequency of the practice marked the Persians from the rest of the community until the beginning of the twentieth century.[27] But even in this regard, Iranian travellers were not always satisfied by the Europeanisation of Tbilisi and especially by the lifestyle transformation of their compatriots. In spite of the relatively closed character of the Persian community in Tbilisi, centuries of co-existence side by side with Christians noticeably affected their customs and mode of life.

Most unacceptable for Iranian travellers (especially in the first half of the nineteenth century) were changes in behaviour and lifestyle within

Tbilisi's Iranian inhabitants after the incorporation of Georgia into the Russian Empire (women's behaviour and clothing, the drinking of alcohol et cetera). Mirza Abul-Hasan Khan Shirazi Ilchi, during his trip to St Petersburg as an emissary of Fath Ali Shah, visited Tbilisi in 1824. He wrote: 'After the conquest of Georgia by Russia, in Tbilisi wine drinking was widespread and local women forgot innocence and honesty.'[28] In reality, wine making and wine drinking were always widespread in Georgia even during Iranian domination. Ilchi believed that the lowering of moral standards was the main result of Russian rule in Georgia. He was outraged by the relaxed manners resulting from the pernicious Russian influence.

Later, in 1863, another Iranian traveller Seyf ad-Douleh stressed:

> In this town a huge amount of pork is eaten and wine is drunk. People are clean and well dressed. In Tbilisi and [other regions] Georgian Muslims, women as well as men, are dressed like local Christians and speak their language. Women, according to Christian tradition, don't cover their faces [. . .] In taverns music is playing [. . .] This country is absolutely different from our country. Here, except for piety and honesty, you can find anything. God forbid Muslims go in this country so that they may not be defiled by the temptation and filth of Satan.[29]

It is worth noting that at the end of the century such assessments became more neutral and even positive towards the emancipation of women.

Later, in 1879 and 1885, other travellers who visited Tbilisi stressed: 'Muslims and non-Muslims mix together. It is very difficult to distinguish them. You can recognise Iranian travellers to Tbilisi only by their merchants' clothing.'[30] 'Muslims live here like Christians, they do not keep their distance from them, they eat the food of Christians and the cattle slaughtered by them, and drink all sorts of strong drinks.'[31] The fact that many Persians in Tbilisi did not abstain from wine is confirmed by publications in the nineteenth-century newspapers.[32]

It must be stressed that at the end of the century this perception had changed. So-called Iranian freethinkers were already interested in the comparative equality of men and women, women's social activities et cetera. At the beginning of the twentieth century Iranian general Majd os-Saltaneh noted approvingly that 'you cannot find in Tbilisi uneducated and illiterate women. There were special schools for girls and after graduation they became secretaries, accountants, musicians and found employment in other professions.'[33]

Two Persian publishing houses operated in Tbilisi – Gheirat and Aigrepin. Tbilisi editors issued Persian textbooks, phrasebooks, classic works of Persian literature, as well as historical works, children's literature, financial accounts of Iran's charitable society and the madrasseh Ettefaq, and even instructions for the sewing machines produced by the Singer company.[34] When the first book was printed in Tabriz in 1817, calligraphists and ulemas reacted extremely negatively to this innovation.[35] Additionally, it was very difficult to obtain printing materials. Therefore, because of this, Tbilisi became one of the major exporters of books to Iran, especially textbooks. Iranian authors gave special attention to the Consulate of Iran in Tbilisi. Majd os-Saltaneh wrote: 'In no city is Iran's state consulate as privileged as in Tbilisi; a special building with magnificent furniture is designated for it. The subjects are well pleased [. . .]. The consulate is a place of ceremonial receptions, paying respect and relaxation.'[36]

In the second half of the nineteenth century Tbilisi became a major telegraph and postal junction, linking the Caucasus and Russia with Iran. After the building of the Tbilisi–Poti railway in 1872 and the Tbilisi–Baku line in 1883, Tbilisi turned into a major railway transit artery of the Caucasus. Rapid development of the city and expansion of the communications network enabled Iran to use Tbilisi in its economic, political and cultural relations both with Russia and Europe. The shortest and safest way to Europe increasingly attracted the attention not only of merchants but also of statesmen of Iran. The fact that during his three journeys to Europe from Iran in 1873, 1878 and 1889 Naser al-Din Shah passed through Tbilisi speaks for itself.[37]

The Persian population in Georgia started growing rapidly from the late nineteenth century, due to an influx of the destitute which were forced to leave Iran, partly because of economic grievances but also through the need for opponents of the shah's regime to flee persecution. Iranian politician and traveller Hasan Taqi Zadeh,[38] who arrived in Tbilisi during the Russo–Japanese War (1904–5), stressed the importance of Tbilisi for Iran as a European city: 'This city was my first gateway to Europe and there, like in Europe, everything was European and Russian. I stayed in Tbilisi approximately one month and learnt lots of useful things.'[39] According to Majd os-Saltaneh, the chief reason for him to move to Tbilisi was that 'as is known to everybody, there are no conditions to receive education in our country at present.'[40]

During the Iranian Constitutional Revolution, there operated in Tbilisi the Society of Iranian Mojaheds (mujahideen). Mojaheds were political opponents of the regime in Iran, who were expelled from their homeland and scattered in different countries. The Iranian author Yahya Daulatabadi wrote about the activities of the Society of Mojaheds in Tbilisi in 1908:

> Some years ago [ideas of] enlightenment were spread in Iran and Iranians who left to go abroad were distinguished in this spread of new ideas. In the Caucasus Iranians, through the help of the Iranian ambassador in Russia at that time Hasan khan Moshir ad–Douleh, created a charitable organisation. They elaborated an excellent charter and presented it to the Russian authorities for signing. As a result madrasseh 'Ettefaq' ('Ettefaq-e Iranian') was opened. But after the dissolution of the National Assembly in Iran, this society was also weakened and now isn't active.[41]

He was also disappointed by the unfavourable conditions for the activities of free-thinking Iranians:

> In the struggle for the prosperity of the country and people in Iran they placed their hopes in Caucasian Muslims and in the Caucasus – on Tbilisi. In Tbilisi there is only one society and the situation is so that till now they cannot solve internal problems, so when will they find time for external affairs?[42]

'The Iranians working in the Caucasus and travelling between Iran and the Russian Empire became a live and mobile link that connected Tbilisi, Baku, Tabriz, and Rasht revolutionary groups.'[43] On the other hand, Caucasians actively participated in the Iranian revolution. 'While Cossack officers, fresh from suppressing the 1905 Revolution in Russia, offered Muhammad Shah the means to destroy the constitutional government in Tehran, Caucasian revolutionaries, fleeing the same Russian conflict, formed the backbone of constitutional resistance during the civil war.'[44]

During the Constitutional Revolution, Iranians not only targeted the Qajars' autocratic power and its abuses, but also turned against its increasing entanglement with foreign powers, notably the Russian Empire.[45] In 1907, for example, a leaflet by the Tiflis organisation of Persian Social Democrats, a revolutionary organisation of Persians in the Russian Empire, admonished people of Tabriz that 'Russian despotism has in its own interest stretched out a hand to the neighboring despot, and both want to destroy the constitution.'[46]

The reformist magazine *Mollah Nasreddin* was published in Tbilisi from 1906 until 1917. It was the first Muslim satirical magazine. This Azerbaijani periodical was 'read across the Muslim world' and had a large circulation in Iran. Mollah Nasreddin contributed much to the political activism in Iran.[47] 'It is important that Tbilisi became the cradle of the Muslim satirical press.'[48]

At the end, it must be stressed that perceptions by Iranians and Europeans of Tbilisi during the nineteenth and early twentieth centuries demonstrate its transformation from a small oriental town at the beginning of the nineteenth century to a European city with 'oriental charm' by the end of the century. In some respect, this evolution reflected changes occurring in Iran and the activities of Iranians in Tbilisi which also had an important impact.

Notes

1. See for example: Kalistrat Salia, *History of the Georgia Nation* (tr. from French). (Paris, 1983); Marie-Felicité Brosset, *Histoire de la Géorgie, depuis l'antiquité jusqu'au XIXe siècle* (tr. from Georgian) (St Petersburg, 1856); David M. Lang, *The Georgians* (London, 1966).
2. See Grigol Beradze, 'Among the Chosen Cities: Tbilisi in the Shi'i Tradition', in *Journal of Persianate Studies*, vol. 1, No. 2 (2008), pp. 206–17.
3. Moritz Deutschmann, '"All Rulers are Brothers": Russian Relations with the Iranian Monarchy in the Nineteenth Century', in *Iranian Studies*, 2013, vol. 46, No. 3 (2013), p. 384.
4. Naser Najem, *Irān dar mian-e tufan* (Tehran, 1334/1915), p. 51.
5. George Sanikidze, 'A Historical Survey of the Georgian–Iranian Relations in the Nineteenth Century' in *Journal of Persianate Studies*, vol. 1, No. 2 (2008), p. 153.
6. Amadée Jaubert, *Mogzauroba somkhetshi da sparsetshi 1805–1806 tslebshi* [*Voyage en Arménie et en Perse fait dans les années 1805–1806*], tr. I. Natchkebia into Georgian. (Tbilisi, 1997), p. 118.
7. See: *Journal d'une voyage dans la Turquie d'Asie et la Perse, fait en 1807 et 1808* (Paris, 1809). *Vocabullario italiano–persico et turco, composto Da Sua Altezza Serenissimo Timuraz*, Principe die Giorgia, pp. 1–52; Guram Sharadze, *Teimuraz Bagrationi*, I–II. (Tbilisi, 1972–4) (in Georgian); Irene Natchkebia.

'Journal d'un voyage of Ange de Gardan and Vocabulario Timurat-Mirza in Journal de l'Empire (1808)', in *Literary Researches*, XXIV (Tbilisi, 2002), pp. 415–20.

8. For the Treaty of Finkenstein and the place of Georgia in this treaty, see Irene Natchkebia. 'La place de Géorgie dans le traité de Finkenstein (1807)', in I. Nathkhebia and F. Hellot-Bellier, *La Géorgie et Tbilissi entre la Perse et l'Europe* (Paris, 2008), pp. 95–114; I. Amini, *Napoléon et la Perse, Les relations franco–persanes sous le Premier Empire dans le context des rivalités entre la France, l'Angleterre et la Russie* (Paris, 1995).
9. Natchkebia, 'traité de Finkenstein', p. 109.
10. *Khaterat-e Perens Arfa*, be kushesh-e Ali Dehbashi (Tehran, 1378/1999). *Georgia in Persian Sources of the Qajar Period. Travelogues and Memoirs*, tr. Marina Alexidze into Georgian (Tbilisi, 2016), p. 319.
11. Irene Natchkebia, 'Tbilissi–Porte de la Perse à la limite des XVIIIe et XIXe siècles', in *Orientalist*, I (Tbilisi, 2001), pp. 196–204.
12. Ch. De Peyssonel, *Essay sur les troubles actueles de Perse et de Georgie* (Paris, 1754), p. 153.
13. Jacques–François Gamba. *Voyage dans la Russie méridionale, et particulièrement dans les provinces situées au delà du Caucase, fait depuis 1820 jusqu'en 1824 par le chevalier Gamba, consul du roi à Tiflis*, I–II (Paris, 1826); Georgian translation: *Mogzauroba amierkavkasiashi* [*Voyage en Transcaucasie*], I, tr. Mzia Mgaloblishvili (Tbilisi, 1987), p. 36.
14. *Safar-name-ye Khosrow Mirza be Petersburg, be qalam-e Mirza Mostafa Afshar (Baha al-Molk), be kushesh-e Mohammad Golbon* (Tehran, 1349/1970), in *Georgia in Persian Sources of the Qajar Period*, p. 96.
15. Detailed analysis of European-Iranian toll-free trade via Georgia, see: George Sanikidze, 'Georgian–Iranian Relations', pp. 155–60.
16. Mirza Mohammad Hoseyn Farahani (Golbon), *Safar-name*, be kushesh-e Hafez Farman Farmayan (Tehran, 1342/1964), in *Georgia in Persian Sources of the Qajar Period*, p. 405.
17. C. Bélanger, *Voyage aux Indes Orientales, par le Nord de l'Europe, les provinces du Caucase, la Géorgie, l'Arménie et la Perse, suivi de détails topographiques et autres sur le Pergou, les îles de Java, de Maurice et de Bourbon, sur le cap de Bonne-Espérance et Sainte-Hélène pendant les années 1827, 1828 et 1829*, I–VIII, 8 et 3 grands atlas (Paris, 1836–1846), II, p. 31.
18. This school - the Gymnasium of Tbilisi was founded in 1830 on the model of the school for nobles which operated from 1804. The gymnasium had direct links with the editorial house of Leipzig. Except general education subjects, students learned foreign languages; there were lessons of music and dances, gymnastics and fencing; there was also an orchestra created by the students. Orthodox and Armenian–Gregorian priests, Roman Catholic and Lutheran pastors, Jewish and Muslim religious teachers also served in the Gymnasium.
19. Alexandre Dumas, *Le Caucase*, tr. T. Kikodze into Georgian (Tbilisi, 1970), pp. 334, 340.
20. Ibid., p. 338.
21. Ernst Orsolle, *Le Caucase et la Perse* (Paris, 1885), p. 43.

22. Ibid.
23. Lyclama à Nijeholt and T. M. Chevalier, *Voyage en Russie, au Caucase et en Perse Pendant les années 1866, 1867 et 1868*, vol. 1 (Amsterdam and Paris, 1872), p. 358.
24. Le Baron de Baye, *Tiflis. Souvenirs d'une mission* (Paris, 1900), p. 9.
25. About Fazel Khan Garusi's life and activities in Georgia see, for example, Marina Alexidze. 'Fazel Khan Garusi in Tbilisi', in M. Alexidze, *the Muslim East in the Nineteenth Century. Studies in The history of Culture, Religion and Life* (Tbilisi, 2011), pp. 57–67.
26. I. Anchabadze and N. Volkova, *Starij Tbilisi. Gorod i gorozhane v XIX veke* [*Old Tbilisi. City and Citizens in the Nineteenth Century*] (Moscow, 1990), p. 259.
27. George Sanikidze, 'Georgian–Iranian Relations', p. 165.
28. Mirza Abul-Hasan Khan Shirazi Ilchi, *Heyrat-name: Safar-name-ye Abul-Hasan Khan Shirazi Ilchi be Landan*, be kushesh-e Hasan Morselvand (Tehran, 1364/1986), in *Georgia in Persian Sources of the Qajar Period*, p. 61.
29. *Safar-name-ye Seyf Maruf be Safar-name-ye Makke, nevesht-e-ye Seyf ad-Douleh Soltan Mohammad*, be tashih va tashiye-ye Ali Akbar Khodaparast (Tehran, 1364/1985), in *Georgia in Persian Sources of the Qajar Period*, p. 159.
30. *Hedayat a-Hajjaj, Safar-name-ye Makketa'lif*: Mohammad Reza Tabatabai TabrIzI, be kushesh-e Rasul Jafariyan, Qum, 1386/2007, in *Georgia in Persian Sources of the Qajar Period*, pp. 349–50.
31. Mirza Mohammad Hoseyn Farahani (Golbon), *Safar-name*, be kushesh-e Hafez Farman Farmayan, Tehran, 1342/1964, in *Georgia in Persian Sources of the Qajar Period*, p. 403.
32. Marina Alexidze, 'Persians in Tbilisi (1801–1921)', in M. Alexidze. *Georgia and the Muslim East in the Nineteenth Century*, p. 21. See for example Georgian newspaper Newspaper *Iveria*, 1886, #55.
33. Majd os-Saltaneh, *Tbilisis aghtsera* [Description of Tbilisi], tr. M. Mamatsashvili from Persian (Tbilisi, 1971), p. 55.
34. Nugzar Ter-Oganov, 'Two Iranian authors, Majd os-Saltāneh and Yahya Dowlatabadi, on Tbilisi', *Tipological Researches*, IV (Tbilisi, 2000), p. 402.
35. Yves Porter, 'Arts du livre et illustration', In Yann Richard (ed.), *Entre L'Iran et L'occident. Adaptation et assimilation des idées et techniques occidentales en Iran* (Paris, 1989), p. 163.
36. Majd os-Saltaneh, *Tbilisis aghtsera*, pp. 80–1.
37. Nugzar Ter-Oganov, 'Two Iranian authors', p. 404.
38. Sayyed Hasan Taqizadeh (1878–1970) was one of the most prominent supporters of the Europeanisation of Iran. He was the founder of the Democratic Party of Iran (1909). During the Pahlavi era, he held several important political positions and contributed to the promotion of Iranian Studies throughout the world. See for example: Nikki R. Keddie (with a section by Yann Richard), *Modern Iran: Roots and Results of Revolution*, revised and updated edition (New Haven, 2003).
39. Seyyed Hasan Taqi zadeh. 'Az yaddashta-ye Taqi Zadeh', in *Yaghm*, No. 1 (283), (Tehran, 1351/1972), pp. 1–7. In *Georgia in Persian Sources of the Qajar Period*, p. 558.

40. Majd os-Saltaneh, *Tbilisis aghtsera*, p. 57.
41. Yahya Daulatabadī, *Hayat-e Yahya*, moqaddame, tashih va taliqat: Mojteba Borzabadi FarAhAnI, J. 3 (Tehran, 1387/2008), pp. 849–55. In *Georgia in Persian Sources of the Qajar Period*, p. 571.
42. Ibid., p. 572.
43. Iago Gocheleishvili, 'Georgian Sources on the Iranian Constitutional Revolution (1905–1911): Sergo Gamdlishvili's Memoirs of the Gilan Resistance', in *Iranian Studies*, vol. 40, No.1 (2007), p. 63.
44. Stephanie Cronin, 'Introduction' in Stephanie Cronin (ed.) *Iranian–Russian Encounters: Empires and Revolutions since 1800* (Abingdon, 2013), p. 21. About the participation of Caucasians in the Iranian Constitutional revolution, see also Moritz Deutschmann, 'Cultures of Statehood, Cultures of Revolution: Caucasian Revolutionaries in the Iranian Constitutional Movement, 1906–1911', in *Ab Imperio*, 2 (2013), p. 190; Iago Gocheleishvili, 'Georgian Sources on the Iranian Constitutional Revolution'; Iago Gocheleishvili, 'Introducing Georgian Sources for the Historiography of the Iranian Constitutional Revolution (1905–1911)', in H. E. Chehabi & Vanessa Martin (eds), *Iran's Constitutional Revolution: Popular Politics, Cultural Transformations and Transnational Connections* (London, 2010), pp. 45–66.
45. Moritz Deutschmann, *Iran and Russian Imperialism: The Ideal Anarchists, 1800–1914* (Abingdon, 2015), p. 163.
46. Arkhiv vneshnei politiki rossiiskoi imperii/Archive of the Foreign Ministry of the Russian Empire (AVPRI), (Moscow), f. 144, op. 488, d. 531, 17b. Quoted in Moritz Deutschmann, *Iran and Russian Imperialism*.
47. See, for example: Ahmad Kasravi, *History of the Iranian Constitutional Revolution (TArikh-e Mashrute-ye Iran)*, vol. I, tr. E. Siegel (Costa Mesa, 2006), p. 224.
48. Alexandre Bennigsen, 'Mollah Nasreddin et la presse satirique musulmane de Russie avant 1917', in *Cahiers du monde russe et soviétique*, vol. 3, No. 3 (1962), p. 505.

CHAPTER 11

GENERATIONAL DIFFERENCES: AMERICAN MEDICAL MISSIONARIES IN IRAN, 1834–1940

Lydia Wytenbroek

American mission work in Iran began in 1834 when the American Board of Commissioners for Foreign Missions (ABCFM) sent a small group of American missionaries to Urumia to establish a mission among the Assyrians of the Church of the East (formerly referred to as the Nestorian Church).[1] The goal of the mission was to 'enable the Nestorian Church [. . .] to exert a commanding influence in the spiritual regeneration of Asia.'[2] The ABCFM hoped that Assyrian Christians, through American-missionary tutelage, would evangelise the rest of Iran.[3] In 1871, the mission was transferred from the ABCFM to the New York-based Presbyterian Board of Foreign Missions and renamed the Mission to Persia.[4] American missionaries hoped to extend their work beyond the Assyrian community in Urumia to other areas of Iran and they opened new stations in Tehran (1872), Tabriz (1873), Hamadan (1881), Rasht (1902), Kermanshah (1911) and Mashhad (1911).[5]

Medical work was an integral part of the American missionary enterprise in Iran from the beginning. When the mission was founded in 1834, missionaries undertook medical and educational work in an effort to make Christianity appealing and gain access to potential Muslim converts. First-generation missionary physicians offered medical services through ad-hoc dispensaries and clinics. They regarded medical work as a means of evangelism and patients were exposed to the Christian message in some form. Often missionary physicians would talk with their patients about Christianity or they would work alongside Iranian evangelists who would share literature and Christian teachings with patients while the patients waited to be seen by a physician. By the early twentieth century, these largely provisional medical services were replaced by modern hospitals and the American medical mission in Iran acquired a prestigious reputation for surgery. Second-generation missionaries were far more interested in founding hospitals than they were in converting patients to Christianity and they argued that medical work was a tangible act of Christian service with intrinsic value. This chapter explores the medical missionary careers of two generations of missionary physicians in Iran. Using missionary correspondence, medical reports and biographies, I argue that changing mission theology led medical missionaries to redefine the purpose of mission medical work.

When the mission was founded in 1834, the ABCFM had no plans to initiate medical work. It was, however, 'anxious to associate a physician with [the mission]'[6] so that there would be someone to look after the health and medical needs of American missionaries. The ABCFM had observed that missionaries who were sent to other mission fields often fell ill and/or died soon after they arrived overseas. It hoped to prevent this by sending a missionary physician who would 'render efficient service in caring for the health of the other [missionaries].'[7] In 1834, it secured Asahel Grant as the first medical doctor to be affiliated with the mission.[8] His main priority was to look after the health and medical needs of the missionary community. By 1839, the American missionary community in Urumia was comprised of four families, all with young children. There was a high incidence of illness in the missionary community and Grant spent much of his time caring for other missionaries.[9]

Although his primary task was looking after the health of other missionaries, Grant quickly realised that medical work was an effective way to advance the religious aims of the mission. When he arrived in Urumia in 1835, he was inundated with requests for medical assistance.[10] He wrote that 'multitudes of the sick of every description daily [crowded his] house for medicinal prescriptions.'[11] Within one year, he reportedly prescribed for 10,000 patients and performed more than 50 cataract operations.[12] Although the mission was established to reach the Assyrian community, Grant reported treating both Christian and Muslim patients who came to his dispensary.[13] Among those he treated were 'many persons of highest rank, and greatest influence, including two princes, and the families of the governor and high [mullahs].'[14] In one instance, he treated the wife of a leading mullah in the city, who later came to thank Grant for caring for his wife after she recovered.[15] Cases like this convinced Grant that the physician was able to 'procure access to places where none but [he] could go.'[16] He became convinced that the physician could use his influence to save patients from 'the endless pains of the second death.'[17] Thus, healing the body was supposedly a way to 'save the soul.'

Despite his views on the usefulness of medicine to the missionary enterprise, Grant actually spent much of his time engaged in non-medical work: preaching, establishing schools and teaching.[18] This was typical of the first generation of American missionary doctors in Iran who 'by no means limited their labors to medical practice.'[19] Grant's successor, Austin Wright, was educated as both a clergyman and a physician. He arrived in Iran in 1840 and practiced medicine, preached regularly and produced literary translations of religious texts.[20] Wright differed from Grant in that he 'had a [stronger] preference for [preaching]' than healing.[21] According to the first American missionary in Urumia, Reverend Justin Perkins, Wright thought that 'the work of the minister was *first* in importance' and he cared more about people's 'perishing immortal souls' than their 'bodies.'[22] Prior to the establishment of mission hospitals, religious work took precedence over the medical work of the mission. The ultimate goal of the Mission at this time was to re-evangelise Assyrians and convert Muslims to Christianity and medical work was only important as a means to achieve this goal.

In 1841, Grant published a book about the Assyrian community in Urumia which reveals his articulation of a discourse that positioned Assyrians as 'less civilised' than Americans. He refers to Assyrian Iranians as 'primitive Christians'[23] and argues that they were 'emerging from that state of obscurity in which they [had] for many ages been almost lost sight by the civilized world.'[24] His articulation of otherness hinged on binary hierarchical oppositions in which social and cultural differences defined Americans as superior to Iranians. Grant comments that Assyrians 'as a people' had 'sunk into the darkness of ignorance and superstition: none but their clergy could read or write; the education of their females was entirely neglected; and they attached great importance to their numerous fasts and feasts, to the neglect of purity of heart and life.'[25] These comments reveal how he represents Assyrian Iranians as Other through cultural tropes. He also seems to link disease to social problems and disorder within the Assyrian community. He writes: 'The climate is naturally very delightful; but, owing to local causes, a poisonous miasma is generated, occasioning fevers and the various diseases of malaria, to which the unacclimated stranger is specifically exposed.'[26] Not only does he point to social problems within the community as a source of disease, but he indicates that they pose a risk to the 'foreign' missionary body.

Given the importance of religious conversion to the work of the mission and Grant's social and cultural understanding of difference, it is not surprising that he used disease as a metaphor for spiritual illness. Historian Esme Cleall argues that missionaries often 'used disease to evoke sin figuratively.'[27] In a letter to his sister, Grant mentioned that he operated to remove cataracts several times a week and while this relieved physical suffering, he hoped that he 'might be made instrumental of opening the eyes of the spiritually blind!'[28] This commentary differs from second-generation missionary surgeons who were more likely to comment on the surgical efficacy of the procedure. For example, the 1905 report on medical work in Tehran notes that 37 cataract operations were performed in the hospital that year. The only case mentioned in detail is that of a seven-year-old boy who had been blind since he was two years of age. The report mentioned the removal of his bilateral cataracts as a success and went on to describe the initial challenges he faced in grasping the colour, size and appearance of objects, but there was no mention of evangelistic impact or metaphors about spiritual sight.[29]

From all accounts, it appears that patients of different ethnicities and religions flocked to missionary-run dispensaries for treatment. It seems likely that patients would have understood missionary physicians as religious healers which was a concept that already existed within the framework of traditional medicine in Iran. Historian Hormoz Ebrahimnejad argues that 'medieval Persian medicine was characterized by its supernatural or religious dimension.'[30] Traditional medicine encompassed physical and spiritual remedies, including charms, amulets, prayers and formulae.[31] Iranians were already accustomed to the involvement of the religious class in medical care and it seems possible that patients may have easily accommodated mission medicine into existing frameworks of health and healing.

The most dominant theory of traditional medicine in the Qajar era was the humoral theory.[32] Grant reported that patients often asked 'a thousand questions' which suggests that patients must have felt that they had some power within the relationship. Grant records the type of questions that patients usually asked, such as whether they should drink milk from a white cow, which was considered cold, or milk from a red cow, which was considered hot. When the patients were given instructions to make a broth, they wanted to know if they should use a hen or a rooster because one was considered dry and the other moist. These inquiries suggest that patients incorporated medical instructions and prescriptions into an understanding of health that hinged on balance between the four humours.

When missionary couple Rev. George and Dr Mary Zoeckler settled in a village outside of Hamadan in 1914, Mary set up a dispensary in the basement of their home. She mostly treated patients with medical conditions, such as pneumonia, measles and skin lacerations.[33] As she became established, she also cared for a greater number of obstetrical cases.[34] Mary's letters indicate that she encountered resistance among patients in Iran because of her gender and American nationality. In her early years as a missionary physician, Mary found that there was 'a very wide spread [sic] prejudice against foreign medicine and foreign methods.'[35] As a result, she was frequently blamed for murdering patients who happened to pass away under her care. It seems that many patients found her gender to be problematic, at least in the earlier years of her medical practice. She notes that they did not seek her out for medical care until they '[realised] that a woman [could] really be a trained physician.'[36] On one occasion, the secretary of a prominent Islamic religious leader, who had always been resistant to the Presbyterian mission, developed a sore on his back that had '[grown] worse under native treatment' so Mary was sent for as a 'last resort.'[37] When the patient recovered six weeks later, the religious leader expressed his gratitude for the work of the missionaries at a public meeting. This suggests that patients were willing to seek out medical care when it offered them tangible, physical benefits even if they did not share the religious beliefs of missionary physicians.

Many missionary physicians in the nineteenth century went on evangelical–medical itineration trips. Mary often made these trips with her husband George to the cities and towns surrounding Hamadan; she often treated patients, while he preached.[38] However, her reports imply that she took the responsibility to proselytise seriously. On a medical-itineration trip in 1925, she 'devoted most of [her] time to evangelistic work and saw only a few patients.'[39] She indicated that this reduction in medical work 'was to the gain {of} the evangelistic work {. . .} {as} many {of the patients} who {had come} {. . .} stayed to listen to the Gospel message.'[40] The following year, she went on a two-week itinerating trip with her husband but 'decided not to take along all {her} medical apparatus' so that she could 'limit {her} medical work to a minimum amount of consultation and prescription work in order to have more time for evangelistic work.'[41] These comments suggest that she viewed medical and evangelistic work as separate types of mission work and that she believed that the medical work could detract from the evangelistic work.

In her early medical reports, she usually mentioned her evangelistic efforts in relation to her work. For example, in her 1923–4 report, she noted that 'the evangelistic work in the city dispensary {had} amounted to very little.'[42] When she had the opportunity to talk about the Gospel to patients, she seems to have done so. In one of her reports, she revealed that when a Muslim woman that she had known 'quite well for some time' suffered a stroke with corresponding paralysis and loss of speech, she went to the woman's home every day and 'read her something from the New Testament.'[43] It is not surprising that Mary would include a discussion on the evangelistic aspects of her work since her reports were being sent to supporters in churches in the United States. But her willingness to engage in other forms of religious work, such as leading Bible study classes, provides evidence that spiritual witness and conversion were important to her. Furthermore, when she reported on the success of the mission, she always spoke in terms of how many people converted to Christianity, never in terms of how many people were healed.[44]

Missionary physicians who arrived in Iran after 1880 were more interested in developing professional medicine than their predecessors had been. This new wave of missionary physicians, unlike the generation before them, largely restricted their mission work to medical activities, although they expanded the scope of their medical work beyond the confines of the dispensary. Second-generation physicians can be distinguished by their desire for, and their efforts to, establish hospitals. They argued that the pressing demands of the medical work necessitated a physical structure that would allow them to treat and safely care for patients. Central to this argument was their desire to perform complex surgeries.

Missionary physician Joseph Cochran typifies the second-generation missionary physician. He was born in Urumia in 1855 to American-missionary parents and sent to the United States to complete his education at 15 years of age. He returned to Urumia in 1878, after graduating with his medical degree from the College of Physicians and Surgeons in New York,[45] and opened a dispensary which was immediately 'thronged' with patients.[46] Within a year, he had 'seen and treated over 3,000 patients.'[47] In 1879, Cochran made an appeal to the Presbyterian Board of Foreign Missions for the construction of a mission hospital.[48] He argued that there was a great opportunity for a Christian surgeon in Urumia as the 'native surgery [was] terribly rough or barbarous' and there was 'no skilled physician within 120 miles in any direction.'[49] It was illegal to perform dissections in Iran and it seems likely that this may have contributed to a lack of physicians in Iran trained in surgery at this time. Although there were many common cases that required surgical intervention, yet Cochran was 'obliged to decline nearly all [surgical] cases' because it was 'folly to perform an operation, and then send the patient home after treatment.'[50] At times, he performed small operations in his dispensary, but it only had two rooms which made it difficult for him to '[treat] and [nurse] patients on whom operations [had] been performed.'[51] He felt it was an 'injustice to [the patient,] [himself] and to the cause of Missions' to turn away patients who needed surgery.[52] The Station supported his proposal for a hospital, believing it would 'be for the best interests of the missionary cause.'[53] In 1882, Westminster Hospital, the first American hospital in Iran, was built in Urumia. Cochran devoted his life to the practice of medicine. He opened a medical school and taught Iranian students how to perform surgery.[54] His engagement with modern medicine represented a new approach to the mission's medical work. He was the first of a growing number of missionary physicians who saw themselves as medical professionals who were interested in advancing modern scientific medicine in the country.

By 1920, American physicians were operating hospitals in Tehran, Rasht, Hamadan, Tabriz, Kermanshah and Mashhad. The development of the hospital as the primary site of scientific medicine dramatically altered the provision of healthcare. The modern hospital required skilled workers, novel technology, diagnostic tools and laboratory services. Each mission hospital established its own training school for nurses and student nurses did much of the practical work on the wards. Missionary physicians in Iran performed complex operations and the mission developed a prestigious reputation for surgery. The 1905 report on the medical work of the Tehran Station noted that 'a large proportion of the patients admitted [to the hospital] were surgical cases.'[56] There was a

Figure 11.1 Cochran Memorial Hospital, Urumia, *c.*1930s.[55]

large number of European-educated Iranian physicians practising in Iran at this time, but American missionaries were able to carve out an exclusive area within the medical field in Iran by focusing on surgery.

As missionary physicians became responsible for increasingly complex hospital systems, they spent little time engaged in other areas of mission work. Missionary physicians came to value medicine as an important social service and argued that it should be motivated by compassion, not conversion. Unlike first-generation missionary physicians, second-generation missionary physicians regarded the practice of medicine as an expression of the Gospel. This shifting notion of medicine as a tool of evangelism to medicine as compassionate Christian service was influenced by changing mission ideology, developments in medical knowledge and an increasing demand for missionary medicine. As the mission underwent the transition from an evangelistic model to a social gospel model, missionary physicians faced tensions between divergent mission objectives. Second-generation missionary physicians were focused on improving medical standards and poor health, but that did not mean that they were not motivated by a religious calling. Faith remained important for many of these physicians and it was the driving force behind their pursuit of medical endeavours. Thus, medical work became the outward expression of an inward faith.

Mission historians have argued that there was a shift in Protestant mission ideology in the early twentieth century when the traditional evangelistic model of missions was gradually replaced by a new model of missions.[57] This new model of missions was influenced by the social gospel movement, which was a religious movement that applied Christianity to social issues. Proponents of the social gospel argued that Christians should express their piety through social service initiatives aimed at eradicating social problems, such as poverty, illness and illiteracy. The movement provided a religious justification to address social problems. The social gospel impulse re-shaped mission ideology. Although missionaries had always engaged in social service work, this work came to be seen as a way to 'reconstruct' societies and 'civilise' non-Christian nations. As a result, medical work came to be valued for its efforts to create healthy citizens and communities. Furthermore, Americans became much more interested in mission medical work at this time and began to donate large sums of money to specific mission medical projects. This reinforced the value of the mission medical work and contributed to the rise of medicine as a defining feature of the mission to Iran.

Mission medicine also offered tangible services that some Iranians utilised and appreciated. The high demand for missionary services reinforced the importance of the medical work. Missionary physicians began to recognise the importance of providing medical care during the cholera epidemics of 1892 and 1904 and this transformed their vision for mission medicine. The mission station in Tehran became the epicentre of relief work in the city during both epidemics. During the 1892 epidemic, the mission hospital, constructed in 1889 but never used because of a lack of medical staff, was 'opened temporarily for the care of cholera patients.'[58] An American physician took charge of the hospital, two male clerical missionaries acted as head nurses and a corps of boys from the mission school, ages 14 to 20, acted as volunteer nurses.[59] Another missionary, Rev Potter, visited patients in their homes.

The medical relief work mobilised all members of the mission, even those who were not trained as medical professionals.

When cholera again reached Tehran in June 1904, the mission hospital on the east side of the city was 'converted from a general hospital into one for cholera cases' and a refuge hospital was opened on the west side of the city.[60] These epidemics transformed American medical mission work from a peripheral activity of the mission to a vital service. They raised the status of the medical work and the mission as a whole. The Shah and elite government officials commended the mission for its relief efforts. Following the epidemic, the Iranian government requested that missionary physician John Frame take charge of a new government hospital in Rasht, which he did for a short while. This suggests that the Iranian government mobilised American personnel in its construction of modern medical services in the country.[61] The experience of providing medical aid during the epidemics also caused missionary physicians to envision themselves as humanitarian workers. Missionary physician Wishard wrote that '[his] motives [for the relief work] were only humanitarian in character.'[62]

With the establishment of mission hospitals and the increasing importance of the mission's medical work, missionary physicians came to articulate difference through biological markers, rather than cultural ones. Photographs depicting the medical work feature Iranians with large tumours and disfiguring sores and lesions and represent a pathologised Iranian body. In medical reports, patients are referred to by their diseases rather than their names. The disease is named and known, but the individual remains unnamed and unknown. As a result, disease becomes coded as Iranian. The diseased Iranian body is juxtaposed with descriptions of missionary surgeons' expertise. In their medical reports, missionary physicians describe the surgical equipment and technology used to 'cure' patients, suggesting that they considered technology crucial to the superiority of modern medicine.

A 1922 evaluative report on the India and Iran Missions, written by Robert Speer and Russell Carter for the Presbyterian Board of Foreign Missions after they visited the mission field, praised the Mission to Iran for paving the way with its surgical work. In their opinion, 'there [was] no other Mission field in the world where the medical work [exerted] a greater influence than in Persia.'[64] However, the report reveals that the place of medical work in the mission had become a contentious issue. Speer and Carter wrote that missionary doctors and evangelists in Iran

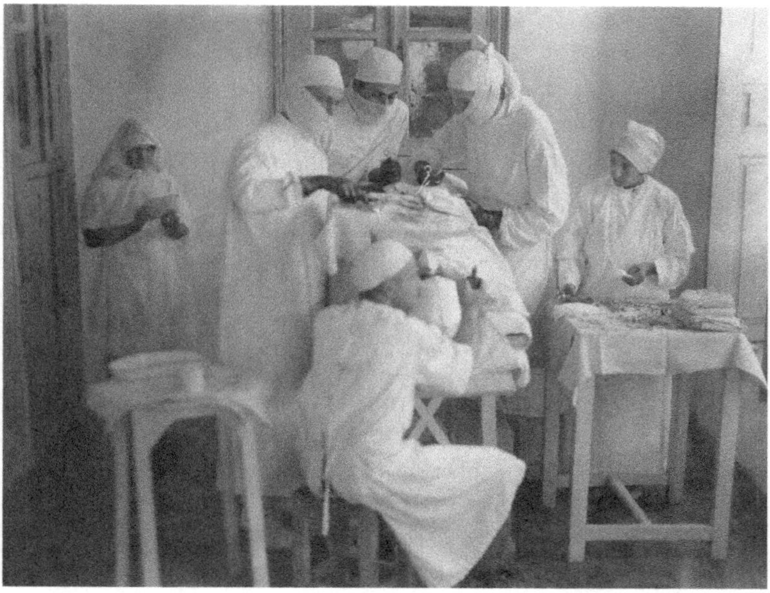

Figure 11.2 Laparotomy performed at the American Mission Hospital in Mashhad (no date).[63]

were full of 'questioning' about the 'efficiency of the medical work as a direct agency of conversion.'[65] This suggests that missionary physicians in Iran faced tensions as they sought to provide medical care within competing models of medical missions. Speer and Carter also noted their disappointment with the small number of people who had converted to Christianity and argued that the 'doctors in charge of the hospitals should regard themselves also as primarily and chiefly responsible for the evangelistic work in the hospitals' which suggests that missionary doctors were not concerned with the evangelistic work. Speer and Carter recommended that missionary physicians 'should seek, instead of the largest volume of operations and treatments, to make their work both in its medical and in its evangelistic efforts qualitatively as efficient as possible.'[66]

These recommendations meant little to missionary physicians in Iran, who were overworked and trying to deal with an increased demand for missionary medical services. Physicians in Iran at this time were interested in 'curing' Iranian bodies, not proselytising. The 1930–1 report of the American Christian Hospital in Mashhad included several quotes regarding the 'place of medical missions in the work of the church' which suggest that missionary physicians felt that medical missions should be motivated by compassion, not conversion. For example, this quote was printed on the front cover of the report: 'As the Christian Church, animated by the same spirit of divine compassion, seeks to follow in [Christ's] footsteps, it should attempt wherever needed, to carry on effectively the ministry of healing. Work done in this spirit is spiritual work.'[67] Missionary physicians argued that 'the medical work should be regarded in itself as an expression of the Spirit of the Master and should not be thought of only as a pioneer of evangelism.'[68] These quotes suggest that medical missionaries in Iran considered their work a direct application of practical Christianity. Missionary physician John Wishard, in 1908, illustrated this view well when he stated: 'human suffering [. . .] needs medical men who make their profession a mission as well as a career.'[69]

Even missionary physician Zoeckler became increasingly preoccupied with her medical work over time. While she continued to make itineration trips, she was unable to 'do evangelistic work' as the demands for medical care were so great.[70] Efforts to integrate evangelism with medical work also failed. On one itineration trip in 1930, so many patients came for assistance that 'all [the] evangelistic staff were pressed into service as assistants or policemen to handle the patients.' Zoeckler indicated that the trip could not be considered successful 'from an evangelistic point of view [. . .] as [the] evangelists were fairly swamped by the amount of medical work to be done.'[71] There was a complete turnabout as evangelists were now pressed to abandon their evangelical work in favour of medical work, rather than the other way around.

By the 1930s, the position of medicine in the mission had changed and the deputation report on medical work in Iran in 1939 noticeably valued medical work in its own right. The deputation committee indicated that 'the ministry of health and healing [belonged] to the essence of the Gospel, and [was] therefore an integral part of the mission to which Christ [had] called, and is calling, His Church.'[72] Furthermore, it stated that 'missionary physicians should not feel that in serving the leaders of a community they [were] failing to render service in the Cause of Christ.'[73] The committee did feel that there should be a closer integration between evangelistic and medical work and it suggested that the mission adopt a policy of having a full-time missionary evangelist to work in each hospital, which seems to have been the approach taken by the mission. The report also praised medical missionaries for advancing 'modern medicine in the country' and suggested that 'Mission hospitals [should] be leaders of [medical] progress' in Iran.[74]

The evangelistic goals of the Mission to Iran never really materialised. Historian Matthew Davis estimates that perhaps 300 to 500 Muslim Iranians converted to Christianity, for a variety of reasons, by 1940.[75] American humanitarian initiatives, however, were extensive and had a significant impact on cultural changes, including the development of healthcare, in Iran.[76] I argue that the shift from dispensary to hospital-based care coincided with a redefinition of mission medical work. Second-generation physicians who were interested in the operation of hospitals and surgical advancements began to define their medical work as 'practical Christianity' and argued that providing medical care was in essence spiritual work.

Notes

1. Justin Perkins, *Missionary Life in Persia: Being Glimpses at a Quarter of a Century of Labors Among the Nestorian Christians* (Boston, MA, 1861), p. 12.
2. Justin Perkins, *A Residence of Eight Years in Persia, Among the Nestorian Christians* (Andover, MA, 1843), p. 31.
3. Matthew Mark Davis, 'Evangelizing the Orient: American Missionaries in Iran, 1890–1940,' PhD diss., Ohio State University (2001), p. 93; Presbyterian Church in the U.S.A. Iran Mission, *A Century of Mission Work in Iran (Persia), 1834–1934* (Beirut, 1936), p. 2.
4. Robert Speer and Russell Carter, 'Report on India and Persia of the Deputation sent by the Board of Foreign Missions of the Presbyterian Church in the U.S.A. to visit these fields in 1921–22' (New York, 1922): p. 323.
5. James Bassett, *Persia: Eastern Mission, A Narrative of the Founding and Fortunes of the Eastern Persia Mission, with a Sketch of the Versions of the Bible and Christian Literature in the Persian and Persian–Turkish Languages* (Philadelphia, 1890), p. 75; Michael Zirinsky, 'A Panacea for the Ills of the Country: American Presbyterian Education in Interwar Iran,' in *Iranian Studies* 26, no. 1 (1993): pp. 119–37; Michael Zirinsky, 'A Presbyterian Vocation to Reform Gender Relations in Iran: The Career of Annie Stocking Boyce,' in *Women, Religion and Culture in Iran*, Sarah Ansari and Vanessa Martin (eds) (Surrey, 2002), p. 51.
6. Perkins, *A Residence of Eight Years in Persia*, p. 30.
7. S. G. Wilson, *Persia: Western Mission* (Philadelphia, 1896), p. 261.
8. Thomas Laurie, *Dr. Grant and the Mountain Nestorians* (Boston, MA, 1853), pp. 16–17.

9. Judith Grant to father, 2 January 1839, as cited in William W. Campbell, *A Memoir of Mrs. Judith S. Grant, Late Missionary to Persia* (New York, 1844), p. 137.
10. Asahel Grant, *The Nestorians; or, The Lost Tribes; Containing Evidence of Their Identity; An Account of Their Manners, Customs, and Ceremonies* (London, 1841), p. 64; Campbell, *Memoir of Mrs. Judith S. Grant*, pp. 104, 111.
11. Asahel Grant to Mother and Sister, 11 May 1836 as cited in Asahel Grant, *Memoir of Asahel Grant, M.D.: Missionary to the Nestorians* (New York, 1847), p. 55; Grant, *Nestorians*, pp. 81–2, 68.
12. Grant, 'Appeal to Pious Physicians', pp. 208–9.
13. Judith Grant to Margaret, 13 April 1836 as cited in Campbell, *Memoir of Mrs. Judith Grant*, p. 111.
14. Grant, 'Appeal to Pious Physicians', p. 208.
15. Sarah Wright McDowell, 'A Century of Medical Work in Iran', given to author by Prof. T. Ricks, transcribed by David McDowell, McDowell Archives, p. 2.
16. Grant, *Nestorians*, pp. 3–4.
17. Grant, 'Appeal to Pious Physicians', pp. 208–9.
18. Perkins, *Eight Years in Persia*, p. 245; Grant, *Memoir*, p. 66.
19. Perkins, *Life in Persia*, p. 128.
20. Ibid., pp. 70, 128; Perkins, *Beloved Physician*, p. 8.
21. Perkins, *Beloved Physician*, p. 25.
22. Ibid., p. 28;
23. Grant, *Nestorians*, p. 79.
24. Ibid., p. 13.
25. Ibid., p. 17.
26. Ibid., p. 20.
27. Esme Cleall, *Missionary Discourses of Difference: Negotiating Otherness in the British Empire, 1840–1900* (New York, 2012), p. 80.
28. Asahel Grant to Mary, 15 June 1836, as cited in Grant, *Memoir*, p. 58.
29. *The Sixty-Eighth Annual Report of the Board of Foreign Missions of the Presbyterian Church in the United States of America* (New York, 1905).
30. Hormoz Ebrahimnejad, 'Religion and Medicine in Qajar Iran', in Robert Gleave (ed.), *Religion and Society in Qajar Iran* (Oxford, 2005), p. 402.
31. Ali Jalali, 'Traditional Medicine and Medicinal Plants in the Qajar Era' in Sahar Barjesteh van Waalwijk van Doorn-Khosrovani, L.A. Ferydoun Barjesteh van Waalwijk van Doorn (Khosrovani) and Manoutchehr M. Eskandari-Qajar (eds), *Qajar Era Health, Hygiene and Beauty* (Rotterdam, 2003), p. 63.
32. Jalali, Traditional Medicine', p. 66.
33. Mary Zoeckler, 'Report of Medical Work for Women, Hamadan Station, 1920–21', Record Group 280, Box 1, Folder 10 (hereafter cited as 280.1.10), Presbyterian Historical Society (hereafter PHS).
34. Mary Zoeckler, 'Report of Medical Work, Daulatabad, Malayir, 1922–1923,' (280.1.10), PHS; Mary Zoeckler, 'Report of Medical Work, 1924–1925', (280.1.10), PHS.

35. Mary Zoeckler, 'Report of Medical Work for Women, Daulatabad Sub-station, 1914–1915', (280.1.10), PHS.
36. Mary Zoeckler to Friends, 22 September 1940, (280.1.8), PHS.
37. Mary Zoeckler, 'Report of Medical work, Daulatabad Sub-station, 1916–1917', (280.1.10), PHS.
38. Mary Zoeckler, 'Report of Medical Work, Daulatabad-Malayir, 1915–16', (280.1.10), PHS.
39. Mary Zoeckler, n.d., (280.1.9), PHS.
40. Mary Zoeckler, 'Report of Medical Work, Daulatabad, Malayir, Persia, 1925–1926', (280.1.10), PHS.
41. Mary Zoeckler to The Women's Guild of North Church, 1 June 1926, (280.1.8), PHS.
42. Mary Zoeckler, 'Report of Medical Work, Daulatabad, Malayir, 1923–1924', (280.1.10), PHS.
43. Mary Zoeckler to Friends of the North Church, 8 February 1922, (280.1.8), PHS.
44. Mary Zoeckler, 'Personal Report, Mary A. Zoeckler, 1923–1924', (280.1.8), PHS.
45. Stephen M. Clement, 'A Hero Physician', (RG 360 Cochran SR), PHS.
46. Robert E. Speer, *"The Hakim Sahib"; The Foreign Doctor; A Biography of Joseph Plumb Cochran, M.D. of Persia* (New York, 1911), p. 54.
47. Joseph P. Cochran to Board, 'A Hospital for Persia', summer 1879 as cited in Speer, *Hakim Sahib*, p. 61.
48. Ibid., p. 61.
49. Ibid.
50. Ibid.
51. Ibid.
52. Ibid.
53. Ibid., p. 63.
54. Clement, 'Hero Physician', (RG 360 Cochran SR), PHS.
55. Hoffman, Rolla Edwards (1887–1974), Papers *c.*1915–49, RG 231, PHS. Used with permission of Hoffman's step-daughter and daughter.
56. *Annual Report* (1905), p. 273.
57. See William Hutchinson, *Errand to the World: American Protestant Thought and Foreign Missions* (Chicago, 1987).
58. *The Fifty-Sixth Annual Report of the Board of Foreign Missions of the Presbyterian Church* (New York, 1893), pp. 161–2.
59. Wilson, *Western Mission*, 310; *Annual Report* (1893), p. 162.
60. John Wishard, *Twenty Years in Persia: A Narrative of Life Under the Last Three Shahs* (New York, 1908), pp. 219–20; *The Sixty-Eighth Annual Report of the Board of Foreign Missions of the Presbyterian Church in the United States of America* (New York, 1905), p. 274.
61. 'Profile of Resht', (91.18.22), PHS.
62. Wishard, *Twenty Years in Persia*, p. 220.
63. Hoffman, Rolla Edwards (1887–1974), Papers *c.*1915–49, RG 231, PHS. Used with permission of Hoffman's step-daughter and daughter.

64. Speer and Carter, *Report on India and Persia*, p. 504.
65. Ibid., p. 504.
66. Ibid., pp. 504–5.
67. 'American Christian Hospital, Meshed, Persia, Annual Report, 1930–1931,' (91.20.1), PHS.
68. Ibid.
69. Wishard, *Twenty Years in Persia*, pp. 216–7.
70. Ibid.
71. Mary Zoeckler to Friends of the North Church, 23 January 1931, (280.1.10), PHS.
72. 'Report of the Second Century Deputation on The Medical Work in Iran,' 5 May 1939, (280.1.6), PHS.
73. Ibid.
74. Ibid.
75. Davis, 'Evangelizing the Orient', p. 94.
76. Zirinsky argues that Presbyterian missionaries, through their social and cultural endeavours, 'encouraged the development of Iran in a modern, American image.' Michael Zirinsky, 'Harbingers of Change: Presbyterian Women in Iran, 1883–1949', in *American Presbyterians* 70, no. 3 (1992): p. 173. See also: Michael Zirinsky, 'A Presbyterian Vocation to Reform Gender Relations in Iran: The Career of Annie Stocking Boyce', in *Women, Religion and Culture in Iran*, pp. 51–69.

CHAPTER 12

A NARRATIVE OF HISTORICAL AND CULTURAL TIES BETWEEN IRAN AND ROMANIA

Elham Malekzadeh

In the twentieth and twenty-first centuries, history took Iran and Romania on two very different trajectories. In 1947, Romania became a Soviet-allied country; 60 years later, it became a member of the European Union. In the space of those 60 years, Iran transitioned from a monarchy to a theocratic republic. These two seemingly unrelated countries do, however, share a common past and heritage. Both Iran's and Romania's territories were dominated by the Ottoman Empire and this mutual enemy led to a rapprochement. This chapter argues that an alliance forged in the fifteenth century sowed the seeds for a relationship which is still on-going. What started off as a purely political relation developed into strong and long-lasting cultural and economic ties. This chapter examines the evolution of Iran's and Romania's relationship through the turmoil and upheaval of the twentieth century's changing geopolitical landscape. It also encourages to re-evaluate perceptions of traditional East–West divides in the light of a broader historical understanding.

The history of modern cultural relations between Iran and Romania dates back to the years after World War I when the publication of studies on Medieval Persian History in Romania was followed by the publication in 1922 of works by celebrated Persian poets such as Saadi's *Gulistan* and Khayyam's *Rubaiyat*. Romania's interest in Iran lies in the history of relations between the two countries. During the Aq Qoyunlu and Qara Qoyunlu Turkic tribal federations (respectively 1378–1501 and 1375–1468),[1] relations between Iran and the Ottoman Empire were hostile and consequently Iranian rulers established amicable relations with the Balkan people, based on mutual animosity of the Ottomans. On the basis of unpublished primary sources in the Iran National Archive, this chapter aims to examine the cultural relations between Iran and Romania during the Pahlavi era when the majority of agreements, exchanges and cultural programmes between the two countries took place. Throughout this study, the manifestations of cultural exchanges between Iran and Romania and the history of their cultural interactions will be reviewed.

Introduction

During the rule of the Aq Qoyunlu and Qara Qoyunlu tribes in Iran, the Ottoman Empire was perceived as the common enemy of both the Iranian rulers and the Balkan people.[2] A link had thus been established among the opponents of the Ottoman sultan and relations were gradually established on the basis of friendship and cooperation. In the fifteenth and sixteenth centuries, an effective cooperation was established between Stephen the Great (*c.*1457–1504), Prince of Moldavia (corresponding to modern-day Romania), and Sultan Uzun Hasan (1471–8), the Aq Qoyunlu ruler, who forged an effective alliance against the Ottoman Sultan Mehmed II (1451–81). In 1472, Uzun Hasan's envoy, on his way to Poland, Hungary, Venice and the Papacy to seek aid against the Turks, delivered a letter from his master to Stephen requesting his support for an expedition against Mehmed II.[3] The prerequisites for collaboration were put in place between the Iranians and the Balkan people to face the Ottomans' expansionist policies. Whilst these policies were being implemented by the Janissaries (*Yeni Chery*) and with the occupation of the Balkan region by the Ottomans, Islamic traditions expanded into these territories. This in turn had a considerable cultural, literary and religious influence on the region and libraries and various religious institutions were among the main centres safeguarding the Islamic heritage. After conquering Constantinople, Sultan Mehmed II moved the capital of his empire there and continued its expansion. After a protracted war with the Serbs and Hungarians, he occupied in 1459 all of Serbia, except

Belgrade. His involvement in Bosnia (Bugumil) made his travel there easier and consequently his stays there became more frequent. After that, Bosnia was the Ottomans' European stronghold and the Bosnian beaches and ports, particularly Dubrovnik, became vital sea bases for Ottoman expeditions to other parts of Europe. As for Sarajevo, it was considered the strongest Ottoman fortress in Europe. Montenegro was then conquered in 1496 by Sultan Bayezid II (1481–1512) and finally Sultan Suleiman the Magnificent (1520–66) conquered what remained of Serbia and then occupied Hungary. From the seventeenth century, Ottoman possessions declined in Europe and from the beginning of the eighteenth century, wars against Russia weakened the Ottomans in Ukraine and the Crimea. As far as the decline in authority was concerned, the Ottomans lost almost all their remaining European territories in 1912–13 and the Ottoman Empire itself ceased to exist in 1922. Contacts forged through the shared concerns of Iranians and the Balkan people regarding the Ottoman threat made way to the development of various institutions and more broadly to the desire to establish relations beyond simple politics. Thus, cultural ties between Iran and Romania in particular became more tangible. At first, the prerequisites to establish the building blocs to this new type of relation between the two countries, who had different types of government, had to be fulfilled. In due course, communications materialised and developed, and the independent states constructed their relations in this new geopolitical context.

By using archival documents on the cultural relations between Iran and Romania, this chapter will try to present a chronological review of the history of this relationship, with the aim of providing grounds for more extensive research on the history of the relations between these two countries for historians and more specifically Romanian Iranologists. Before beginning my discussion, it must be noted that the interest of Romanian orientologists in Iran and Iranian history begins in 1795, with the translation of a volume on geography, entitled *General Geography of the World*, which portrayed Iranians as hospitable and eagerly in pursuit of science, technology and knowledge. More importantly, the volume discussed the religious differences between Shi'i Iranians and Sunni Turks,[4] as well as the cultural differences between the two nations. The author believed that the religious difference between Iranians and Turks was the main factor in their differences of behaviour, tradition and code of conduct.

Documents on the History Of Cultural Relations between Iran and Romania

In the twentieth century, a turning point occurred in the history of cultural relations between Iran and Romania. Authors and Oriental scholars in both countries benefitted from the lingering heritage of Ottoman rule over Romania and were able to exploit its rich archival material. In this way, the highest cultural and intellectual exchanges between Iran and Romania became manifest through a focus on Persian literature, especially through translations of Persian poetry.

Romania's independence in 1881[5] was immediately recognised by the Iranian government. In 1901, during the reign of the Qajar shah, Mozaffar ad-Din, the Iranian government opened an embassy in Bucharest and officially announced the highest level of relations between Iran and Romania. Moavenoldoleh Ghaffari, the then Chief minister whose official position was acknowledged in other Balkan countries, was created the first Iranian ambassador to Romania.[6] Cultural relations during the period were relatively modest, but interest by Romanian scholars and writers in Persian literature and language grew, as evidenced by the number of translations of classical Persian poetry into Romanian. It was in the same period that translations of the works of a number of famous Iranian poets such as Saadi and Khayyam, particularly sections of their works on the history of Iran and Romania in ancient times, attracted the attention and interests of Romanian orientologists towards Iran and Iranian culture. This process trickled down to a broader, non-specialised public in Romania who were thus gradually introduced to the culture and civilisation of Iran. More significant relations between Romania and Iran developed in the second half of the twentieth century as the geopolitical reality of the Cold War led to economic opportunities. As the present chapter argues, political, cultural and economic relations between Iran and Romania were closely intertwined.

Cultural exchanges benefitted from the fact that Romania houses valuable Persian documents. The Romanian Cultural House in the city of Kolohe thus curates important Persian manuscripts including copies of Saadi's *Gulistan*, *Bustan* and other lyrical works attributed to him, Hafez's poems and the romance of Joseph and Zulaikha from Jami's *Haft Awrang*.[7] The influence of Persian culture on Romanians is visible in George Kantakozino's autobiography. Kantakozino relates his journey to the Middle East in 1938 and, more importantly for us, half of the contents of the book concerns Persian literature and culture and Iran's Islamic heritage.

After Ghaffari, Iran sent three other ambassadors to Romania. In 1922, however, due to economic problems arising from the aftermath of World War I and because of internal disturbances, Iran decided to close its embassy in Romania to save resources. This closure was only to last ten years: in 1932, the Iranian embassy in Bucharest re-opened. In 1941, beligerant governments dragged Iran into World War II, meaning that political relations between Iran and Romania were cut off, so the Iranian embassy in Romania was closed. At the end of the war, an Iranian ambassador by the name of Abbas Farvahar was sent to Yuguslavia and an accredited embassy was established in Bucharest. Three years later, Iran's ambassador in Poland was accredited in Romania and ultimately from 1961 the Iranian embassy was fully re-established. Their activities were lower key than hitherto to save resources and, in 1962, its affairs assigned to Iran embassy in Belgrade. Since 1966, the Iranian embassy in Romania has been stable in its activities and since then has continued its affairs.

Reza Shah's government encouraged the establishment of political communications with countries perceived as inferior by European powers as a response to small countries feeling humiliated by powerful European governments. He made this rapprochement visible by sending the Iranian Red Lion and Sun emblem to be displayed at the gate of these countries' embassies; Romania was seen to be an important country and thus received this significant Iranian status symbol.

The establishment of the communist system in the Eastern Bloc seemed to be, in theory, an obstacle in the path of relations between Iran and Romania. In practice, however, Reza Shah's efforts to strengthen the ties between the two countries – partly as a snub to France – were not actually impeded. But it is likely that Communism coloured the views of Romanian academics who, in their studies of ancient and contemporary Iran – which they would refer to as the New Iran – mostly adopted leftist approaches. Following the cultural cooperation regarding Iranology, the Middle East Studies department of the National Culture Academy of Romania was founded in Bucharest and in early days, one member of staff was assigned with the task of conducting scientific studies and research on Persian manuscripts, particularly Ferdowsi's *Shahnameh*. The result would be the creation of the journal Studia *et* Acta Orientalia, published by the Société des Sciences

Historiques et Philologiques de la République Populaire de Roumanie and whose first number would be published in 1958.

During World War II, Iranian neutrality was breached as the Allies occupied Iran's territory, which led in 1941 to Reza Shah's abdication. Iran was able to maintain its relationship with Romania through the intercession of Japan whose embassy had been chosen to represent the interests of Romania in Iran. Yet again, the focus was on cultural exchanges. A report sent from the embassy of Romania to the Iranian government in 1953, emphasised the importance of cultural relations between the two countries. The Romanian airwaves were put to use in the promotion of Iran. Radio Bucharest played Iranian music in order to further familiarise the Romanian people with Iranian culture and civilisation. However, Iranian authorities were also aware of Romanian cultural programmes in the mainstream press that did not project a favourable view of the Persian language. In 1958, a report was sent from the Iranian Minister of Interior to the Prime Minister and other ministers of concern, informing them of the contents of Radio Romania, broadcast in Persian from Bucharest, in the city of Qasr-e Shirin. The report contained information that the radio programme in question propagated the socialist views of the Ba'ath Party in Iraq and aired negative content on the Persian language. As a result, the cultural section of the radio went under examination by the Ministry of War.[8] After one month, the ministry issued a statement on behalf of the War Minister, General Vosuq, on 19 November 1958, which declared that the content of the Persian radio of Romania must be sent to the Iranian government and in the future, all such material, including radio advertising must be sent to Iran's Ministry of War.[9] The report also indicated that the government of Romania had published the works of Iranian poets and provided a detailed account on an upcoming festival, which was to be held in Romania for the commemoration of the 700th anniversary of Saadi's *Gulistan*.[10] An earlier report sent to Iran on 27 February 1958 by the Romanian ambassador to Iran, Yun Gregsco, had already mentioned the Socialist Republic of Romania's commitment to the canonical Persian poet's commemoration and its plan to print Saadi's *Gulistan* in large numbers.[11] In the same year, in commemoration of leading Persian figures such as Saadi, Ferdowsi, Hafez and Jami, governmental journals published an anthology of their best poetry. One year later, in 1959, the Romanian government decided to facilitate the study of the Persian language for young Romanians, through the publication of a volume on Persian grammar and Romanian–Persian dictionaries.

The Iran–Romania cultural exchange programmes continued and were carried out by the authorities of both countries in subsequent years. Both governments agreed to guarantee the implementation of cultural activities. Between 1966 and 1969, the highest level of cultural cooperation was carried out between Iran and Romania. The discourse of commissions in controlling such plans reveals the extent of these cultural interactions.[12] The cultural agreement that was signed between Iran and Romania on 15 August 1967 set the basis for agreements that were to follow in later years.[13] Recommendations and opinions were compiled as a cultural plan of action for the 1960s and 1970s and they were presented to the Iranian embassy in Bucharest. The Iranian ministry of education was in charge of carrying out cultural activities and was therefore the focal point of consultation. After exchanges with the officials in charge of scholarships and the cultural relations sector in the Ministry of Foreign Affairs in 1970, it was announced that the Iranian embassy in Bucharest was to be in charge of training camps and extra-curricular exchanges. The National Scouts Organisation of Romania had agreed to receive four to five Iranian specialists to discuss the nature of the extra-curricular activities in 1970. The plan was to send two Iranians to Romania for 30 days during the academic year and two to three Iranians for the summer vacation. Their expenses were to be covered by the National Scouts Organisation of Romania and the Iranian government would only cover their travel expenses.[14]

Officials in the ministry of education examined the invitation and announced the result of their investigations as follows:

(1) The plan would enable the exchange of teachers and experts in technical fields including mechanics and the food, water and soil industries. (At the time, Romania was the biggest exporter of tractors to Iran.)
(2) The government agreed to send a young Romanian mathematician to teach at Tehran University.
(3) Four annual scholarships were to be awarded for a maximum period of four years (two scholarships for Tehran University and two scholarships for the Pahlavi University) to Romanian students.

(4) It was agreed that three Romanian specialist instructors would reside in Iran for a period of one month and a half, during which they would visit schools in rural areas and give recommendations on education curricula and facilities.
(5) A Persian-language course was to be established in either Bucharest University or Cluj University. For this reason, one full-time instructor was to be sent to Romania, with the salary provided by the Romanian government for a period of three to four years. The Iranian government favoured Cluj University because the students there were mainly Hungarian and German minorities and through them, more non-Romanians would be able to participate in the course and study Persian.
(6) Specialists would be sent to Romania to study local Romanian music and dance.
(7) One librarian would be sent to examine and document a list of Persian manuscripts in the libraries of the Romanian Academy, Cluj University and Moldavian monasteries.
(8) One art specialist would be sent to compile a list of Iranian artefacts in the National Museum of Bucharest and the Peles Castle in Sinaia.
(9) One specialist would be sent to Romanian cultural centres, and would study Romanian rural houses.
(10) One specialist would be sent to Romania to study the main institution specialising in the printing and distribution of school textbooks.
(11) In the sports sections, recommendations were made to appoint a basketball coach and purchase sports and training films.

Attempts made by the Iranian embassy in Bucharest to implement these cultural recommendations led to the development of economic relations and investments in different economic sectors such as oil and steel plants and gas piping projects. It also resulted in the establishment of permanent exhibitions of goods and economic investment opportunities of Romania in Iran. The same cultural cooperation continued in the 1970s, leading to the signing of joint economic and cultural projects including various works on Iranology.[15] The above-mentioned activities, which were carried out for the development of economic cooperation, also resulted in the signing of scientific, technical and cultural agreements between Iran and Romania. As a result, between 1969 and

1976, many bills were passed by Romania on civil and economic plans and cultural budgets were allocated. The rate of cooperation was clearly growing. A conference bringing together the ambassadors and cultural and commercial delegates of Romania was organised. The Romanian president made a speech emphasising the will to continue in the direction of creating strong relations between the two countries. In response, the Iranian embassy in Bucharest asked the foreign ministry to allocate the necessary funding for investing in cultural sections.[16] In addition, the Iranian embassy in Romania issued a statement regarding cultural proposals and recommendations of top Iranian universities, including Tehran University and the Pahlavi University in Shiraz.

The proposals read as follows:

(1) Concert and theatre exchanges were to be organised between the two countries between 1968 and 1969. The focus was on folkloric and artistic exchanges, including Romanian Marionette theatres.
(2) Iran was to hold an exhibition of Iranian handicrafts in Bucharest in 1968. In return, Bucharest would hold exhibitions to display Romanian decorative arts in Tehran in 1969.
(3) In 1968, Iran would hold a photography exhibition in Bucharest. In the same year, Romania would hold an exhibition in Tehran.
(4) Both countries were to exchange soloists in 1968 and 1969.
(5) Museum exchanges were to be arranged between the two countries.
(6) Literary exchanges, publications of literary works and publication of articles on culture and art were to be encouraged in both countries.

In the education sector, the universities of the two countries agreed to exchange professors and educational professionals. In the media sector, there were agreements to exchange journalists between 1968 and 1969 for a period of seven to ten days. In the health sector, the Iranian and Romanian ministries of Health were to exchange medical specialists for a period of three weeks. In the sports sector, arrangements were to be made for having at least five sports exchanges per year. At the end of the agreement, it was mentioned that if there were any changes, they were to be settled through political negotiations. As a result of the above agreements, the first step by the Iranian delegates in Bucharest was to schedule a course on teaching Romanian to the embassy staff of Iran and the Iranians in Romania in 1970 and to follow up the activity, which had started in 1967 in a more serious way. The goal was to provide more familiarity with the civilisation and culture of Romania. In the meantime, the works of Iranian authors and writers were to be published and made accessible to researchers and specialists who were interested in the history, literature and culture of Iran.[17]

Furthermore, Mohammad Reza Pahlavi issued an ordinance in 1968 that included the implementation of the cultural agreement law between Iran and Romania, which was carried out for eight years, up to the last years of the Pahlavi rule. The plan led to the holding of permanent exhibitions and several reciprocal visits of officials of both countries to each other's historical sites. In the meantime, suitable conditions were provided for Romania to invest in industrial sectors, including the oil industry. During the years before the 1979 Islamic Revolution, the cultural interactions of the two countries continued. As mentioned before, despite the establishment of a communist government in Romania which was contradictory to the ideological structure of the political system in Iran and considering the pressures of the Western governments in safeguarding their political and economic interests, it is significant that the Iranian government, both during Reza Shah's and Mohammad Reza Shah's time, maintained its diplomatic, economic and cultural interactions with Romania. While Romania was in the Soviet bloc, it had better relations with Iran in comparison with other countries.

After the Islamic Revolution, not only were the relations maintained, but the interactions also continued their expansion in the cultural, scientific, economic and political arenas. Romania and its universities were presented as a scientific destination to Iranian students who were dispatched abroad for studies. In many instances, married students stayed in Romania with their families. Academic relations developed into more personal ones and Iranians' interactions with their Romanian counterparts grew stronger and deeper as familiarity with each other's codes and traditions grew.

With the collapse of the communist government in Romania, the relations were set in a new template of cultural interactions through the establishment of joint cultural programmes organised by the Iranian and Romanian embassies; some of the resulting activities are still in place today. Among them, one may recall a variety of events such as cultural weeks, traditional musical ceremonies, teaching Persian language and literature and in turn providing courses of Romanian language and literature, holding scientific and cultural seminars, religious rituals, Iranian handicrafts exhibitions, photography exhibitions, creating twin cities such as Yazd and Isfahan. As in many other cities across the world, the twinning of cities led to valuable and symbolical cross-cultural events. To mention but a few examples, the bust of Omar Khayyam was erected in one of Bucharest's main public parks, Iranian books were translated, guidebooks on Iran were published for Romanian tourists, Iranian film festivals were held, films and documentaries on Iran were broadcast to a Romanian audience, scholarships and awards for Persian language and literature were created.

Conclusion

Building on the intimate diplomatic relations, economic concerns and scientific and cultural interactions during the Pahlavi era, the Islamic Revolution encouraged a large number of businessmen and young people in search of work to go to Romania. The strengthening of the relations between Iran and Romania meant that the impact was no longer just localised. As a result, Iran's relations with other Balkan countries started to develop. During and after the Islamic Revolution, Iran faced international sanctions imposed by Western countries. During this period, it sought to modernise its scientific and technological skills. Romania provided an answer to the problem as Iran could send students and young workers there to acquire some of the skills it needed. Hence, Romania is one of the main destinations for Iranian travellers.

Given the lack of prior research investigating Iran and Romania's cultural relations, the present chapter can arguably be considered as the first published research on the subject. The study conducted here confirms not only the appeal of Iranian culture and Iran's capacity to export it, but also its resonance and influence across countries, such as Romania, which used to be part of the Ottoman Empire. The Persian language had a considerable impact on the language of the Ottoman Empire and thus the Balkans, where the Turkish conquerors spread dozens of Persian words into local languages, including Romanian. But this study also points to a gap. Other European countries such as France and Great Britain enjoyed long-lasting cultural, political and social relations with Iran, which resulted in the efforts of intellectuals, such as Edward Fitzgerald, the translator of *The Rubaiyat of Omar Khayyam*, to introduce Iran's seminal contributions to global culture. Yet, contrary to what happened in Romania, Iran remains a mystery for the vast majority of people in these countries because of the absence of state initiative.

Notes

1. For more information on these Turkic tribes, see V. Minorsky, 'Jihān-Shāh Qara-Qoyunlu and His Poetry' in *Bulletin of the School of Oriental and African Studies*, vol. 16, No. 2 (1954), p. 277.
2. 'Balkan' in Turkish means 'mountains', with the Balkans including Albania, Bulgaria, Croatia, Bosnia-Herzegovina, Serbia, Kosovo, Montenegro, Romania and Greece and Western Turkey. See Masoud Moradi, 'International Cooperation in Solving the Issue of the Balkans (1875–6)', in *Shenakhtjournal*, Summer 2003, Issue 38, pp. 141–4. Strategically, the Balkan Peninsula is significant both geographically, economically and geopolitically, with a diverse and evolving ethnic diversity. After World War II, the Balkans was largely within the Soviet sphere of influence. After the collapse of communism in Romania in December 1989, Romania shifted to presidential democracy and capitalism, joining NATO in 2004 and the European Union in 2007.
3. Aurel Decei, *Istoria Imperiului otoman* (Bucharest, 1978), pp. 164–7.
4. Viorel Bachako, 'Iran in the First Romanian Geography Books', in Mohammadali Soti (tr.), Ayandeh Journal, 5th fol., p. 29.
5. Subhan Pakpur, *The Ottoman History* (Qom, 2014), pp. 114–15.
6. Houshang Mahdavi, *Tarikh e ravabet e khareji e Iran: az ebteday e doran e safaviye ta payan e dovvom e jahani* (The History of Iranian Foreign Affairs: From the Beginning of the Safavid Eara until the end of World War II) (Tehran, 2013), p. 326.
7. Valdiana Juana, 'Cultural and Historical Relations Between Iran and Romania', in *Faculty of Literature Jounals*, Issue IV, p. 13.
8. Document no. 290/3447, Archive of the National Library of Iran.
9. Document no. 290/2131, Archive of the National Library of Iran.
10. Document no. 20119/297, Archive of the National Library of Iran.
11. Document no 297/201192, Archive of the National Library of Iran
12. Document no. 297/46145, Archive of the National Library of Iran.
13. Ibid.
14. Ibid.
15. Document no. 297/46142, Archive of the National Library of Iran.
16. Document no. 16022/220, Archive of the National Library of Iran.
17. Document no. 297/50552, Archive of the National Library of Iran.

CHAPTER 13

THE GREAT SATAN AND THE AXIS OF EVIL: THE POLITICS OF DEMONISATION IN IRAN AND THE UNITED STATES

Laleh Gomari-Luksch

To achieve foreign policy goals, both Iran and the United States have made use of a strategy that constructs a nationalist identity through the demonisation of the Other. This chapter argues that 'radical othering' increases popular support for foreign policy objectives as it consequently legitimises it. I make use of post-structuralist theoretical framework in identifying how the demonisation has facilitated the construction of national identities in Iran and the USA and its implications. I examine the legitimisation of the American policy on Iran and Iran's USA policy in the context of the War on Terror and Tehran's nuclear programme respectively using discourse analysis. The findings indicate that the demonisation of the Other has led to the successful achievement of each country's foreign policy goals while simultaneously affecting Iranian–American relations. In some periods, the legitimisation of the foreign policy worked to escalate tensions between the two, but since 2013, a shift in the discourses had made direct talks possible.

Introduction

Iran–US relations have been in the spotlight for many years, especially gaining momentum during the Ahmadinejad period due to the Iranian nuclear crisis. Before the Islamic Revolution in Iran in 1979, the United States was a close ally of Tehran. However, it was this very alliance that had pulled them apart after some Iranian students took Americans as hostage in their embassy in Tehran shortly after the Revolution. Since then, hostile relations became a norm between the two countries and it was only at the height of the Iranian nuclear crisis that Washington and Tehran began direct talks. Although many studies have been made about the bitter relationship between the two countries,[1] much less has been written on the justification of the two countries in maintaining such a hostile relationship. This chapter seeks to answer the following question: which constructed meanings legitimise foreign policies in the US and Iran regarding their relationship since 2002? What actions have these constructed identities made possible? How have these meanings changed over time?

Myths surrounding the Iran–US relationship were discussed in depth by Beeman (2005) and Ansari (2006). Beeman emphasised the role of 'conflicting strategies of discourse' in upholding hostile relationship with each other. The Iranian discourse of resistance and American discourse of accommodation have been etched in each country's national identities, which affect their foreign policy, and hostility rises as they are 'pressed to abandon their postures'.[2] Ansari (2006), on the other hand, wrote about the history of the relationship of Iran and the US while examining national myths, particularly Iran's national myth of victimisation in the hands of the West as well as the American image of Iran leading to failures in US foreign policy.[3] This chapter is along similar lines as it examines both sides of the relationship, however, I analyse the demonisation and the foreign policy failures through a different perspective using a post-structuralist approach. I focus on equivalential chains of identity found in the discourses of political elites. This allows me to elaborate on the creation of a Self and an Other that are in binary opposition to each other, justifying the policies, which is distant from Beeman's 'conflicting strategies of discourse' and Ansari's historical narration and exposition of myths. Such identity construction through the description of an evil Other and an opposite Self legitimises policies in Iran and the United States regarding their relationship with each other. I also discuss the ways in which the discourse has changed over time leading to direct talks regarding the nuclear programme. I argue that on both sides, the construction of equivalential chains of identity have been quite similar, with the evil Other being a threat while the Self is the victim. Furthermore, there have been changes on both sides as will be discussed below, especially during moments of perceived rapprochement such as after the election of President Barack Obama in 2008 and President Hassan Rouhani in 2013.

I provide a brief historical background of Iran–USA relations in the next section, followed by a post-structuralist theoretical framework underpinning this research. I then discuss Iran's enemy image, identity and foreign policy legitimisation in followed by a section on the United States. Then the changes in discourse in both Iran and the US that surrounded the direct talks are highlighted. The last section concludes this chapter.

Brief Historical Background of Iran–US Relations

At the beginning of the twentieth century, Iran's oil attracted the attention of Britain and, after World War II, the United States. Iran and the US enjoyed a special type of friendship during the Pahlavi regime, as the Americans were a strong supporter of the Shah. However, US patronage became a double-edged sword as opposition built up against such a relationship, particularly Western control of Iran's oil. This conflict intensified when the Iranian independence movement was revived in the 1950s. Mohammad Mosaddeq was appointed Prime Minister and he nationalised the oil industry, much to the dismay of Britain and the United States. Thus, the two powers set up Operation Ajax in 1953 to oust Mosaddeq through a coup that is now entrenched as a bitter memory for the Iranian people.[4] This created further resentment of the United States within the public sphere in addition to popular grievances within Iran against the Shah, who had close ties with Washington. Such resentment of the West, internal social inequalities and the Shah's alienation from his own people led to the Islamic Revolution in 1979 headed by Ayatollah Khomeini, which overthrew the monarchy.[5] Due to their relentless support for the Shah, the American government became known in Iran through the portrayal of Khomeini as the 'Great Satan', effectively redefining the relationship of Tehran with Washington. Not long after the Islamic Revolution, a group of students took Americans hostage in the US embassy in Tehran, holding them captive for 444 days, which did irreparable damage to Iran's image in the United States. The US response was swift: they froze Iran's assets, effectively severed diplomatic ties with Tehran and refused to recognise the legitimacy of the establishment of the Islamic Republic. Moreover, during the Iran–Iraq war that ensued, the United States and its allies provided unconditional support to Saddam Hussein although arms were sold to Iran by the USA under the Reagan administration's controversial Iran–Contra Affair. By the late 1980s, Iran had learned to distrust the great powers even more and harboured insecurity towards the rest of the world.[6] Tehran remained neutral during the Gulf War of 1990–1 as it wanted to rebuild the country and restore ties with its neighbours. By that time, the Rafsanjani government reached out to the United States, but the efforts were met with new trade sanctions in the form of the Iran–Libya Sanctions Act (ILSA) due to Iran's alleged sponsorship of terrorism.[7] There was a moment of near-reconciliation during Khatami's administration in 2000, but the attacks of 11 September 2001 prompted President Bush to declare Iran as part of the 'Axis of Evil'. Soon after, Iran's nuclear programme was exposed, creating a further complication between the two countries. Ahmadinejad's government took the issue to a different level and refused to settle the nuclear programme on nationalist grounds, prompting the USA, the UN and the EU to impose harsh sanctions on Iran, which targeted a larger sector of the Iranian economy, in order to bring Tehran back to the negotiating table. From 2002, the Bush administration embarked on the 'War on Terror' – a military intervention in the Middle East aimed at eliminating the threat of terror emanating from groups such as Al Qaeda and the Taliban. The continuation of this war is still evident today in the fight against ISIL. When Rouhani was elected in 2013, Iran resumed direct talks with the US regarding the nuclear programme, leading to the JCPOA in July 2015.

Post-Structuralism, Discourse and Identity Construction

A post-structuralist approach allows the identification of constructed identities that justify certain foreign policy actions, legitimising the Iran–USA relationship. Post-structuralists hold 'that identities, interests and behaviour of political agents are socially constructed by collective meanings, interpretations and assumptions about the world'.[8] As such, language takes on a vital role considered to be a non-neutral instrument shaping the social world and we use language 'to communicate realities external to us' forming identities through 'discourse and interactions'.[9] Post-structuralists conceive of societies as structured largely by their dominant discourses, which produce stories or narratives about what is and what is not desirable, legitimate and acceptable.[10] Dominant discourses and narratives in turn, entail power in a linguistically hegemonic sense, making them capable of intruding and manipulating the people's perception of objective reality. This creates a distinction between 'us' and 'the Other', which reinforces the interests of those in a position of power in the society, namely the political elites. Questions such as 'Who are we?', 'What do "we" do?' and 'Who are they?' are thus of significance given the relation between culture, national identity and the country's foreign policy.[11] Answering those questions helps constitute the dominant discourses, which political elites circulate in a society. The political elites then become the dominant actors taking the collective representation of meanings, identity in particular, as objective realities that shape their actions. It is here that the characterisation of the Other enables the manufacture and reinforcement of certain beliefs in the society by turning the beliefs into facts once incorporated into a dominant discourse, legitimising certain actions. In the case of Iran, this action pertains to the pursuit of the nuclear programme, whilst for the United States, it refers to the 'War on Terror'. Taking these concepts into consideration, one could argue that historical agency lies both in the discourses themselves and in the political elites using the discourses as they mutually reinforce each other to be used as justifications for foreign policy. Discourses that shape identity through collective meaning and collective memory in themselves are perpetuated by constantly being connected to the language used within the social sphere but their dominance is secured mostly by the decision of a political figure to use them for a political purpose such as justifying foreign policy.

Discourse can be defined 'as a particular way of talking about and understanding the world'[12] or 'practices that systematically form the objects of which they speak'[13] and are thus significant systemic practices that configure social representations and their identities. Discourses are aspects of the world which represent meanings that shape 'social realities' through the use of language and are all interconnected elements of the social realm.[14] This social world is constituted by language, which forms 'social identities and social relations'.[15] Identities and relations within the social world are represented by signs that have meanings which are not fixed. Through discursive struggles, however, discourses compete in order to dominate. Once a discourse, with its underlying signs and meanings, achieves dominance, it is called a 'hegemonic discourse' and it temporarily stops 'the fluctuations in the meaning of the signs'.[16] At this point, meaning becomes permanent for a short period of time, as if being frozen for a moment in the social world, until another set of signs and meanings heats it up and dissolves it. Here the issue of historical agency lies with the political leader that chooses to maintain the dominant discourse where meaning becomes fixed for the time it is needed to justify a policy.

There are two ways in which the frozen moment of meanings or 'hegemonic discourses' in the social world can be understood. Laclau and Mouffe call them the 'logic of equivalence' and the 'logic of difference'.[17] In the logic of equivalence political space is divided into two distinct 'antagonistic poles' wherein which certain meanings coagulate; it is a simplification of political space. The logic of equivalence works by 'creating equivalential identities that express a pure negation of a discursive system' which splits a 'system of differences' and institutes a 'political frontier between two opposed camps'.[18] The logic of difference, on the other hand, expands the political space, increasing its complexity, dissolving the antagonistic equivalential chains of identities.[19] Simply put, the logic of equivalence creates division between a Self and an opposite Other, while logic of difference creates unity: an 'Us' or 'We'.

The logic of equivalence is most prominent in Iran's relentless pursuit of the nuclear programme and the 'War on Terror' of the United States, which are both constituted by a construction of a Self, i.e. national identity, and 'the Other', pertaining to the evil enemy. Once the identities are temporarily fixed, certain foreign policy actions become legitimate. In the case of Iran, this is the stubborn quest for the nuclear programme despite all the sanctions. For the United States, its is the 'War on Terror' along with all its complications such as isolation on the part of Iran and mobilisation of allies on the part of America, notwithstanding the enormous costs of such endeavours. The minute dissolution of the antagonistic equivalential chains of identities can also be observed since the election of President Obama and President Rouhani, leading to the direct talks regarding the nuclear programme. Although this dissolution has not been clearly marked by the creation of a logic of difference, it is significant enough to justify a change in policy.

For the analysis section that follows, I examined the speeches of political elites of US and Iran. For the Iran case, the majority is comprised of the Iranian New Year speeches of the Supreme Leader, Ali Khamenei, since 2002. I have also taken some speeches of Mahmoud Ahmadinejad and Hassan Rouhani at the United Nations. For the US, I analysed the yearly State of the Union Address of the Presidents of the United States, George W. Bush and Barack Obama, since 2002. The speeches I have chosen reflect the hegemonic discourse and some of the competing discourses as will be shown below. Statements of the highest-ranking political elites were chosen as they contain the most dominant political discourses. Articulations of these elites are stronger in terms of affecting the overall discourse and impacting a larger audience in comparison to other lower-key officials. These hegemonic discourses from the political elites contain equivalential chains of identities for both countries, which represents the core of this research.

The Great Satan, Iranian Identity and Legitimisation of the Nuclear Programme

Following President Bush's 'Axis of Evil' speech in January 2002, the Supreme Leader, Khamenei, reinstated the term 'Great Satan' to refer to the United States, which appeared in conjunction with being the 'main supporter of tyrannical and oppressive regimes in the world'.[20] Bush was particularly demonised by being characterised as speaking 'like a person who is thirsty for the blood of human beings,' who 'threatened and accused other governments'.[21] For the Supreme Leader, the American military intervention in Iraq in 2003 was 'a clear sign of bullying and oppression on the part of the United States' to further 'its illegitimate interests'.[22] Such endeavours, according to Khamenei, make America 'arrogant' as it considers 'itself entitled to trample on the rights and interests of other nations and promote its own interests by using its military power'.[23] This 'arrogance' of the US is a recurring theme in the majority of Khamenei's speeches and is usually linked to American intervention in the internal affairs of other countries, such as that of the 1953 coup in Iran. Khamenei regards America as 'a threat to global peace and security' due to its 'desire for domination'.[24] With regard to the nuclear programme, Khamenei repeatedly said that the United States wants to hinder development and progress in Iran as Washington opposes Tehran's independence in terms of energy production.[25] The United States is considered to be opposed to a 'powerful, developed, independent and Islamic Iran enjoying modern technologies'.[26]

The United States wants to prohibit Iran from using nuclear technology – which is a right of the Iranian nation.[27] Khamenei defines the enemy's tactic to be that of aggression and hostility in the form of sanctions, depriving Iran of achieving progress and becoming a great nation.[28] Such sentiments were reflected by Ahmadinejad in his speeches at the UN, where the United States was characterised to be one of the 'hegemonic powers'[29] and 'bullying powers'[30] with the desire to dominate, impose 'exclusionist policies on international decision making mechanisms'[31] and monopolise technological progress as an instrument of power,[32] thus putting 'hurdles in the way of the peaceful nuclear activities of the Iranian nation'.[33]

The Iranian identity, the Self, has been defined against the characteristics of the enemy. Khamenei claims that the Islamic Republic has particularly achieved scientific progress due to the sanctions as the country was 'awakened ... to the realities' that forced it to become independent'.[34] It is a nation that is 'much stronger than 15, 20 or 27 years ago' showing that the enemy has failed.[35] Such great progress and achievements have been a constant feature of the Iranian identity, where setbacks in the form of threats and harsh sanctions are seen to be challenges that must be overcome by the Iranian nation through strength, vigilance and unyielding character.[36] Ahmadinejad equated the nuclear programme with the nationalisation of Iranian oil in the 1950s glorifying the nuclear programme and deeming it to be more valuable than the movement to nationalise the oil.[37] Iran's 'active diplomacy' as a tool for making 'great achievements' at least in terms of regional issues has also been emphasised by Khamenei,[38] which steadily became a feature of Iran's identity especially throughout the negotiations on the nuclear programme since 2013.

Such a unified personification and characterisation of the enemy as well as the Self in the speeches of Khamenei and Ahmadinejad had justified the persistence for the success of the nuclear programme, which eventually led to a deadlock in negotiations and the sanctions. Since 1979, Iran had persevered to take its own course and continue with minimal reliance on the West, particularly the United States. They have been adamant in their opposition to the demands of the United States and have not cooperated with them for decades following the Islamic Revolution. This suggests that since such cooperation has not occurred in the past, it cannot be expected that they would cooperate with the United States and give in to their demands regarding the nuclear programme in such a short span of time when hostile relations have existed as far as the Iranian regime is concerned. Through the creation of an evil Other – an enemy that is the United States – the Iranian government's persistence on the nuclear programme was legitimised despite the ensuing sanctions and hardship for the country. This also justified Iran's policy of not having direct talks with American officials, although this second issue has been a recurrent theme since the Islamic Revolution. It has more to do with the perceived injustices Iran has suffered at the hands of the Western powers, which was one of the driving forces of the Islamic Revolution. However, as will be shown later, the discourses changed preceding the direct talks with the United States during the Rouhani administration.

The Axis of Evil, American Identity and Legitimisation of the 'War on Terror'

Following the 11 September 2001 attacks, the former US President, George W. Bush, has classified terrorist groups as enemies of the country, particularly Hezbollah, Hamas and Al Qaeda. In his State of the Union speech in 2002, Bush emphasised that there was an 'Axis of Evil' constituted by Iran, Iraq and North Korea, which support and ally themselves with the terrorist groups.[39] Thus, Iran, Iraq and North Korea were identified to be 'outlaw regimes' – a threat to America and the world as they seek weapons of mass destruction and provide the terrorist groups with such arms.[40] Iraq's 'brutal dictator', Saddam Hussein, who allegedly supported terrorists, was especially in the spotlight for possessing lethal weapons that should be disarmed,[41] eventually leading to the US military intervention in Iraq. The Iranian regime, which is constituted of an 'unelected few' repressing the Iranian people's freedom,[42] has also been a constant element in the State of the Union speeches until the end of Bush's term. It is 'a government that represses its people, pursues weapons of mass destruction, and supports terror',[43] 'remains the world's primary state sponsor of terror, pursuing nuclear weapons while depriving its people of the freedom they seek and deserve'.[44] The Iranian nation is 'held hostage by a small clerical elite that is isolating and repressing its people' as the Iranian rulers 'oppress a good and talented people'.[45] In sum, the Iranian government was characterised as an oppressive regime that represses its own citizens in the majority of the speeches analysed. The Iranian government, however, has consistently been separated from the positively depicted 'good' Iranian people – a pattern also recognisable in the speeches of Khamenei with regard to the United States.

The American Self in contrast to the enemy is the defender of peace and freedom. In order to keep America safe and secure, the American nation had to embark on a 'War on Terror',[46] which targets the terrorist groups, as well as the 'Axis of Evil' who support the terrorists. The USA could not afford to be indifferent to the existence of Evil regimes supporting terrorists as the consequences would be catastrophic.[47] President Bush defined the two objectives of this 'War on Terror'. First, 'shut down terrorist camps, disrupt terrorist plans and bring terrorists to justice' and second, 'prevent the terrorists and regimes who seek chemical, biological or nuclear weapons from threatening the United States and the world'.[48] It is the United States and their allies 'that stand between a world at peace and a world of chaos and constant alarm' and America accepts the responsibility to 'defend the safety of' the American people as well as 'the hopes of all mankind'.[49] 'America is on the offensive against the terrorists who started this war', which entails confronting the regimes 'that harbour and support terrorists and could supply them with nuclear, chemical, or biological weapons'.[50] President Bush further reiterated that America shall 'not rest until this enemy (Al-Qaida) has been defeated'.[51] In addition to such tasks, the US will 'support democratic movements in the Middle East and beyond, with the ultimate goal of ending tyranny in our world'.[52] Such a description of the American 'Self' had justified the Bush administration's foreign policy or 'the Bush Doctrine', which not only aimed at eliminating terrorists but also legitimised the US intervention in Afghanistan and Iraq. An important element in the Bush Doctrine relating to the former president's description of the Iranian regime is rooted in 'a strong belief in the importance of a state's domestic regime in determining its foreign policy'; hence, 'knowing that North Korea, Iran, and Syria are brutal dictatorships tells us that they will seek to dominate their neighbours, sponsor terrorism, and threaten the United States'.[53] Thus, looking at the equivalential chains of identity and how Iran's regime has been described by Bush, the speculation that the US was seeking regime change in Iran during the Bush administration is not completely unfounded.

The Legitimisation of Direct Talks

The election of Rouhani in 2013 saw a significant shift in Iran's rhetoric towards the world. The United States as an enemy was not as emphasised in his speeches but maintained almost the same degree of negativity in the speeches of Khamenei, indicating a competing discourse that struggles for dominance. On the one hand, Khamenei continues to focus on the enmity and hostility of the United States[54] as well as differing goals in the region[55] and believes that 'America's policy in the region is to create insecurity'.[56] On the other hand, Rouhani reiterated in his UN speech that 'Iran seeks constructive engagement with other countries based on mutual respect and common interest, and within the same framework does not seek to increase tensions with the United States',[57] which indicated a potential opening up of bargaining space on the Iranian side.[58] While direct talks were being held, Rouhani stressed Iran's determination to 'continue negotiations with our interlocutors'.[59] After the nuclear deal, the Supreme Leader declared 'that "Death to America" does not mean death to the people of America' but rather 'death to American policies and to arrogance'.[60] On the American side, 'diplomacy', 'diplomatic solution' and 'diplomatic efforts' have been words regularly used when discussing Iran since Obama became president in 2009.[61] Iran's support for terrorism has gradually disappeared and an insistence on Iran's meeting its obligations as defined by the P5 + 1 with regard to the nuclear programme[62] replaced negative attributions. Although far from a 'logic of difference' emerging in order to unify the otherwise two opposite poles of Self and evil Other, the dominant discourses since the election of Rouhani in 2013 have shifted away from demonisation, which follows the 'logic of equivalence'.

Conclusion

Since 2001, the evil Other has been a constant subject of the speeches of the political elites in Iran and the United States, referring to each other and thus legitimising their relationship. During the Bush and Ahmadinejad administrations, demonisation was at its peak in both countries, justifying their hostile policies – US sanctions and Iran's persistence with the nuclear programme – leading to a deadlock in the nuclear negotiations. During this period, both governments characterised each other as a threat as well as both being oppressive regimes, demonstrating that the equivalential chains of identities were very similar. At any point, both the Iranian and the US governments defined their Self to be the victim of the evil Other, which prompted both countries to pursue certain policies much to the dismay of the other. After the election of Obama, the American tone towards Iran changed and negative attributes were replaced by terms such as 'diplomacy'. By the time Rouhani took office, Iran followed suit and diplomacy dominated the discourses within Iran leading to the Joint Comprehensive Plan of Action (JCPOA) in July 2015. Although examining the legitimisation of Iran and US policies through a post-structuralist approach could help us understand the justifications of both countries with regard to their foreign policy, other approaches, such as securitisation or role theory, could provide an alternative perspective and perhaps supplement my approach. At the time of writing, a new Other seems to be in the making in the form of ISIL – which is the enemy of both the United States and Iran. Perhaps with the passage of time, this enemy could unify the two countries and dissolve the polarised equivalential chains of identity even for a short period indicating that negotiations and cooperation with each other will not be confined to the nuclear programme but rather extended to regional issues. At the opposite end, a return to the demonisation strategies of Bush and Ahmadinejad could undermine the progress made so far, reinforcing the characterisation of the notorious evil Other.

Notes

1. See the works of Ali Ansari, *Confronting Iran: The Failure of American Policy and the Next Great Crisis in the Middle East* (New York, 2006); Barbara Slavin, *Bitter Friends, Bosom Enemies: Iran, the U.S., and the Twisted Path to Confrontation* (New York, 2007); William O. Beeman, *The "Great Satan" vs. the "Mad Mullahs": How the United States and Iran demonize each other* (Westport, Conn., 2005); Donette Murray, *US foreign policy and Iran: American–Iranian relations since the Islamic revolution* (London, 2007); Christian Emery, *US Foreign Policy and the Iranian Revolution The Cold War Dynamics of Engagement and Strategic Alliance* (London, 2013).
2. Beeman, *The "Great Satan"*, p. 190.
3. Ali Ansari, *Confronting Iran.*
4. Ibid.
5. Ali Ansari, *Modern Iran since 1921: the Pahlavis & After* (London, 2003).
6. Adam Tarock, *Iran's Foreign Policy Since 1990: Pragmatism Supersedes Islamic Ideology* (Commack, N.Y, 1999), p. 45.
7. Lukas Kasten, Laleh Gomari-Luksch, 'An Eye for an Eye: Bargaining Theory, Mistrust, and the Iranian Nuclear Crisis' in Andreas Bock and Ingo

Henneberg (eds), *Iran, die Bombe und das Streben nach Sicherheit* (Baden-Baden, 2014), p. 232.

8. Emmanuel Adler, 'Seizing the Middle Ground. Constructivism in World Politics', in *European Journal of International Relations* 3 (1997), pp. 319–63.
9. Fred Chernoff, *Theory and Metatheory in International Relations: Concepts and Contending Accounts* (New York, 2007), p. 156.
10. Ibid.
11. Valerie M. Hudson, *Foreign Policy Analysis: Classic and Contemporary Theory* (Lanham, 2007), p. 104.
12. Marianne Jørgensen and Louise Phillips, *Discourse Analysis as Theory and Method* (London, 2002), p. 1.
13. Michel Foucault, *The Archaeology of Knowledge and the Discourse on Language* (New York, 1972; 1989), p. 54.
14. Norman Fairclough, *Analysing Discourse: Textual Analysis for Social Research* (London, 2003): p. 3; Jennifer Milliken, 'The Study of Discourse in International Relations: A Critique of Research and Methods', in *European Journal of International Relations* 5 (1999), p. 229.
15. Jørgensen and Phillips, *Discourse Analysis*, pp. 8–9.
16. Ibid., p.28.
17. Ernesto Laclau and Chantal Mouffe, *Hegemony and Socialist Strategy: Towards a Radical Democratic Politics*, 2nd edn (London, 2001), p. 130.
18. David R. Howarth, Aletta J. Norval, Yannis Stavrakakis, *Discourse Theory and Political Analysis: Identities, Hegemonies, and Social Change* (Manchester & New York, 2000), p. 11.
19. Laclau and Mouffe, *Hegemony and Socialist Strategy*, p. 130.
20. Ali Khamenei, Leader's Address to Education Ministry Officials, 7/17/2002 (2002). Available online at http://english.khamenei.ir/news/159/Leader-s-Address-to-Education-Ministry-Officials. [Accessed 27 June 2017].
21. Ibid.
22. Ali Khamenei, Leader's Address on New Year's Day, 3/21/2003 (2003) Available online at http://english.khamenei.ir/news/133/Leader-s-Address-on-New-Year-s-Day. [Accessed 27 June 2017].
23. Ibid.
24. Ali Khamenei, Leader's Speech at the Shrine of Imam Ridha (a.s.), 3/21/2006 (2006) Available online at http://english.khamenei.ir/news/1982/Leader-s-Speech-at-the-Shrine-of-Imam-Ridha-a-s. [Accessed 27 June 2017].
25. Ali Khamenei, Leader's Address to a Large Gathering in Mashhad, 3/21/2005 (2005a) Available online at http://english.khamenei.ir/news/95/Leader-s-Address-to-a-Large-Gathering-in-Mashhad. [Accessed 27 June 2017].
26. Khamenei, Leader's Speech at the Shrine of Imam Ridha.
27. Khamenei, Leader's Address to a Large Gathering in Mashhad.
28. Ali Khamenei, Leader's Speech at Imam Ridha's (a.s.) Shrine, 3/21/2007 (2007). Available online at http://english.khamenei.ir/news/1656/Leader-s-Speech-at-Imam-Ridha-s-a-s-Shrine. [Accessed 27 June 2017]. Ali Khamenei, Leader's Speech in Mashhad, 3/21/2009 (2009). Available online at http://english.

khamenei.ir/news/1076/Leader-s-Speech-in-Mashhad [Accessed 27 June 2017]. Ali Khamenei, Leader's Speech at Imam Ridha's (a.s.) Shrine, 3/20/2012 (2012). Available online at http://english.khamenei.ir/news/1620/Leader-s-Speech-at-Imam-Ridha-s-a-s-Shrine [Accessed 27 June 2017]. Ali Khamenei, Leader's Speech at Imam Ridha's (a.s.) Shrine, 3/21/2013 (2013). Available online at http://english.khamenei.ir/news/1760/Leader-s-Speech-at-Imam-Ridha-s-a-s-Shrine. [Accessed 27 June 2017].

29. Mahmoud Ahmadinejad, Address by H. E. Dr. Mahmood Ahmadinejad President of the Islamic Republic of Iran at the Sixtieth Session of the United Nations General Assembly, 9/14/2005 (2005). Available online at http://iran-un.org/en/2005/09/14/14-september-2005/ [Accessed 27 June 2017]. Mahmoud Ahmadinejad, Address by His Excellency Dr. Mahmoud Ahmadinejad President of the Islamic Republic of Iran before the 61st Session of the General Assembly, 9/19/2006 (2006) Available online at http://iran-un.org/en/2006/09/19/19-september-2006/. [Accessed 27 June 2017].
30. Mahmoud Ahmadinejad, Address by His Excellency Dr. Mahmoud Ahmadi-Nejad President of the Islamic Republic of Iran before the 63rd Session of the UN General Assembly, 9/23/2008 (2008). Available online at http://iran-un.org/en/2008/09/23/23-september-2008/. [Accessed 27 June 2017].
31. Ahmadinejad, Address before the 63rd Session of the UN General Assembly.
32. Ahmadinejad, Address at the Sixtieth Session of the United Nations General Assembly.
33. Ahmadinejad, Address before the 63rd Session of the UN General Assembly.
34. Khamenei, Leader's Speech at the Shrine of Imam Ridha, (a.s.), 3/21/2006.
35. Khamenei, Leader's Speech at Imam Ridha's (a.s.) Shrine, 3/21/2007.
36. Khamenei, Leader's Address on New Year's Day, 3/21/2003, Ali Khamenei, Leader's Address to Residents of Kerman, 5/1/2005 (2005b). Available online at http://english.khamenei.ir/news/92/Leader-s-Address-to-Residents-of-Kerman. [Accessed 27 June 2017]; Khamenei, Leader's Speech at the Shrine of Imam Ridha; Khamenei, Leader's Speech in Mashhad, 3/21/2009; Khamenei, Leader's Speech at Imam Ridha's (a.s.) Shrine, 3/20/2012; Khamenei, Leader's Speech at Imam Ridha's (a.s.) Shrine, 3/21/2013.
37. Mahmoud Ahmadinejad (2007): Speech on a Missionary Conference in the Holy Month of Ramadhan (In Farsi), 9/6/2007. Available online at http://www.president.ir/fa/print.php?ArtID=10617. [Accessed 27 June 2017].
38. Khamenei, Leader's Speech at Imam Ridha's (a.s.) Shrine, 3/20/2012.
39. George W. Bush, Address Before a Joint Session of the Congress on the State of the Union, 1/29/2002 (2002). Available online at http://www.presidency.ucsb.edu/ws/index.php?pid=29644. [Accessed 28 June 2017].
40. Ibid.
41. George W. Bush, Address Before a Joint Session of the Congress on the State of the Union, 1/28/2003 (2003). Available online at http://www.presidency.ucsb.edu/ws/index.php?pid=29645. [Accessed 28 June 2017].
42. Bush, Address Before a Joint Session of the Congress on the State of the Union, 1/29/2002.

43. Bush, Address Before a Joint Session of the Congress on the State of the Union, 1/28/2003.
44. George W. Bush, Address Before a Joint Session of the Congress on the State of the Union, 2/2/2005 (2005). Available online at http://www.presidency.ucsb.edu/ws/index.php?pid=58746. [Accessed 28 June 2017].
45. George W. Bush, Address Before a Joint Session of the Congress on the State of the Union, 1/28/2008 (2008). Available online at http://www.presidency.ucsb.edu/ws/index.php?pid=76301. [Accessed 28 June 2017].
46. Bush, Address Before a Joint Session of the Congress on the State of the Union, 1/29/2002.
47. Ibid.
48. Ibid.
49. Bush, Address Before a Joint Session of the Congress on the State of the Union, 1/28/2003.
50. George W. Bush, Address Before a Joint Session of the Congress on the State of the Union, 1/20/2004. (2004). Available online at http://www.presidency.ucsb.edu/ws/index.php?pid=29646. [Accessed 28 June 2017].
51. Bush, Address Before a Joint Session of the Congress on the State of the Union, 1/28/2008.
52. Bush, Address Before a Joint Session of the Congress on the State of the Union, 2/2/2005.
53. Robert Jervis, 'Understanding the Bush Doctrine', In *Political Science Quarterly* 118 (2003), pp. 365, 375.
54. Khamenei, Leader's Speech at Imam Ridha's (a.s.) Shrine, 3/21/2013.
55. Ali Khamenei, Leader's Speech at the Holy Shrine of Imam Ridha (a.s.), 3/21/2015 (2015a). Available online at http://english.khamenei.ir/news/2025/Leader-s-Speech-at-the-Holy-Shrine-of-Imam-Ridha-a-s. [Accessed 28 June 2017].
56. Ibid.
57. Hassan Rouhani, Statement by H. E. Dr. Hassan Rouhani President of the Islamic Republic of Iran at the Sixty-Eighth Session of the United Nations General Assembly, 9/24/2013 (2013). Available online at http://iran-un.org/en/2013/09/24/24-september-2013-2/. [Accessed 28 June 2017].
58. Kasten, Gomari-Luksch, 'An Eye for an Eye'.
59. Hassan Rouhani, Statement by H. E. Dr. Hassan Rouhani, The President of the Islamic Republic of Iran Before the 69th Session of the UN General Assembly, 9/25/2014 (2014). Available online at http://iran-un.org/en/2014/09/25/25-september-2014/. [Accessed 28 June 2017].
60. Ali Khamenei, "Death to America" means death to American, 11/3/2015 (2015b). Available online at http://english.khamenei.ir/news/2298/Death-to-America-means-death-to-American-policies-and-arrogance. [Accessed 28 June 2017].
61. Barack Obama, Address Before a Joint Session of the Congress on the State of the Union, 1/27/2010 (2010). Available online at http://www.presidency.ucsb.edu/ws/index.php?pid=87433, Barack Obama (2011): Address Before a Joint Session of the Congress on the State of the Union, 1/25/2011. Available online

at http://www.presidency.ucsb.edu/ws/index.php?pid=88928. [Accessed 28 June 2017]. Barack Obama, Address Before a Joint Session of Congress on the State of the Union, 1/24/2012 (2012). Available online at http://www.presidency.ucsb.edu/ws/index.php?pid=99000. [Accessed 28 June 2017]. Barack Obama, Address Before a Joint Session of Congress on the State of the Union, 2/12/2013 (2013). Available online at http://www.presidency.ucsb.edu/ws/index.php?pid=102826. [Accessed 28 June 2017].

62. Ibid.

SECTION 4

VISUAL AND MEDIA REPRESENTATIONS

CHAPTER 14

ZAN-I FARANGI, A SYMBOL OF OCCIDENT: THE EUROPEAN WOMEN IN *FARANGI SAZI* PAINTINGS (1666–94)

Negar Habibi

Introduction

The main aim of this chapter is to interpret the seventeenth-century Safavid perception of Europeans, concentrating precisely on the presence of Western women in the works of art commonly known as *farangi sazi*.[1]

Among several genres co-existing in Iranian painting in the second half of the seventeenth century, a limited number of artists adopted a new pictorial language, most likely by observing European works of art.[2] Employing light and shadow effects and an evocation of geometric perspective, these paintings are clearly distinct from other Iranian artistic types. They do no longer faithfully follow the prototypes of Iranian classical painting, nor correspond to the pictorial conventions of European art.

The so-called *farangi sazi* paintings contained a considerable number of Western women. For a period of 15 years between 1673 and 1688–9 (the dating of signatures testifies) the *farangi sazi* masters like Ali Qoli Jebādār and Mohammad Zaman (both active in the late seventeenth century) completed several paintings with female subject matters.[3] There are at least 13 of these paintings: seven are Biblical story illustrations,[4] four are portraits of Western women or perhaps ladies of

European nobility,[5] and two have their origin in Occidental mythologies.[6] Two paintings have an annotation in which it is mentioned that this was intended to be offered to a high-ranking member of the royal court (*Jahat-i Sarkar-i navvab*) and one was done at the command of the king (*Hasb al-amr*). It is notable, however, that the patron's name is not mentioned in any of these paintings.

Safavid sources do not easily let us know for whom and for what purpose these paintings of female subjects were created, necessitating a study of the general perception of the European women in the late Safavid Iran.

The Iranian Occidentalist Paintings

A short historical review of Safavid chronicles proves that Europeans were neither appreciated, nor considered a subject of great interest for Iranians in the second half of the seventeenth century. At the end of the sixteenth century, Hasan Romlu (Shah Tahmasp's chronicler) mentions for the first time Europe and the Europeans mostly when referring to the Portuguese settling in the East.[7] While Safavid sources are filled with the presence of the Turks, Uzbeks and Mughal Indians, Europeans occupy little space, with the vaguest possible descriptions.[8] The main interest of the chroniclers and historians was Safavid dynastic events, where information about the West was of no significance.[9] It raises this idea that for the Safavids, observing the neighbouring Muslim powers, with a more immediate political and economic effect to the Iranian territory, was considered more important than the study of *Farangis*, these non-Muslim pagans, naturally inferior. In fact, the Safavid considered the Europeans both economically and culturally inferior to the Iranians. Thus, the Europeans' circulations, travels and international trades were seen mostly as the need to fulfil their deficiency in the primary and essential materials or manufactured objects. Then, if they were in Iran it was either for vital necessity or for espionage.[10]

The reign of Abbas I (r.1588–1629) is the key moment of meeting between the pre-modern Iran with seventeenth-century Europe. The artistic outcome of this moment of encounter, where two parts of the globe still exchange as equals, is felt in some pages of paintings. That exchange on an equal footing, however, was temporary. The conflicts that Iran experienced from the fall of the Safavids until the arrival of the Qajars, tipped the scales in favour of the West.

This discovery of Europe and European exoticism plays undoubtedly a fundamental role in the creation of the so-called *farangi sazi* paintings. The reign of Shah Soleiman (r.1666–94) witnessed a significant increase in the production of works of art with Western subject matters. The same period curiously coincided with a political and civilisational underestimation of the Europeans.[11] Indeed, it seems that neither Shah Soleiman nor his court was interested in the prospect of establishing new political ties with Europe.[12] Several European and Russian envoys came to Iran, bringing different political and military proposals between 1670 and 1685. Shah Soleiman rejected them all. Not only was the king not seduced by the offers of the West, but also European envoys had to wait several months before being received by the king.[13] As Chardin points out, making foreign envoys wait long periods before receiving an audience with the Safavid Shah was a deliberate policy to strengthen the impression of magnificence and majesty of the Iranian court.[14]

Iranian visual sources, however, do not confirm this situation. The court of Shah Soleiman seems visibly more enthusiastic for Western art and goods. Not only were several pages of paintings made on the basis of Western historical, mythological or religious anecdotes, but also in 1668–9, Shah Soleiman asked Charles II of England to send him, in addition to enamellers, watchmakers, goldsmiths and armorers, a *naqqash-i bala dast* or a talented painter.[15]

The so-called *farangi sazi* paintings were created in a mixed atmosphere of disdain for European policy, as a result of the Safavid superiority complex and of enthusiasm for the exotic Western customs, habits and people. These paintings represent some exotic aspects of a strange and alien world, without really worrying about representing it in all its complexity or pretending to demonstrate a deep knowledge of the West. It seems that they were almost content to present a Western cultural strangeness where men and women wear attractive dresses and caps while behaving generally very differently from what was seen as a respectful, religiously and traditionally legitimate relationship between the two sexes in Iran.

It seems that the late seventeenth-century Safavids, selectively, chose and adapted the most striking and fascinating aspects of the Western world, by mixing them with their own tastes and aesthetics. It would then be a sort of Iranian transient mode, like the fashionable *turcoiserie* or *chinoiserie* in the West at about the same time, and what was to develop in the nineteenth century into Orientalism. Considering that European visual culture manifests with more strength in European subject matters paintings of *farangi sazi*, one may legitimately wonder whether we should perceive an Occidentalism in Iranian painting.[16] The parallel is interesting, because in the Orientalist vision, it was not only about a large, vague and undefined East, but also about a fascination for exotic colours, clothes and attitudes dictated by the costumes and architecture with the codes radically different from those of the West.

Meanwhile, with a certain irony, depictions of nudes and characters in erotic attitudes are one of the major themes that are found in Safavid Occidentalist paintings as well as in European Orientalism.[17] Whereas Greco–Roman mythology offered more freedom to European artists, the naked women of Iranian traditional painting were also often related to the ancient literature and strictly limited to them. In most cases, it was about Shirin taking a bath or similar scenes of bathing such as the bathers of *Haft Peikar* (seven portraits) or the magical and enchanting naked women of *Eskandar Nameh* coming out of the sea every night.[18] From the seventeenth century, however, away from literary texts, European engravings became new sources of inspiration for Iranian artists. Two paintings signed by Reza Abbasi, datable to 1590–2, are the first examples of the elongated female nudes in Iranian painting. Inspired by Marcantonio Raimondi's Cleopatra, this subject was replicated several times during the seventeenth century, not only by the artist himself, but also by many others.[19]

Representations of the naked female body (especially those in isolated pages), directly related to a European context, increased especially in the Occidentalist paintings created during the reign of Shah Soleiman. Either they are European women whose neckline dresses and feathered hats are characteristically Westernising, like the turban and cashmere shawl can be 'oriental' in European paintings or, when reclining, they are accompanied mostly by men in European outfits, with the majority identifiable as Portuguese.[20]

One may then wonder if these Occidentalist features play for Muslim Iran the same role as the odalisques and slaves sold at the Orientalist artistic bazaar, but a century in advance. If the naked or half-naked women were perceived as a Western delegacy and also an eligible fantasy, since it concerns geographically foreign and exotic women who follow an infidel religion.

As A. Landau reminds us the foreigners passing in Safavid Isfahan were almost exclusively men. So while the representations of Western men may be more or less taken from a real life individual, images of European women were constructed on the basis of the oral descriptions or visual highlights. 'The Safavid male subjugated indeed the European female to his own gaze long before Western imperialism.'[21] As Landau highlights, the Safavid single-sheet paintings seriously question the traditional assumptions concerning 'who sexualized whom?'[22] This issue could be seen through various sources, such as Safavid texts and anecdotal evidence written by men, such as the attitude of two Iranian envoys of Shah Abbas I, Musa Beig in Holland and Naqdi Beig in England, being known as insatiable womanisers.[23]

Safineh-i Soleimani (*The Ship of Soleiman*) one of the few Iranian Safavid travelogues confirms the observation of Safavid men towards European women. Written by Ibn-i Mohammad Ebrahim Mohammad Rabi, it is about the travel of the Iranian Ambassador Hossein Beig in an English ship to Siam in the last years of the seventeenth century.[24] Part of the story is devoted to European women, their absolute beauty and exoticism in the eyes of Iranian men: 'The Frank women have faces that beam like the sun and are round like the moon, hidden with the veil of modesty.'[25]

He points out that:

> Surely such women must be encouraged. Their beautiful straight backs sway like cypress trees and bring a rush of sap into the dry garden of these old lovers' hearts. The rose–red glimmer of their cheeks, cheeks like those of heaven's Houris, sparked new life in the breasts of the company of friends. Thus the light of their beauty was admitted and they participated in the festivities despite the fact that they were women.[26]

The remarkable point in these lines is certainly the approach of the writer to describe these women as Houris who transform every place into paradise.[27] This approach is quite similar to that found in *farangi sazi* paintings. The author, like the painter, employs the same rhetoric and literal images to describe the *farangi* women as it used to be traditionally for Leila or Shirin since the eleventh century. His material, European women, is different, strange and exotic, while his expression is common and remains in fact very traditional.

Zan-i farangi and its Diverse Persian Interpretations

The seventeenth-century representation of European women could be perceived from the Safavid masculine eye. It remains however to see if it was always about a subject of common fantasy and eroticism.

One of the murals of the southern Talar of Chehel Sotun palace in Isfahan, for example, shows a woman and a man drinking wine in European clothes. The neck of the woman's dress is so open that her breasts are entirely exposed (Figure 14.1). Women with bare torsos are also on the walls of the Armenians' houses in New Jolfa of Isfahan. One wall of the house of Sukias shows two scenes of banqueting and feasting among several men and women, all dressed as Europeans. The men, fully clothed, tighten their arms around bare-chested women and offer them wine glasses (Figure 14.2). One may wonder if these images aim to represent prostitutes.

It is essential to remember that in Safavid Iran, the prostitutes dressed like other women, but wore shorter veils and were less covered than respectable women.[28] According to Chardin, it was their behaviour that made them readily detected.[29] *The Famous Sakineh* painted by Jani Farangi Saz is probably a portrait of a famous courtesan of the time.[30] The image shows an almost bare-headed woman, as her long hair is visible. The Kaempfer album assigned by Jani Farangi Saz, also represents a *qahbeh-yi bazar* or a bazaar prostitute, which shows a woman completely covered, except for her face. Her long black hair also spills out from under her veil.

The topless or half nude women of mural or single sheet paintings do not appear to be always associated with a specific social category. Similarly, it is not obvious to categorise them according to their particular costume. It is noteworthy that the dancers of large murals of the Chehel Sotun palace are fully dressed, while their functions could not be exercised by honest and respectable women.[31] It is worth considering the gestures of the women in the paintings, which could signify their place in society. Thus, the women in European dress shown on wall paintings of the Armenians' houses could include prostitutes, particularly considering their different attitudes. They are probably drunk with other drunken men who are trying to fondle their breasts. We must, however, ask the question as to whether almost entirely nude European women represented in the Safavid Occidentalist paintings may be considered as prostitutes or if they fall in another category with more blurred lines as to private sensuality.

Figure 14.1 Southern talar of Chehel Sotun, Isfahan, seventeenth century.

Figure 14.2 House of Sukias, south wall of northern talar, New Jolfa, Isfahan, seventeenth century.

Suzanna and the Elders signed by Ali Qoli Jebādār (Figure 14.3) and *Venus and Cupid* signed by Mohammad Zaman both show nude women. However, neglecting their nakedness and considering their postures, we observe that these women share some points in common.[32] The general poses of the characters are certainly identical to their European models, but the overall composition of the pictures and the backgrounds are all modified. These women under a tree and next to a spring or a lake may remind us of Shirin taking her bath, shown several times in Iranian painting for centuries. It therefore seems important to ask the question whether there is a contagion of classical imagery of Shirin extending to the Occidentalist paintings of the late seventeenth century.

Venus and Suzanna could probably recall the scenes of Shirin taking a bath to an Iranian reader: a new interpretation of this favourite story arose, inspired by European representations. In parallel, it could also be considered as the acclimatisation and integration of Suzanna and Venus into a new Iranian context. This idea is particularly supported by other late seventeenth-, eighteenth- or nineteenth-century representations of Shirin.[33] It is important to remember that Suzanna and Venus are among the most frequently represented women in European art and culture. Their beauty and their popularity in the West were probably known in Safavid Iran. The resemblance of Shirin and these popular nudes in the Western culture could perhaps inspire Iranian patrons and artistes to create a new version of this well-liked story. While it is impossible to confuse Shirin with a courtesan, naked females represented in so-called *farangi sazi* paintings could probably not be taken all for prostitutes.

Besides, some *Farangi* women represented in Safavid Occidentalist paintings seem likely to not necessarily refer to a specific person, but rather to European women in general. Here the female clothes and fashion accessories, etiquette and the prestigious aspect of courtly life in general attract the Persian eyes. According to written sources, Safavid women and men were very careful with sartorial elegance.[34] The Iranian passion for clothes also extended to foreign suits, especially those of Europeans. Tavernier reported that he had taken the portrait of his wife to the court of Shah Abbas II (1642–66), so the Shah could see the European female manner of clothing.[35] Kaempfer reported the kidnapping of eight *Farangi* women in Isfahan neighbourhoods in 1685;

Figure 14.3 *Suzanna and the Elders*, Ali Qoli Jebādār, *c.*1673.

the reason given by the Royal Court was the desire of the women of the harem to know the culture and clothes of the *Farangi* ladies.[36] It is noteworthy that although travellers' accounts mention the desire of the king to know the Western costume, it is also possible that the women of the seraglio wished also to know more about their European counterparts. Iranian women had the (perfectly natural) curiosity to know better how their Western peers dressed. Shah Abbas I, for example, brought a French tailor to the Royal Court to make necklines embellished with lace and artificial flowers.[37]

Conclusion

The Safavid mental world vis-à-vis the Europeans considered both their men and women as inferior to the Iranians. But at the same time, the European customs, clothes and traditions, especially those of women, could be considered as the most exotic and alien to the Iranian public. The desire of some single-sheet paintings to present some aspects of European culture, not in an exhaustive or scientific way, but rather to capture some piquant traits is what would give an Occidentalist character to certain Persian paintings of the second half of the seventeenth century. These paintings used the fantasies of Europe to create an exotic visual world.

We may not, however, be able to consider all these paintings as the pure fascination of a masculine eye for Western women, where not all the bare torsos or naked women were aimed to appease an erotic need. It is highly probable that the patrons (men and women) who commissioned these images had a semantic understanding of the European images. It is important to keep in mind that the emergence of such new subjects came about by selecting and choosing imported images in order to achieve a synthesis. The viewers or patrons of these paintings were neither the simple admirers of European works of art, nor passive towards Western cultural novelties. In some cases, such as for example Suzanna or Venus, it is perhaps possible to identify them as the new interpretation of Shirin taking a bath. One may suggest that it is with her that Iranian artists and patrons of the late seventeenth century have found some similarities with bathers or some other European nudes.

At the same time, one may propose the possibility that the noble and courtly European women could be observed by their Iranian homologues. Thus, we may consider these paintings not only as a purely Iranian interpretation, but also as a singular reading precisely tailored to the personality and the social position of the patrons. The European women may then not only be observed by the Safavid men, but also by the women.

Notes

1. Literally 'making' or 'building' in 'the European way', the term is a combination of *Farangi*, the adjective of *Farang*, and *Sazi* the present stem of *sakhtan* (building or making). For more information about *Farang* and *Farangi* see Abd-al-Mohammad Rouhbakhshan, *Farang and Farangi in Iran* (Tehran, 1388/2009). See also A. Dehkhoda (1372–73/1993–94), *Loghat Nāmeh*, 37 vols (1325/1956–57/78, Tehran), vol. 10, p. 1587. The expression of *Farangi Sāzi* is mentioned neither in the Safavid written sources nor in that of the later years. However, it is used by the majority of our contemporary scholars in order to describe and define some of the paintings done in the second half of the seventeenth century. For more information, see Eleanor Sims, 'Five seventeenth century oil paintings' in *Persian and Mughal Art* (London, 1976), pp. 221–48; Sheila R. Canby, 'Farangi Sāz, the impact of Europe on Safavid painting', in *Silk and Stone: The Art of Asia*, the Third Hali annual (London, 1996), pp. 46–59; Amy S. Landau, *Farangi sāzi at Isfahan: the court painter Muhammad Zamān, the Armenians of New Julfa and Shāh Soleymān (1666–1694)*, Thesis Dissertation, Oxford University, 2007; Axel Langer (ed.), *The Fascination of Persia, The Persian–European Dialogue in Seventeenth-Century Art & Contemporary Art from Tehran* (Zurich, 2013), pp. 170–237; Negar Habibi, *ʿAli Qoli Jebādār et l'occidentalisme safavide: une étude sur les peintures dites farangi sāzi, leurs milieux et commanditaires sous Shāh Soleimān (1666–94)* (Leiden, 2017).
2. For more information on the artistic characteristics of this century, see for example Basil William Robinson 'A Survey of Persian Painting (1350–1896)', in Ch. Adle (ed.), *Art et société dans le monde Iranien* (Paris, 1982), pp. 68–71; see also Massumeh Farhad 'Searching for the New: Later Safavid Painting and the Suz u Gawdaz (Burning and melting) by Na'i Khabushani', in *The Journal of the Walters Art Museum* 59 (2001), p. 115.
3. For a bibliography of Mohammad Zaman see for example Landau, *Farangi sāzi at Isfahan*, especially pp. 60–75 where she gives a complete list of studies on the life of the artist. For a biography of A. Jebādār, see Negar Habibi, 'A Saheb Mansab Painter? A Reconsideration of ʿAli Qoli Jebādār's career', *Iran* 54 (2016), pp. 143–58.
4. Russian Academy of Sciences, Institute of Oriental Manuscripts, album E-14, f. 93r; John Rynalds Library, Ryl Indian Drawings 6; the Indo–Persian album sold at Hôtel Drouot, 23 June 1982, lot H, n° 7; Russian Academy of Sciences, Institute of Oriental Manuscripts, album E-14, fol. 89r; Arthur M. Sackler Museum, 1966.6, Boston.
5. Russian Academy of Sciences, Institute of Oriental Manuscripts, album E-14, f. 93r; Collection of Hossein Afshar, London; Metropolitan Museum of Art, Album Davis, 30.95.174.24; The Art and History Trust, Arthur and M. Sackler Gallery, Smithsonian institution, LTS 1995.2.118.
6. Russian Academy of Sciences, Institute of Oriental Manuscripts, album E-14, f. 86r.

7. See Mansur Sefatgol, 'Farang, Farangi and Farangestan: Safavid Historiography and the West (907–1148/1501–1736)', in W. Floor and E. Herzig (eds), *Iran and the World in the Safavid Age* (London, 2012), p. 358; see also Rudi Matthee, 'Between Aloofness and Fascination: Safavid Views of the West', in *Iranian Studies* 31 (1998b), pp. 219–46; Sussan Babaie, 'Visual Vestiges of Travel: Persian Windows on European Weaknesses', in *Journal of Early Modern History* 13 (2009), p. 116.
8. The Western travelogues (e.g. J. Chardin, Jean-Baptiste Tavernier, R. Du Mans, etc.) give us a considerable account about the presence of Europeans in Iran. However, as S. Babaie points out, there is a great imbalance between the imposing number of Europeans' overseas visits and that of other continents inhabitants, including the Safavid Iranians; see Babaie, 'Visual Vestiges of Travel', p. 116.
9. M. Sefatgol, 'Farang, Farangi and Farangestan', pp. 361–2.
10. Jean Chardin, *Voyages du Chevalier Chardin en Perse et les autres lieux de l'Orient*, L. Langlès (ed.), Paris, 1811, vol. III.429–30; several European travelogues mention the Iranian inferior look towards the Europeans, some of which are cited by R. Matthee, 'Between Aloofness and Fascination', especially pp. 241–4; See also M. Sefatgol, 'Farang, Farangi and Farangestan', pp. 357–64.
11. See Rudi Matthee, 'Iran's Ottoman Diplomacy During the Reign of Shāh Sulayman I (1077–1105/1666–94)', in K. Eslami (ed.), *Iran And Iranian Studies, Essays in Honor of Iraj Afshar* (New Jersey, 1998c), pp. 154–5, 158.
12. Ibid., pp. 152, 160.
13. J. Chardin, *Voyages du Chevalier Chardin*, V.491, see also R. Matthee, 'Iran's Ottoman Diplomacy', p. 159. Sebastian Knab, Archbishop of Nakhichevan and German envoy of Pope Innocent XI or the representative of the Emperor Leopold I (1655–1705) of Austria, mentions that other European envoys had to wait at least two years to be served with the negative response of Shah Soleiman following their requests for an anti-Ottoman coalition; see R. Matthee, 'Iran's Ottoman Diplomacy', pp. 157–8 and p. 160.
14. J. Chardin, *Voyages du Chevalier Chardin*, V.491.
15. R. Matthee, 'Between Aloofness and Fascination', p. 236, in footnote 79, A. Landau, *Farangi sāzi at Isfahan*, p. 190; the letter is published in L. Fekete, Einführung in die persische Paläographie. 101 persische Dokumente, d. G. Hazai (Budapest, 1977), pp. 529–33.
16. I know that by using this term for these paintings they may be compared with the movement of Europology or *farang shenasi* known in Iran since 1948, especially with studies of F. Shadman, which is a comprehensive study on any aspect of the West. Let me stress that the Occidentalist theme of some Safavid paintings does not tend to reach a detailed and specific knowledge of Europe, such as that of European Orientalists in the eighteenth and nineteenth centuries. I would caution all trends that could be extracted from this expression, which would tend to believe that the Iranians wanted to 'discover' Europe, as the later Westerners did for the East. As for the

attempts of Iranians to know the West, see for example Mohammad Tavakoli-Targhi, *Refashioning Iran, Orientalism, Occidentalism and Historiography* (Houndmills, 2001), pp. 38–44. For the knowledge of Muslims about Europe and vice versa see for example Edward Said, *Orientalism* (London, 1978); see also Lewis, Bernard, *The Muslim Discovery of Europe* (New York, 1982).

17. See C. Peltre, *Dictionnaire culturel de l'Orientalisme* (Paris, 2003); C. Peltre, *Orientalisme* (Paris, 2005).
18. See Vera Kubicková, *Persian Miniatures*, tr. R. Finlayson-Samsour (London, 1959), fig. 24; See also Basil William Robinson, *Persian Painting in the John Rylands Library* (London, 1980), figs. 1196, 1997, p. 302.
19. One of these two paintings is currently at the Freer Gallery (FGA 54.24) and the other is in a private collection. See Sheila R. Canby, *The Rebellious Reformer* (London, 1996), Cat. 7, 8 and Fig. 28; S. Babaie, 'Visual Vestiges of Travel', pp. 124–5; A. Langer (2013), p. 180. For a definition of the nudes, see Kenneth Clarke, *The Nude: A study of Ideal Art* (London, 1956).
20. The nudes represented in Iranian painting are the subject of several recent studies, including those of S. Babaie and Amhy Landau. Babaie, 'Visual Vestiges of Travel', S. Babaie, 'Frontiers of Visual Taboo: Painted Indecencies in Isfahan', in F. Leoni and M. Natif (eds), *Eros and Sexuality in Islamic Art* (Dorchester, 2013); Amy Landau, 'Visibly Foreign, Visibly Female: The Eroticization of the *zan-i farangi* in seventeenth-century Persian painting', in F. Leoni and M. Natif (eds), *Eros and Sexuality in Islamic Art* (Dorchester, 2013), 99–130; see also Nimet Hamdy Allam, 'The Development of Nude Female Drawing in Persian Islamic Painting', in Akten des VII. International kongresses fur Iranische kunst une archalologie (Munich, 1979), 431–4, Canby, *The Rebellious Reformer*, p. 32 and Habibi, *ʿAli Qoli Jebādār et l'occidentalisme safavide*, pp. 121–35.
21. A. Landau, 'Visibly Foreign, Visibly Female', pp. 100 and 106; see also footnotes 11 and 12.
22. Ibid.
23. See Matthee, 'Between Aloofness and Fascination', p. 242; For Musa Beig, see U. Vermeulen, 'L'ambassade persane de Musa Beg aux Provinces-Unies (1625–1628)', in *Persica* 7 (1975–8): 145–53. For Naqdi Beig, see Denis Wright, *The Persians Amongst the English* (London, 1985), pp. 1–8.
24. J. O'Kane reproduced the manuscript in English in 1972. See also Christoph Marcinkowski 'The Safavid Presence in the Indian Ocean: A Reappraisal of the Ship of Solayman, a Seventeenth-Century Travel Account to Siam', in W. Floor and E. Herzig (eds), *Iran and the World in the Safavid Age* (London, 2012),
25. *Safineh Soleimani*, tr. John O'Kane (London, 1972), P. 37.
26. Ibid.
27. Ibid.
28. There were between 12,000 and 14,000 prostitutes in Isfahan. They were omnipresent in Safavid Iran, in particular because they danced and sang in the

private and public ceremonies. According to Chardin it seems that the status of prostitutes was different from that of other urban and nomadic women; see Chardin, *Voyages du Chevalier Chardin*, II.205.

29. J. Chardin, *Voyages du Chevalier Chardin*, II.210–3, 215–6, VII.417; W. R. Ferrier, 'Charles I and the Antiquities of Persia: The Mission of Nicholas Willford', in *Iran* VIII (1970), p. 395; John Fryer, *A new Account of East India and Persia, Being nine years' travels 1672–1681*, William Crooke (ed.) (London, 1967), III.128.
30. British Museum (1974, 0617, 0.1.37).
31. The dance of women dated probably to the Achaemenid era, although it had a bad reputation, particularly in the Islamic era. It was normally courtesans and prostitutes who were involved in dance and music, unlike respectable women. See R. Matthee, 'Prostitutes, Courtesans, and Dancing girls: women entertainers in Safavid Iran', in R. Matthee and B. Baron (eds), *Iran and Beyond, Essays in Middle Eastern History, in Honor of Nikkie R. Keddie* (California, 2000), pp. 121–51, p. 139; see also Anthony Shay, 'Dance and Non-Dance: Patterned Movement in Iran and Islam', in *Iranian Studies*, 28 (1995), pp. 61–78.
32. *Suzanne and the Elders*, Ali Qoli Jebādār, the Indo–Persian Album sold at Hotel Drouot, 23 June 1982, salle 7, L.G.B.T., experts: J. Soustiel, M. -C. David, lot H, n° 7, private collection. *Venus and Cupid*, signed Mohammad Zaman, 1676/77, the Russian Academy of Sciences, the Institute of Oriental Manuscripts, Album E-14, fol. 86r.
33. See for example *Khamseh* of Nezami, Pierpont Morgan Library, M. 469, fol. 90.
34. For Iranian women's clothes of the seventeenth century, see: J. M. Upton, 'Notes on Persian Costumes of the Sixteenth and Seventeenth Centuries,' in *Metropolitan Museum Studies* 2 (1929–30), pp. 206–20; Hermann Goetz, 'Persians and Persian Costumes in Dutch Painting of the Seventeenth-Century', in *The Art Bulletin*, 20 (1938), pp. 2246–53 and especially Figures 1073–4; J. Housego, 'Honour is According to Habit: Persian Dress in the sixteenth and seventeenth centuries', in *Apollo* 93 (1971), pp. 204–9; 'Historical Lexicon of Persian Clothing', in *Encyclopaedia Iranica*, vol. V, pp. 856–65; Jennifer Scarce, 'Vesture and Dress, Fashion, Function and Impact', in C. Bier (ed.), *Woven from the Soul, Spun From the Heart, Textile Arts of Safavid and Qajar Iran 16th–19th centuries* (Washington DC, 1987), pp. 33–57, particularly pp. 38, 44–6; Leyla S. Diba 'Clothing in the Safavid and Qajar periods', in *Encyclopaedia Iranica*, vol. V (1992), p. 790.
35. Jean-Baptiste Tavernier, *Les six voyages de J. B. T. en Turquie, en Perse et aux Indes* (Paris, 1676), p. 490.
36. Engelbert Kaempfer, *Am hofe des persischen grosskonigs (1684–85)*, Walther Hinz (ed.) (Leipzig, 1940), p. 52; he mentions also that these women were treated very well and were not abused by the king. On the same page, Kaempfer also points out that in 1683, the court had kidnapped 20 Armenian girls.

C. Le Brown does not give us any specific detail, but mentions that these girls were intended for the harem of the king, see Cornelius Le Brun, *Voyage de Corneille le Brun par la Moscovie, en Perse, et aux Indes Orientales* (Amsterdam, 1718), I.236.

37. N. Naficy, 'Iranian Art and Its Sociological Setting, Painting in Zand and Qajar periods', in *Akten des VII. International kongresses fur Iranische kunst une archalologie* (Munich, 1979), pp. 466–70.

CHAPTER 15

MEETING OF ANTHROPOLOGY AND RACIAL IDEOLOGY IN HOLLYWOOD: DISCOVERING 'THE FORGOTTEN PEOPLE' AND REMEMBERING 'THE LOST TRIBE' IN *GRASS* (1925)

Ali Sadidi Heris

In 1924, '[t]wo men and a woman sought and found the Forgotten People' known as Bakhtiari, a nomadic tribe in south-western Iran. They documented their semi-annual migration in what is now considered as one of the early examples of feature-length ethnographic films: *Grass: A Nation's Battle for Life*. The cited sentence above is one of the intertitles at the beginning of this silent film that positions the American filmmakers as explorers and discoverers of these people, that are the subject of the film, portrayed as lost and isolated from the rest of the human world. The goal of this chapter is to analyse the construction of this presentation of the Bakhtiari people in the film. In particular, the focus will be on this layered representation through its shared links with scientific endeavours and aspects of Anthropological and Culture Studies. Through elaborating on the claims put forward in reference to the people, *Grass* will be situated as an early example that adopts anthropological claims in the domain of cinema. In addition, the reception of the film during release will be referenced to further complement the perception of

Bakhtiaris and Iranians in general, at the time in the US. Several assessments on ethnography and social anthropology will be utilised for this aim to re-evaluate the claims in *Grass* from a critical standpoint. I argue that *Grass* should be perceived as a meeting point of popular understandings and 'scientific' achievements of anthropology tied with the political significations of the ideology that shaped its context.

It was in the spring of 1922 that Robert Flaherty released his highly acclaimed documentary film *Nanook of the North*. It was the result of a series of shootings that began originally in 1914 and portrayed the life of an Inuit called Nanook living with his family in northern Canada and their existential struggle to access food. Regarded as the first feature-length ethnographic film, its success sparked an interest in 'racial films' in the United States: 'Hollywood was willing to invest in films of ethnographic romanticism, time machines into a faraway present which represented a simpler, "savage" past'.[1] This encouraged many others, even those with no experience in film, to pursue similar paths and document other 'exotic' and 'primitive' non-Western indigenous peoples' struggle with nature.

Merian C. Cooper, the main figure behind the making of *Grass*, was an American aviator who only through hearing about the success of Flaherty's film and without even seeing it was inspired to shoot his own. During his youth, Cooper attended the US Naval Academy that led him to join the Air Service during World War I. In 1919, he volunteered to act as a pilot to battle the Soviet invasion of Poland, in which he was taken hostage and kept in prison for a while.[2] While imprisoned in Moscow, Cooper revealed his identity to Marguerite Harrison who was acting as a spy for American intelligence but guised as an Associated Press correspondent. Prior to the signing of the Versailles Peace Treaty, Harrison also spied for the United States in Germany throughout the War. Cooper's other associate in making *Grass*, Ernest B. Schoedsack served in World War I as an army photographer and camera operator. Schoedsack is considered as one of the first airborne combat photographers. During the Polish–Soviet War he filmed newsreel footage of the Polish fighters. It was in Warsaw that he met with Cooper and they decided together to document a tribe's battle against nature after the success of Flaherty's *Nanook*. Cooper, as an adventurer who always dreamed of becoming an explorer, spent days at the American Geographical Society searching for a 'less known' region that would provide him with this opportunity. Cooper's decision to concentrate on the nomadic tribes that settled in a vast region between the Persian Gulf and the Black Sea directed his attention towards the Kurdish tribes residing in Mesopotamia as he was amazed by the natural lure of the mountainous region of Kurdistan.[3] This indicated that he would be proceeding to move towards the east, which in itself fulfilled the criteria specified by Hollywood for ethnographic film. Later, he teamed up with Schoedsack as agreed and Marguerite Harrison who worked as a reporter for the *Baltimore Sun* at the time. Harrison, also, acted as the financial supervisor of the film alongside Cooper, the only reason why Schoedsack accepted her to be involved.[4]

The film crew's arrival in Ankara, through Istanbul, coincided with the early stages of the newly established Republic in Turkey. The Turkish state which had managed to erect itself after a series of exhausting battles against Western imperial powers, looked with suspicion upon these three foreigners who were desperate to get filming permission from the government. Failing to do so, they decided to move south to the British-administered Iraq and meet with Sir Arnold Wilson and Gertrude Bell, the influential British policy makers who suggested they document the Bakhtiari tribes of southern Iran. Following several negotiations that took place between the British officers and the ruling khans of the tribe, Cooper and his team set foot in Iran to participate in the semi-annual migration of the Baba Ahmadi tribe of the Bakhtiari.[5] This migration process consisted of an estimated 50,000 people and 500,000 animals passing from the snowy mountainous regions of Zagros, climbing Zardeh Kuh, rising to over 4,000 metres, before finally crossing the longest river in Iran, the Karun. What the name Bakhtiari brought to the minds of Westerners was only limited to a few lines in various travelogues of eighteenth- and nineteenth-century voyagers who had visited the region. Gene R. Garthwaite describes it thus:

> The name alone brings to mind many, and often conflicting, images, for which Victorian travellers are primarily responsible. Their accounts provided readers with the vicarious thrill of accompanying the dauntless but largely uncivilized and unprincipled herdsmen in their ceaseless and seemingly ageless quest of pastures for their flocks.[6]

The links between ethnographic film, a visual representative medium, and ethnography, a defining practice of cultural anthropology, have been analysed ever since the former was shaped following the invention of the moving picture. Karl Heider, a visual anthropologist who has studied these links, argues, 'ethnographic film must be judged in relation to ethnography, which is, after all, a scientific enterprise.'[7] This is an indication of an overarching theme in most discussions regarding the nature of ethnographic film: the balance between the entertaining and the scientific in the film. Heider clearly prioritises the latter in favour of an informative and objective approach. Heider's conclusion is that in ethnographic film the cinematography must come second to the ethnography which is the main reason for producing the film: 'Film is the tool and ethnography the goal.'[8] However, the problems arise when the sociocultural and geopolitical differences between the ethnographer filmmaker and the indigenous people as the subject of the film are taken into account. Hence, in discussing ethnographic films, the prevailing attitudes in anthropology and social science regarding ethno–racial divisions and boundaries should be taken into account. This gap or disconnection is largely due to the ontological and epistemological differences between the ethnographer and the indigenous people as the subject of the study.

In order to evaluate *Grass* as a result of ethnographic construction, it is necessary to do so in accordance with ethnography and anthropology itself, as Heider puts it. For this purpose, arguments put forward by Baykan Sezer and Bernard Cohn will be used as a guideline for this analysis. Sezer's distinctive role in generating a local approach to social science outside of the Western academic spectrum, enabled him to formulate a wide corpus of work for this aim. Thus, his indigenous position in understanding ethnography and social anthropology allowed him to develop arguments for a local social science of a region that until that point was considered outside the scholarly knowledge-producing domain. On the other hand, it can be said that Cohn pursued a similar goal from within the tradition of academic anthropology and attempted to historicise the multiple approaches in the discipline. Hence, Sezer and Cohn act as counterparts when discussing anthropology and social sciences. In this sense, Sezer's and Cohn's arguments on ethnography will serve the aims of this chapter to further analyse the mentioned gap between the researcher and the topic of the research in ethnography, since both highlighted the shortcomings of Social Sciences as developed in the Western context when used to study a non-Western indigenous group.

Ethnography as an Imperial Project of Ethno–Racial Classifications

In one of his essential texts, originally published in 1985, titled *Sosyolojinin Ana Başlıkları* (*The Main Titles in Sociology*), Sezer aims to evaluate the development of sociology from an analytic standpoint vis-à-vis other fields of social science such as ethnography and anthropology. At a first glance, he argues, the two disciplines of sociology and ethnography or cultural anthropology share common grounds. If, he asks, the overarching goal of both is to study people and societies, then, why two distinct disciplines have been constructed? Sezer's answer is simple since, he acknowledges, one is intended to study the modern, developed, industrialised Western societies, while the other is put forth to study the primitive, underdeveloped, traditional non-Western people: 'it can be said that sociology becomes the science of Western societies, and ethnography the science of non-Western societies.'[9] The assumption in social sciences, Sezer argues, is that modern Western societies bear all the answers and explanations within themselves and are not in need of non-Western societies' systems of knowledge.

Sezer indicates that the interest towards non-Western societies in the West began a long time before the ethnographic studies of the nineteenth century. There is an enormous body of work composed by many Western travellers and adventurers that had wandered the East and had recorded their experiences. Adding to their numbers are ambassadors and military men that represented Western imperial forces and conducted the first ethnographic studies that relied heavily on first-hand observations. However, the crucial point here would be the urgent need that arose in the nineteenth century in the West to acknowledge non-Western societies. This was largely due to the expansion of Western domination globally that demanded such knowledge to be formed in order to manage the colonised world. Hence:

> The new administration fields required the data and insights collected from the first observations to be organized systematically. This systematic articulation was expected to inscribe efficiency over non-Western peoples and ease the ability to manage them. To sum up, the validity of conclusions derived from this systematization is essential and necessary. This necessity has given, to those studies, the impression of being *scientific*.[10]

According to Sezer, there is one unproblematised assumption that Ethnographical Studies are based on and that is the multiplicity of ethno–racial compositions of societies in the world. A whole range of diverse theoretical practices has been built on this assumption. However, this assumption has not been problematised, Sezer argues, and has been accepted as an explanation in itself. Even the name of this new discipline, 'ethnography', is emphasising this idea as well as sustaining the belief in it through time.

From the Western spectrum of knowledge, Bernard Cohn built up his arguments on similar approaches to anthropology as Sezer's. In his pursuit to outline and elaborate an 'anthropology of colonial knowledge', Cohn attempted to 'historicize the analytical schemas and institutional arenas of colonial knowledge and practice.'[11] It is important to remember that Cohn's main focus was the British colonial rule in India and take into account the problematic implications of adopting his evaluations directly to the Iranian case because of it; however, his emphasis on 'epistemological difficulties' in creating coherent scientific understandings of non-Western peoples by Westerners is of use here. Indeed he argues that the British by coming to India 'unknowingly and unwittingly invaded and conquered not only a territory, but an epistemological space as well.'[12] Cohn draws upon a wide range of data such as reports, documents, artefacts, regulations, statistics, investigations as well as interactions among languages, legal codes, histories and so on, to document different ways of categorising and classifying indigenous people by anthropologists. Cohn, also, highlights the links between the development of anthropology and European colonial activities: 'Throughout the colonial period, some anthropologists argued, in a highly ambivalent fashion, that they had a particular role to play in mediating between the colonial subjects and rulers.'[13] He argues that they established this aim by accepting the assumption that the societies they were interacting with or governing 'could be known and represented as a series of facts.'[14] Through constructing certain coherent accounts based on these 'facts', they claimed to have engaged in scientific and analytic endeavour.

In the following section, while arguing the presentation of the Bakhtiari in *Grass*, instances of this appropriation of knowledge will be outlined to delineate how the ontological and epistemological gaps were conquered in order for the Western imperial gaze to adjust and adapt the non-Western in its own classifications. In that case, it can be said that both Sezer and Cohn argue against a perception of social sciences being value-free and objective, since both invite to consider the 'beneficiaries' of the assessments put forward in these disciplines.

The Bakhtiari as True Aryans: Racial Theory and Ethnography

In accordance with the above-mentioned arguments, I will attempt to evaluate the approach and attitude of the filmmakers of *Grass* towards the Bakhtiari. Therefore, with references to intertitles of the film, some of the arguments rooted in Ethnographic Studies will be outlined.

The film starts with these two intertitles:

> *The* way of the world is west.
>
> Long the sages have told us how our forefathers, the Aryans of old, rose remote in Asia and began conquest of earth, moving ever in the path of the sun.
>
> Back in the East behind us are the secrets of our own past, and a tradition of our brothers still living in the cradle of the race – a long since Forgotten People.

The racial identification here, Aryans, is used to describe the Bakhtiari people as well as defining them alongside 'forefathers' of Western societies. Previously, this identification had deeper roots in British colonisation of India and the Middle East and it also shares connections with the scholarly and scientific studies of the nineteenth century. The notion of the Aryan race, in opposition to the Semitic race, was developing in the academic circles of the time, for instance its origin is estimated to date back to the linguistic studies of the eighteenth century, notably with the idea of the Indo–European languages. Later on, figures such as Max Müller, German-born philologist considered as the founder of Indology or Indian Studies, provided it with extensive historical background. Müller was appointed to edit the translations of an enormous collection of old Indian Sanskrit texts that resulted in *Sacred Books of the East* in 49 volumes.[15]

The intertwining of political pursuits with intellectual interests regarding issues of language, race and spirituality was behind the establishment of the Theosophical Society by Colonel Henry Olcott, Helena Blavatsky and William Q. Judge in 1875 which published extensively on the idea of Aryan race. The Theosophical movement and its outputs influenced the development of disciplines such as linguistics in the academic milieu as well as the reception of Eastern religio–historical texts. Blavatsky believed that India was ready for spiritual regeneration as she claimed to have access to thousands more Sanskrit texts than Müller did.[16] In her book *The Secret Doctrine*, originally published in 1888, Blavatsky appoints the Aryan race with the mission of spreading civilisation in today's world. Following in Blavatsky's steps, Annie Besant who became president of the society in 1907, declared five civilisations throughout history in chronological order were founded by the Aryans: the Indian civilisation, the Mesopotamian civilisations, the Persian Empire, the Roman Empire and, finally, contemporary European civilisation. In addition, Aryans were migrating westward throughout history and were building empires and civilisations at each stop. Besant placed the Western colonial empires as the Aryans' fifth great civilisation.[17] Blavatsky's and Besant's ideas and notions would potentially bring the internalisation of the British modern/colonial rule by the local people as intended in the imperial policies of the time. Peter van der Veer puts it thus: 'In colonized India the idea of race had to be combined with that of culture or civilisation to explain why the British as "younger brothers" of the Aryan family had to guide the "older brothers" to the civilisation.'[18] This justification is clearly implied in one of the articles by Besant as she discusses the issue of ethno–racial affiliations between the Indians and the British:

> Nor must we forget that the Indian is our equal, and not our inferior. We must meet him on equal terms, and not as if we belonged to a higher race. We are all of the same race, the Aryans. Of that root stock of the Aryan we are a later branch.[19]

The overlapping similarities in the subjection of the Indians by Besant and Blavatsky to the positioning of the Bakhtiari in *Grass* are noteworthy. Throughout the film, the Bakhtiari are portrayed as being on 'equal terms' racially, albeit belonging to an earlier 'branch' that places them in the same historic era as the 'forefathers' of Western civilisation. Just as the Aryans had started out in India migrating toward the West according to Blavatsky, the Bakhtiari had belonged to the times of Mesopotamian and ancient Persian civilisations. For this reason, they represent the 'past' for Westerners and they still inhabit the 'traditions' of earlier Aryans, in an unchanging way to this day. Alternatively, Cooper expands on the idea of the Bakhtiari as Aryans in a memoir he published following the release of the film in 1925 outlining the journey in more detail, titled *Grass*. In chapter 4 of his memoir, Cooper mentions that the Bakhtiari are probably descendants of the 'noble Aryans' who lived in Iran, which would make this migration belong to 'our Aryan ancestors from thousands of years ago.'[20] Furthermore, Cooper considers 'the firm posture' and 'beautifully shaped elements of the face' of the Bakhtiari members as proof of their ancient roots. However, he acknowledged his failure in gathering the necessary historical and sociocultural information regarding the tribe before the journey and performed an extended research when he was back in New York. Cooper's main reference here is the book *Persia and the Persian Question* by George N. Curzon. Lord Curzon, who held various administrative offices on relations with India and Iran including Viceroy of India between 1899–1905, had travelled to every corner of Iran and gathered his observations in two volumes. Curzon begins by positioning the Bakhtiari as 'a people without a history, a literature, or even a tradition' that 'presents a phenomenon in face of which science stands abashed.'[21] Not only Curzon confronts difficulties 'to lift the curtain of an inscrutable past' regarding the people, but also indicates doubts over categorising the Bakhtiari in one of the ethno–racial classifications: 'Are they Turks? Are they Persians? Are they Semites?' Yet, he concludes that '[i]t is sufficient to believe that they are Aryans by descent, and to know that they have lived for centuries in their present mountains.'[22] This recurring theme of 'Bakhtiari as Aryan' was also present in the reviews of the film done by American critics. In a review of the film *Grass* published in the weekly *The Literary Digest*, the writer has this to say when highlighting the lack of any protagonist in the film: 'There is no beautiful hero and heroine, no story other than the epic struggle of a tribe of primitive Aryans with the forces of nature that seem too powerful for human efforts to combat.'[23]

The unproblematised assumption in ethnography that perceives all people according to distinct ethno–racial classifications, as argued by Sezer, reproduces itself in Curzon's effort to include the Bakhtiari in one of the formulated groups. This particular articulation of a 'scientific racism', as coined by Wulf D. Hund, that combines cultural with biological arguments was developing since the Enlightenment.[24] Hund argues that ethnography and ethnographic exhibitions were one of the tools in popularising racial theory.[25] Curzon's assertions as an observer, ethnographer and colonial administrator are transferred into Cooper's ethnographic film on the tribe. The European racial thought or 'scientific racism' was imported in Iranian intellectual circles long before Cooper and his crew attempted to produce *Grass*.[26] However, the Bakhtiari tribe and specifically the Baba Ahmadi sub-tribe documented throughout the film, had no self-identification as Aryans or as descendants of an Aryan race. Cooper, in his book, mentions Rahim, the only member of the tribe who could communicate with them in English during the migration. Rahim proudly states that 'they – the Bakhtiari – are the true Iranians.'[27] The connotations of being a 'true Iranian', in the thought of the tribe members in comparison to the thought of Westerners, are an instance of the gap in epistemological and ontological differences these two groups held. In this sense, as argued by Cohn, Cooper's and Curzon's epistemological world 'was part of the European world of social theories and classificatory schema that were formed, in part, by state projects to reshape the lives of their subjects at home and abroad.'[28] Cooper, by grounding his presentation of the Bakhtiari on the speculative arguments of Curzon, carried on the same flaws and biases to his own work. Instead of attributing this to his carelessness or misunderstanding of Curzon's arguments, it actually reveals his eagerness to situate himself in the same line of knowledge production on the non-Western that was conceived as scholarly and scientific. Hence, his film would be successful in attracting the attention of institutions such as academia; a fact that was reflected in exhibitions that he organised in several universities throughout the US to screen the film.

The Life of Thousands of Years Ago: Cultural Evolution and Myth of 'Lost Tribes'

Another approach in *Grass* to identify the Bakhtiari has its roots in the ethnographic and cultural studies of the late nineteenth century. The journey that the filmmakers took from the USA to Iran, through Turkey and Iraq, is described in *Grass* with the following intertitle: '*But going ahead, we were turning the pages backwards* – on and on further back into the centuries –/ Till we reached the first Chapter, arrived at the very beginning'. The further eastwards they were travelling, the further they were going back in history. In other words, they were not only in motion through space but also through time. This linear spatialised perception of time was the result of evolutionist tendencies. In the nineteenth century, many anthropologists and social scientists attempted to apply Darwinist evolutionary principles to their studies. To establish 'scientific' claims in their fields, anthropologists and social scientists viewed the evolutionist approach in natural science as a scientific tool that needed to be adopted. This was a ubiquitous approach to explain the variety of differences that existed in communities geographically dispersed throughout the world. In this case, linear cultural development was the main principle that would apply to all peoples and rationality was the measure of this progress. The works of Lewis Henry Morgan and Edward B. Tylor were crucial in the organisation of this view known as cultural evolutionism. Tylor who is credited with being the founder of cultural anthropology, argued that while humans evolve biologically, the progress of innate rational faculties also improve the societies they belong to. Since 'all societies evolve in a single direction towards complexity, progress and civilisation', some would be more 'complex', 'advanced' and 'civilised' than others.[29]

In his arguments on ethnography and anthropology, Sezer highlights the premise that peoples and societies inhabit different levels of progress on the same single linear timeline of development, the end of the line being Western society and all the others occupying spots between the start line and the end. This is where Sezer arrives at the conclusion that there are no differences among Western and non-Western societies in social science, because 'the Western society is *the society*';[30] just as in *Grass*, '*the* way of the world is West'. Various states exist in the development of Western societies and the reason for the diversity today is the different stands on the progression of this monotype society. Hence, the Bakhtiari people with their lifestyle and traditions represent a time when 'the way of the world' was East, but now has been put behind or 'forgotten' by the advances Western civilisation has achieved: '*We know them by the ancient life of tent and tribe and herd, the life of three thousand years ago.*'

There is a scene in *Grass* that places Marguerite Harrison, the only person from the crew shown in front of the lens and portrayed as a modern Western woman, next to the local Bakhtiari women in their indigenous clothing. The contrast between these two worlds emphasises the 'historical gap' that is assumed. The myth of an isolated, lost, forgotten and uncontacted tribe that has now got in touch with the civilised modern world is repeated in this scene. This myth functions each time an explorer and adventurer makes the claim of having discovered such a tribe as Cooper and Schoedsack do in *Grass*. Naturally, the first viewing of the film in America took place in The Explorers Club of New York on the night of 24 January 1925. Jesse L. Lasky, motion picture producer and founder of Paramount Pictures, watched the film that night and decided to purchase it for release, regretting he had not done so with *Nanook*.[31] Above all, at the end of the film, a document dated 5 June 1924, bearing the signatures of the Bakhtiari tribal chiefs as well as the American Consul in Iran re-emphasise the myth through the following statement:

> Dima, Persia, June 5th, 1924.
> M.C. Cooper, E.B. Schoedsack and M.E. Harrison are the first foreigners who have made the 46 day migration with the Baba Ahmadi tribe of the Bakhtyari, over the Zardeh Kuh trail from the Jungari district in Arabistan to the Chahar Mahal valley in Ehleck.
> Amir Jang, Prince of the Bakhtyari.
> Haidar Khan, Chief of the Baba Ahmadi.
>
> Sworn to before me by Amir Jang, Prince of the Bakhtyari at Tehran the 20th day of June, 1924.
> Robert W. Imbrie, Vice Consul of the United States.

This is indicating that the ethnographic value of this documentation relied heavily on the fact that it was performed for the very first time by three Westerners. Cooper draws again on this point in his memoir when he writes: 'I think Haidar was correct in saying that we were the first to have migrated with the Baba Ahmadi tribe over this route.'[32] The urge to document the contact with an 'uncontacted tribe' through administrative institutions and political representatives is where the line between fiction and reality or geopolitical and scientific studies is blurred in ethnography.

The repetitive argument regarding the Bakhtiari's way of life belonging to 'thousands of years ago', ubiquitous in the film, books written on the film by Cooper and Harrison, as well as the reviews of the film at the time of release, all point to the need to keep the Bakhtiari as far and distant as possible.[33] According to Johannes Fabian, the evolutionist perception of time is a 'naturalized-spatialized Time which gives meaning (in face of a variety of specific meanings) to the distribution of humanity in space' and is constructed to distance the observed from the 'Time of the Observer'.[34] Indeed the filmmaking approach of Cooper and Schoedsack was 'Keep it distant, difficult, and dangerous.'[35] Thus, *Grass* and the early examples of ethnographic film acted as time machines that would take the viewer on a safe journey from the seat of the cinema to far off distances through time and space. The filmmaker would gather footages of 'exotic' and 'unknown' places and peoples in order to entertain the audience with adventurous trips. This was done to the extent that after a certain point the fictitious or real nature of the information provided would become irrelevant, if not secondary. This would reverse the formula of Heider for ethnographic film effectively, combining entertainment and science while drawing upon ideological connotations that had shaped its context.

Conclusion

Cooper, Harrison and Schoedsack all had backgrounds in various military and intelligence services. While Cooper and Schoedsack were fighting in the military force, Harrison was providing the government with intelligence. The shift they made after the war, to leave behind careers in the military and intelligence, visiting instead the lesser-known parts of the world, such as the Middle East, can be seen as an attempt to introduce these regions to the American audience. Thomas Doherty also argues this point when he perceives the exploration film 'on the most obvious level' as 'a transparent projection of American frontier vision onto new worlds in an age of territorial limitations.'[36] The decision to draw on ethnography and anthropology belies the seemingly innocent scientific curiosity of the project, as in reality it resulted in an increase in the United States' influence in the region. Hollywood's involvement carried the anthropological databank into a new medium resulting in works like *Nanook* and *Grass*. The Cooper and Schoedsack duo would move on to produce other ethnographic and fiction films with similar motivations peaking with the success of their most iconic fiction film, *King Kong* in 1933. As Naficy states: 'The wide dissemination of such ideologically loaded projections of non-Western people would ensure that these ideologies would become part of the political unconscious of Westerners, helping, in the words of Edward Said, to ideologically "produce" the "East," or the "Orient".'[37] Thus, following Said's arguments, certain mechanisms of the 'Orientalist' perspective had gained dominancy in Hollywood's approach to the matter that, in return, had placed the US as an extension of its European imperial counterparts.

In her article on *Grass*, Amy Malek draws parallels with the 1976 remake titled *People of the Wind* that portrays the migration of the Bakhtiari. She analyses the tension between entertainment value and ethnographic value, only this time two anthropologists are consulting the filmmaker Anthony Howarth. Malek demonstrates that despite the advantages the latter film had, both regarding technological advancements and the scholarly attention to the Bakhtiari people, *People of the Wind* fails to deliver a 'more ethnographic' film in terms of content and approach. She concludes that the struggle between education and entertainment is still a serious blow to ethnographic filmmaking in terms of scholarly engagement.[38] However, to draw on Rony's assertions, while the ethnographic film archive seems to be a mere collection of visual documents, the world does not act in a value-free manner: 'the circulation of images presupposed by the archive implicates social, historical and political relations of dominance.'[39] This brings forth the necessity of taking into account the geopolitical structure of the world while evaluating the current function of ethnography and anthropology, since, as put by Fabian: 'production of knowledge occurs in a public forum of intergroup, interclass, and international relations.'[40] In other words, the function of ethnography is to systemise the data collected on non-Westerners in a way that would contribute to shape and organise the world based on a set of values and criteria that would maintain Western imperial dominance. Overall, ethnography *is* a form of appropriation by the imperial gaze and ethnographic film is a visual manifestation of that.

It can be said that *Grass* is one of the first examples of overlap between subjective anthropological studies and an ideologically constructed presentation to re-order the global scene according to US imperialism that met in the entertainment-film-industry milieu of Hollywood.

Grass is the filmic expression of an imaginary that constitutes the cultures of the non-Western peoples as the object of study for the knowing subjects of the West. The cultures of the Bakhtiari are transferred into Western anthropology and the constructed representation is then dispatched back to where it came from as ethnographic study. In this way, it also manages to overcome what Cohn defines as the epistemological divide that exists between the representation of the Bakhtiari in the West and their self-identification. Through *Grass* and its pioneer *Nanook*, the medium of film was utilised to perform as a new component of the long tradition of data collection in ethnography. Eventually, the presence of America in regional politics of the Middle East increased significantly and, even though, there are no direct links between the two, the discourse that was influential in British imperial colonisation had now translated itself into another transatlantic imperial force that replaced its predecessor on the global scene. To put it more simply, *Grass* can be perceived as a product of the long line of missionaries, men of letter and travellers of sixteenth and seventeenth centuries to the military men and scientifics of the eighteenth and nineteenth centuries had now landed on the then-newly found medium of film.

All quotations from non-English sources have been translated. Emphases in the originals are included.

Notes

1. Fatimah Tobing Rony, *The Third Eye: Race, Cinema and Ethnographic Spectacle* (Durham, 1996), p. 133.
2. Paul M. Jensen, 'Cooper, Merian Coldwell' in *American National Biography Online* (2000). Available at www.anb.org/articles/18/18-01970.html [Accessed 12 June 2016].
3. Mark Cotta Vaz, *Living Dangerously: The Adventures of Merian C. Cooper, the Creator of King Kong* (New York, 2005), pp. 111–12.
4. Schoedsack expressed his discomfort regarding Harrison's presence during the filmmaking in an interview published in *American Cinematographer*: 'Marguerite Harrison was a fine, courageous and adventurous woman, and was really not very much trouble to us, but she just didn't belong in this sort of a show. She only saw the Bakhtiari tribesmen as dirty, wandering fellows who sometimes beat their wives.' in Ernst B. Schoedsack, 'Grass: The Making of an Epic', in *American Cinematographer*, 64 (1983), pp. 40–4 & 109–14, p. 112.
5. Vaz, *Living Dangerously*, pp. 117–18.

6. Gene R. Garthwaite, *Khans and Shahs: A History of the Bakhtiyari Tribe in Iran* (New York, 2009), p. 1.
7. Karl G. Heider, *Ethnographic Film: Revised Edition* (Austin, 2006). p. 4.
8. Ibid., p. 3.
9. Baykan Sezer, *Sosyolojinin Ana Başlıkları / Main Titles in Sociology* (Istanbul, 2016), p. 43.
10. Ibid., p. 45.
11. Nicholas Dirks, 'Introduction', in Bernard Cohn, *Colonialism and its Forms of Knowledge* (Princeton, 1996), p. x.
12. Bernard Cohn, *Colonialism and its Forms of Knowledge* (Princeton, 1996), p. 4.
13. Ibid., p. 11.
14. Ibid., p. 4.
15. R. C. C. Fynes, 'Müller, Friedrich Max (1823–1900)' (*Oxford Dictionary of National Biography*, 2004). Available at www.oxforddnb.com/view/article/18394. [Accessed 20 April 2016].
16. Christopher M. Hutton and John E. Joseph, 'Back to Blavatsky: The impact of theosophy on modern linguistics', in *Language & Communication*, vol. 18 Issue 3 (1998), p. 183.
17. Annie Besant delivered a series of lectures at the Annual Convention of the Theosophical Society, at Adyar, during December 1903 entitled: *The Pedigree of Man*. Available at www.anandgholap.net/Pedigree_Of_Man-AB.htm [Accessed 15 June 2016].
18. Peter van deer Veer, 'Hindus: a superior race', in *Nations and Nationalism*, 5 (1999), pp. 424–5.
19. Annie Besant, 'Coloured Races in the Empire', in *The Indian Review*, 14 (1913), pp. 288–94, p. 29.
20. Merian C. Cooper, *Grass* (New York, 1925), in *Mostanad Alaf: Se Revayat va Yek Moghaddameh / The Documentary Grass: Three Narratives and One Introduction*, Ahmad Alasti (ed. and tr.) (Tehran, 2015), p. 115.
21. George N. Curzon, *Persia and the Persian Question*, vol. 2 (London, 1966, originally published in 1892), p. 273.
22. Ibid., p. 274.
23. The Literary Digest, 'An Epic Movie of Man's Fight with Nature' (25 April 1925), p. 27.
24. Wulf D. Hund, 'Negative Societalisation: Racism and the Constitution of Race', in Wulf D. Hund, Jeremy Krikler, David Roediger (eds), *Wages of Whiteness & Racist Symbolic Capital* (Berlin, 2010), p. 58.
25. Ibid., p. 70.
26. For more on this point: Reza Zia-Ebrahimi, *The Emergence of Iranian Nationalism: Race and the Politics of Dislocation* (New York, 2016).
27. Cooper, *Grass*, p. 115.
28. Cohn, *Colonialism and its Forms of Knowledge*, p. 11.
29. Rumina Rai, *Introduction to Cultural Studies* (Mumbai, 2010) pp. 24–5.
30. Sezer, *Sosyolojinin Ana Başlıkları*, p. 43.
31. Bahman Maghsoudlou, *Alaf: Dastan-haye Shegeft va Nagofteh* (Tehran, 2010) pp. 405–46; also published in English: *Grass: Untold Stories* (Costa Mesa, 2009).

32. Cooper, *Grass*, p. 201.
33. Harrison, in her memoir regarding the trip, mentions that the place they had gone to was where 'the human civilisation had stayed still for two thousand years.' Marguerite Harrison, *There's Always Tomorrow: The Story of a Checkered Life* (New York, 1935), in Alasti, *The Documentary Grass*, p. 227.
34. Johannes Fabian, *Time and the Other* (New York, 2014), p. 25.
35. Vaz, *Living Dangerously*, p. 7.
36. Thomas Doherty, 'The Age of Exploration: The Hollywood Travelogue Film', in *Cineaste*, 20 (1993), pp. 38–40, p. 38.
37. Hamid Naficy, 'Lured by the East: Ethnographic and Expedition Films About Nomadic Tribes - The Case of Grass', in Jeffrey Ruoff (ed.), *Virtual Voyages: Cinema and Travel* (Durham, 2006), p. 133.
38. Amy Malek, *'"If you're going to educate 'em, you've got to entertain 'em too": An Examination of Representation and Ethnography in Grass and People of the Wind'*, in *Iranian Studies*, 44 (2011), p. 325.
39. Rony, *The Third Eye*, p. 68.
40. Fabian, *Time and the Other*, p. 143.

CHAPTER 16

'SORAYA CRIED FOR THREE DAYS': THE MANY FACES OF IRANIAN-GERMAN ROYALTY IN THE GERMAN POPULAR PRESS IN THE 1950S AND 1960S

Birgit Röder

Soraya Esfandiary-Bakhtiari was the second wife of the Shah of Iran Reza Pahlavi (1919–80). Her father, Khalil Esfandiary-Bakhtiari was the Imperial Ambassador of Iran in the Federal Republic of Germany from 1951–61 and came from one of the most high-ranking aristocratic Persian families. By contrast, her mother, Eva Karl, came from an unambiguously middle-class German background. Soraya grew up in Isfahan and Berlin, attended elite boarding schools in Montreux, Lausanne and London, and was fluent in German, Farsi, French and English. A cosmopolitan figure on the world stage, she always insisted that she felt equally at home in the cultures of both Germany and Iran, that is to say in both the oriental and occidental world. At the age of 17 she was officially enrolled as a student of German literature at the University of Bonn while at the same time taking acting lessons in the hope of making a career in the performing arts. Her obvious intelligence was complemented by an exotic Ava Gardner-like beauty and an engaging personality. From her glamorous marriage in 1951 as an 18 year old right up to her equally dramatic divorce some seven years later, she enjoyed the status of a cult figure in the eyes of the rightwing tabloid press in Germany who – in a tacit allusion to her mixed race origins – dubbed her 'the German empress on the peacock throne'.[1] In addition, Soraya's predicament invoked memories of the extremely popular Bavarian Princess Elizabeth who, following her marriage to her cousin Franz Joseph I had, in 1854 become Empress of Austria and Queen of Hungary. Indeed there is a striking similarity between the kind of cult following that Elizabeth ('Sissi') enjoyed in the mid-nineteeth century and that which came to be associated with Soraya a hundred years later.

The Shah already had a daughter, Shahnaz, from his first marriage with the Egyptian princess Fawzia, but the patrilineal structures of the Iranian monarchy meant she could not succeed her father to the throne. Nonetheless, this daughter was living proof of the Shah's fertility and, of course, of Soraya's inability to conceive – ostensibly the grounds for her divorce in 1958.[2] Although Soraya had a series of relationships following her separation from the Shah, she never remarried and had no children. In accordance with her own wishes, she is buried alongside her parents and brother in a cemetery in Munich – another reason why she is popularly regarded by many Germans as 'one of ours'. Every detail of her life both during her marriage to the Shah and following her divorce was obsessively monitored by the German press; but the ways in which her image was constructed in the press at different points in history were, at least to some extent, conditioned by the changing view of Iran in the West generally and in the Federal Republic in particular.

Given the extent to which Soraya's public persona in Germany was mediated via a carefully selected series of images, it is perhaps fitting that the start of her relationship with the Shah can be traced back to a photographic image. As the first nine years of his marriage to the Egyptian princess Fawzia had not resulted in a male heir, the Shah was presented with a seemingly endless stream of photographs of potential wives who had been pre-vetted by his mother, twin-sister and cousin. Reza Pahlavi had a reputation as a notorious playboy and womaniser (not only before but also during his three marriages); nonetheless the photo of Soraya appears to have made an impression on him as she, together with her family, were invited to Tehran for a meeting with the man who would become her future husband. Soraya was quick to accept the Shah's offer of marriage (in fact the Shah asked her father for her hand in marriage only hours after the initial meeting) and that was probably one of the reasons why their relationship was widely reported as an instance of love at first sight.[3] Whether or not that was actually the case can only be a matter for speculation because Soraya's autobiography clearly follows a political and commercial agenda. However, presenting this carefully engineered relationship in terms of a series of romanticised clichés addressed the needs and desires of patriarchal and politically conservative factions in both the Federal Republic and Iran. Crudely put, Soraya's greatest asset was her potential to produce a male heir and – in a manner reminiscent of the arranged feudal alliances of the pre-modern world – to shore up the Pahlavi dynasty in Iran while at the same time stabilising a political relationship between the Federal Republic and Iran that would become increasingly precarious. However, once it became clear that Soraya's reproductive organs were not up to the job, she would fall victim to the same operations of patriarchal scheming that had originally catapulted her into a position of power.

1946 had seen the marriage of Eva Duarte to the Argentinian president Juan Peron; in 1953 Jackie Bouvier married the American president John F. Kennedy; and three years later Grace Kelly married Prince Rainier of Monaco. With Soraya's marriage to the Shah in 1951 the Federal Republic also had its own glamorous 'First Lady' on the postwar global stage. However, Soraya's image as a transnational icon of glamour and power politics in the popular press also needs to be seen in the context of the political and historical situation of the Federal Republic in the decade immediately following the end of World War II. The period 1949–61 in West Germany was characterised by a deeply conservative political agenda under the leadership of Chancellor Konrad Adenauer and his rightwing Christian Democrats (CDU). At one level, Adenauer's policies were designed to ensure the continued viability of a capitalist western-oriented German state in the face of the perceived threat of Eastern Bloc expansionism (a threat which for West Germans was crystallised in the division of Germany and the existence of its communist neighbour the German Democratic Republic). The geopolitical dynamics of the early phase of the Cold War explain not only the Marshall Plan of 1947 that in turn led to the so-called 'economic miracle' of the mid to late 1950s, but also the rapid integration of the Federal Republic into NATO in 1955 – just ten years after the collapse of Hitler's Third Reich. As a result, a country that had lain in ruins in 1945 was, at least in the West, transformed into a prosperous state that whole-heartedly embraced American-style capitalism and consumerism, and whose rehabilitation within the family of Western nations was confirmed by membership of the European Economic Group in 1957.

Achieving such geopolitical goals went hand in hand with the implementation of a raft of equally conservative domestic policies designed to 'normalise' those social and gender relations in Germany that had been disrupted by the trauma of World War II. As in other countries, the war had forced women to abandon their traditional roles as wives and mothers and to gain a sense of independence and self-worth by skilling up and assuming positions of responsibility in production and manufacturing. The situation was compounded by the large number of men who had either lost their lives in combat or whose experiences at the front and in Prisoner of War camps had left them so traumatised that they were scarcely able to pick up the threads of their pre-war lives.[4] One of the tasks the Adenauer government set itself was the rehabilitation of the male population, a process which centred by and large on the revival of the patriarchal family model with all that this implies. As women increasingly made way in the workplace for male returnees, they were confronted with an alternative role model, the perfect housewife with a weakness for American-style consumerism, a role model that found its fullest expression in such figures as Doris Day.[5]

Seen in this context, the Shah's marriage to Soraya served as an ideal embodiment of the essentially patriarchal values underpinning the domestic policies of the staunchly Catholic Konrad Adenauer and his CDU government, while at the same time conjuring up pre-war associations with paternalistic modes of government in which the ruling family was inseparable from the concept of the nation itself. Adenauer's own style of authoritarian leadership in which a willingness to compromise was regarded as a sign of weakness was also mirrored, at least to some extent, in the autocratic figure of the Shah. But in the 'German empress' Soraya, a German nation whose values and sense of identity had been thrown into confusion by the trauma of the Nazi dictatorship, was invited to embrace a different and distant culture that had enjoyed a long and rich tradition extending back over more than 2,500 years. In many respects Soraya was also the perfect embodiment of a fantasy of modern femininity in postwar Germany: an exotic beauty who had enjoyed the benefits of a Western education, who went skiing in Switzerland and whose wardrobe was overseen by top designers in Paris, Rome and Milan. At the same time she was portrayed as an individual who embraced Western notions of female emancipation and whose efforts to improve the rights of women in her Iranian homeland provoked not only the fury of the mullahs but also the criticism of the

Shah's equally conservative mother. However, those aspects of her personality that were at odds with such images of emancipated femininity went largely unreported in the German tabloid press. For example, despite her initial objections, ultimately Soraya did conform to the patriarchal customs of the Iranian royal family and submitted to a pre-nuptial gynaecological examination to prove that she was indeed a *virgo intacta*. Likewise, she had few qualms in exploiting her glamour and celebrity status to boost the popularity of her husband – a man who effectively enjoyed the status of an absolute ruler – thereby shoring up a reactionary political system that was quite at odds with the new postwar understanding of democracy in her other (German) 'homeland'.[6] However, the German tabloid press's fascination with the Persian Other and its idealisation of the structures of political and familial power associated with the Shah's family serviced a range of German needs and desires during the Adenauer era. Indeed it is striking that during the 1950s and 1960s the popular press in Germany almost always refers to Persia – and not Iran – when reporting on the Shah or any member of the Pahlavi family. This is because in German the term *Persien* – evoking as it does images of the poetry of Omar Chajjam, Hafez, Saadi and the often erotically charged stories narrated by Scheherazade – has far more exotic and sumptuous connotations than 'Iran'. But behind this veil of mysterious erotic exoticism lay concealed the fantasy of a supposedly timeless realm of reactionary conservative values that, in Adenauer's postwar Germany, was once more in high demand. References in the tabloid press to Soraya, empress and empire – all terms that evoked memories of a pre-1914 German Empire untainted by Hitler's legacy – conjured up an array of eternal values the origins of which could be traced back to a world that seemed to have existed from time immemorial and which was impervious to change.

The extent to which the image of Soraya in the tabloid press was an artificial construction is reflected in the contradictory nature of these images themselves. In an edition of the popular weekly magazine *Wochenend* of November 1954 we learn that 'Soraya is unbelievably popular in Persia. With her natural air she has conquered the hearts of school children, impoverished peasants, carpet weavers in Tabriz, and the rose growers of Shiraz.'[7] As we shall see, such superficial reporting masked the fact that, having sought temporary refuge in Rome from widespread anti-Shah demonstrations, the real reason for the return of Soraya and her husband to Iran was the need to address the impending crisis surrounding the nationalisation of Iran's oil reserves. Three years later, however, in 1957 the same magazine carried the following report: 'In Persia, the beautiful Soraya, beloved by everyone across the world is not popular. Not only is she at loggerheads with the close members of her political entourage, but the bulk of the population – for the most part supporters of Mosaddeq – now detest her'.[8] That is just one of many examples of the way in which a predominantly rightwing tabloid press exploited Soraya's image in order to elicit popular support for the vested interests of a transnational authoritarian elite that spanned both Iran and the Federal Republic. In the 1954 article Soraya is portrayed as the mother of the nation and as a figure devoted to children and ordinary people; in keeping with such conservative class-bound fantasies, the image is deployed to prop up an existing political hierarchy by positing an unconditional relationship of mutual love and admiration between the aristocratic ruler and her subjects from the lower orders. Accordingly *Weltbild* comments: 'And ordinary people, guided by their infallible sense for what is genuine and true took Soraya to their hearts.'[9] Maintaining the myth of an elite upper class devoted to the well-being of the lower classes was, of course, just one of the ways in which the German tabloid press sought to deflect criticism from the conservative agenda of the rightwing Adenauer government in the Federal Republic of the early 1950s.

In 1951 the liberally minded patriot, Dr Mohammad Mosaddeq, had been appointed Prime Minister in Iran. During his period in office a number of progressive social reforms were implemented, of which by far the most important was the nationalisation of the Iranian petrochemical industry which, up until that point, was controlled by the British-based Anglo–Persian Oil Company, the AIOC. Popular anti-British and anti-Western sentiment was on the rise and prompted a series of increasingly virulent anti-Shah demonstrations that in turn prompted the Shah to seek refuge first in Baghdad and then in Rome. In 1953, however, the intervention of President Eisenhower and the CIA led to the removal of Mosaddeq from power and, under the new prime minister General Zahedi, the petroleum industry was de-nationalised and a consortium was set up to oversee access to Iran's oil reserves – an arrangement that was highly advantageous to both the USA and Great Britain. In return the USA pledged itself to supporting the Shah and his luxurious lifestyle.[10]

Portraying Soraya as the mother of the Persian nation as the 1954 article in *Wochenend* did just months after the oil crisis sent out a clear subtext: the Shah and his wife are back on their rightful throne, ruling over a grateful and submissive populace and Iranian oil reserves are, once again, in safe (Western) hands. For the citizens of a German state that was increasingly dependent on regular oil supplies in order to fuel its 'economic miracle' the message was one of reassurance. Although the reports of the 1954 and 1957 articles in the magazine *Wochenend* would appear at first sight to be diametrically opposed to one another, they are in fact both underpinned by essentially the same concerns, namely the mobilisation of an anti-MosaddEqn (and anti-nationalisation) agenda. By appealing to popular sentiment and describing how the universally adored Soraya is now despised by Iran's pro-Mosaddeq population, the 1957 article aims to neutralise any critique of the attempts of the Shah and his Western backers to reverse the nationalisation of the Iranian oil industry and to undermine support for progressive democratic movements.

Adenauer's government and the rightwing tabloid press in Germany had always been vehemently opposed to the political agenda of Mosaddeq who enjoyed the support of the communist Tudeh Party; but following the break-up of Soraya's marriage – her 'unjust and barbaric rejection' as it was described – the tabloid press in Germany started to portray the Pahlavi regime in a different light. With reports of Soraya's allegedly brutal treatment at the hands of the Shah – under pressure from his family to comply with the country's laws of succession – it was not long before the fantasy image of the land of Scheherazade propagated by the press began to crumble. However, the fact is that Soraya was not officially rejected. Under Islamic law the Shah had the option of marrying a second wife who, it was hoped, would produce a (male) heir. Soraya refused to accept this proposed arrangement so the Shah divorced her although he granted her the title of Royal Princess of Iran and guaranteed her a luxurious jet-set lifestyle. In Germany, the run up to Soraya's divorce attracted intense press coverage, especially in the tabloid press. In April 1958 an article in the weekly news magazine *Stern* under the highly evocative title '1001 Powers' ('1001 Macht') – a barely concealed allusion to the stories of Scheherazade – claimed that an anti-Shah putsch was about to take place and also speculated about the break-up of the Shah's marriage. The Iranian government responded with a formal protest to the Federal Republic that the article insulted both the Shah and his nation. The government was shocked to be confronted by the Persian threat that they would break off diplomatic relations if no action was taken. Something that had seemed to be a mere triviality had suddenly taken on an altogether different dimension. Accordingly, Foreign Minister Heinrich von Brentano informed the Federal Chancellor, Konrad Adenauer, of the disastrous political consequences that could ensue from a dispute with Persia. Tehran, he suggested, might seek to establish diplomatic relations with the neighbouring GDR, an initiative that had the potential to persuade a large number of Arab states in the Middle East to recognise the sovereignty of the fledgling socialist state.

In an attempt to prevent a further decline in German–Iranian relations the German foreign minister Heinrich von Brentano paved the way for legal action against the magazine. However, the Adenauer government was confronted with the possibility of a political catastrophe. Good relations between Iran and the Federal Republic had been established by means of a series of reciprocal state visits. Unlike Great Britain and the USA, Germany had not maintained a military presence in Iran and Adenauer regarded the three Islamic states of Turkey, Pakistan and Iran as a bulwark against the Soviet Union and communist China. At the same time, because of the efforts of the Federal Republic to develop good relations with Israel, opportunities for cooperation with Arab states in the Middle East were limited. Last but not least, Adenauer, the Shah and Soraya enjoyed a close personal friendship (in 1957 the German chancellor had been invited to Iran on a state visit where he had enjoyed the hospitality of the royal couple). For all of these reasons Adenauer had no interest in antagonising Iran.

Accordingly, in 1958 his government proposed new legislation – the so-called *Lex Soraya* – that would make it a criminal offence to make assertions regarding the private lives of foreign heads of state in cases where such claims could have a detrimental effect on the relations between that state and the Federal Republic. Even if such negative reporting had a basis in actual fact, it still could not be published if it potentially undermined diplomatic relations. The liberal press protested that this was merely an excuse to suppress critical reports relating to the Pahlavi regime, including accounts of the dire poverty of great parts of the population, widespread corruption, the training of the notorious secret police SAVAK by the CIA and the excessive use of torture. In *Neues Deutschland*, the main communist newspaper in the neighbouring German Democratic Republic, the 'Lex Soraya' was denounced as a return to a Nazi-style approach to propaganda and dubbed the

'Lex Goebbels'.[11] Ultimately, there was so much political pressure from liberal and left–wing factions that the Adenauer government had no choice but to abandon the proposed legislation.[12]

Soraya's departure from the peacock throne was lamented in the most melodramatic tones in the German popular press: 'It is this that is the real dilemma for the Emperor and Empress, that otherwise happy couple. It is the population at large and the Mullahs who are unhappy. The private relationship of two individuals who love each other is being transformed into a political issue.'[13] The discontent of the populace and the Mullahs ostensibly stemmed from Soraya's inability to produce a male heir. At one level the tabloid rhetoric appears to suggest that private happiness is all that matters and is something quite distinct from concerns of state. But as the article unfolds it becomes clear that beneath the surface a harsh critique of Islamic culture and religion is being articulated. Because Soraya is incapable of producing an heir and will not accept the presence of a second wife as a rival she has no choice but to go. The underlying implication is that Soraya's victimhood highlights the supposed superiority of the ethical values of Christianity in the West over the quasi-medieval, barbaric practices of Islamic Iran and the East;[14] and perhaps not surprisingly the German mass media sided with Soraya who, in stark contrast to the Islamic culture of Iran, was depicted as modern and tolerant. Just eight years earlier the tabloid press had used Soraya to construct a mythical image of Persia as a land of tradition and erotic exoticism; now the image of 'Soraya the victim' was deployed to mobilise an alternative myth of the Oriental world as barbaric, cruel and oppressively patriarchal. Accordingly *Wochenend* suggests to its readers: 'Was one of the reasons Soraya was exiled because her "western outlook" posed a threat to certain members of the royal entourage?'[15] But replacing one ideological construct with another, an equally artificial myth still required the negotiation of the most flagrant contradictions. For as an article of weekly magazine *Wochenend* from 1958 reports: 'It is the human suffering associated with Soraya's fate that touches every heart. The tragedy of an empress who, whenever she wants, can enjoy everything the world has to offer – save one thing: the happiness of motherhood'.[16] And when Farah Diba, the Shah's third wife finally succeeded in 1960 in producing the coveted male heir to the throne, the headline in the popular German magazine *Frau im Spiegel* reads 'Farah: [. . .] a mother and fairy princess all in one!'[17]

While the tabloid press deployed the image of Soraya as a means of exposing the patriarchal dimension of what it regarded as a clearly inferior and backwards-looking culture in Islamic Iran, it ignored the extent to which this critique of the Orient depended upon an uncritical acceptance of the equally patriarchal attitudes underpinning the conservative restorative agenda of Adenauer's 'modern' democracy. In postwar West-German discourse the term *Doppelverdiener* (double income family) was already stigmatised and was used to suggest that married women in regular employment were essentially acting in a way that was anti-social and contrary to the spirit of family life and was even used as an argument for their exclusion from the workplace. The underlying cause of such attitudes was a sharp rise in the number of male POW-returnees and refugees searching for work. Accordingly, it was proposed that on the one hand, women should seek employment in lower-status and less demanding jobs 'more suited to women'; and on the other, by terminating the employment of those female employees who were married. This gender-based approach to employment was the hallmark of the Adenauer government in particular which saw women, first and foremost, as wives and mothers and suggested their self-fulfilment was to be sought and found in the domestic sphere. Conservative factions, including the Catholic Church, regarded the employment of women as a key factor in the decline of family life; and this combination of traditional patriarchal attitudes and the gender-specific demands of the German labour market in the 1950s conspired to exclude women from the workplace and to deny them any real form of economic agency.

While the rightwing tabloid press expressed their sympathy and regret at Soraya's inability to bear children (and, albeit indirectly, at her 'failure' to fulfil the duties of a royal wife), at the same time it sought to downplay the obvious similarities between Western patriarchal views of women and prevailing attitudes in Iran during the 1950s and 1960s. Given the prominent position Soraya occupied in the cultural imagination of both the Federal Republic and Iran, a greater willingness on the part of the press to recognise the constructed nature of both female and Oriental stereotypes could have paved the way for a smoother social and political transition following the collapse of the Shah's regime. But what Soraya's case demonstrated above all is that, whether in the Orient or the Occident, the manipulation of patriarchal culture and the propagation of essentialist views of femininity are crucial to the successful functioning of all authoritarian regimes.

Notes

1. In the 1950s and 1960s, the tabloid press in Germany enjoyed a readership of around 20 million. During the Persian empress's lifetime, this sector of the newspaper industry was often referred to as the 'Soraya Press'.
2. As the Shah's close family relatives were either half-brothers and/or female, the problem of finding a male heir to the throne became even more intense following the death of the Shah's younger brother Ali Reza in a plane accident in October 1954.
3. The portrayal of Soraya's first meeting with the Shah as an occasion in which the couple's destiny was sealed established an enduring trope and one that was not confined to the popular press. In his biography *Soraya* (translated by Rita Perli from the French original title *Soraya, la malediction des étoiles*), the journalist, Henri de Stadelhofen, describes their first meeting as follows: 'She bowed before the ruler and then stared straight into his eyes. Between the green-eyed gaze of Soraya and the brown-eyed countenace of the Shah there was an almost magnetic attraction, and she realised that she would belong to this man and that her ambition would be subsumed by love.' (pp. 105–6, my translation). See Henri de Stadelhofen, *Soraya* (Lausanne, 1983). Another biography goes even further: 'The Shah', so we are told 'gave the young woman a kiss, a tender kiss that held out the prospect of love and a deep and lasting desire' (p. 42, my translation) See: Walter W. Krause, *Kaiserin aus Liebe* (Munich, 1955). The film *Soraya* (Ludovico Gasparini, 2003) confirms that this sentimental trope continues to hold sway even in the twenty-first century. However, it is striking that in her autobiography, Soraya herself refuses to endorse such sentimental accounts of their first meeting: 'What was important to me was the Shah himself. I found him attractive and highly intelligent; and although it was hardly love at first sight, it's true that there was an immediate connection between us. That was the most important thing for me.' (p. 69, my translation). See: Soraya Esfandiary *Meine eigene Geschichte* (Olten, Stuttgart, Salzburg, 1963). In an interview reproduced in *Der Schah* (translated by Linda Hollingstedt from the French original title *L'irresistibile Acsension de Mohmmed Reza Shah d'Iran*) and published 12 years later in 1975 Soraya continued to maintain that 'It would not be accurate to say that I fell in love with him on our first meeting' (p. 220, my translation). See: Gérard de Villier, *Der Schah* (Munich, 1975).
4. This crisis in postwar German masculinity is the subject of numerous postwar films and works of literature, e.g. the films *Die Mörder sind unter uns* (*The Murderers are Among Us*, Wolfgang Staudte, 1946) and *Canaris* (Alfred Weidenmann, 1954), Wolfgang Borchert's drama *Draußen vor der Tür* (*The Man Outside*, 1949) and Heinrich Böll's novel *Das Brot der frühen Jahre* (*The Bread of those Early Years*, 1955).
5. For a detailed analysis of American consumerism and postwar gender relations in Germany see: Erica Carter, *How German is she? Postwar German Reconstruction and the Consuming Woman* (Michigan, 1997).
6. In his famous and controversial study *Persien, Modell eines Entwicklungslandes oder Die Diktatur der Freien Welt (Persia, a model of a developing nation or the dictatorship*

of the Free World) which was published in January 1967 and includes a postscript by Hanz Magnus Enzensberger (translated as *Iran, The New Imperialism in Action*) the German–Iranian scholar and journalist Bahman Nirumand describes a very different country in which the brutal suppression of any form of Western-backed opposition against the Pahlavi regime was part of the everyday political reality. See: Bahman Nirumand, *Persien, Modell eines Entwicklungslandes oder Die Diktatur der freien Welt* (Reinbek, 1967).

7. *Wochenend*, 33/1954. All subsequent translations from the German newspapers are my own.
8. *Wochenend*, 19/1957.
9. *Weltbild*, 20/1954.
10. For a comprehensive analysis of the relation between the Shah, the politics of oil production and the West see: *Spiegel Geschichte 2/2010, Persien*, especially the chapter 'Treibstoff der Feindschaft.'
11. *Neues Deutschland*, May 1958.
12. The draft legislation was heavily criticised by organisations representing the interests of print journalism (the 'Presserat') on the grounds that it represented an unwelcome intervention into the freedom of the press and it was rejected by the Upper House ('Bundesrat') of the government in Bonn. There representatives of the Federal states commented that the provisions of the bill were so loosely formulated that it would be impossible for individuals to grasp when they had actually broken the law; as such the bill amounted to a form of censorship that contradicted the constitution of the Federal Republic. Accordingly, the draft legislation was unanimously rejected.
13. *Wochenend*, June 1957.
14. In an article in *Wochenend* such a view is openly articulated: 'Even today that old Oriental penchant for intrigue and double-dealing is still alive and well', *Wochenend*, 43/1956. Nor was it just the tabloids that resorted to such a disparaging tone. Even the highly regarded broadsheet the *Süddeutsche Zeitung* adopted a not dissimilar attitude: 'The Middle East which, following the introduction of direct flight connections, trade deals and Western clothing, had lost much of its air of mystery, is once again regaining its enigmatic, cruel and inscrutable aura'. See *Süddeutsche Zeitung*, March 1958.
15. *Wochenend*, April 1958.
16. *Wochenend*, January 1958.
17. *Frau im Spiegel*, 25/1967.

CHAPTER 17

PERSEPOLIS: THE SHAH'S NATIONAL FICTION

Margaux Whiskin

Social Rupture

The tension between past and future was particularly acute in Iran under the Pahlavi dynasty. This was a society in change. Following the path of modernisation set by his father, Mohammad Reza Shah launched on 6 January 1963 the White Revolution which aimed to regenerate Iran through a series of economic and social reforms. The very term revolution reflected the Shah's aim of a radical transformation. The backdrop was the narrative of decline under the Qajars used as scapegoats to explain Iran's backwardness.[1] But revolutions are traumatic events and this one was no different. Riots against the White Revolution started in June 1963, but they were not so much a protest against the reforms themselves as the way they were being implemented. The Shah's revolution was being imposed from the top instead of coming from the bottom, making the trauma of change even more acute. Economic growth was undeniable, but the benefits were unevenly spread across Iranian society. The countryside was severely neglected, leading to rural migration to urban areas. A consequence of the government's control over food prices was a reduction in farm incomes, pushing out the most vulnerable in rural societies, mainly nomads and peasants with no land of their own, who were forced to leave their villages to seek work in the cities.[2] The mediation between rural communities and State was also reconfigured through administrators with whom the local population had no previous connection, taking the place of the local gentry, thus leading to dysfunctional communication.[3] Rural flight had a knock-on effect on urban life. Housing became less and less affordable, the cost of rents soared and resources such as electricity, water and gas became stretched; and this led to a growing discontent amongst the urban middle classes.[4] The Shah kept pushing on with his reforms, believing that his success as a ruler would be measured by these. In his chapter 'Westernization: Our Welcome Ordeal', the Shah listed over 20 pages of examples of economic and social developments as so many trophies to his rule. In the conclusion to his long list of achievements, he recognised that the pace of change he had set was challenging:

> Experienced observers often tell me that in few other countries of the world can one find such an amazing tempo of physical and cultural change. When they return to Persia after an absence of say five years, or even only two years, they are astounded at the differences. [...] Especially in a country with such venerable traditions as ours, rapid change naturally brings its strains and stresses. These are the price we must pay for Westernization and modernization. But I do not propose that we abandon our great heritage. On the contrary, I have every confidence that we can enrich it.[5]

The rapid pace is here a source of pride for the Shah as it demonstrates his country's high potential. There is also a brief acknowledgment of the tensions brought about by this tremendous leap forward, but tradition and heritage are not presented as being antithetical to Westernisation and modernisation. On the contrary, Iranian heritage would be made even stronger by modernisation. The dramatic contrast between ancient and modern took on an almost aesthetic dimension. In *Mission for My Country*, the Shah described Shiraz where one could admire the verses of Hafiz and the municipal water system. In Isfahan, the visitor could see the camels grinding grain and modern textile mills. In Tehran, the Shah waxed lyrical about the caravans ('Lucky is he who can see a caravan, and hear its camel bells, as it passes under the full moon') and the university built by his father.[6] The aesthetic potential of these dramatic oppositions would be more effectively exploited by Claude Lelouch in his film *Iran* (1973), a silent documentary juxtaposing shots of traditional and modern Iran.

The Shah was aware of criticisms of the pace he had set, but argued that the advice of going slower was patronising and underestimated Iranian abilities.

> It is argued that the thing to give [Persian villagers] is the type common in the mid-nineteenth century. Don't waste time thinking about tractors or modern implements, because the villagers wouldn't know how to operate them, still less to maintain them. [. . .] The economically backward countries should learn to walk before they try to run. At least as concerns my own country, I profoundly disagree.[7]

The Shah believed the tension between past and future would be resolved through himself by the fact that he was continuing the Persian monarchy and at the same time propelling Iran forward. He had resolved the opposition between monarchy and revolution by believing that he embodied both. As Ansari neatly puts it, 'he was a revolutionary dynast, guided both by God and by an interpretation of radical socialism'.[8] His speech on 6 November 1978, when facing his own downfall, reiterated his belief that monarchy and revolution were brought together in his person, rather than being two opposite forces: 'The revolution of the Iranian people cannot fail to have my support as the monarch of Iran and as an Iranian.'[9] The notion that Iranian national identity was anchored within the person of the Shah and so consequently could not be altered by the tension between tradition and progress, was contained in the term *Shahanshahi* which the Shah thus described in *Towards the Great Civilisation*:

> In Iranian culture, the Iranian monarchy means the political and geographic unity of Iran in addition to the special national identity and all those unchangeable values which this national identity has brought forth. For this reason no fundamental change is possible in this country unless it is in tune with the fundamental principles of the monarchical system.[10]

The Shah's sudden decision in 1976 to set a new calendar could be seen as an expression of his revolutionary enthusiasm. After all, the French revolutionaries had declared that the year of the proclamation of the First Republic was no longer 1792, but year I, thus making a point of very visibly ignoring Christian tradition. The Shah did exactly the same: the point of reference was no longer Islam but the Persian monarchy, starting with the reign of Cyrus the Great. The historical accuracy of this new calendar did not matter.[11] This decision was a practical demonstration of the principle of *Shahanshahi*. What was at the very heart of Iranian national identity, its unchangeable core, was not Islam, but the figure of the Shah. 1976 was no longer 1355 according to the Islamic calendar, but 2535. As Ansari points out, the dating of the new calendar doubly served the Shah's purpose as this meant that the year 2500 corresponded to 1941, the year marking the beginning of his reign. 'Thus while Cyrus the Great spawned the first 2500 years of Iranian history, Mohammad Reza Shah would define the next 2500 years.'[12] However, far from reinforcing the sense of Iranian identity by bridging past and present, the new calendar entrenched social rupture.

The French historian Pierre Nora was witnessing in the 1970s a break within his own society, manifesting itself in an increasingly anxious relationship with the past. Tradition, custom, the passing on of knowledge and skill from one generation to the next, were no longer a praxis and this loss was being counterbalanced by conscious acts of preservation. Because memory was no longer lived, it had to be preserved and institutionalised. Memory was becoming a national obsession:

> Our curiosity about the places in which memory is crystallized, in which it finds refuge, is associated with this specific moment in French history, a turning point in which a sense of rupture with the past is inextricably bound up with a sense that a rift has occurred in memory. But that rift has stirred memory sufficiently to raise the question of its embodiment: there are sites, *lieux de mémoire*, in which a residual sense of continuity remains. *Lieux de mémoire* exist because there are no longer any *milieu de mémoire*, settings in which memory is a real part of everyday experience.[13]

The rift in France, described by Pierre Nora, was even more brutal in Iran where forceps were used to forcefully bring forth modernity. Consequently, a sense of continuity with the past had to be reaffirmed; and, as in France, this was done through what Nora refers to as sites of memory.

Sites of Memory

The 2,500-year celebration of the Persian Empire consecrated Persepolis and Pasargadae as Iran's two great sites of memory. They contained the remains of the old Achaemenid kings, but now they were also the national repository of Iranian identity. These two sites, less than 50 km apart, were two capitals, two sites of burial and two remnants of the First Persian Empire. However, this apparent coherence is inconveniently undermined by the fact that these are hybrid sites with shifting identities. Persepolis, from the Greek meaning 'Persian city', is known to Iranians as Takht-e-Jamshid, meaning in Farsi the 'throne of Jamshid', a mythical king from Ferdowsi's *Shanameh* and with no connection with the Achaemenids. Persepolis is a site combining two traditions, European and Iranian, historical and literary. As for Pasargadae, it combined pre-Islamic and Islamic traditions until the site was reconfigured for the Celebrations. After the Arab Conquest, Pasargadae as a burial site extended to include Muslim tombs which were all removed to leave only Cyrus' tomb standing.[14] Homogenisation of the sites corresponded to a homogenisation of Iranian identity, which again was imposed from the top. As Amanat remarks, the State suppressed minority identities in order to shape this unifying national identity; minority groups, such as nomads, were culturally and linguistically dismantled, whilst on the other hand military service and national school curricula helped to create common national reference points.[15]

The solid presence of these stone monuments belies their malleability as repositories of memory which by its very essence is pliant, inconstant, vague and subject to manipulation: 'memory is indeed form more than content, a stake constantly available, a series of strategies, a being-there important less for what it is than for what you do with it.'[16] The Cyrus Cylinder, which appeared at the centre of the emblem for the Celebrations and was flown from London on loan for the occasion, perfectly encapsulates Nora's point on the importance of form over content, of an object valued more for the ways in which it can be used than for what it actually is. The Shah used the cylinder as though the clay had never been baked and was soft enough to receive inscriptions 2,500 years later. The Shah presented Cyrus the Great as the father of the Persian Empire, but maybe more importantly as the founder of values the West had made its own. Cyrus thus became the founder of the world's first nation state, he was the defender of international tolerance, justice, respecting the rights, customs and laws of all his subject nations. He ruled in the spirit of today's United Nations and, as the cylinder attests, he was the first to establish human rights, a claim echoed by the British press who referred to it as Iran's Magna Carta.[17]

The shaping of the Iranian national identity involved a careful selection process. A national fiction was being created with a coherent narrative demonstrating a past–present–future continuity and upholding the portrayal of a strong Iran.[18] And this national fiction was told during the Persepolis celebrations. The most blatant omission was Iran's Islamic inheritance. Amanat suggests that the focus on pre-Islamic Iran was a way to exorcise another narrative, that of the decline of Iran since the beginning of the Islamic period, made even more prominent after the Qajar rule, but also because it had more modern applications such as boundary disputes with Iraq and a reaction to its neighbours' anti-Shi'i feelings.[19] The hope was that this glorious past would eventually rub off.[20] The Shah was not only the descendant of Cyrus but a second Cyrus leading his people through historic times. Identification with the Iranian past predated the Pahlavis, but what was new was the considerable sustained effort Mohammad Reza Shah made to harness that past to serve his own vision of Iran.[21] Consciously he addressed the past–present–future continuity in his three main books: *Mission for My Country* (1960), *The White Revolution* (1967) and *Towards the Great Civilisation* (1977). He offered a more spectacular demonstration at the Persepolis Celebrations.[22]

On the Screens

History and memory in such events are not held completely separate, despite having radically different aims and methods. The Celebrations sparked a renewed interest in Iran's ancient history and archaeological sites, and Iranologists were consulted and their advice taken to create the impression that the parade was historically accurate.[23] But history served the purpose of memory by providing it with the factual details to which it could cling. The costumes, facial hair, poses were stylised using historical sources to give the impression to the spectators that the past was being resurrected and becoming tangible. As Nora explains, this reliance on history is a trait of modern memory:

> Modern memory is first of all archival. It relies entirely on the specificity of the trace, the materiality of the vestige, the

> concreteness of the recording, the visibility of the image. The process that began with writing has reached its culmination in high-fidelity recording. The less memory is experienced from within, the greater its need for external props and tangible reminders of that which no longer exists except *qua* memory – hence the obsession with the archive that marks an age and in which we attempt to preserve not only all of the past but all of the present as well.[24]

Television played a key role in the Persepolis Celebrations. French television technology was used for the filming and retransmission of the Celebrations, in exchange of which France was hoping Iran would buy its colour television technology.[25] Very few people were direct spectators. A few officials were invited to the ceremony at Pasargadae on 12 October 1971. As for the events in Persepolis, these were witnessed only by Iranian officials and the foreign monarchs and heads of state. The Iranian people were only allowed to follow on their television sets. This in a way was no different from the normal military parades, which would be broadcast on television, whilst only a happy few would have the privilege of directly seeing the Shah reviewing his troops.[26] What was different, however, was that the Celebrations were broadcast in 30 other countries. The Celebrations were an international affair and Iran, now at the very centre of the map, had to put on a good show. The Shah had been cultivating his public persona abroad. Despite bemoaning the American media's interest in mundane and superficial details, such as the colour of his tie or the interior decoration of his office, instead of focusing on his political vision, the glamorised portrayal he received in return well served his interests abroad by attractively presenting him as a modern man.[27] He was hoping that something on similar lines would happen for his country, as a result of the celebrations.

The Celebrations had to be archived, but considering their importance and the need of adapting to the new way people responded to events, they also had to appear on the cinema screen: 'Our memory is intensely retinal, powerfully televisual. The much-touted 'return of the narrative' in recent historical writing has to be linked to the ubiquity of visual images and film in contemporary culture [. . .].'[28] The Shah commissioned films to be made of the Celebrations for Western viewers, the most famous being *Flames of Persia* by Shahrokh Golestan, with Orson Welles as narrator. As Watson argues, the Pahlavi regime did not attempt to create from scratch a representation of Iran, but instead it recycled familiar Oriental tropes. *Flames of Persia* functioned on this principle. Setting the Oriental scene, the film opens on desert scenes and mentions 'beautiful women' 'with silvery voices and melting eyes, eyes like the eyes of the gazelle which leaps over the tarnished gold of the mountain side', 'Persian gardens scented with jasmine' and 'the nightingale serenading lovers'. As the film progresses to the actual Celebrations, the spectator leaves traditional Persia and enters modern Iran with rather lengthy information about the different events and the camp itself, and busy split-screen effects attempting to stand both for technological innovation and the dynamism of the festivities.[29]

The Double Parade

Mohammad Reza Pahlavi opened the first chapter of his book *Mission for My Country* on an anecdote from his childhood, at a Swiss boarding school. 'Our milkman asked me one day which country I came from, and when I told him Persia, he said: "Oh yes, I have heard of Persia. That's in America!"'[30] The recalling of this incident was the Shah's open acknowledgement of his sense of shame that Iran was closed in on itself and not internationally known. It is also presented as a seminal moment when the Shah received his mission, namely, making Iran known to the rest of the world and restoring it on the international scene, as it had once been and as it now deserved to be. The chapter 'My Ancient and Modern Homeland' in *Mission for My Country* offers a portrait in very broad brushstrokes of Iran, emphasising both its current and past achievements and more particularly its international influence, whether scientific, linguistic, horticultural, culinary, military or administrative, and by offering a crash course on Iranian history through its dynasties. The message clearly formulated is that Iran's contribution to the world is considerable. The chapter also points to both Iran's distinctness from and its closeness to the West, whilst presenting Iran as its very cradle:

> Certainly no one can doubt that our culture is more akin to that of the West than is either the Chinese or that of our neighbours the Arabs. Iran was an early home of the Aryans from whom most Americans and Europeans are descended, and we are racially quite separate from the Semitic stock of the Arabs. Our language

> belongs to the Indo–European family which includes English, French, German and other major Western tongues.[31]

The Shah considered Iran to have 'a culture much older, and in some respects more mature, than those of the Western nation themselves.'[32] This constituted a more determinant superiority: if the West was now civilising Iran by sharing its scientific and technologic advancements, Iran would then be in the position to return the favour by civilising the West in a more fundamental way. In the same way as his person solved the tension between tradition and modernity, the Shah believed Iran could offer 'a fresh synthesis of East and West, old and new.'[33] After having been taken aback and silenced by the milkman's ignorance a few decades earlier, the Shah had finally been able to offer his response, not just to one Swiss worker but to the whole world. The Celebrations express the same desire to erase the portrayal of Iran as some backwater hardly worth noticing and share with the world the Shah's own vision of his country. For Mohammad Reza Pahlavi, Iranian national identity was not a domestic issue; it was an international affair. Yet, he was mistaken in this. The national identity the Shah was so keen on showing abroad, was not being embraced by his own people. The fact that he was facing outward instead of inward only increased the sense of alienation between the Iranians and their monarch.

Amanat notes two opposing attitudes towards the West in the shaping of Iranian identity under the Pahlavis. The first was a generally uncritical embrace of Western values and ways of life as the miracle remedy to Iranian decline. The second was a rejection of the West seen as corrupting Iran and diluting its specificity, especially its Islamic inheritance.[34] These two antithetical positions eventually were no longer framed in terms of for/against the West, but for/against the Pahlavi regime. The Shah had very clearly turned westward and was perceived as hostile towards Islamic leaders and traditions which were seen as part of Iranian culture and identity. In reality, the issue was not about the Shah rejecting Islam. He tried to cultivate the public image of being a deeply pious man, especially by regularly going on pilgrimage to Shi'i holy sites and of being favoured by God by being granted divine guidance in his captaincy of the State. What the Shah wanted was to be the main figure of authority on Islam so as to control religious affairs and so keep a lid on the unruly clerics who kept getting in the way of his modernisation programme.[35]

The Shah's relationship with foreign countries was, from the very start, less than straightforward. Fearing Reza Shah, his father, would enter in an alliance with Germany during World War II, the Allies forced Reza Shah to abdicate on 16 September 1941, in favour of his son, Mohammad Reza Shah whose reign began under the sign of foreign interference. The British and the Americans intervened with the coup against Mosaddeq on 19 August 1953. The US presence and influence became even more visible and continued to be so. Westernisation had now left its mark on the urban landscape of the main cities with Western shops and brands making their way onto the shelves. This difficult cohabitation became increasingly resented by the Iranians, affronted by the Americans' lack of cultural sensitivity.[36] To make matters worse, Americans working on military projects in Iran were granted diplomatic immunity in October 1964, which offered Khomeini the opportunity to condemn the unjust difference in treatment between foreigners and the Shah's own people:

> Does [the Iranian nation] know that the Assembly, at the initiative of the government, has signed the document of enslavement of Iran? It has acknowledged that Iran is a colony; it has given America a document attesting that the nation of Muslims is barbarous, it has struck out all our Islamic and national glories with a black line. By this shameful vote, if an American adviser or the servant of an American adviser should take any liberty with one of the greatest specialists in Shiah law [. . .] the police would have no right to investigate. If the Shah run over an American dog, he would be called to account but if an American cook should run over the Shah, no one has any claims against him.[37]

Still firm in his belief of enjoying a privileged connection with his people as the embodiment of their identity and values, but also feeling that he needed American support to reach his Great Civilisation, the Shah paid no heed to Khomeini and refused to see the growing sense of alienation amongst the Iranians.[38] He dismissed the threat of Westernisation as being a threat to Iranian identity by presenting it as merely a series of scientific, industrial and economic developments rather than transforming society in any fundamental way. Westernisation was the necessary step towards progress and modernisation rather than the imposition of a specific culture, set of values or way of life. 'Now in order to understand the Western impact upon Persia, one must remember that "Westernization" in its present-day sense is new to the Western nations themselves.'[39] In other words, the Shah had dissociated Westernisation from the West. Yes, there had been foreign interference in the past, especially with Britain and Soviet Russia, but that was all over since Stalin's death and Mosaddeq's fall.[40] The real corrupting foreign influence was what the Shah called the new totalitarian imperialism which spawned counterfeit nationalists bent on destroying freedom and all that which he had so patiently built.[41]

The Persepolis Celebrations did nothing to encourage the Iranians to share the Shah's vision of Westernisation. On the contrary, the alienation between the people and their monarch was no longer just felt, it became clearly visible on hundreds of thousands of television screens. Persepolis and Pasargadae were closed to the public and more than 1,000 people, suspected of wanting to disrupt the event, were arrested beforehand. As the camera shots made clear, there was not one but two parades: the historical military parade of all the different Persian dynasties and the parade of the foreign guests. Their reception, their accommodation in luxury tents, as would have been done in the old days, feature as importantly as the various events they attended.[42] It was for them that the Shah was telling so dramatically and flamboyantly his national fiction in order to convince the world that Iran was on its way to becoming once again a great civilisation, but not only this, also to request the recognition of the world's debt to Iran's past contributions and to celebrate its international legacy.

However, the Shah's fiction took on a meaning different from the one originally intended. The press focussed on the luxury of the celebrations which were referred to in the *Daily Mail* as 'The Biggest Beano Since Babylon'.[43] Accounts of the menu of the banquet were particularly rich in detail.[44] The emphasis on luxury led to a condemnation of displays of vanity and the spending of astronomical sums of money:

> Dust settles on the Shah's picnic. [...] It would be easy to hail this as the greatest non-event of our time, a creation of a royal despotism taking advantage of the bedazzled mass media. It was a Field of the Cloth of Gold without a purpose. It was the Congress of Vienna without any business. It was a picnic of unparalleled vulgarity. [...] The whole thing took place in a sort of safari park surrounded by barbed wire and newly planted trees and tall lights

> and about two battalions of soldiers. Except for the Press on the fringe, this was a private ceremony, and with sophistication the Press were used as the substitute for the 'mob.' [. . .] Then there was a banquet in the tent city. The French were in charge there of the design, the cooking and the drink. In fact, it would scarcely have honoured a motel on the outskirts of Detroit. [. . .] All this was not quite the vanity of a man who has no kingly blood. It was an expensive and carefully calculated act of State.[45]

Accusations of human rights violations had led to embarrassing cancellations, such as Pompidou's, but also to inconvenient newspaper articles:[46]

> No pardons in Iran. Amnesty International yesterday regretted that the Persian Government had failed to grant a pardon to political prisoners on two recent ceremonial occasions – the 2,500th anniversary of the foundation of the Persian Empire and the Shah's birthday on October 26. Amnesty estimates that between 1,000 and 4,000 people were imprisoned before the celebrations.[47]

A few months after the Celebrations, the traditional portrayal of Oriental rulers as cruel and sadistic continued being applied to the Shah, appearing in articles with headlines such as 'Firing Squads Kept Busy' which informed readers that:

> Coupled with the reported executions are accounts of physical torture, verified by several Western lawyers and observers who travelled to Tehran for the courts-martial of political prisoners. A French lawyer was told by prisoners that they had been tortured by, among other techniques, being placed on a heated metal table.[48]

Orientalism had backfired and become a story of brutality, excess and decadence. This version has constituted the main narrative of the Persepolis Celebrations neatly presented as the beginning of the end, made even more dramatic by the retrospective interpretation of the gust of wind rising during the Shah's address to Cyrus, as a bad omen.[49]

Celebrations as a Site of Memory

Such an interpretation of the Celebrations makes for a good story and for this very reason makes it suspect. Talking of the 1989 Bicentenary of the French Revolution, Mona Ozouf argued that it is unfair to turn into ridicule the pick-and-choose historical selection of commemorations and their too obvious political aims, as such events can hardly operate otherwise.[50] Afkhani reminds us that, on the occasion of the Celebrations, infrastructure benefitting the Iranian population was developed and Iranian Studies were strongly encouraged.[51] Afkhani's argument, like the Shah's enumeration of reforms, does not weigh enough in the balance. More importantly, memory has yet again taken hold of history and used it for its own purpose. The 2,500-year Celebration of the Persian Empire has itself become a site of memory.[52] In Western countries, it has maintained its fascinating hold on the imagination and has come to stand for the collapse of the Persian monarchy, as the turning point from the Old to the New Regime. Making use of the rich visual footage, documentaries have been produced, such as Serge Viallet's *Mystères d'Archives – 1971: Les Fastes du Shah d'Iran à Persepolis* and Hassan Amini's *Decadence and Downfall: The Shah of Iran's Ultimate Party.* In June 2007, the New Zealand artist Michael Stevenson exhibited an installation at Art Basel 38. The installation consisted in the reconstruction of one of the tents used during the Persepolis Celebrations to accommodate guests, but as it would be 36 years later. The tent was now but a skeletal structure, naked, stripped of its past glory and standing as a folly, an ornamental ruin and a vanity, reminding the public of the passing of time and the fact that high as well as low will return to dust: 'I think it is very interesting that you look at a structure like this and immediately fantasise about its demise.'[53] Stevenson intended his installation to repeat the narrative of the Celebrations as being the beginning of the end, as can be seen in the transcript of his conversation with the engineer Rüdiger Ihle. Stevenson and Ihle seem at first to be discussing the structural soundness of the tent. However it becomes quickly apparent, through terms such as 'collapse', 'turning moment' and 'revolution', that the tent has become a metaphor for Mohammad Reza Pahlavi's reign.

Reflecting on his rule, the Shah in exile expressed the hope that his vision would not be completely destroyed:

> Our Great Civilization appears as no more than a myth today. It seems to be finally dead. In fact it continues to exist like those mighty rivers which disappear under mountains and are believed to be lost and whose reappearance amazes.[54]

One of the Shah's legacies did survive, but it was the Persepolis Celebrations, not the Great Civilisation, which were invoked by Stevenson's installation. The skeletal tent frame, a fantasy of demise, offers a clear illustration of Nora's claim that sites of memory are constantly changing, offering a synthesis of life and death, '[capturing] the maximum possible meaning with the fewest possible signs' and ' [resurrecting] old meanings and [generating] new ones'.[55]

Notes

1. The strength of this narrative of decline is highlighted by discussions on the choice of bride for Mohammad Reza Shah. Following tradition, the bride should have been the daughter of the deposed ruling family, which would have meant that the next Shah would have had Qajar blood. This was ruled out by a constitutional amendment 'forbidding any person from the Qajar lineage to come back to the throne', in Houchang Nahavandi, *Iran: The Clash of Ambitions*, tr. Martine Jackson (Slough, 2006), p. 343.
2. See Dilip Hiro, *The Iranian Labyrinth* (New York, 2005), p. 106.
3. See Ali M. Ansari, *Modern Iran Since 1921, The Pahlavis and After* (Harlow, 2003), p. 194.
4. See Hiro, *The Iranian Labyrinth*, pp. 106–7.
5. Mohammad Reza Pahlavi, *Mission for My Country* (London, 1961), p. 160.
6. Ibid., p. 28, see also p. 27.
7. Ibid., p. 135.
8. Ansari, *Modern Iran*, p. 194.
9. Quoted by Ansari in *Modern Iran*, p. 206. This notion would be later picked up by Tony Shafrazi declaring 'I'm a Revolutionary Monarchist', quoted in Michael Stevenson, *Celebration at Persepolis* (Bristol, 2008), p. 46.
10. Quoted by Ansari, *Modern Iran*, p. 190.
11. As Dilip Hiro points out, 2,500 years of Persian Empire was historically inaccurate, as it did not take into account the period from 640 to 1501 during which there was no kingship in Iran. See Hiro, *The Iranian Labyrinth*, p. 103.
12. Ansari, *Modern Iran*, p. 189.
13. Pierre Nora, 'Between Memory and History', in Pierre Nora (ed.), *Realms of Memory*, vol. I Conflicts and Divisions, tr. Arthur Goldhammer (New York, 1996), p. 1.

14. See documentary by Serge Viallet, *Mystères d'Archives – 1971: Les Fastes du Shah d'Iran à Persepolis* produced by Arte France and the Institut National de l'Audiovisuel, first shown on 20 August 2011, mn. 7.03–7.56.
15. See Abbas Amanat, 'Iranian Identity Boundaries, A Historical Overview', in Abbas Amanat and Frazin Vejdani (eds), *Iran Facing Others, Identity Boundaries in a Historical Perspective* (New York, 2012), pp. 21–2.
16. (My translation). 'la mémoire en effet est un cadre plus qu'un contenu, un enjeu toujours disponible, un ensemble de stratégies, un être-là qui vaut moins par ce qu'il est que par ce que l'on en fait', Pierre Nora, 'Présentation', in Pierre Nora (ed.), *Lieux de Mémoire*, vol. 1 La République (Paris, 1984), p. xviii. See also Nora, 'Between Memory and History', p. 3.
17. See Pahlavi, *Mission for My Country*, p. 21 and Mohammad Reza Pahlavi, *The Shah's Story*, tr. Teresa Waugh (London, 1980), pp. 16–17.
18. I am borrowing Pierre Nora's expression 'roman national' in Pierre Nora, 'L'ère de la commémoration', in Pierre Nora (ed.), *Lieux de Mémoire*, vol. 3 Les Frances (Paris, 1992), p. 1008.
19. See Amanat, 'Iranian Identity Boundaries', p. 21.
20. Nora noticed a similar process in France: 'The grander France's origins were, the more they magnified the grandeur of the French. Through the past we venerated ourselves.' In Nora 'Between Memory and History', p. 12.
21. See Amanat, 'Iranian Identity Boundaries', pp. 4–10.
22. See Ansari, *Modern Iran*, p. 190.
23. See Amanat, 'Iranian Identity Boundaries', p. 21.
24. Nora, 'Between Memory and History', p. 8.
25. See Viallet, *Mystères d'Archives*, mn 24.24–25.00.
26. See Sandra Mackey, *The Iranians, Persia, Islam and the Soul of the Nation* (London, 1996), p. 245.
27. See Pahlavi, *Mission for My Country*, p. 139; see too Mackey, *The Iranians*, pp. 246–7.
28. Nora, 'Between Memory and History', p. 13.
29. See James A. F. Watson, 'Stop, Look, and Listen: Orientalism, Modernity, and the Shah's Quest for the West's Imagination', in *The UBC Journal of Political Studies*, 17 (2015), pp. 27–8.
30. Pahlavi, *Mission for My Country*, p. 15.
31. Ibid., p. 18.
32. Ibid., p. 132.
33. Ibid.
34. See Amanat, 'Iranian Identity Boundaries', pp. 23–4.
35. See Ansari, *Modern Iran*, pp. 187–8, Mackey, *The Iranians*, pp. 254–7 and Hiro, *The Iranian Labyrinth*, p. 104.
36. See Hiro, *The Iranian Labyrinth*, pp. 95–112. See Mackey, *The Iranians*, pp. 240, 250–3, 258–9.
37. Quoted in Mackey, *The Iranians*, p. 248.
38. Mackey, *The Iranians*, pp. 252–3.
39. Pahlavi, *Mission for My Country*, p. 135.
40. See Ibid., pp. 118–19.

41. See Ibid., pp. 127–8. In his final book, *The Shah's Story*, the Shah returned the accusation of foreign corruption to the Iranian revolutionaries: 'the Iranian people should protect themselves from fatal contagion whilst continuing to learn from other people. They should have rejected, and still should reject, the negative and nihilistic aspects of so-called "civilizations" which bear within themselves the seeds of self-destruction. A community which loses its own soul no longer exists.' Palhavi, *The Shah's Story*, p. 124.
42. The Minister Alam thus explained the choice of tents as accommodation: 'It replicates our kings' historically setting up tents on their travels in the desert and conforms to our nomadic traditions.' Quoted in Gholam Reza Afkhani, *The Life and Times of the Shah* (London, 2009), p. 407.
43. Vincent Mulchrone, *Daily Mail*, 11 October 1971, p. 6.
44. 'On the menu for the banquet of all time: Peacocks, caviar, roast lamb and quails' eggs. Of all the problems facing yesterday, none was quite so exotic as how to keep 90 peacocks cool in the shade with the temperature in the seventies. The birds are the Shah's surprise for his royal guests at the banquet of all time next Thursday. [. . .] They will be roasted and then presented complete with their tail fans, symbol of the Iranian throne, according to Maxim's, the Paris restaurant which is preparing the banquet. [. . .] The quails' eggs will be stuffed with the golden Imperial caviar, rare stuff which puts ordinary Beluga into the fish-and-chip class. Then a mousse of crayfish tails, followed by stuffed roast lamb and truffles. There will then be a blessed pause, during which guests may refresh themselves with a champagne water ice. Then back to their moutons, or rather their peacocks, served with a nut and truffle salad. If they have an odd corner left there will be creamed figs with raspberries in port wine.' Vincent Mulchrone, *Daily Mail*, 12 October 1971, p. 4.
45. Patrick O'Donovan, *The Observer*, 17 October 1971.
46. See note 30 in Nahavandi, *Iran: The Clash of Ambitions*, p. 697.
47. The *Guardian*, 11 November 1971, p. 4.
48. Neal Ascherson in The *Observer*, 19 March 1972.
49. This particular reading of the event can be found in William Shawcross, *The Shah's Last Ride* (London, 1989), pp. 24–33.
50. See Mona Ozouf, 'Célébrer, Savoir et Fêter', in *Le Débat*, 57 (1989), 16–31.
51. See Afkhani, *The Life and Times of the Shah*, pp. 414–5.
52. Nora states that the notion of sites of memory can be applied to concrete things, such as buildings, as well as to abstract and intellectually constructed creations, such as events. See *Les Lieux de Mémoire*.
53. Stevenson, p. 14.
54. Pahlavi, *The Shah's Story*, p. 126.
55. Nora, 'Between Memory and History', p. 15.

CHAPTER 18

VAMPIRES, VEILS AND THE WESTERN GAZE: GENDER IMAGES AND THE NOTION OF BEAUTY FROM QAJAR TO POST-REVOLUTIONARY IRAN

Maryam Aras

Since the establishment of the Islamic Republic, Iran's image in the West has been embodied by the veiled female body. From heavily chadored Pasdaran women representing a religiously conservative symbolic order, to colourfully veiled young women often illustrating the critical dialogue, diverse versions of the female Islamic body have been portrayed in Western media coverage. Only recently, through Instagram accounts like @therichkidsoftehran, has the West become aware of a post-revolutionary generation deeply influenced by Hollywood-beauty idolisation and an imagined Western lifestyle. This westernisation of Iranian upper-class pop culture, paired with an illegal, yet active homosexual community in urbanised Iran raises the question of how – against an authoritarian political order and its homophobic rhetoric – this abjection of the traditional Islamic body could come into existence.

In the summer 2014 when the Instagram account @therichkidsoftehran confronted the online world with a body image of Iranian youth culture to that point only known to Iran's insiders, the reactions throughout the Iranian diaspora were more ambiguous than the general media coverage.[1] In a mainly critical social-media discussion, in which classism and the overt display of material wealth had been the focus of the original posting, a young female user (judging by the profile) posted the following comment in defence of the pictures of private pool parties, sunbathing beauties and street-style shots:

> I think the point of this instagram account was to show another side of persians and iran / to show ignorant americans and europeans that not everyone in that country is all about war and hijab and covering up and launching missiles / to show you people that Iran is not the same as iraq and afghanistan / to show people that Persians are just like any other american or European even better . . .
>
> This is how majority of people in iran LOOK and LIVE !!! SERIOUSLY !!!! Like 80 per cent of the population![2]

Although a simple refutation of the numbers given would be tempting to make, statistics will not be the focus of this chapter. What I consider worth further investigation is the commentator's perception of 'good' or 'even better' living and looking.

Consequently, some of the questions that will be investigated here are: How did this Iranian body image develop under the present political order? How did the regime's official ideal of the female body become rejected to such a broad extent by Iranian youth culture? It is clear that these pictures of private bodies reflect a beauty ideal more influenced by Hollywood, Western fashion blogs and recent globalised pop cultural ideals than the official dress code of the Islamic Republic. Hence, the Islamic body has become an abject figure. Beyond that, how should we read those bodies?

As apparent from the quoted posting above, the usage of terms as 'Western', 'Eastern' or 'Islamic' mainly refers to ideas and values with which they are commonly associated within the context of this chapter. I do not wish to essentialise geographical spaces or cultural communities. Moreover, this chapter hopes to stress the need for transparency and clarification in matters of 'East' and 'West' as matters of perception.

As a consequence of this aim, the present chapter will begin by exploring the Iranian concept of beauty in Qajar Iran (1785–1925), a period in which Iran's contact with Europe intensified and observations about its counterpart were recorded and read, respectively. In a selective manner I will work my way through Iranian cultural history, touching on the modernist discourse of the Constitutional Revolution (1905–11), the westernised male body and the re-veiling of the female body in the course of the Iranian Revolution. This genealogy of beauty and body politics in modern Iran and the investigation of the aforementioned questions will also bring forth a gendered dimension to my analysis.

In order to give space to a perspective that is liminal in itself, that contains characteristics of both insider and outsider eyes, I will review different types of representations of the veiled female body by Iranian diasporic artists Marjane Satrapi (who is a representative of the first-generation diaspora) and Ana Lily Amirpour (who belongs to the second generation outside Iran) in the last part of this chapter. Focusing on Amirpour's feature film *A Girl Walks Home Alone at Night* I will put emphasis on a creative reading of the female body that transcends stereotypes of veiled backwardness and subverts the ideas and ideals of both Islamic orthodoxy and Western cultural superiority.

The analytical leitmotiv applied in this chapter is Julia Kristeva's concept of abjection. The abject is a place between subject and object, the reaction to a breakdown in meaning or, within a post-structualist context: 'What disturbs identity, system, order. What does not respect borders, positions, rules.'[3] It is a useful psychoanalytical tool to understand the collective abandonment of the political regime's body ideal in contemporary Iranian youth culture.

Beauty and Gender Images in Qajar Iran

The concept of beauty in early Qajar Iran, as appears through contemporary texts, was highly idealised and closely linked to male love and desire. Following Afsaneh Najmabadi's seminal work *Women with Moustaches and Men without Beards* (2005) a certain set of facial and bodily features was considered beautiful and desirable. For example: moon-faced (*mah tal'at*), cypress-statured (*sarv qamat*), ruby lips (*la'l lab*), bow-eyebrows (*kaman abru*), narcissus-eyed (*narges chashm*) and narrow-waisted (*kamar barik*).[4] These features were not gender specific – they were used to describe beautiful women as well as men. To be an object of desire for adult men depended more on youth than on gender. Beauty icons were the female *huri* and the male *ghelman* (actually plural for *gholam*: servant, but used in singular form). In Qur'anic verses, they are the servants of paradisiac pleasures.[5] The *ghelman* is not as directly described as a renderer of sexual pleasures as the *huri* is, but he shares the same cultural spot as a wine-server, musician and dancer.[6] Consequently, in Persian and Arabic literature, especially in Sufi literature, the *ghelman* was embellished with sexual connotation.[7] The human embodiment of the *ghelman* was called *amrad*. A face was considered the most beautiful with the first traces of a moustache (*khatt*, often intensified with make-up on female faces), whereas the fully-grown beard marked adult manhood.[8]

Homoerotic relationships were institutionalised in forms of brotherhood and sisterhood vows. *Kolsum Naneh* is a collection of women's beliefs and rituals, supposedly written by Mollah Agha Jamal Khwansari, born in 1605. He attributes advice and knowledge to five religiously learned women, their presbyter and title-character named Kolsum Naneh. Although of Safavid origin, manuscripts of the collection still circulated in Qajar Iran.[9] The last of 15 chapters deals with the courtship among women and the procedure of sisterhood vows. Its opening reads like a contemporary blend of then homosocial practices and popular belief:

> Kolsum Nane and the other wise women agree that every woman is bound to have a *khahar khandeh* [intimate girlfriend], because if she dies without having had intimate relationships with other women, she cannot hope to go to paradise.[10]

The same-sex practices of the elite were often read by European travellers as proxy-heterosexuality caused by women's seclusion.[11] Commentaries on sexual mores in European travelogues of Iran were written accordingly.[12] Jean Chardin's *Journal du Voyage en Perse* from the late seventeenth century was probably the best-known example, Joseph Michel Tancoigne's travelogue from 1807–9 was similar in tone and so was James Morier's *Adventures of Hajji Baba of Ispahan* from 1828.[13]

The Iranian responses were diverse: from travelogues describing hidden homosexuality in Europe,[14] to the disappearance of the male beloved from portrait paintings and love poetry.[15] '"Another gaze" entered the scene of desire', as Najmabadi states.[16]

I am not suggesting that beside the procreational heterosexual marriage, same-sex relationships were common throughout Iranian society until the late nineteenth century. However, it is certainly significant that here were ways of naming these diverse gender images and positionalities, which means that the connected practices were culturally accepted at that time.

The Veiled Body as a Marker of Backwardness

With the dawn of the Constitutional Movement, homosocial life and homoerotic relationships were seen as one of the main reasons for scientific and societal backwardness in Iran by many Iranian intellectuals.[17] Romantic heterosexual marriage became the ideal rather than the former institution of mainly procreational purpose.[18] Taj al-Saltana, the daughter of Naser al-Din Shah was a prominent voice of the Constitutional Movement. She was considered one of the most beautiful women of her time at the royal court. In her memoires she recalls a journey through the Tabriz region and idealises the marriages of the rural folk:

> I saw men and women everywhere working side by side in the villages, the women unveiled. [. . .] There are no prostitutes in any of the villages, because as long as a man and a woman are not equal in wealth, neither will marry the other. Besides, since the women do not cover their faces, mates are able to choose one another for themselves. [. . .]
>
> They will observe all the love, sincerity and unaffectedness of life toward one another and always live in happiness and good fortune, leaving to posterity honourable and proud descendants. The character of rural folk and desert dwellers is a hundred thousand times better than that of city people. [. . .] The veiling of women in this country has spawned and spread thousands upon thousands of corrupt immoral tendencies.[19]

In 1929 Reza Shah's compulsory order for men to wear Western-style clothing caused as much popular and clerical outrage as the prohibition of women's veiling seven years later.[20] The prohibition of the veil however, could not be enforced and was withdrawn in 1941. Since modernity was, as Najmabadi points out, sought to be achieved through heterosociality,[21] not only the veil was linked to Iranian backwardness and had to be abandoned, the *amrad* (beardless adolescent with first traces of a moustache, usually considered the passive part in a homoerotic relationship[22]) had to be also erased from the public sphere and the national memory. At the same time the new fashion of shaving and wearing the European-style suit made Iranian men look like *amrads*.

Therefore, the religious discourse was concerned with the problem of looking like a non-Muslim other.[23] Clean-shaven men wearing bow-ties were called *fokoli* (meaning bow-tie) or *farangi'-ma'ab* (oriented towards the West) and became the abject figures in conservative circles and press, especially after the defeat of the Constitutional Revolution.

It is significant in this period that although the participation of women in society and women's education were considered to be the landmarks of modernity, the body that became the battlefield of ideas was the male body. The *amrad* became the abject figure in the late nineteenth century and the *fokoli*, the westernised dandy, followed the same path more than a century later.

The Veiled Body as a Marker of Anti-Imperialism

While the westernisation of the male body was brought about mostly through Europeanisation, the westernisation of the female body evolved mostly through American influence. During the late 1940s, the United States slowly took over Britain's quasi-colonial position in Iran. Luxury products Americanised the everyday life of the Iranian upper and middle classes. The social gap widened significantly during the two decades after World War II and established a situation of Western cultural domination or, of cultural alienation, to stress the reciprocity of the alienated situation between Americans and a less wealthy Iranian majority.[24]

Particularly after the 1953 coup d'état against Mosaddeq, intellectuals started to criticise – and often self-criticise – that the adapted mores of the upper class were only superficially progressive and that they came without true democratic achievements. In the polemic essay *Gharbzadegi* ('Westoxication' or 'Occidentosis', the term became the catch-cry of the early revolution and was originally coined by Ahmad Fardid[25]), the essayist, once activist of the communist Tudeh Party and novelist Jalal Al-e Ahmad characterises the 'illness' of Iranian society as follows:

> Unless the work of men and women and their services to society are equally valued and paid, unless, alongside men, women assume responsibility for administering a sector of society (other than the

> home, a private function shared between men and women), unless material and spiritual equality is established between the sexes, we will have succeeded only in swelling an army of consumers of powder and lipstick – the products of the West's industry – another form of occidentosis.[26]

Reading *Gharbzadegi* today is an odd experience: though the reader is well aware of the profound impact this manifesto–essay has had on the course of historical events in Iran, most readers outside the Islamic Republic's belief system will feel estranged by its sheer polemic style, its black-and-white argumentation. However, as Hamid Dabashi stresses, one cannot overestimate the power *Gharbzadegi* once had on Western or western-style educated young intellectuals and religious seminary students alike.[27] It bears witness of the zeitgeist of the young disillusioned post-coup generation and its author (who died ten years prior to the revolution whose intellectual figurehead he then became) embodied this generation's multifaceted and enigmatic character: torn between the hardship he had witnessed as a child when his father Sheykh Ahmad was absolved of his notarial functions (as all clerics were) and he himself had to contribute to the family's income by working as a watch-maker after leaving primary school,[28] and between his political ideals of gender equality and emancipation. Characteristically, he articulated the latter's claims gladly but did not always translate them into his personal life. Faced with the inability of his novelist-wife Simin Daneshvar and himself to conceive children, Al-e Ahmad wrote in his self-reflection *sangi bar guri (A Stone upon a Grave)*:

> There are two men inside myself: one educated, modern writer and social critic of the twentieth century and the other an 'Eastern man' (*mard-e sharqi*) who inherits the cry of tradition, history and desires and all things related to religious and common law. Like my father and brother used to be and the sons-in-law are. Like the neighbours and cultural colleagues and ministers and all merchants and businessmen. Even the shah.[29]

He could not bear not to be a father, moreover not to be a father of a son with curly hair, he continued. He even considered marrying his extra-marital partner he met in Europe as a second wife, in case she would become pregnant with his child.[30]

In this atmosphere of political incitement, it was the female body that carried the meaning of the political order. Despised by both leftwing intellectuals and political clerics, Farah Diba Pahlavi represented the lead of material wealth and Western lifestyle during the 1960s and 70s. As much as she was admired in the Western yellow press for her French-couture wardrobe and her elegant hair up-do, she embodied the decadent Westernised female body that was the figure of abjection for both the Iranian intelligentsia and Khomeini and his followers. When by October 1971 the self-orientalisation[31] of the Pahlavis and the depiction of Farah as the Persian fairytale empress culminated in the 2,500 anniversary celebrations of the Persian Empire, religious rhetoric had found its way back into political day-to-day discourse.

With representatives of the intelligentsia (re)discovering Iranian Shiism as a language of political resistance, the veil was rediscovered as well. Not to re-establish homosociality, but to express dissent with the Pahlavi regime and to proclaim anti-imperialist and/or religious virtues in opposition to the Western lifestyle of the elite. Significantly, the veil did not return with its former implications: women were not supposed to go back to the harem, they did not need to be beautiful at all, instead they were supposed to be companions to their husbands and brothers, revolutionaries in chadors. This shift intensified during the war years 1980–8, during which French photographer and filmmaker Jean Gaumy visited Iran. In a training camp for Basij women outside Tehran he took a picture of female fighters during a shooting exercise.[32] The black-and-white picture is of a curious nature: the first two women visible in a row, wearing (supposedly) black cloaks and chadors and holding rather large automatic pistols contain notions of both menacing Muslim otherness and female empowerment. Three women at the left margin of the picture are obviously waiting for their turn on the gun. With their chadors tightly wrapped around their bodies, they look like the archetype female body that was to become the signifier of the Islamic Republic in the West. Yet the veiled bodies they are waiting to become, pointing a gun determinedly to a target outside the frame, are the female revolutionary 'sisters' idealised inside Iran. To a certain extent, their dipiction was a continuation of the modernist discourse of the Constitutional Movement, but religiously oriented.

At the same time, this new symbolic order came about with invented tradition.[33] In order to create a new Islamic identity, the sexual history of Iran had to be re-written and the veil, the former marker of homosociality (and therefore linked with same-sex practices) became the marker of heteronormativity and religiously approved monogamous marriage. Beside the legal inferiority of women, the non-existence of homoeroticism in Iranian culture became the invented tradition of the Islamic Republic.

The former, however, did not go unchallenged. Soon after the very beginning of the Islamic Republic, the last public uprising against compulsory veiling and a religiously determined State began on 8 March 1979, lasting five days and attracting the participation of tens of thousands.[34] A number of European and American feminists came to show their public support, among them Kate Millett. In her memoir *Going to Iran* (1982) Millett remarks upon the large attendance of male activists in the demonstrations as well as upon the physical struggle they and the female demonstrators had to engage in against armed gangs of the newly formed Hezbollahi Movement. She also mentions killings of homosexuals in the streets.[35] In their study *Foucault and the Iranian Revolution*, Janet Afary and Kevin B. Anderson provide an in-length analysis of Michel Foucault's temporarily undifferentiated support for Khomeini and a complete translation of the series of articles on Iran and the revolution Foucault had published in the Italian *Corriere della Sera*. Also included is an open letter of the Iranian feminist Atoussa H. from November 1978, published in *Le Nouvel Observateur*. It reads:

> Living in Paris, I am profoundly upset by the untroubled attitude of French leftists toward the possibility of an 'Islamic government' that might replace the bloody tyranny of the shah. Michel Foucault, for example, seems moved by the 'Muslim spirituality' that would advantageously replace, according to him, the ferocious capitalist dictatorship that is tottering today. After twenty-five years of silence and oppression, do the Iranian people have no other choice than between the SAVAK and religious fanaticism?[36]

The Abjection of the Islamic Body

Today, there is an official social order in which homosexuality is assumed not to exist.[37] In contrast, trans-sexuality is regarded as an illness of body and soul and therefore curable. In the early 1980s Khomeini released a fatwa for a struggling pious trans-sexual, Maryam Khatoon Molkara, stating mankind was allowed to modify its nature.[38] In order to re-establish the heteronormative binary order, surgical sex changes are half-covered by state insurance. Homosexuality on the other hand, continues to be seen as abnormal.[39]

Moreover, the political order reduces the human body and its performativity to be in line with its own interpretation of Sharia laws. Foremost, the female body. Consequently, it is the female body that struggles everyday with the limits of this order and is ultimately forced into the private realm. A glance into this upper-class private realm and the degree of how far limits of public dressing have been pushed, reveals that the Islamic body, the ideal of the ruling political order, has become abject. In Iranian upper- and middle-class youth culture, the reality of the political order is 'a reality, that if I acknowledge it, it annihilates me. There, abject and abjection are my safe-guards. The primers of my culture.'[40]

The female Islamic body has, again, become a symbol of Islamic backwardness – to Western mainstream media and a large part of its consumers as well as to a large part of upper-class Iranians. Adding another dimension, it has been suggested that a somewhat 'Western' dress code and the use of beautifying measures designed to match up-to-date beauty ideals would point to a bearer's politically dissident attitude. Returning to the phenomenon of *The Rich Kids of Tehran* I would like to propose a different reading. The display of Western luxury fashion brands, surgically or non-surgically optimised bodies and expensive lifestyle tools is clearly a privilege of upper-class youths.[41] Following Arghavan's research on *Tehrani Cultural Bricolage* (Arghavan, 2013), he identified five categories of female and male young Tehranis among the participants of his survey: distinctive boys, hedonistic boys, pretentious boys, distinctive girls and ordinary girls.[42] For the 'distinctive' categories he summarises:

> They grow up in society's wealthiest families and their socioeconomic background allows them to freely choose every aspect of their lives. [. . .] Because they try to minimise the chance of confrontation with the dominant Islamic and traditional order, it is very hard to regard them as being overtly resistant against the dominant culture.[43]

Taking the less wealthy participants into account, he observes that large groups of Tehran's youth have constructed their own cultural worlds in which modern and Western values and the Iranian and Islamic traditions coexist harmoniously, such as the participation in Ashura ceremonies along with Valentine's Day celebrations.[44] Concluding, Arghavan states: 'these young people just want to be fashionable.'[45]

In her case-study 'Shopping for Freedom in the Islamic Republic' Ariane Sadjed conducts similar (though broader) research but takes her analysis one step further (Sadjed, 2012, in German). She characterises consumerism in Iran as a means for battling for social positions:

> The nature of consumerism of the Iranian population is not subversive but represents a conflict between social classes that is traditionally connected with the West. The aestheticisation of this conflict by Western media coverage deepens the cleavages within Iranian society and points to the factual and symbolic monopoly of interpretation by the West in terms of what resistance should look like and which political positions are preferable to others.[46]

Representations of the Veiled Female Body

The Western convention to depict the female Islamic body as a signifier of the Iranian political order is also reflected in some works of Iranian diasporic artists, as in the first *Persepolis* graphic novel by Marjane Satrapi (2000). Although the veiled female body is not the only depiction of the female figure in this work, it is a major feature of it. At the beginning of the story, little Marjane is pondering about religion and shares her innocent point of view with the reader, stating: 'I really didn't know what to think about the veil. Deep down I was very religious but as a family we were very modern and avant-garde'.[47] The graphic shows her with a split face – one side unveiled with her bob-haircut and a ruler and gear wheels in the background (symbolising science and learning), on the other side of her face her hair is covered by a chador and has stylised Islamic ornaments drawn around the head – a blurrily orientalised version of herself. While she and her mother experience the private–public realm split with the beginning of the Islamic Republic very distinctly (her short veil always looks like a costume on Marjane's mother), other female bodies are depicted in a rather essentialist way: religious bodies wearing the chador (such as the female revolutionary guards) are abject figures. Through little Marji's eyes, these female bodies in chadors become mere faces wrapped in vast black cloth, obscure *gestalten*. Figures that consist only of blackness and do not have the chance to change their identities, as herself, her mother and other female bodies within the story do. The graphic of little Marjane wearing her wrongly spelled 'Punk is not ded'-badge on a denim jacket overshadowed by two enormous and threatening black figures has already become iconic in Western pop culture.[48] But, besides the irony of the Islamic Revolution (symbolised by the women in the chadors) paying so much attention to a little girl with a wrongly spelled (Westernised) badge, the depiction of religious bodies through the child's eyes remains mainly essentialist.

As the choice of title for the Greek (and in most Western languages) common version of the ancient Achaemenid capital and today archaeological site suggests, the graphic novel and even more so the animated film appear to be made for a Western audience. Apart from its technically outstanding making, it is often referred to as an educational movie about the Iranian Revolution. Since public screenings in Iran remained limited to a few censored occasions, the general reception of the film is difficult to measure.[49] The reactions by diasporic audiences seemed to be mostly positive.

The American–Iranian filmmaker Ana Lily Amirpour offers a very different take on the veiled body in her first feature film *A Girl Walks Home Alone at Night* (2014). Aesthetically heavily influenced by Western independent pop culture, Amirpour develops an original, creative way of dealing with the West's favourite symbol for the Islamic regime: the Girl (with a capital G) in the black chador is a vampire. She is roaming *Bad City, Shahr-e Bad*, on her skateboard. Here, the female Islamic body is not a figure of abjection, it is a figure of subversion. And it is the chador that makes the Girl a vampire: it empowers her and it makes her an avenger of womanhood. Although she is not always that vampire – in her teen bedroom she is almost an ordinary girl. Only at sunset she transforms into the vampire, puts on her black eye make-up and slips over her chador/cape. Her vampire personality is a performance. Amirpour manages to satirise the symbolic of the Islamic Republic and of the diasporic community on many levels simultaneously, not only by emphasising the Iranian private-public realm schizophrenia but also in terms of gender politics. Apart from the attractive but often lost anti-hero Arash, all male characters are abject figures: Arash's father is a desperate old heroin addict named Hossein and the procurer is a parody of a Tehrangeles yob with an inscripted body, the word 'Sex' tattooed on his neck, right above the Farkiani symbol on his chest. Atti 'the

Prostitute' is dressed like a regular Tehrani woman with a tightly pulled manteau/trenchcoat and a casually worn *roosari* (headscarf). In one of the most biting scenes, Hossein 'the Junkie' begs Atti to dance for him and she proceeds, loosening her hair and moving sensually to the song 'Cheshme man' by pre-revolutionary superstar singer Dariush. Amirpour deconstructs notions of diasporic nostalgia by using this iconic tune to be danced to by a beautiful woman in back light, for a man by the name of the highest Shi'i martyr. However, the dancing beauty is a prostitute and the man with the holy name is a junkie. Nothing is like it used to be (or never was), Amirpour seems to say, and eventually the Girl comes to Atti's rescue and kills Hossein 'the Junkie'.

The second main character is the setting itself, *Shahr-e Bad*, an extremely dark representation of Tehran – or suburban United States look-alike, full of corruption, death, drugs and sexual abuse – with a mass grave surrounding the city and massive dilapidated oil pumps marking the day in their machinic autarky. But it is also home to the female vampire and her pop culturally branded bedroom, therefore – as Farshad Zahedi has convincingly argued – a hybrid interval space between homeland and host land, as the female vampire body in her naval stripe shirt underneath the chador/cape neither stands for a stereotypical film-noir femme-fatal vampire, nor subdues to orthodox religious body politics.[50]

Amirpour plays with the chador, the very symbol of the Islamic regime in the West, in an allegedly naïve way and subverts its common connotations of oppression by giving it an almost sensual look-and-feel when it is floating around the Girl's body while she is skateboarding.[51] The Western pop cultural phenomenon of the vampire is used here to reconquer the self-determination of the female body. A veiled body can mean anything. Re-signification and hybridisation are two strategies constantly at work in Amirpour's film, in favour of a new, interstitial reading of the veiled female body.

The variety of Iranian reviews the film received, however, offers some illuminating insights. A number of reviews by private bloggers seem to have been taken offline. A review by the independent moviemag.ir website reads sympathetically, seems aware of interviews the director has given and draws a differentiated picture of Amirpour's work:

> The film does not pursue any political agenda. But of course, when it comes to the chador, there are certain sensitivities. The chador can mean two things here: It can provide freedom and

> independency for the Girl or it can give dignity to her blood-sucking side.

The article is categorised under 'Review and Analysis – Foreign Film' (*naqd va barresi – film-e khareji*).[52] A video review by the religiously conservative roshangari.ir website is as flatly negative as it is suspicious of attacks on everything Iranian–Islamic. The reviewer remarks upon the setting: 'If somebody doesn't know Iran, this film will give him/her a very wrong impression. *Shahr-e bad* is an allegory for Iran, it is cold, soulless, bare of any beauty – a dreadful symbol for Iran.'[53] Referring to the Girl he says:

> If somebody doesn't know about Islamic veiling, this film will be an absolute deception since only the girl who is a vampire wears the complete Islamic chador, the chador represents everything bad in the film. This is an insult to the Iranian–Islamic identity.[54]

As flat as the given interpretation may be, its fear of giving 'a bad image' of Iran is revealing. Like-minded Mehrnews, a news agency close to the Revolutionary Guards, titles on its website 'The West goes to War against Iran by means (literally: with the weapon) of Cinema/ a Veiled Girl in the Shape of a Bloodsucker'. A medium as Mehrnews reporting on a foreign independent film allows the conclusion to be drawn that the film had been so widely watched that it could not be ignored and that consequently the agency felt urged to condemn it publicly.[55]

Further Thoughts

Today, the Islamic body along with its reality has become abject. It is, in Kristeva's words, 'a weight of meaninglessness, about which there is nothing insignificant, and which crushes me.'[56] Escaping this public realm, Iranian upper-class pop culture has created a cultural order of its own, which is ceaselessly at once constituted and threatened by the political order and its signifier, the veiled female body, a representation tied by affects. Although the globalisation of the fashion and beauty industry may provide some insights concerning ephemeral trends also present in Iran, it does not serve as a universal exegesis. The concept of beauty in contemporary Iran bears aspects of orientalisation and westernisation at the same time. 'The Persian princess' is a popular motif of self-presentation on social-media platforms and a graphic example of an ideal Oriental (exotic) body measured by Western beauty standards. It disposes all features of 'Oriental' beauty that seem desirable according to Western standards and has eliminated all othering characteristics, exhibiting a perfect make-up, largely painted eyes, a snub nose, framing eyebrows and a glittering crown. In the words of American–Iranian author Dina Nayeri: 'Because the mandatory hijab leaves nothing but the small circle of the face as a canvas for beauty and self-expression, Iranian women have become obsessed with their faces. They want their features to be delicate, symmetrical, and European.'[57]

At the same time the sheer constructedness of the 'Persian princess' motif points to further layers of meaning: as the 'statement' by the @therichkidsoftehran Instagram account reveals, it is a concept of beauty modelled to please the Western gaze[58] and to distance itself from all 'Eastern' otherness:

> We don't belong to any organization or to any political group. Rich Kids of Tehran shows the lifestyle in Tehran and other cities in Iran. Many think we ride Camels and most can't even tell the difference between Arabs and Persians, our motive is simple: Rich Kids of Tehran. We ride Italian and German Wheels and we dress Chanel, Gucci, Louboutin and Tom Ford. We have the ultimate sanctions on us and despite all those sanctions by the west we still show you how we dress, look, our cars and houses. Everywhere has the less-unfortunates before you start talking about the poor![59]

I want to argue that this idea of 'Persian beauty' is a consequence of what Zia-Ebrahimi has conclusively described as a self-orientalisation that takes root in a lack of desire for detachment from Europe coupled with an inferiority complex that caused an internalisation of orientalism's prejudices towards Islam and the 'East'.[60] In other words: Why is it desirable for Iranian women (and men) to look European? Nayeri's word association 'delicate, symmetrical, European' points directly to the self-orientalisation of the Iranian body. In consequence, the counterpart would read 'crude, clumsy, Eastern'. This, ultimately, implies the abjection of the Eastern-Iranian self. Easterness, therefore, is 'the impossible within.'[61] 'I abject *myself*', as Kristeva puts it, 'within the same motion through which "I" claim to establish *myself*.'[62]

However, considering the 'Princess' motif and its constructedness I want to argue that 'everyday European' beauty is not enough as a role model for the self-Orientalised body today. The beauty ideal as present in upper-class Iran as in some diasporic communities alike, is already an aesthetic system, a new social order of Hollywood and Tehrangeles, of Dubai and Instagram, a beauty that is even 'better', even more beautiful than representations of Western beauty. It is an idealised Western beauty with an 'exotic touch' coming true. A third body[63] that combines the very best of East and West. A body which has been optimised throughout modern history and does not hesitate to display the work behind this process, as Nayeri evokes rhinoplasty as 'the Iranian rite of passage' that is shared by thousands of Iranian women.[64] Thus the 'Persian Barbie princess' may be one recent and common real-life personification of this third body. The fantasmatic character of this very aesthetic becomes even more blatantly taken to the next level, even if not as frequently used: following the 'fantasi' trend, Hollywood icons and fairy tales are brought to life through body building, coloured contact lenses or plastic surgery – as the press coverage of the 'donkey ear' operation (*amal-e zibayi gush-e olaghi*) recreating Peter Jackson's elves and hobbits impressively illustrates.[65]

Notes

1. http://www.dailymail.co.uk/news/article-2916388/Our-lives-aren-t-like-Homeland-Argo-Instagram-s-Rich-Kids-Tehran-250-000-cars-10m-homes-opulent-lifestyles-attack-view-think-ride-camels.html and http://nypost.com/2014/10/08/rich-kids-of-tehran-instagram-showcases-life-of-iranian-elite/ [Accessed 25 July 2016].
2. Source: Facebook.
3. Kristeva, Julia, *Powers of Horror: An Essay on Abjection* (New York, 1984), p. 4.
4. Najmabadi, Afsaneh, *Women with Moustaches and Men without Beards. Gender and Sexual Anxieties of Iranian Modernity* (Berkeley and Los Angeles, 2005), p. 11.
5. Ibid., p. 13.
6. Ibid.
7. Ibid., pp. 13–15.
8. Ibid., p. 15.
9. The Qajar Women Archive features a manuscript of Kolsum Naneh from 1830 or 1831 that is the property of the Majlis Library, Museum and Document Centre, Tehran: http://www.qajarwomen.org/en/items/1018A43.html to view the manuscript: http://iiif.lib.harvard.edu/manifests/view/drs:44579176$1i both accessed 12 July 2016.

10. Khwansari, Molla Agha Jamal, *Kolsum Nane. Sitten und Gebräuche der Frauen im Orient und ihr Aberglaube.* Tr. and ed. by Bahram Choubine and Judith West (Paris, 1998), p. 125 (in German). Translations are my own, if not marked otherwise.
11. Najmabadi, *Women with Moustaches*, p. 34.
12. Ibid.
13. Ibid., pp. 34–7.
14. Ibid., p. 37.
15. Ibid., p. 38.
16. Ibid.
17. Ibid., pp. 133–5.
18. Ibid., p. 156.
19. Taj Al-Saltana, *Crowning Anguish. Memoirs of a Persian Princess. From the Harem to Modernity*, tr. Anna Vanzan and Amin Neshati, Abbas Amanat (ed.) (Washington, 2003), p. 204.
20. Janet Afary, *Sexual Politics in Modern Iran* (Cambridge, 2009), pp. 155–8.
21. Najmabadi, *Women with Moustaches*, p. 147.
22. Afary, *Sexual Politics*, pp. 88–95.
23. Najmabadi, *Women with Moustaches*, p. 138.
24. See Gronke, Monika, *Iran – A Short History from Islamization to the Present* (Princeton, 2008), p. 125. In her original German version, Gronke uses the term of *kulturelle Überfremdung*, which is not fully reflected in either 'cultural domination' (Ibid., p. 125) or in my own apposition of 'cultural alienation' since it bears the notion of over-alienation plus the reciprocity of the alienated situation between the American representatives in Iran and the Iranian upper class on one side and a huge religious section of the population on the other side. Compare: Gronke, Monika, *Geschichte Irans – Von der Islamisierung bis zur Gegenwart* (Munich, 2003), p. 105.
25. Jalal Al-e Ahmad, *Occidentosis*, tr. R. Campbell (Berkeley, 1984), p. 16 and Hamid Dabashi, *Theology of Discontent* (New York and London, 1993), p. 76.
26. Al-e Ahmad, *Occidentosis*, p. 70.
27. Dabashi, *Theology of Discontent*, p. 76.
28. Al-e Ahmad, *Occidentosis*, p. 9.
29. Jalal Al-e Ahmad, *Sangi bar guri* (Tehran, 1981), p. 70, as quoted in Michael Hillmann, *A Western Take on Jalal Al-e Ahmad (Jalal Al-e Ahmad az Chashme Gharbi), Second Part* (in Persian) available at: http://www.madomeh.com/site/news/news/3176.htm [Accessed 24 July 2016].
30. Ibid.
31. For the concept of self-orientalisation and Iranian nationalism see: Zia-Ebrahimi, Reza, 'Self-Orientalization and Dislocation: The Uses and Abuses of the "Aryan" Discourse in Iran', in *Iranian Studies*, vol. 44 (2011), pp. 445–72.
32. For the photograph see: http://pro.magnumphotos.com/C.aspxVP3=SearchResult&VBID=2K1HZO6U75N2HK&SMLS=1&RW=1280&RH=615#/SearchResult&VBID = 2K1HZO6U7CT2WV&SMLS = 1&RW = 1280&RH = 615&POPUPIID = 2S5RYDWALH_0&POPUPPN = 14.

33. See Eric Hobsbawm and Terence Ranger (eds), *The Invention of Tradition* (Cambridge, 1983).
34. Janet Afary and Kevin Anderson, *Foucault and the Iranian Revolution: Gender and the Seductions of Islamism* (Chicago, 2005), p. 111.
35. Ibid., pp. 112–13.
36. Ibid., p. 209.
37. The probably best-known example of public denial of homosexuality in Iran is former President Ahmadinejad's speech at Columbia University on 24 September 2007, in which he stated: 'In Iran we don't have homosexuals like in your country'; https://www.youtube.com/watch?v = xou92apNN4o [Accessed 28 July 2016], 3.50.
38. Floor, Willem, *A Social History of Sexual Relations in Iran* (Washington, 2008), p. 358.
39. See Najmabadi, Afsaneh, *The Truth of Sex* (12 January 2005), available at: http://iranian.com/Najmabadi/2005/January/Sex/index.html [Accessed 27 July 2016].
40. Kristeva, *Powers*, p. 2.
41. I want to thank Mahnaz Yousefzadeh for pointing up the need for specification of my former argument as made in my conference paper at the preceding 'Iran and the West' conference at Warwick, 1–3 July 2015.
42. Mahmoud Arghavan, 'Tehrani Cultural Bricolage. Local Traditions and Global Styles of Tehran's Non-Conformist Youth' in Annabelle Sreberny and Massoumeh Torfeh (eds), *Cultural Revolution in Iran. Contemporary Popular Culture in the Islamic Republic* (London, 2013), pp. 35–9.
43. Ibid., pp. 35–6.
44. Ibid., p. 29.
45. Ibid., p. 40.
46. Sadjed, Ariane, *Shopping for Freedom in der Islamischen Republik – Widerstand und Konformismus im Konsumverhalten der iranischen Mittelschicht* (*Shopping for Freedom in the Islamic Republic: Resistance and Conformism in Iranian Middle-Class Consumer Behaviour*) (Bielefeld, 2012), p. 202.
47. Satrapi, Marjane, *Persepolis* (New York, 2003), p. 6.
48. It is, for example, specifically mentioned in this short review on MTV by Jennifer Vineyard (19 December 2007) available at: http://www.mtv.com/news/1576819/persepolis-tells-the-story-of-growing-up-during-the-islamic-revolution-with-laughing/ [Accessed 11 October 2016].
49. ABC Australia, *Rare Iran screening for controversial film 'Persepolis'* (16 February 2008) available at: http://www.abc.net.au/news/2008-02-16/rare-iran-screening-for-controversial-film/1044548 [Accessed 11 October 2016].
50. Zahedi, Farshad, 'Diasporic Space and the Weight of Memory in Films Made by Exilic Iranian Female Directors' to-date unpublished paper, presented at the *Annual Conference of the Italian Society for Middle Eastern Studies (SesaMO)*, 17 March 2016 at the University of Catania.
51. See interview with the director for Vice Media: http://www.vice.com/video/talking-to-the-star-and-director-of-a-girl-walks-home-alone-at-night-000 [Accessed 26 July 2016].

52. Karimi, Meysam, *Naqd va barresi film-e dokhtari dar shab tanha be khane miravad*, available at: http://moviemag.ir/cinema/movie-reviews/world/10166-%D9%86%D9%82%D8%AF-%D9%88-%D8%A8%D8%B1%D8%B1%D8%B3%DB%8C-%D9%81%DB%8C%D9%84%D9%85-%D8%AF%D8%AE%D8%AA%D8%B1%DB%8C-%D8%AF%D8%B1-%D8%B4%D8%A8-%D8%AA%D9%86%D9%87%D8%A7-%D8%A8%D9%87-%D8%AE%D8%A7%D9%86%D9%87-%D9%85%DB%8C-%D8%B1%D9%88%D8%AF-(-A-Girl-Walks-Home-Alone-at-Night-) [Accessed 24 November 2016].
53. Pourmas'ud, Alireza, *Tahlil va barresi film-e dokhatri dar shab tanha be khane miravad* (28.6.1394), available at: http://roshangari.ir/video/36298 [Accessed 24 November 2016].
54. Ibid.
55. Mehrnews, *Gharb ba selah-e sinama be jang-e iran amad* (05.11.1392), available at: http://www.mehrnews.com/news/2221052/%D8%BA%D8%B1%D8%A8-%D8%A8%D8%A7-%D8%B3%D9%84%D8%A7%D8%AD-%D8%B3%DB%8C%D9%86%D9%85%D8%A7-%D8%A8%D9%87-%D8%AC%D9%86%DA%AF-%D8%A7%DB%8C%D8%B1%D8%A7%D9%86-%D8%A2%D9%85%D8%AF-%D8%AF%D8%AE%D8%AA%D8%B1-%D9%85%D8%AD%D8%AC%D8%A8%D9%87-%D8%A7%DB%8C-%D8%AF%D8%B1-%D9%82%D8%A7%D9%85%D8%AA-%DB%8C%DA%A9%A9 [Accessed 24 November 2016].
56. Kristeva, *Powers*, p. 2.
57. Nayeri, Dina, *The Complicated Beauty of the Persian Nose* (24 November 2014) available at: http://www.vice.com/en_uk/read/shes-so-najoor-0000467-v21n10 [Accessed 27 July 2016].
58. I thank Savka Andic for making me aware of this point. The original 'statement' after the account went online is echoed in the social-media comment quoted at the beginning of this chapter.
59. https://www.instagram.com/p/x5ic1MPN69/?taken-by=therichkidsoftehran [Accessed 28 January 2016].
60. Zia-Ebrahimi, Reza, 'Self-Orientalization and Dislocation: The Uses and Abuses of the "Aryan" Discourse in Iran', in *Iranian Studies*, vol. 44 (2011), p. 468.
61. Kristeva, *Powers*, p. 5.
62. Ibid., p. 3.
63. The notion of a 'third body' is not mine but was introduced by Margaux Whiskin during a discussion. I am borrowing it gratefully.
64. Nayeri, *The Complicated Beauty*.
65. http://www.asriran.com/fa/news/379222/%DA%AF%D9%88%D8%B4-%D8%A7%D9%84%D8%A7%D8%BA%DB%8C-%D8%AC%D8%AF%DB%8C%D8%AF%D8%AA%D8%B1%DB%8C%D9%86-%D8%B9%D9%85%D9%84-%D8%B2%DB%8C%D8%A8%D8%A7%DB%8C%DB%8C-%D8%AF%D8%B1-%D8%A7%DB%8C%D8%B1%D8%A7%D9%86-%D8%B9%DA%A9%D8%B3 [Accessed 21 August 2017].

AFTERWORD

ISFAHAN 1976–8: A PERSONAL RECOLLECTION

Andrew Knapp

I specialise in French, not in Iranian, politics and contemporary history. These recollections, therefore, are in no sense an academic article. They may have the merit of directness; they make no claim to rigour.

In the last years of the Pahlavi regime, Iran attracted tens of thousands of expatriate workers, teachers, trainers and technicians, drawn by the promise of high wages at a time of economic downturn in the West. Many were young, male and single. I was one: a teacher of English with the British Council in Isfahan, appointed in 1976, the year of my graduation. This was a moment of major expansion for the British Council in Iran, as demand for ELT was very high; in Isfahan the number of teachers rose from two to nine. Most of our pupils were individuals, aged anything from 14 up, who sought to improve their educational or professional prospects. We also had a few company contracts, for example with the Iran Fertilizer Company. On a smaller scale (in every way), I gave a six-week intensive course to a group of miniaturists, who were preparing to study the design and printing of banknotes with Thomas de la Rue, in Basingstoke.

Before: Iran and its Disaffected Elite

I had visited Iran three times before 1976. My father was a Politics don at Oxford who began working on the Middle East in the mid-1960s.

As a family man, he liked, when possible, to take his wife and sons with him on his travels. So in 1966, 1970 and 1973, we made our way to Iran in a camping-car, the first time on a seven-month tour which had started in Tunis, via Cairo and Beirut, the other two on briefer summer visits along the classic Turkish route via Bazargan.

The camping-car suggests adventure, and so in some ways it was; we did camp in eastern Turkey, and beneath the mausoleum of Oljeitu at Sultaniya. But for much of our time in Iran, Farhad Diba looked after us. A former pupil of my father's, Ferry Diba was a figure both close to the regime – as the cousin of the Shahbanou Farah – and a potential 'dissident' – as the nephew of Mohammad Mosaddeq. And the sort of people we mixed with, at Ferry Diba's lunch parties at Shemiran, were of a piece with this: a cosmopolitan, wealthy, but also disaffected elite. Ferry's friend Ahmad Farougi Qajar was, for obvious reasons, no great supporter of the regime. Nor, probably, was Iraj Hedayat, whose thriving Yek-o-Yek food processing firm, founded in 1967 on his estate at Pasargadae, soon attracted the unwelcome attention of a rapacious royal family which liked successful entrepreneurs only if they got their cut. When, in 1975, Iran became a real one-party state, Ferry's circle referred to the new Rastakhiz party, the Party of National Resurgence in English, as the Party of National Regurgence.

Ferry Diba, of course, had to leave in 1979, and the business empire created by his father Abolhassan was confiscated by the clergy. Ferry has since settled in Spain, where he has created what he wants to be the most comprehensive library in the world of things Iranian.

Orientalism and Modernity

It was Ferry who shaped my view of the regime: hostile but hardly radical. My broader view of the country, by 1976, might be called Orientalist, though Edward Said would not publish his seminal work for another two years. Two books shaped this perception: Robert Byron's *The Road to Oxiana*, a travel book based on a visit in 1933–4 and still, I believe, seen as necessary reading for the educated Brit travelling to Iran; and Arthur Upham Pope's *Persian Architecture*. Pope's excellent single-volume study introduced me to squinches and mosaic faience, and incidentally taught me a little Iranian history. In this respect it was complemented, for the twentieth century, by impromptu paternal tutorials about the Constitutional Revolution, Reza Shah, the Anglo–Russian occupation and Mosaddeq. Meanwhile the camping-car had taken us to many of the buildings Pope described: not just the big mosques and palaces around the Maidan in Isfahan, but also the Darb-e-Imam and Harun-e-Vilayet, and further afield Sultaniya, the mosque of Gohar Shad in Mashad (for a few seconds) and the Gonbad-i-Qabus. I had drunk tea with students in a Madrassa in the Isfahan bazaar, met by chance. I wanted nothing better than to live close to these buildings.

And to acquire the artefacts. Not yet feeling wealthy enough or established enough to buy carpets, I inclined to miniatures and to the printed cloths, the *qalam-qah*, for which Isfahan was famous. So the bazaar beckoned: you could get still get old ones if you knew where to look.

At the same time I was aware that 'Orientalist' Iran, insofar as it existed at all, was being overtaken by modernity. In March 1976 the *Architectural Review* had published a special issue whose leading chapter bore the dramatic title 'Can Isfahan survive?'. Its author, Sherban Cantacuzino, pointed out how, while the big monuments were cherished as tourist attractions, the urban fabric which bound them together was increasingly being sacrificed to the motor-car. Most dramatically, the bazaar itself had been chopped in two by a road, with no serious attempt to bind up the wounds that this act of destruction had left. I was sufficiently struck by this to want to draw it to the attention of some of my more advanced students, by writing a simplified (but still rather long) version of the main article and making a reading project out of it; with what success I shall never know.

The Western Presence

The Western presence had grown exponentially in Isfahan since 1973 and was estimated at about 10,000. More, then, than a few English teachers. The major reasons for this were the huge influx of wealth into Iran following the oil price rise, and the decision of the United States to sell state-of-the-art weaponry to the Shah. So although there were some civilian projects in the region, many of the Western personnel – chiefly Americans – were linked to the defence contractors: Bell Helicopter, Grumman, General Dynamics. They were there to teach Iranians English, then to teach them to fly aircraft, to maintain the helicopters and the F14s, and to cut dead Iranians out of the wreckage when, as sometimes happened, they crashed them into the mountains.

Figure A.1 Avenue: Hatef Street.

I encountered Americans everywhere, and particularly in the bars of the Irantour or the Kourosh hotels, but many lived in speedily-built satellite towns in the desert. A visit to one of these revealed a passable reproduction of American suburbia: a teenage American girl in shorts mowed an absurdly green front lawn, copiously watered from some rapidly diminishing underground source. Many Americans were Vietnam veterans, for whom the new contracts with Iran offered the chance to make a better living ($2,000 a month) than at home, and perhaps also to avoid settling down. 'I was in the 'Nam for three years', one veteran told me, 'I've been in Iran for two years and let me tell you, I hate those goddam Farsis': not a universal attitude among Isfahan's Americans, but common enough.

The Paykan People

If the Western presence had expanded, so had what today might be called an aspirational middle class: people whom the wife of the director of the British Council in 1973 referred to, not very kindly, as the 'Paykan People': materialistic, status-conscious, seeking to educate themselves or their children in Britain or America. These people were my bread and butter; their aspirations allowed me to live and work in Isfahan. But of course I disapproved of them because they seemed attached to the *wrong* traditions. From the perspective of the (quite recently) sexually liberated West, their continuing attachment to traditional models of the family and roles for women (even if the *chador* was not de rigueur, the idea that a woman could ride a bicycle was a step too far) appeared deeply retrograde. At the same time they appeared to kick away the best of their past, unaware of what they were losing. Symptomatic of this, perhaps, was the contrast between our views of Afghanistan, where I spent two Now-Ruz holidays. My Iranian students clearly thought it a dirty, benighted country, stuck in the Middle Ages. This, of course, was its charm for me.

This odd inversion between Iranian modernity and Western traditionalism was expressed in other ways, too. On arrival in Isfahan I bought a bicycle – a big robust Chinese model with rod brakes and a double crossbar. This seemed an admirable way to get about: Isfahan is a flat town where the distances were not excessive. My students thought it very *infra dig* and wondered why I, as a Brit and therefore obviously well-off, did not drive a motor-car.

Or consider how we sat. Most of my British and American friends furnished their homes with foam mattresses, covered with traditional printed cloths from the bazaar and a greater or lesser number of carpets depending on income and length of stay. Our white walls were adorned with a few miniatures or hangings. We were young, so getting down to

Figure A.2 Pavilion.

the floor wasn't yet a problem; and reclining on a mattress made it all the easier to slide gently into unconsciousness after a pleasant Friday afternoon smoking dope, as we all did. We thought of all this as traditional. Iranians, meanwhile, went for chairs and tables, and if they were imitation Louis XV, so much the better; a betrayal of their heritage, in our view.

Isfahan's favoured night spot, the Hezar-o-Yek Shab, was perhaps a symbol of the divisions. It was, rather against the odds, a good place. The more progressive Iranian families and the expatriates might encounter one another there. But the two groups danced separately, at different times of the evening, to different music.

This might be the stuff of a sitcom had the gulf not run much deeper. Within a few months – certainly by the end of my first year in Iran – I had come to mistrust Iranians. My housemates and I took to playing a game, characterising peoples as inhabited by two extremes. For the Iranians it was rudeness and flowery politeness: the offhand attitudes encountered in ordinary shops on the one hand, and on the other, the Iranians who called us their best friends after just one meeting. By comparison, I considered that the British were both polite and straightforward; the notion that we could be devious or hypocritical in our dealings with Iranians barely crossed my mind. But another, important reason for my mistrust was the Iranians' relationship with the West: my sense that for Iranians, I was of interest chiefly as a vehicle for the Western prosperity they wanted to get their hands on. Despite occasional pleasant encounters, like an autumn picnic (early in my time in Isfahan) with Iranians studying to be teachers of English at the University, this meant that I didn't make Iranian friends. I am far from proud of this reaction, all too common among British and Americans. At least the realisation dawned that if I didn't trust Iranians, I shouldn't be spending too long in their country. So in 1977 I made arrangements to return to the UK the following year.

Neither was my failure, equally common among expatriates, to learn Farsi a source of pride. I had enough to hold a very simple conversation and to do basic shopping. I think I was reasonably polite within my limited vocabulary, although *Simple Colloquial Persian*, a book produced for employees of the Anglo-Iranian Oil Company and the source of much of my vocabulary, was full of instructions to servants. That the Iranians wanted to practise their English on expatriates is a partial excuse for us not doing more. But the fact is that I didn't put in the effort, preferring either to drink and smoke with my expatriate friends, or to read English novels (I got through all 12 volumes of Anthony Powell's *A Dance to the Music of Time* in a few weeks), rather than engage seriously with the language of my country of residence.

Sex and the Gay Scene

No account would be complete without some mention of sex. Western women I knew might take (male) Iranian lovers; I neither expected nor sought such relationships with Iranian women, though that did not preclude very discreet admiration. But by far the most common type of sexual contact between expatriates and Iranians took place between men. Isfahan had a thriving gay scene, centred in part on the bar of the Irantour Hotel. Gay Western acquaintances seemed to have little difficulty attracting Iranian partners, some gay, some straight but frustrated. One friend had to jump out of a window when his lover's wife arrived home unexpectedly; he found himself in a graveyard without his underpants. The most beautiful colleague even acquired a sugar-daddy, a wealthy turquoise merchant who enabled him, in return for a weekly evening session, to bank his whole salary and to take holidays in Egypt, where he became an assiduous frequenter of bath-houses. The poor turquoise merchant was reportedly shot in 1979.

Orientalism Again

Did I find my Orientalist's Iran? Yes, a little. I bought more *qalam-qah*. I lived in beautiful, slightly run-down, houses with (English and American) friends. And early in the morning at weekends I would ride my bicycle over the Marnan bridge and along the glorious country roads west of town to the Ateshgah. I loved the place. It was my own fault if I failed to connect as well with the people.

Politics

Talking politics with my housemates, we agreed that Iran ought to have a lot going for it: it had natural resources, a tradition of urban living and one of the world's oldest cultures. And yet it was a mess. We put this down chiefly to the regime. We underestimated the role of the West.

Figure A.3 Chemin creux.

Did I see the revolution coming? Yes and no. Nothing since my arrival left me in much doubt about what sort of regime was in charge. Before my teaching started, I was told to expect an informer – not a full-timer, just someone on whom SAVAK had found a way to put pressure – in every class. A teacher could mention the Prime Minister, Amir Abbas Hoveyda, and the class would chuckle gently; but the Shah and SAVAK itself were most definitely off limits. The story that went round about SAVAK was that they would ask you if you preferred Coke or Fanta, meaning which sort of bottle you would prefer them to stick up your arse.

I spent the summer holidays of 1977 in the UK, sorting out a D.Phil. application and playing in that year's least successful show on the Edinburgh Fringe. Peter Avery, the Cambridge specialist on Iran, gave me lunch. He was bullish about the future: 'Business is looking up', he said. His optimism seemed to me misplaced. If I had articulated my views, I would have said that the countryside had been abandoned, forcing a disaffected lumpenproletariat into the cities, and that the Paykan people had had enough of SAVAK. And that the regime was rotten and that its modernisation had included some perfectly gratuitous gestures which had offended key constituencies. For example, the switch

Figure A.4 Fire.

from the Islamic to the so-called Pahlavi calendar or even the introduction of daylight saving time ('which time is it you want me to tell you, God's time or the Shah's time?'). Or the razing of a great swathe of the bazaar in Mashhad, to make way for the lawns that now surrounded the Shrine of Imam Reza: very pretty lawns, reminiscent of Pisa, but you can imagine what the bazaaris thought.

And then, early in 1978, the demonstrations started, first in Qom, and were repressed with some ferocity. Kayhan International blamed 'Islamic Marxists', which seemed a nonsense. But I had heard of Khomeini, thanks to reading Marvin Zonis, and so thought I could identify the mosque as the only body in civil society that had neither been co-opted nor repressed by the regime. The 40-day mourning period appeared as a perfect framework for the propagation of demonstrations across the country. It seemed only a matter of time before they reached Tehran. Then, I expected, it would all be like 1963: a bloodbath and then everyone would go home. I did not expect what followed: that the people of Tehran would carry on regardless after Black Friday in September 1978, that the oil workers would go on strike, that the Shah would 'lose his nerve'.

But by then, I was gone, my contract with the British Council, which I had chosen not to renew, having ended in July. Three weeks after that, Isfahan was under martial law.

BIBLIOGRAPHY

Primary Sources

Document no. 297/201192, Archive of the National Library of Iran.

Document no. 220/16022, Archive of Documents and National Library of Iran.

Document no. 290/3447, Archive of Documents and National Library of Iran.

Document no. 290/2131, Archive of Documents and National Library of Iran.

Document no. 16022/220, Archive of Documents and National Library of Iran.

Document no. 297/50552, Archive of Documents and National Library of Iran.

Document no. 297/46142, Archive of Documents and National Library of Iran.

Document no. 297/46145, Archive of Documents and National Library of Iran.

Al-e Ahmad, Jalal, *Sangi bar guri* (Tehran, 1981).

——— *Occidentosis: A Plague from the West*, tr. R. Campbell (Berkeley, 1984).

Ammianus Marcellinus, *History* (three vols), tr. John C. Rolfe (Cambridge [Mass.], 1935–40).

Arberry, A.J. (ed.), *The Legacy of Persia* (Oxford, 1953).

Bassett, James, *Persia: Eastern Mission, A Narrative of the Founding and Fortunes of the Eastern Persia Mission, with a Sketch of the Versions of the Bible and Christian Literature in the Persian and Persian-Turkish Languages* (Philadelphia, 1890).

Baye, Le Baron de, *Tiflis. Souvenirs d'une mission* (Paris, 1900).

Bélanger, C., *Voyage aux Indes Orientales, par le Nord de l'Europe, les provinces du Caucase, la Géorgie, l'Arménie et la Perse, suivi de détails topographiques et autres sur le Pégou, les îles de Java, de Maurice et de Bourbon, sur le cap de Bonne-Espérance et Sainte-Hélène pendant les années 1827, 1828 et 1829*, I–VIII, 8 et 3 grands atlas (Paris, 1836–46).

Beradze, Grigol (ed.), *Georgia in Persian Sources of the Qajar Period: Travelogues and Memoirs*, tr. Marina Alexidze (Tbilisi, 2016).

Blavatsky, Helena, *The Secret Doctrine*, three vols (Wheaton, IL, 1978–9).

The Book of a Thousand Judgements, tr. into Russian by Anahit Perikhanian, tr. from Russian into English by Nina Garsoïan (Costa Mesa, 1997).

Campbell, William W., *A Memoir of Mrs. Judith S. Grant, Late Missionary to Persia* (New York, 1844).

Carter, Russell and Speer, Robert, *Report on India and Persia of the Deputation sent by the Board of Foreign Missions of the Presbyterian Church in the U.S.A. to visit these fields in 1921–22* (New York, 1922).

Chardin, Jean, *Voyages du Chevalier Chardin en Perse et les autres lieux de l'Orient*, 10 vols (Paris, 1811).

Curzon, George N., *Persia and the Persian Question*, vol. 2 (London, 1966, originally published in 1892).

Dehkhoda, A., *Loghat Nāmeh*, 37 vols (1325/1956–57/78, Tehran).

Dio Cassius, *Roman History* (9 vols), tr. Earnest Cary (London, 1914–27).

Dumas, Alexandre, *Le Caucase*, tr. T. Kikodze (Tbilisi, 1970).

Elishe, *History of Vardan and the Armenian War*, tr. Roberts W. Thomson (Cambridge [Mass.], 1982).

Ellison, Ralph, *Invisible Man* (New York, 2010).

Enzensberger, Hans Magnus, 'Unsere weißen Hände' in Nirumand, Bahman, *Persien, Modell eines Etnwicklunglandes oder Die Diktatur der Freien Welt* (Hamburg, 1967).

——— 'Gemeinplätze die Neue Literatur betreffend', in *Kursbuch* 11 (1968): pp. 187–97.

Esfandiary, Soraya, *Meine eigene Geschichte* (Olten, Stuttgart, Salzburg, 1963).

Ferdowsi, *Shahnameh*, tr. Dick Davis (London, 2006).

Fryer, John, *A new Account of East India and Persia, Being nine years' travels 1672–1681*, William Crooke (ed.), 3 vols (London, 1967).

Gamba, Jacques-François, *Voyage dans la Russie méridionale, et particulièrement dans les provinces situées au delà du Caucase, fait depuis 1820 jusqu'en 1824 par le chevalier Gamba, consul du roi à Tiflis* (Paris, 1826).

——— *Mogzauroba amierkavkasiashi*, I, tr. Mzia Mgaloblishvili (Tbilisi, 1987).

Gardane, Paul-Age-Louis de and Mirza, Timurat, *Journal d'un voyage dans la Turquie d'Asie et la Perse, fait en 1807 et 1808* (Paris, 1809).

Grant, Asahel, *The Nestorians; or, The Lost Tribes; Containing Evidence of Their Identity; An Account of Their Manners, Customs, and Ceremonies* (London, 1841).

——— *Memoir of Asahel Grant, M.D.: Missionary to the Nestorians* (New York, 1847).

Harrison, Marguerite, *There's Always Tomorrow: The Story of a Checkered Life* (New York, 1935).

Hegel, Georg Wilhelm Friedrich, *Philosophy of History*, tr. John Sibree (New York, 1902).

Heliodorus, *An Ethiopian Romance*, tr. Moses Hadas (Philadelphia, 1957).

Herodian, *History of the Empire, Volume II: Books 5–8*, tr. C.R. Whittaker (Cambridge, MA, 1970).

Herodotus, *The Histories*, tr. Robin Waterfield (Oxford, 1998).

Jaubert, Amadée, *Mogzauroba somkhetshi da sparsetshi 1805–1806 tslebshi* [*Voyage en Arménie et en Perse fait dans les années 1805–1806*], tr. I. Natchkebia (Tbilisi, 1997).

Josephus, Flavius, *Jewish Antiquities* (nine vols), tr. Louis H Feldman, Ralph Marcus, Allen Wikgren, H. St. J. Thackery (London, 1927–65).

Justin, *Epitome of the Philippic History of Pompeius Trogus*, tr. J.C. Yardley (Atlanta, 1994).

Kaempfer, Engelbert, *Am hofe des persischen grosskonigs (1684–85)*, Walther Hinz (ed.) (Leipzig, 1940).

Karim, Persis M. (ed.), *Let Me Tell You Where I've Been. New Writing by Women of the Iranian Diaspora* (Chicago, 2006).

Karim, Persis M. and Khorrami, M. M. (eds), *A World Between. Poems, Short Stories, and Essays by Iranian–Americans* (New York, 1999).
Khakpour, Porochista, *Sons and Other Flammable Objects* (New York, 2007).
Krause, Walter W., *Kaiserin aus Liebe* (Munich, 1955).
Laurie, Thomas, *Dr. Grant and the Mountain Nestorians* (Boston [MA], 1853).
The Literary Digest, 'An Epic Movie of Man's Fight with Nature', 25 April 1925, pp. 27–8.
Le Brun, Cornelius, *Voyage de Corneille le Brun par la Moscovie, en Perse, et aux Indes Orientales* (Amsterdam, 1718).
Lyclama à Nijeholt, Chevalier T. M., *Voyage en Russie, au Caucase et en Perse Pendant les années 1866, 1867 et 1868*, vol. 1 (Amsterdam & Paris, 1872).
Mahjub, Mohammd-Ja'far, 'Goftar darbare-ye ba'zi farangan va mostafrangan', in *Iran Nameh*, 12 (1994): pp. 673–714.
Malcolm, John, *Sketches of Persia* (London, 1861).
Meinhof, Ulrike, 'Offener Brief an Farah Diba,' in *Konkret* 6 (1967): pp. 21–2.
Menander, *The History of Menander the Guardsman*, tr. R.C. Blockley (Liverpool, 1985).
Nafisi, Azar, *Reading Lolita in Tehran: A Memoir in Books* (New York, 2008).
Nirumand, Bahman, *Persien, Modell eines Entwicklunglandes oder Die Diktatur der Freien Welt* (Hamburg, Reinbek, 1967).
——— *The New Imperialism in Action* (New York, 1969).
Orsolle, Ernst, *Le Caucase et la Perse* (Paris, 1885).
os-Saltaneh, Majd, *Tbilisis aghtsera*, tr. M. Mamatsashvili (Tbilisi, 1971).
Pahlavi, Mohammad Reza, *Mission for My Country* (London, 1961).
——— *The Shah's Story*, tr. Teresa Waugh (London, 1980).
The Paikuli Inscription, tr. Prods Skærvø (Munich, 1983).
Perkins, Justin, *A Residence of Eight Years in Persia, Among the Nestorian Christians* (Andover, MA, 1843).
——— *Missionary Life in Persia: Being Glimpses at a Quarter of a Century of Labors Among the Nestorian Christians* (Boston, MA, 1861).
Peyssonel, Ch. De, *Essay sur les troubles actueles de Perse et de Georgie* (Paris, 1754).
Plutarch, *Plutarch on Sparta*, tr. Richard J. A. Talbert (London, 1988).
Presbyterian Historical Society, 'American Christian Hospital, Meshed, Persia, Annual Report, 1930–1931,' (Record Group 91, Box 20, Folder 1).
——— 'Report of the Second Century Deputation on The Medical Work in Iran, 5 May 1939,' (Record Group 280, Box 1, Folder 6).
——— Clement, Stephen M., 'Hero Physician,' (360 Cochran SR).
——— Frame, John, 'Profile of Resht,' (Record Group 91, Box 18, Folder 22).
——— Hoffman, Rolla Edwards (1887–1974), Papers c. 1915–49, Record Group 231.
——— Zoeckler, Mary, 'Report of Medical Work for Women, Daulatabad Sub-station, 1914–1915,' (Record Group 280, Box 1, Folder 10).
——— Zoeckler, Mary, 'Report of Medical Work, Daulatabad-Malayir, 1915–16,' (Record Group 280, Box 1, Folder 10).
——— Zoeckler, Mary, 'Report of Medical work, Daulatabad Sub-station, 1916–1917,' (Record Group 280, Box 1, Folder 10).
——— Zoeckler, Mary, 'Report of Medical Work for Women, Hamadan Station, 1920–21'.
——— Zoeckler, Mary, 'Report of Medical Work, Daulatabad, Malayir, 1922–1923,' (Record Group 280, Box 1, Folder 10).

——— Zoeckler, Mary, 'Report of Medical Work, Daulatabad, Malayir, 1923–1924,' (Record Group 280, Box 1, Folder 10).
——— Zoeckler, Mary, 'Report of Medical Work, 1924–1925,' (Record Group 280, Box 1, Folder 10).
——— Zoeckler, Mary, 'Report of Medical Work, Daulatabad, Malayir, Persia, 1925–1926,' (Record Group 280, Box 1, Folder 10).
——— Zoeckler, Mary, Letter to Friends of the North Church, 23 January 1931 (Record Group 280, Box 1, Folder 10).
——— Zoeckler, Mary, Letter to Friends, 22 September 1940 (Record Group 280, Box 1, Folder 8).
Procopius, *Wars*, tr. H. B. Dewing (Cambridge, MA, 1914).
Rachlin, Nahid, *Foreigner* (New York & London, 1978).
Saadi, *Moslicheddin Sa'dis Rosengarten*, tr. and ed. K. H. Graf (Leipzig, 1846).
——— *Der Rosengarten*, tr. D. Bellmann, following tr. of K. H. Graf, revised (Leipzig, 1982).
——— گلستان سعدی *Golestân-e Sa'di*, Persian critical edn by Gholam-Hossein Yusofi (Tehran, 1989).
——— *Der Rosengarten*, tr. K. Göpel, following tr. S. O. Ali-Shah (Berlin, 1997).
——— *Der Rosengarten*, tr. D. Bellmann, following tr. K. H. Graf, revised (3rd edition) (Munich, 1998).
——— *Gulistan*, tr. Edward Rehatsek (Tehran, 2004).
Safineh Soleymāni, tr. John O'Kane (London, 1972).
Salignac de la Mothe-Fénelon, François de, *De l'Education des Filles* (Paris, 1687).
——— *Dialogues des morts anciens et modernes, avec quelques fables, composez pour l'éducation d'un prince*, vol. I (Paris, 1718).
——— *Les Aventures de Télémaque* (Paris, 1730).
——— *Dialogues of the Dead* (London, 1760).
Satrapi, Marjane, *Persepolis* (New York, 2003).
Sue, Eugène, *Mysteries of Paris* (New York, 2015).
Tabari, *The History of al-Tabari: Volume V: The Sasanids, the Byzanties, the Lakmids, and Yemen*, tr. C. E. Bosworth (New York, 1999).
Tacitus, *Annals* (in 3 vols), tr. John Jackson (London, 1931–7).
Taj Al-Saltana, *Crowning Anguish. Memoirs of a Persian Princess. From the Harem to Modernity*, tr. Anna Vanzan and Amin Neshati (Washington, 2003).
Tavernier, Jean-Baptiste, *Les six voyages de J.B.T. en Turquie, en Perse et aux Indes* (Paris, 1676).
Teimuraz, *Vocabullario italiano–persico et turco, composto Da Sua Altezza Serenissimo Timuraz, Principe die Giorgia* (Paris, 1809).
Wilson, S. G., *Persia: Western Mission* (Philadelphia, 1896).
Wishard, John, *Twenty Years in Persia: A Narrative of Life Under the Last Three Shahs* (New York, 1908).
Wolf, Christa, *Cassandra. A Novel and Four Essays* (New York, 1988).
Woolf, Virginia, *A Room of One's Own/Three Guineas* (London, 2000).
Zoeckler, Mary, Letter to Friends of the North Church, 8 February 1922.
——— 'Personal Report, Mary A. Zoeckler, 1923–1924'.
——— Letter to The Women's Guild of North Church, 1 June 1926.
Zonaras, *The History of Zonaras: from Alexander Severus to the Death of Theodosius the Great*, tr. Thomas M. Banchich and Eugene N. Lane (Abingdon, 2009).

Secondary Sources

Abbas, Sadia, *At Freedom's Limit: Islam and the Postcolonial Predicament* (New York, 2014).

Abrahamian, Ervand, *Iran Between Two Revolutions* (Princeton, 1982).

Abu-Lughod, Lila, *Do Muslim Women Need Saving?* (Cambridge, MA, 2013).

Adler, Emmanuel, 'Seizing the Middle Ground. Constructivism in World Politics', in *European Journal of International Relations* 3 (1997): pp. 319–63.

Al Afghani, Jamal al Din, 'The Reign of Terror in Persia', in *The Contemporary Review*, 41 (1892): pp. 238–48, reprinted in L. Ridgeon (ed.), *Religion and Politics in Modern Iran* (London, 2005): pp. 1–13.

Afary, Janet, *Sexual Politics in Modern Iran* (Cambridge, 2009).

Afary, Janet and Anderson, Kevin, *Foucault and the Iranian Revolution: Gender and the Seductions of Islamism* (Chicago, 2005).

Afkhani, Gholam Reza, *The Life and Times of the Shah* (London, 2009).

Ahmadzadeh, Hashem, *Nation and Novel: A Study of Persian and Kurdish Narrative Discourse* (Uppsala, 2003).

Ahmed, Rehana, *Writing British Muslims: Religion, Class and Multiculturalism* (Manchester, 2015).

Ahmed-Ghosh, Huma and Donadey, Anne, 'Why Americans Love Azar Nafisi's Reading Lolita in Tehran', in *Signs*, 33 (2008): pp. 623–46.

Aka, Ismail, *Timurid*, tr. Akbar Saboori (Tehran, 2011).

Akhundzade, Mirza Fatali, *Alefba-ye Jadid va maktubat* (Baku, 1963).

Alasti, Ahmad (ed. and tr.), *Mostanad Alaf: Se Revayat va Yek Moghaddameh / The Documentary Grass: Three Narratives and One Introduction* (Tehran, 2015).

Alexidze, Marina, *The Muslim East in the Nineteenth Century. Studies in The history of Culture, Religion and Life* (Tbilisi, 2011).

Allam Hamdy, Nimet, 'The Development of Nude Female Drawing in Persian Islamic Painting', in *Akten des VII. International kongresses fur Iranische kunst une archalologie* (Munich, 1979): pp. 430–8.

Aloob, Abdelwahab M., *The Persian Social Novel from 1900 to 1941*, PhD dissertation (University of Michigan, 1988).

Amanat, Abbas, *Pivot of the Universe: Nasir Al-Din Shah Qajar and the Iranian Monarchy, 1831–1896* (London, 1997).

Amanat, Abbas and Vejdani, Farzin (eds), *Iran Facing Others, Identity Boundaries in a Historical Perspective* (New York, 2012).

Ambrosius, Lloyd E., *Wilsonianism: Woodrow Wilson and his Legacy in American Foreign Policy* (New York, 2002).

Amini, I., *Napoléon et la Perse, Les relations franco–persanes sous le Premier Empire dans le contexte des rivalités entre la France, l'Angleterre et la Russie* (Paris, 1995).

Anchabadze, I., Volkova, N., *Starij Tbilisi. Gorod i gorozhane v XIX veke* (Moscow, 1990).

Anderson, Benedict, *Imagined Communities. Reflections on the Origins and Spread of Nationalism* (London & New York, 2006).

Ansari, Ali M., *Modern Iran Since 1921, The Pahlavis and After* (Harlow, London, 2003).

——— *Confronting Iran: The Failure of American Policy and the Next Great Crisis in the Middle East* (New York, 2006).

——— (ed.), *Perceptions of Iran: History, Myths and Nationalism from Medieval Persia to the Islamic Republic* (London, 2013).

——— 'Myth, History and Narrative Displacement in Iranian Historiography' in Ali M. Ansari (ed.), *Perceptions of Iran: History, Myths and Nationalism from Medieval Persia to the Islamic Republic* (London, 2013): pp. 5–23.

Anvar, Abdollah, *Fehrest-e No'sakh-e Khatti ketabkhaneh-ye melli-e Iran*, vol. 4 (Tehran, 1992).

Asdourian, Pascal, *Die politischen Beziehungen zwischen Armenien und Rom von 190 v. Chr. bis 428 n. Chr: ein Abriss der armenischen Geschichte in dieser Periode* (Venice, 1911).

Asgari, Afshin Matin, 'The Academic Debate on Iranian Identity: Nation and Empire Entangled', in Abbas Amanat and Farzin Vejdani (eds), *Iran Facing Others, Identity Boundaries in a Historical Perspective* (New York, 2012): pp. 173–92.

Arghavan, Mahmoud, 'Tehrani Cultural Bricolage. Local Traditions and Global Styles of Tehran's Non-Conformist Youth' in Sreberny, Annabelle and Torfeh, Massoumeh (eds), *Cultural Revolution in Iran. Contemporary Popular Culture in the Islamic Republic* (London, 2013): pp. 27–42.

Arnason, Johann P., 'East and West: From Invidious Dichotomy to Incomplete Deconstruction', in Gerard Delanty and Engin F. Isin (eds) *Handbook of Historical Sociology* (London, 2003): pp. 220–34.

Azhand, Yaghob, *History of Iran, Timurid period* (Tehran, 2008).

Babaie, Sussan, 'Visual Vestiges of Travel: Persian Windows on European Weaknesses', in *Journal of Early Modern History*, 13 (2009): pp. 105–36.

——— 'Frontiers of Visual Taboo: Painted Indecencies in Isfahan', in F. Leoni and M. Natif (eds), *Eros and Sexuality in Islamic Art* (Dorchester, 2013): pp. 131–56.

Bachako, Viorel, 'Iran in the First Romanian Geography Books', in Mohammadali Soti (tr.), Ayandeh Journal, 5th fol: pp. 21–32.

Bachleitner, Norbert, "Übersetzungsfabriken". Das deutsche Übersetzungswesen in der ersten Hälfte des 19. Jahrhunderts', in *Internationales Archiv für Sozialgeschichte der deutschen Literatur (IASL)*, 14 (1989): pp. 1–49 Available at http://complit.univie.ac.at/fileadmin/user_upload/abt_complit/%C3%9 Cbersetzungsfabriken_pdf.pdf [Accessed 24 September 2015].

Baker, Mona, *In Other Words – A Coursebook on Translation* (London, 2007).

Bakhshandeh, Ehsan, *Occidentalism in Iran* (London, 2015).

Bakhtin, Mikhail, *Problems of Dostoevsky's Poetics*, ed. and tr. Caryl Emerson (London, 1984).

Banita, Georgiana, 'Affect, Kitsch and Transnational Literature: Azar Nafisi's Portable Worlds' in Sarah Sackel et al. (eds), *Semiotic Encounters: Text, Image and Transnation* (Amsterdam, 2009): pp. 87–102.

Bayani, Shirin, *History of Jalayer* (Tehran, 2003).

Beeman, William O., *The "Great Satan" vs. the "Mad Mullahs": How the United States and Iran demonize each other* (Westport [Conn.], 2005).

Bellmann, Dieter, 'Nachwort', in *Der Rosengarten* (Leipzig, 1998): pp. 349–70.

Bennigsen, Alexandre, 'Mollah Nasreddin et la presse satirique musulmane de Russie avant 1917', in *Cahiers du monde russe et soviétique*, 3 (1962): pp. 505–20.

Bennoune, Karima, 'Secularism and Human Rights: A Contextual Analysis of Headscarves, Religious Expression, and Women's Equality Under International Law', in *Columbia Journal of Transnational Law*, 45 (2007): pp. 367–426.

——— *Your Fatwa Does Not Apply Here: Untold Stories from the Fight Against Muslim Fundamentalism* (New York, London, 2015).

Besant, Annie, 'Coloured Races in the Empire', in *The Indian Review*, 14 (1913): pp. 288–94.

Beradze, Grigol, 'Among the Chosen Cities: Tbilisi in the Shi'i Tradition', in *Journal of Persianate Studies*, 1 (2008): pp. 206–17.

Bhabha, Homi K. (ed.), *Nation and Narration* (London, 1990).

Bigwood, J. M., 'Queen Mousa, Mother and Wife (?) of King Phraatakes of Parthia: A Re-evaluation of the Evidence', in *Mouseion*, 4 (2004): pp. 35–70.

——— 'Some Parthian Queens in Greek and Babylonian Documents', in *Iranica Antiqua*, 43 (2008): pp. 235–74.

Bivar A. D. H., 'The Political History of Iran under the Arsacids', in E. Yarshater, *The Cambridge History of Iran, The Seleucid, Parthian and Sasanian Periods*, vol. III (Cambridge, 1983): pp. 21–99.

Blank, Richard (ed.), *Schah Reza – der letzte deutsche Kaiser* (Reinbek, 1979).

Boudakian, Jessica, 'An Interview with Porochista Khakpour', in *Modern Language Studies*, 39 (2009): pp. 10–25.

Brecht, Bertolt, *Schriften zum Theater. Über eine nicht-aristotelische Dramatik* (Frankfurt, 1957).

Brizzi G., 'Considerazioni di storia mesopotamica da un passo di Giuseppe Flavio (Ant. Jud. XVIII, 314–79)', in *Cahiers du Centre Gustave Glotz*, 6 (1995): pp. 61–80.

Brosset, Marie-Felicité, *Histoire de la Géorgie, depuis l'antiquité jusqu'au XIXe siècle* (St Petersburg, 1856).

Boeft, J. den, Drijvers, J.W., Hengst, D. den and Teitler, H. C., *Philological and Historical Commentary on Ammianus Marcellins XXIII* (Groningen, 1998).

Brown, Wendy, 'Civilizational Delusions: Secularism, Tolerance, Equality', in *Theory and Event*, 15 (2012): p. 5.

Browne, Edward G., *A Literary History of Persia*, vol. 2 (Maryland, 1997).

Bulliet, Richard W., 'Iran Between East and West', in *Journal of International Affairs*, 60 (2007): pp. 1–14.

Burn, A. R., 'Persia and the Greeks', in Ilya Gershevitch (ed.), *The Cambridge History of Iran: Volume 2: The Median and Achaemenian Periods* (Cambridge, 1985).

Burrell, R. M., *Iran: Political diaries 1881–1965*, vol. II (Melksham, 1997).

Burwell, Catherine. 'Reading Lolita in Times of War: Women's Book Clubs and the Politics of Reception' in *Intercultural Education*, 18 (2007): pp. 281–96.

Cameron, Averil, 'Herodotus and Thucydides in Agathias', in *Byzantinische Zeitschrift*, 57 (1964): pp. 33–52.

——— 'Agathias on the Sasanians', in *Dumbarton Oaks Papers*, vol. 23/24 (1969/1970): pp. 67–183.

Canby, Sheila R., *The Rebellious Reformer* (London, 1996).

——— 'Farangi Sāz, the impact of Europe on Safavid Painting', in Jill Tilden (ed.), *Silk and Stone: The Art of Asia* (London, 1996): pp. 46–59.

Cawkwell, G., *The Greek Wars: The Failure of Persia* (Oxford, 2005).

Camus, Pierre-Marie, *Ammien Marcellin: Témoin des Courants Culturels et Religieux à la fin du IVe Siècle* (Paris, 1967).

Canepa, Matthew, 'Technologies of Memory in Early Sasanian Iran: Achaemenid Sites and Sasanian Identity', in *American Journal of Archaeology*, 114 (2010): pp. 563–96.

Chatterjee, Partha, *The Nation and its Fragments: Colonial and Postcolonial Histories* (Princeton, NJ, 1993).

Chahuan, Eugenio, 'An East–West Dichotomy: Islamophobia', in *Palestine-Israel Journal of Politics, Economics and Culture*, 12 (2005): pp. 47–52.

Chaumont, M. L., *L'Arménie entre Rome et l'Iran I. De l'avènement d'Auguste à l'avènement de Dioclétien*, in H. Temporini and W. Hasse (eds), *Aufstieg und Niedergang der römischen Welt*, II, 9, 1 (Berlin and New York 1976): pp. 71–194.

Chernoff, Fred, *Theory and Metatheory in International Relations: Concepts and Contending Accounts* (New York, 2007).

Chevasco, Berry, 'Lost in Translation: The Relationship between Eugene Sue's *Les Mystères de Paris* and G. W. M. Reynolds's *The Mysteries of London*', in Anne Humpherys and Louis James (eds), *G. W. M. Reynolds: Nineteenth-century Fiction, Politics, and the Press* (Aldershot, 2008): pp. 135–47.

Christensen, Arthur, *L'Iran sous les sassanides* (Copenhagen, 1944).

Clarke, Kenneth, *The Nude: A study of Ideal Art* (London, 1956).

Cleall, Esme, *Missionary Discourses of Difference: Negotiating Otherness in the British Empire, 1840–1900* (New York, 2012).

Coetzee, J. M., *Giving Offence: Essays on Censorship* (Chicago and London, 1996).

Cohen, N. G., 'Asinaeus and Anilaeus, Additional Comments to Josephus' Antiquities of the Jews', in *Annual of the Swedish Theological Institute*, 10 (1976): pp. 30–7.

Cohn, Bernard, *Colonialism and its Forms of Knowledge* (Princeton, 1996).

Cole, Juan R. I., 'Invisible Occidentalism: Eighteenth-Century Indo–Persian Constructions of the West', in *Iranian Studies*, 25 (1992), pp: 3–16.

Colpe, C., 'Die Arsakiden bei Josephus', in O. Betz, K. Haacker and M. Hengel (eds), *Josephus – Studien, Untersuchungen zu Josephus, dem antiken Judentum und dem Neuen Testament, Otto Michel zum 70. Geburtstag gewidmet* (Göttingen, 1974): pp. 97–108.

Coulston, J. C., 'Roman, Parthian and Sassanid Tactical Developments', in Philip Freeman and David Kennedy (eds), *The Defence of the Roman and Byzantine East: Part I* (Oxford, 1986): pp. 59–75.

Cronin, Stephanie (ed.), *Iranian–Russian Encounters: Empires and Revolutions since 1800* (London, 2013).

Cruickshank, John (ed.), *French Literature and Its Background: The Early Nineteenth Century*, vol. 4 (London, 1969).

Dabashi, Hamid, *Brown Skins, White Masks* (London, 2011).

——— *Theology of Discontent* (New York and London, 1993).

Dabrowa, E., *La politique de l'état parthe à l'égard de Rome – d'Artaban II à Vologèse I (ca 11 – ca 79 de n. è.) et les facteurs qui la conditionnaient* (Cracow, 1983).

——— 'Les premiers "otages" parthes à Rome', in *Folia Orientalia*, 24 (1987): pp. 63–71.

Damrosch, David, *What is World Literature* (Princeton, 2003).

Daryaee, Touraj, 'Ethnic and Territorial Boundaries in Late Antique and Early Medieval Persia (Third to Tenth Century)' in Florin Curta (ed.), *Borders, Barriers and Ethnogenesis: Frontiers in Late Antiquity and the Middle Ages* (Turnhout, 2005): pp. 123–38.

——— 'Marriage, Property and Conversion among the Zoroastrians: From Late Sasanian to Islamic Iran', in *Journal of Persianate Studies*, 6 (2013): 91–100.

——— 'From Terror to Tactical Usage: Elephants in the Partho–Sasanian Period', in Vesta Curtis, Elizabeth Pendleton, Michael Alram and Touraj Daryaee (eds), *The Parthian and Early Sasanian Empires: Adaptations and Expansion* (Oxford, 2016): pp. 36–41.

Darznik, Jasmin, 'The Perils and Seductions of Home: Return Narratives of the Iranian Diaspora', in *MELUS*, 33 (2008): pp. 55–71.

Dashti, Ali, *The Realm of Sa'di*, tr. S. Dashti (Costa Mesa, 2013).

Davis, Dick, *Epic and Sedition: The Case of Ferdowsi's Shahnameh* (Washington, DC, 1992).

——— 'Iran and Aniran: The Shaping of a Legend', in Abbas Amanat and Farzin Vejdani (eds), *Iran Facing Others: Identity Boundaries in a Historical Perspective* (Basingstoke, 2012), pp. 39–50.

Davis, Matthew Mark, *Evangelizing the Orient: American Missionaries in Iran, 1890–1940*, PhD diss. (Ohio, 2001).

Debevoise, N. C., *A Political History of Parthia* (Chicago, 1938).

Decei, Aurel, *Istoria Imperiului otoman* (Bucharest, 1978).

DePaul, Amy, 'Re-Reading Reading Lolita in Tehran', in *MELUS*, 33 (2008): pp. 73–92.

Deutschmann, Moritz, '"All Rulers are Brothers": Russian Relations with the Iranian Monarchy in the Nineteenth Century', in *Iranian Studies*, 46 (2013): pp. 383–413.

——— 'Cultures of Statehood, Cultures of Revolution: Caucasian Revolutionaries in the Iranian Constitutional Movement, 1906–1911', in *Ab Imperio*, 2 (2013): pp. 165–90.

——— *Iran and Russian Imperialism: The Ideal Anarchists, 1800–1914* (Abingdon, 2015).

Dhaliwal, Sukhwant, Nagarajan, Chitra and Varma, Rashmi, 'Editorial', in *Feminist Dissent*, 1 (2016): pp. i–v.

Dignas, Beate and Winter, Engelbert, *Rome and Persia in Late Antiquity: Neighbours and Rivals* (Cambridge, 2007).

Dirks, Nicholas, 'Introduction', in Bernard Cohn, *Colonialism and its Forms of Knowledge* (Princeton, 1996): pp. ix–xviii.

Dizadji, H., *Journey from Tehran to Chicago: My Life in Iran and the United States, and a Brief History of Iran* (Bloomington, 2010).

Dodgeon, Michael H. and Lieu, Samuel N. C., *The Roman Eastern Frontier and the Persian Wars: A.D. 226–363* (London, 1991).

Doherty, Thomas, 'The Age of Exploration: The Hollywood Travelogue Film', in *Cineaste*, 20 (1993): pp. 38–40.

McDonough, Scott, 'Were the Sasanians Barbarians? Roman Writers on the "Empire of the Persians"', in Ralph W. Mathiesen and Danuta Shanzar (eds), *Romans, Barbarians and the Transformation of the Roman World: Cultural Interaction and the Creation of Identity in Late Antiquity* (Farnham, 2011): pp. 55–66.

Ebrahimnejad, Hormoz, 'Religion and Medicine in Qajar Iran,' in Robert Gleave (ed.) *Religion and Society in Qajar Iran* (Oxford, 2005).

Eco, Umberto, *Mouse or Rat? Translation as Negotiation* (London, 2003).

Egilsrud, Johan, *Le Dialogue des Morts dans les Littératures Françaises, Allemande et Anglaise (1644–1789)* (Paris, 1934).

Ehrhardt, N., 'Parther und partische Geschichte bei Tacitus', in J. Wiesehöfer (ed.), *Das Partherreich und seine Zeugnisse, Beiträge des internationalen Colloquiums. Eutin (27. –30. Juni 1996)* (Stuttgart, 1998): pp. 295–307.

El Amine, Loubna, 'Beyond East and West: Reorienting Political Theory through the Prism of Modernity', in *Perspectives on Politics*, 14 (2016): pp. 102–20.

Elahi, Babak, 'Translating the Self: Language and Identity in Iranian–American Women's Memoirs', in *Iranian Studies*, 39 (2006): pp. 461–80.

Elliott, T. G., *Ammianus Marcellinus and Fourth Century History* (Toronto, 1983).

Eltahawy, Mona, *Headscarves and Hymens: Why the Middle East needs a sexual revolution* (London, 2015).

Emery, Christian, *US Foreign Policy and the Iranian Revolution The Cold War Dynamics of Engagement and Strategic Alliance* (London, 2013).

Fabian, Johannes, *Time and the Other* (New York, 2014).

Fairclough, Norman, *Analysing Discourse: Textual Analysis for Social Research* (London, 2003).

Farhad, Massumeh, 'Searching for the New: Later Safavid Painting and the Suz u Gawdaz (Burning and melting) by Na'i Khabushani', in *The Journal of the Walters Art Museum*, 59 (2001): pp. 115–30.

Farneti, Roberto, 'Cleavage Lines in Global Politics: Left and Right, East and West, Earth and Heaven', in *Journal of Political Ideologies*, 17 (2012): pp. 127–45.

Farokh, Kaveh, *Shadows in the Desert: Ancient Persia at War* (Oxford, 2004).

Farzaneh, M. F., *Ashna'ee ba Sadegh Hedayat, Ghes'mat-e av'val: An'cheh Sadegh Hedayat be Man Goft* (Paris, 1988).

Ferrier, Ronald W., 'Charles I and the Antiquities of Persia: the Mission of Nicholas Willford', in *Iran*, 8 (1970): pp. 51–7.

——— *A Journey to Persia: Jean Chardin's Portrait of a Seventeenth-Century Empire* (London & New York, 1996).

Floor, Willem, *The History of Theater in Iran* (Washington, 2005).

——— *A Social History of Sexual Relations in Iran* (Washington, 2008).

Flower, Michael, 'Herodotus and Persia', in Carolyn Dewald and John Marincola (eds) *The Cambridge Companion to Herodotus* (Cambridge, 2006): pp. 274–89.

Fornara, Charles W., 'Studies in Ammianus Marcellinus: II: Ammianus' Knowledge and Use of Greek and Latin Literature', in *Historia: Zeitschrift für Alte Geschichte*, 41 (1992): pp. 420–38.

Fotouhi, Sanaz, *The Literature of the Iranian Diaspora: Meaning and Identity since the Islamic Revolution* (London, 2015).

Foucault, Michel, *The Archaeology of Knowledge and the Discourse on Language* (New York, 1972, 1989).

Frye, R. N., *The History of Ancient Iran* (Munich, 1983).

Garthwaite, Gene R, *Khans and Shahs: A History of the Bakhtiyari Tribe in Iran* (New York, 2009).

Genette, Gérard, *Paratexts – Thresholds of Interpretation.* tr. J. E. Lewin. (Cambridge, 2001).

Gerleman, Gillis, 'Der Nicht-Mensch. Erwägungen zur hebräischen Wurzel N B L', in *Vetus Testamentum*, vol. 24, Fasc. 2 (1974): pp. 147–58.

Ghasemi, Farid, *Kitab* (Tehran, 2001).

Gignoux, Philippe, 'Etude des variants textuelles des inscriptions de Kirdīr, Genèse et datation', in *Le Muséon*, 86 (1973): pp. 192–216.

——— *Les Quatre Inscriptions du Mage Kirdīr: Textes et Concordances* (Paris, 1991).

Gilmartin, K., 'Corbulo's campaigns in the East: an analysis of Tacitus' Account', in *Historia*, 22 (1973): pp. 583–626.

Goethe, Johann W., 'Translations (1819)', tr. Sh. Sloan, in L. Venuti (ed.) *The Translation Studies Reader* (London, 2012): pp. 64–6.

Gocheleishvili, Iago 'Georgian Sources on the Iranian Constitutional Revolution (1905–1911): Sergo Gamdlishvili's Memoirs of the Gilan Resistance', in *Iranian Studies*, 40 (2007): pp. 59–85.

——— 'Introducing Georgian Sources for the Historiography of the Iranian Constitutional Revolution (1905–1911)', in H.E. Chehabi & Vanessa Martin (eds), *Iran's Constitutional Revolution: Popular Politics, Cultural Transformations and Transnational Connections* (London and New York, 2010): pp. 45–66.

Goetz, Hermann, 'Persians and Persian Costumes in Dutch Painting of the Seventeenth Century', in *The Art Bulletin*, 20 (1938): pp. 280–90.

Gomari-Luksch, Laleh and Kasten, Lukas: 'An Eye for an Eye: Bargaining Theory, Mistrust, and the Iranian Nuclear Crisis', in Andreas Bock and Ingo Henneberg (eds), *Iran, die Bombe und das Streben nach Sicherheit* (Baden-Baden, 2014): pp. 225–47.

Goodblatt, D., 'Josephus on Parthian Babylonia (Antiquities XVIII)', in *Journal of the American Oriental Society*, 107 (1987): pp. 605–22.

Gould, Rebecca, 'Engendering Critique: Postnational Feminism in Postcolonial Syria', in *Women Studies Quarterly*, 42 (2014): pp. 209–29.

Graf, Karl H., 'Vorrede', in Sa'di, *Rosengarten* (Leipzig, 1846): pp. ix–xxii.

Grassian, Daniel, *Iranian and Diasporic Literature in the 21st Century. A Critical Study* (North Carolina, 2013).

Greatrex, Geoffrey, 'The Dates of Procopius' Works', in *Byzantine and Modern Greek Studies*, 18 (1994): pp. 101–14.

Greenwood, 'Sasanian Echoes and Apocalyptic Expectations: A Re-Evaluation of the Armenian History Attributed to Sebeos', in Alice Rio (ed.), *Law, Custom and Justice in Late Antiquity and the early Middle Ages. Proceedings of the 2008 Byzantine Colloquium* (London, 2011): pp. 323–97.

Gregoratti, L., 'Parthian Women in Flavius Josephus' in M. Hirschberger (ed.), *Jüdisch-hellenistische Literatur in ihrem interkulturellen Kontext, Akten der Tagung, Düesseldorf, 10.–11. Februar 2011* (Frankfurt, 2012): pp. 183–92.

——— 'The Journey east of the Great King, East and West in the Parthian Kingdom', *Parthica*, 15 (2013): pp. 43–52.

——— 'The Kings of Parthia and Persia, Some Considerations on the "Iranic" Identity in the Parthian Empire', *Digital Archive of Brief Notes & Iranian Review 2015*, 1 (2015): pp. 14–6.

——— 'A Tale of two Great Kings: Artabanus and Vologaeses' in A. Krasnowolska and R. Rusek-Kowalska (eds), *Studies on the Iranian World I, Before Islam* (Cracow, 2015 (b)): pp. 203–10.

——— 'Sinews of the other Empire: Parthian Great King's rule over vassal Kingdoms' in H. Teigen and E. Seland (eds), *Sinews of Empire: Networks in the Roman Near East and Beyond* (Oxford, 2017): pp. 95–104.

——— 'The Arsacid Empire', in T. Daryaee (ed.), *King of the Seven Climes: A History of the Ancient Iran World (3000 BC – 651 CE)* (Irvine, 2017): pp. 125–53.

Gronke, Monika, *Geschichte Irans – Von der Islamisierung bis zur Gegenwart* (Munich, 2003).

——— *Iran – A Short History from Islamization to the Present* (Princeton, 2008).

Habibi, Negar 'A Saheb Mansab Painter? A Reconsideration of ?Ali Qoli Jebādār's career', *Iran* 54 (2016): pp. 143–58.

———, *Ali Qoli Jebādār et l'occidentalisme safavide: une étude sur les peintures dites farangi sāzi, leurs milieux et commanditaires sous Shāh Soleimān (1666–94)* (Leiden, 2017).

Hack, U., Jacobs, B. and Weber, D., *Quellen zur Geschichte des Partherreiches* (Göttingen, 2010).

Haillant, Marguerite, *Culture et Imagination dans les Œuvres de Fénelon "Ad Usum Delphini"* (Paris, 1983).

Hall, Stuart, 'Cultural Identity and Diaspora', in Rutherford, Jonathan (ed.), *Identity. Community, Culture, Difference* (London, 1990): pp. 222–37.

Hanaway, William L., *Persian Popular Romances before the Safavid period*, PhD dissertation (Columbia, 1970).

Hapke, Laura, *Girls Who Went Wrong: Prostitutes in American Fiction, 1885–1917* (Bowling Green, 1989).

Hart, James, *Who One Is: Existenz and Transcendental Phenomenology* (New York, 2009).

Hastedt, Glenn P. and Kaussler, Bernd, *US Foreign Policy Towards the Middle East: The Realpolitik of Deceit* (London, New York, 2017).

Heider, Karl G, *Ethnographic Film: Revised Edition* (Austin, 2006).

Henrichot, Michel, 'Mars aux Enfers: la Guerre Vue des Dialogues des Morts', in Jean Garapon (ed.), *Armées, Guerre et Société dans la France du XVIIe Siècle* (Tübingen, 2006), 139–50.

Hiro, Dilip, *The Iranian Labyrinth* (New York, 2005).

Hobsbawm, Eric and Ranger, Terence (eds), *The Invention of Tradition* (Cambridge, 1983).

Hoffman, Diane M., 'Self and Culture Revisited: Culture Acquisition among Iranians in the United States', in *Ethos*, 17 (1989): pp. 32–49.

Houshang Mahdavi, Abdolreza, *History of Iranian Foreign Relations from the Safavid Era to the End of Second World War*, vol. 3 (Amirkabir, 1985).

Howard-Johnston, James, 'The Two Great Powers in Late Antiquity: A Comparison', in Averil Cameron (ed.), *The Byzantine and Early Islamic Near East: III: States, Resources and Armies* (Princeton, 1995): pp. 157–226.

Howarth, David R., Norval, Aletta J. and Stavrakakis, Yannis, *Discourse Theory and Political Analysis: Identities, Hegemonies, and Social Chang*e (Manchester and New York, 2000).

Hudson, Valerie M., *Foreign Policy Analysis: Classic and Contemporary Theory* (Lanham, 2007).

Hund, Wulf D., 'Negative Societalisation: Racism and the Constitution of Race', in Wulf D. Hund, Jeremy Krikler, David Roediger (eds), *Wages of Whiteness & Racist Symbolic Capital* (Berlin, 2010): pp. 57–96.

Hutton, Christopher M. and Joseph, John E. 'Back to Blavatsky: The impact of theosophy on modern linguistics', in *Language & Communication*, vol. 18, Issue 3 (1998): pp. 181–204.

Jalali, Ali, 'Traditional Medicine and Medicinal Plants in the Qajar Era' in Sahara Barjesteh van Waalwikjk van Doorn-Khosrovani, L.A. ferydoung Barjestehn van Waalwijk van Doorn (Khosrovani) and Manoutchechr M. Eskandari-Qajar (eds) *Qajar Era Health, Hygiene and Beauty* (Rotterdam, 2003).

James, Simon, 'Evidence from Dura Europos for the Origins of Late Roman Helmets' in *Syria*, T. 63, Fasc. 1/2 (1986): pp. 10–34.

——— *Excavations at Dura-Europos 1928–1937: Final Report VII: The Arms and Armour and other Military Equipment* (Oxford, 2004).

Jervis, Robert, 'Understanding the Bush Doctrine', in *Political Science Quarterly*, 118 (2003): pp. 365–88.

Jordheim, Helge, 'Verdenslitteratur og litteraturforskningens kairós: Goethe, Auerbach, Said - og vi' in *Norsk Litteraturvitenskapelig Tidsskrift*, 9 (2006): pp. 11–36.

Jørgensen, Marianne and Phillips, Louise, *Discourse Analysis as Theory and Method* (London, 2002).

Juana, Valdiana, 'Cultural and Historical Relations Between Iran and Romania', in *Faculty of Literature Journals*, Issue IV, pp. 12–30.

Kahrstedt, U., *Artabanos III. und seine Erbe*, Dissertationes Bernenses I 2, Bern, A. Francke (1950).

Kaldellis, Anthony, *Procopius of Caesarea: Tyranny, History, and Philosophy at the End of Antiquity* (Philadelphia, 2004).

Kamil Banak, 'Mushfiq Kazimi's Novel The Horrible Tehran: Romantic Fiction or Social Criticism' in *Asian and African Studies*, 13 (1977): pp. 147–52.

Kantzios, Ippokratis, 'The Politics of Fear in Aeschylus' "Persians"', in *The Classical World*, 98 (2004): pp. 3–19.

Karim, Persis M., 'Talking with a Pioneer of Iranian American Literature: An Interview with Nahid Rachlin', in *MELUS*, 33 (2008): pp. 153–7.

Karras-Klapproth, M., *Prosopographische Studien zur Geschichte des Partherreiches auf der Grundlage antiker literarischer Überlieferung* (Bonn, 1988).

Karimi-Hakkak, Ahmad, *Recasting Persian Poetry: Scenarios of Poetic Modernity in Iran* (Salt Lake City, 1995).

Kashani-Sabet, Firoozeh, 'Cultures of Iranianness: The Evolving Problem of Iranian Nationalism,' in Nikki Keddie and Rudi Matthee (ed.), *Iran and the Surrounding World* (Seattle, 2002): pp. 162–81.

Kasravi, Ahmad, *History of the Iranian Constitutional Revolution (Tārikh-e Mashrute-ye Iran)*. vol. I, tr. E. Siegel (Costa Mesa, 2006).

Katouzian, Homa, *Sa'di: The Poet of Life, Love and Compassion* (Oxford, 2006).

Kattan, Jeanne and Saliba, Therese, 'Palestinian Women and the Politics of Reception', in Amal Amireh and Lisa Suhair Majaj (eds), *Going Global: The Transnational Reception of Third World Women Writers* (New York, 2000): pp. 84–111.

Kazemi, Morteza Moshfeq, Tehran-e Makhuf (Tehran, 1924).

——— Ruzegar va andisheh-ha (Tehran, 1971).

Keddie, Nikki R., *Modern Iran: Roots and Results of Revolution* (New Haven, 2003).

Keener, Frederick M., *English Dialogues of the Dead, A Critical History, An Anthology, and A Check List* (London and New York, 1973).

Keller, William J., 'Xenophon's Acquaintance with the History of Herodotus', in *The Classical Journal*, 6 (1911), 252–9.

Kelly, Gavin, *Ammianus Marcellinus: The Allusive Historian* (Cambridge, 2008).

Keshavarz, Fatemeh. *Jasmine and Stars: Reading More than Lolita in Tehran* (Wilmington, 2007).

Khamei, Anvar, *Khaterat-e Ruznameh-negar* (Tehran, 2001).

Khwansari, Molla Agha Jamal, *Kolsum Nane. Sitten und Gebräuche der Frauen im Orient und ihr Aberglaube*, tr. Choubine, Bahram and West, Judith (Paris, 1998).

Kim, Myunghee and Mirilovic, Nikola, 'Ideology and Threat Perceptions: American Public Opinion Toward China and Iran', in *Political Studies*, 65 (2017): pp. 179–98.

King, Ashton, *War of the Persians in Chalderan and Greece*, tr. Zabihullah Mansouri (Negarestan, 2006).

Kouhestani-nejad, Masoud, *Akhbar va E'lan-e Ketab va ketabkhaneh be Revayat-e Matbu?aat: 1285–1304* (Tehran, 2016).

Kristeva, Julia, *Powers of Horror: An Essay on Abjection* (New York, 1984).

Kubicková, Vera, *Persian Miniatures*, tr. R. Finlayson-Samsour (London, 1959).

Laclau, Ernesto and Mouffe, Chantal, *Hegemony and Socialist Strategy: Towards a Radical Democratic Politics* (London, 2001).

Landau, Amy S., *Farangi sāzi at Isfahan: the court painter Muhammad Zamān, the Armenians of New Julfa and Shāh Soleymān (1666–1694)*, Thesis Dissertation (Oxford, 2007).

——— 'From Poet to Painter: Allegory and Metaphor in a Seventeenth-century Persian Painting by Muhammad Zaman, Master of *Farangi-Sazi*', *Muqarnas* 28 (2011): pp. 101–13.

——— 'Visibly Foreign, Visibly Female: The Eroticization of the *zan-i farangi* in seventeenth-century Persian painting', in F. Leoni and M. Natif (eds), *Eros and Sexuality in Islamic Art* (Dorchester, 2013): pp. 99–130.

——— 'Reconfiguring the Northern European Print to Depict Sacred History at the Persian Court', in Thomas Da Costa Kaufmann and Michael North (eds), *Mediating Netherlandish Art and Material Culture in Asia* (Amsterdam, 2014): pp. 65–82.

——— 'Man, Mode, and Myth: Muhammad Zamān ibn Haji Yusuf', in A.S. Landau (ed.), *Pearls on a String: Artists, Patrons, and Poets* at *the Great Islamic Courts* (Baltimore, 2015): pp. 167–203.

Landau, Emilie, 'US Counter-Proliferation Policy: The Case of Iran' in Inbar, Efraim and Rynhold, Jonathan (eds), *US Foreign Policy and Global Standing in the 21st Century: Realities and Perceptions* (London, New York, 2016): pp. 198–212.

Lang, David M., *The Georgians.* (London, 1966).

Langer, Axel (ed.), *The Fascination of Persia, The Persian–European Dialogue in Seventeenth-Century Art & Contemporary Art from Tehran* (Zurich, 2013).

——— 'European Influences on Seventeenth-Century Persian Painting: Of Handsome Europeans, Naked Ladies, and Parisian Timepieces', in A. Langer (ed.), *The Fascination of Persia, The Persian–European Dialogue in Seventeenth-Century Art & Contemporary Art from Tehran* (Zurich, 2013): pp. 170–237.

Lerouge, Ch., 'L'image des Parthes dans le monde greco–romain. Du début du Ier siècle av. J.-C. jusqu'à la fin du Haut-Empire romain', in *Oriens et Occidens*, 17 (Stuttgart, 2007).

Mackey, Sandra, *The Iranians, Persia, Islam and the Soul of the Nation* (London, 1996).

Maghsoudlou, Bahman, *Grass: Untold Stories* (Costa Mesa, 2009).

——— *Alaf: Dastan-haye Shegeft va Nagofteh* (Tehran, 2010).

Mahdavi, Shirin, 'Amusements in Qajar Iran', in *Iranian Studies*, 40 (2007): pp. 483–99.

Malek, Amy, '"If you're going to educate 'em, you've got to entertain 'em too": An Examination of Representation and Ethnography in Grass and People of the Wind', in *Iranian Studies*, 44 (2011): pp. 313–25.

Maleki, Abbas and Tirman, John (eds), *US-Iran Misperceptions: A Dialogue* (New York, 2014).

Mandanipour, Shahriar, *Censoring An Iranian Love Story* (London, 2011).

Marciak, M., 'Seleucid–Parthian Adiabene in the Light of Ancient Geographical and Ethnographical Texts', in *Anabasis. Studia Classica et Orientalia*, 2 (2011): pp. 179–208.

——— 'The cultural environment of Adiabene in the Hellenistic, Parthian, and Sasanian Periods', in *Parthica*, 16 (2014): pp. 111–50.

——— 'Das Konigreich Adiabene in hellenistisch-parthischer Zeit', in *Gymnasium*, 122 (2015): pp. 57–74.

Marcinkowski, Christoph, 'The Safavid Presence in the Indian Ocean: A Reappraisal of the Ship of Solayman, a Seventeenth-Century Travel Account to Siam', in

W. Floor and E. Herzig (eds), *Iran and the World in the Safavid Age* (London, 2012): pp. 379–406.

Maricq, André, 'Res Gestae Divi Saporis', in *Syria*, T. 35, Fasc. 3/4 (1958): pp. 295–360.

Marmulla, Henning, 'Re-Thinking the Writer's Role: Hans Magnus Enzensberger and Cuba or A Story of Self-Censorship,' in Ingrid Gilcher-Holtey (ed.), *A Revolution of Perception?: Consequences and Echoes of 1968* (New York, 2014): pp. 17–34.

Matthee, Rudi, 'The Safavid, Afshar, and Zand Periods', in *Iranian Studies* 31 (1998): pp. 483–93.

——— 'Between Aloofness and Fascination: Safavid Views of the West', in *Iranian Studies*, 31 (1998b): pp. 219–246.

——— 'Iran's Ottoman Diplomacy During the Reign of Shāh Sulayman I (1077–1105/1666–94)', in K. Eslami (ed.), *Iran And Iraninan Studies, Essaie in Honor of Iraj Afshar* (New Jersey, 1998c): pp. 148–77.

——— 'Prostitutes, Courtesans, and Dancing girls: women entertainers in Safavid Iran', in R. Matthee and B. Baron (eds), *Iran and Beyond, Essays in Middle Eastern History, in Honor of Nikkie R. Keddie* (California, 2000): pp. 121–51.

——— 'The Safavids under Western Eyes: Seventeenth-Century European Travellers to Iran', in *Journal of Early Modern History*, 13 (2009), pp. 137–72.

Maxwell, Richard, *The Mysteries of Paris and London* (Charlottesville, 1992).

Mercer, Kobena (ed.), *Exiles, Diasporas & Strangers* (Cambridge & London, 2008).

Milani, Farzaneh, *Veils and Words. The Emerging Voices of Iranian Women Writers* (New York, 1992).

Milliken, Jennifer, 'The Study of Discourse in International Relations. A Critique of Research and Methods' in *European Journal of International Relations*, 5 (1999): pp. 225–54.

Minorsky.V, 'Jihān-Shāh Qara-Qoyunlu and His Poetry' in *Bulletin of the School of Oriental and African Studies*, 16 (1954): pp. 271–97.

Miransari, Ali, 'The Constitutional Revolution and Persian Dramatic Works: An Observation on Social Relations Criticism in the Plays of the Constitutional Era' in H. E. Chehabi and Vanessa Martin (eds), *Iran's Constitutional Revolution: Popular Politics, Cultural Transformations and Transnational connections* (London, 2010): pp. 239–48.

Moaddel, Mansoord (ed.), *Values and Perceptions of the Islamic and Middle Eastern Publics* (New York, Basingstoke, 2010).

Moore, Steven, '[The Eastern Novel:] Persian', in *The Novel: An Alternative History: Beginnings to 1600* (New York & London, 2011): pp. 499–527.

——— 'Persian Fiction', in *The Novel: An Alternative History, 1600–1800* (New York & London, 2013); pp. 527–32.

Moradi, Masoud, 'International Cooperation in Solving the Issue of the Balkans (1875–6)', in *Shenakhtjournal*, Summer 2003, Issue 38: pp. 141–68.

Moretti, Franco, *Atlas of the European Novel 1800–1900* (London and New York, 1998).

——— *Distant Reading* (London and New York, 2013).

Motadel, David, 'Iran and the Aryan Myth', in Ali M. Ansari (ed.), *Perceptions of Iran: History, Myths and Nationalism from Medieval Persia to the Islamic Republic* (London, 2013): pp. 119–45.

Murray, Donette, *US foreign policy and Iran: American–Iranian relations since the Islamic revolution* (London, 2007).

Murray, G. N., 'Zack Snyder, Frank Miller and Herodotus: Three Takes on the 300 Spartans', in *Akroterion*, 52 (2007): pp. 11–35.

Naficy, Hamid. 'Lured by the East: Ethnographic and Expedition Films about Nomadic Tribes - The Case of Grass', in Jeffrey Ruoff (ed.), *Virtual Voyages: Cinema and Travel* (Durham, 2006): pp. 117–38.

Naficy, N., 'Iranian Art and Its Sociological Setting, Painting in Zand and Qajar periods', in *Akten des VII. International kongresses fur Iranische kunst une archalologie* (Munich, 1979): pp. 466–70.

Nafisi, Azar. 'Fiction: Open Space in a Closed Society' in *New Perspectives Quarterly*, 22 (2005): pp. 12–14.

Nahavandi, Houchang, *Iran: The Clash of Ambitions*, tr. Martine Jackson (Slough, 2006).

Najem, Naser, *Irān dar miān-e tufān* (Tehran, 1334/1915).

Najmabadi, Afsaneh, *Women with Moustaches and Men without Beards. Gender and Sexual Anxieties of Iranian Modernity* (Berkeley and Los Angeles, 2005).

Nanquette, Laetitia, Orientalism Versus Occidentalism: Literary and Cultural Imaging Between France and Iran Since the Islamic Revolution (London, 2013).

——— 'Cultural and Translation Exchanges Between Iran and the West (France, Germany, Great Britain, the United States)', in *Publishing in Persian language in Iran, Afghanistan, Tajikistan, Uzbekistan, Europe and the United States* (International Alliance of Independent Publishers, 2015): pp. 111–30.

Natchkebia, Irene, 'Tbilissi – Porte de la Perse à la limite des XVIIIe et XIXe siècles', in *Orientalist*, 1 (Tbilisi, 2001): pp. 196–204.

——— 'Journal d'un voyage of Ange de Gardan and Vocabulario Timurat-Mirza in Journal de l'Empire (1808)', in *Literary Researches*, 25 (2002), pp. 415–20.

——— 'La place de Géorgie dans le traité de Finkenstein (1807)' in I. Nathkhebia and F. Hellot-Bellier, *La Géorgie et Tbilissi entre la Perse et l'Europe* (Paris, 2008): pp. 95–114.

Nateq, Homa, *Karnameh-ye Farhangi-ye Farangi dar Iran* (Paris, 1996).

Navabpour, A. R., *A Study of Recent Persian Prose Fiction with Special Reference to the Social Background*, PhD dissertation (Durham, 1981).

Neusner J., *A History of the Jews in Babylonia I: The Parthian Period* (Chico, CA, 1984).

Nicolle, David, *Sasanian Armies: The Iranian Empire, early 3rd to mid–7th centuries AD* (Stockport, 1996).

Nora, Pierre (ed.), *Lieux de Mémoire*, vol. 1 La République (Paris, 1984).

——— *Realms of Memory*, vol. I Conflicts and Divisions, tr. Arthur Goldhammer (New York, 1996).

Olbrycht, M. J., *Parthia et ulteriores gentes. Die politischen Beziehungen zwischen dem arsakidischen Iran und den Nomaden der eurasischen Steppen* (Munich, 1998).

——— 'Das Arsakidenreich zwischen der mediterranen Welt und Innerasien, Bemerkungen zur politischen Strategie der Arsakiden von Vologases I. bis zum Herrschaftsantritt des Vologases III. (50–147 n. Chr.)' in E. Dabrowa, *Ancient Iran and the Mediterranean World: Proceedings of an international conference in honour of Professor J. Wolski held at the Jagiellonian University, Cracow, in September 1996* (Cracow, 1998 (b)): pp. 123–59.

——— 'The Political-Military Strategy of Artabanos/Ardawān II in 34–7', in *Anabasis: Studia Classica et Orientalia*, 3 (2012): pp. 160–78.

——— 'The genealogy of Artabanos II (AD 8/9–39/40), King of Parthia', in *Miscellanea Anthropologica et Sociologica*, 15 (2014): pp. 92–7.

——— 'Parthians, Greek Culture, and Beyond', in K. Twardowska, M. Salamon, S. Sprawski, M. Stachura, S. Turlej (eds), *Within the Circle of Ancient Ideas and Virtues. Studies in Honour of Professor Maria Dzielska* (Cracow, 2014 (b)): pp. 129–42.

——— 'Vologases I, Pacoros II and Artabanos III: Coins and Parthian History', in *Iranica Antiqua*, 51 (2016): pp. 215–33.

Ostby, Marie, 'De-censoring an Iranian–American "Memoir": Authorship and Synchronicity in Shahriar Mandanipour's Censoring an Iranian Love Story', in *Iranian Studies*, 46 (2013): pp. 73–93.

Ozouf, Mona, 'Célébrer, Savoir et Fêter', in *Le Débat*, 57 (1989): pp. 16–31.

Pakpur, Subhan, *The Ottoman History* (Qom, 2014).

Parsinejad, Iraj, *Mirza Fath Ali Akhundzadeh and Literary Criticism* (Tokyo, 1988).

Passmore, Leith, *Ulrike Meinhof and the Red Army Faction: Performing Terrorism* (New York, 2011).

Pedersen, Jan, *Subtitling Norms for Television* (Amsterdam, 2011).

Peltre, Christine, *Dictionnaire culturel de l'Orientalisme* (Paris, 2003).

——— *Orientalisme* (Paris, 2005).

Pfeiffer, Heinrich, *Ausländische Studenten an den wissenschaftlichen Hochschulen in der Bundesrepublik und West-Berlin, 1951–1961* (Wiesbaden, 1962).

Pfordt, M., *Studien zu Darstellung der Außenpolitik in den Annalen des Tacitus* (Frankfurt, 1998).

Porter, Yves, 'Arts du livre et illustration', in Yann Richard (ed.), *Entre L'Iran et L'occident. Adaptation et assimilation des idées et techniques occidentales en Iran* (Paris, 1989): pp. 157–70.

Pourmokhtari, Navid, 'A Postcolonial Critique of State Sovereignty in IR: the contradictory legacy of a "West-centric" discipline', in *Third World Quaterly*, 34 (2013): pp. 1767–93.

Pourshariati, Parvaneh, *Decline and Fall of the Sasanian Empire: The Sasanian–Parthian Confederacy and the Arab Conquest of Iran* (New York, 2008).

Pujol, Stéphane, *Le Dialogue d'Idées au Dix-Huitième Siècle* (Oxford, 2005).

Questa, C., *Studi sulle fonti degli Annales di Tacito* (Rome, 1960).

Rai, Rumina, *Introduction to Cultural Studies* (Mumbai, 2010).

Rajak T., 'The Parthians in Josephus', in J. Wiesehöfer (ed.), *Das Partherreich und seine Zeugnisse, Beiträge des internationalen Colloquiums. Eutin (27.–30. Juni 1996)* (Stuttgart, 1998): pp. 309–24.

Rai, Rumina, *Introduction to Culture Studies* (Mumbai, 2010).

Robinson, Basil William, *Persian Painting in the John Rylands Library* (London, 1980).

——— 'A Survey of Persian Painting (1350–1896)', in Ch. Adle (ed.), *Art et société dans le monde Iranien* (Paris, 1982): pp. 13–89.

Rolfe, John C., 'Introduction' in Ammianus Marcellinus, *History* (in three vols), tr. John C. Rolfe (Cambridge, MA, 1935): pp. ix–xlvii.

Rony, Fatimah Tobing, *The Third Eye: Race, Cinema and Ethnographic Spectacle* (Durham, 1996).

Rosenberg, Emily S. 'World War I, Wilsonianism, and Challenges to U.S. Empire', in *Diplomatic History*, 38 (2014): pp. 852–63.

Rouhbakhshan, Abd-al-Mohammad, *Farang and Farangi in Iran* (Tehran, 1388/2009).

Rowe, John Carlos, 'Reading Reading Lolita in Tehran in Idaho', in *American Quarterly*, 59 (2007): pp. 253–75.
Rubin, Zeev, 'The Roman Empire in the *Res Gestae Divi Saporis*', in Edward Dabrowa (ed.), *Ancient Iran and the Mediterranean World: Studies in Ancient History* (Cracow, 1998): pp. 177–85.
Sabbah, Guy, *La Méthode d'Ammien Marcellin: Recherches sur la Construction du Discours Historique sur les History* (Paris, 1978).
Sadjed, Ariane, *Shopping for Freedom in der Islamischen Republik – Widerstand und Konformismus im Konsumverhalten der iranischen Mittelschicht* (*Shopping for Freedom in the Islamic Republic: Resistance and Conformism in Iranian Middle-Class Consumer Behaviour*) (Bielefeld, 2012).
Said, Edward, *Reflections on Exile And Other Essays* (Cambridge, 2001).
——— *Orientalism* (London, 2003).
Saleh, Gholam hosein Mirza (ed.), *Khaterat-e Shaykh Ebrahim-e Zanjani* (Tehran, 2000).
Salia, Kalistrat, *History of the Georgian Nation*, tr. Katharine Vivian (Paris, 1983).
Sancisi-Weerdenburg, Heleen, 'The Personality of Xerxes, King of Kings', in Egbert J. Bakker, Irene J. F. Jong and Hans van Wees (eds), *Brill's Companion to Herodotus* (Leiden, 2002), 579–90.
Sanikidze, George, 'A Historical Survey of the Georgian–Iranian Relations in the Nineteenth Century' in *Journal of Persianate Studies*, 1 (2008): pp. 148–73.
Scarce, Jeniffer, 'Vesture and Dress, Fashion, Function and Impacti', in C. Bier (ed.), *Woven from the Soul, Spun From the Heart, Textile Arts of Safavid and Qajar Iran 16th–19th centuries* (Washington, DC, 1987): pp. 33–57.
Schippmann, K., *Grundzüge der parthischen Geschichte* (Darmstadt, 1980).
Schleiermacher, Friedrich, *Kritische Gesamtausgabe: 1. Abt. 11: Schriften und Entwürfe Akademievorträge* (Berlin, 2012).
Schleiermacher, Friedrich, 'On the Different Methods of Translating', tr. S. Bernofsky, in *The Translation Studies Reader*, Lawrence Venuti (ed.) (London, 2012): pp. 42–63.
Schneider, Rolf Michael, 'Orientalism in Late Antiquity: The Oriental in Imperial and Christian Imagery', in Josef Wisehöfer and Philip Huyse (eds), *Eran ud Aneran: Studienzu den Beziehungen zwischen dem Sasanidenreich und der Mittelmeerwelt* (Stuttgart, 2006): pp. 241–78.
Schoedsack, Ernst B, 'Grass: The Making of an Epic', in *American Cinematographer*, 64 (1983): pp. 40–4 and 109–14.
Schuurman, Paul, 'Fénelon on Luxury, War and Trade in the Telemachus', in *History of European Ideas*, 38 (2012): pp. 179–99.
Seager, Robin, *Ammianus Marcellinus: Seven Studies in His Language and Thought* (Columbia, 1986).
Sefatgol, Mansour, 'Farang, Farangi and Farangestan: Safavid Historiography and the West (907–1148/1501–1736)', in W. Floor and E. Herzig (eds), *Iran and the World in the Safavid Age* (London, New York, 2012): pp. 357–64.
Sellwood, D., *An Introduction to the Coinage of Parthia* (London, 1980).
Sepehran, Kamran, *Rad-de Pa-ye Ta'zal'zol: Roman-e Tarikhi-e Iran 1300–1320* (Tehran, 2002).
Sezer, Baykan, *Sosyolojinin Ana Başlıkları* (Istanbul, 2016).
Shahbazi, A. Shapur, *Ferdowsi: A Critical Biography* (Costa Mesa, 1991).
Sharadze, *Guram, Teimuraz Bagrationi*, I–II. (Tbilisi, 1972–74).

Sharif, Ali-Asghar, *Khun-baha-ye Iran*) (Tehran, 1925).

Shawcross, William, *The Shah's Last Ride* (London, 1989).

Shay, Anthony, 'Dance and Non-Dance: Patterned Movement in Iran and Islam', in *Iranian Studies*, 28 (1995): pp. 61–78.

Shayegan, R., *Arsacids and Sasanians: Political Ideology in Post-Hellenistic and Late Antique Persia* (Cambridge, 2011).

Shepherd, Dorothy, 'Sasanian Art', in Ehsan Yarshater (ed.), *The Cambridge History of Iran 3(2): The Seleucid, Parthian and Sasanian Periods* (Cambridge, 1983): pp. 1055–112.

Shore, F.B., *Parthian Coins and History: Ten Dragons Against Rome* (Quarryville [PA], 1993).

Sidwell, Barbara, *The Portrayal and Role of Anger in the Res Gestae of Ammianus Marcellinus* (Adelaide, 2008).

Simpson, St John, 'Mesopotamia in the Sasanian Period: Settlement Patterns, Arts and Crafts', in J. Curtis (ed.), *Mesopotamia and Iran in the Parthian and Sasanian Periods: Rejection and Revival: c. 238 BC–AD 642* (London, 2000): pp. 57–79.

Sims, Eleanor, 'Five seventeenth century oil paintings', in B.W. Robinson (ed.), *Persian and Mughal art* (London, 1976): pp. 221–48.

Slavin, Barbara, *Bitter Friends, Bosom Enemies: Iran, the U.S., and the Twisted Path to Confrontation* (New York, 2007).

Slobodian, Quinn, *Foreign Front: Third World Politics in Sixties West Germany* (Durham, 2012).

Sommer, M., 'La crisi romano–partica del 53–64 d.C.: la prospettiva "orientale"', in *ὅρμος - Ricerche di Storia Antica*, 1 (2009): pp. 220–5.

Soukup, Uwe, *Wie starb Benno Ohnesorg: Der 2. Juni 1967* (Berlin 2007).

Speer, Robert E., 'The Hakim Sahib' *The Foreign Doctor; A Biography of Joseph Plumb Cochran, M.D. of Persia* (New York, 1911).

Spivak, Gayatri Chakravorty, 'Acting Bits/Identity Talk', in *Critical Inquiry*, 18 (1992): pp. 770–803.

Stadelhofen, Henri de, *Soraya*, tr. Rita Perli (Lausanne, 1983).

Stevenson, Michael, *Celebration at Persepolis* (Bristol, 2008).

Strugnell, E., 'Thea Musa, Roman Queen of Parthia', in *Iranica Antiqua*, 43 (2008): pp. 275–98.

Syme, R., *Tacitus* (Oxford, 1958).

Tahir Gürçağlar, Şehnaz, 'What Paratexts Don't Tell – The Uses of Paratexts in Translation Research', in T. Hermans (ed.), *Crosscultural Transgressions – Research in Translation Studies II – Historical and Ideological Issues* (Manchester, 2002): pp. 44–60.

——— 'Paratexts', in Y. Gambier and L. van Doorslaer (eds): *Handbook of Translation Studies*, vol. 2 (Amsterdam, 2011): pp. 113–16.

Talatoff, Kamran, *The Politics of Writing in Iran: A History of Modern Persian Literature* (Syracuse, 2000).

Tarock, Adam, *Iran's Foreign Policy Since 1990: Pragmatism Supersedes Islamic Ideology* (Commack, NY, 1999).

Tavakoli-Targhi, Mohammad, *Refashioning Iran, Orientalism, Occidentalism and Historiography* (Basingstoke, 2001).

Ter-Oganov, Nugzar, 'Two Iranian authors, Majd os-Saltāneh and Yahyā Dowlātabādi, on Tbilisi', in *Typological Researches*, 4 (2000): pp. 399–408.

Thackston, Wheeler M., 'Translator's Preface', in *The Gulistan of Sa'di* (Maryland, 2008).

——— 'Bibliography of Sa'di's Gulistan', in *The Gulistan of Sa'di* (Maryland, 2008): pp. 182–9.

Thompson, E. A., *The Historical Work of Ammianus Marcellinus* (Cambridge, 1947).

Tortonese, Paolo, 'The Mysteries of Paris' in Franco Moretti (ed.), *The Novel, Volume 2: Forms and Themes* (Princeton, 2006): pp. 181–8.

Trnka, Jamie, *Revolutionary Subjects: German Literatures and the Limits of Aesthetic Solidarity with Latin America* (Berlin, 2015).

Tyma, Adam W., 'This is Sparta! Mediated Mythology as Pedagogy in *300*', in *Journal of Communication Inquiry*, 39 (2015): pp. 5–20.

Upton, J. M., 'Notes on Persian Costumes of the Sixteenth and Seventeenth Centuries,' in *Metropolitan Museum Studies* 2 (1929 to 1930), pp. 206–20.

Vasunia, Phiroze, 'Between East and West: Mobility and Ethnography in Herodotus' Proem', in *History and Anthropology*, 23 (2012): pp. 183–98.

Vaz, Mark Cotta, *Living Dangerously: The Adventures of Merian C. Cooper-the Creator of King Kong* (New York, 2005).

Veer, Peter van deer, 'Hindus: a superior race', in *Nations and Nationalism*, 5 (1999): pp. 419–30.

Venuti, Lawrence, *The Translator's Invisibility – A History of Translation* (London, 2008).

——— (ed.), *The Translation Studies Reader* (London, 2012).

Verstandig, A., *Histoire de l'Empire Parthe (-250/227)* (Brussels, 2001).

Villiers, Gérard de, *Der Schah*, tr. Linda Hollingstedt (Munich, 1975).

Wagenknecht, Maria D., *Constructing Identity in Iranian–American Self-Narrative* (New York, 2015).

Warmington, B. H., 'Ammianus Marcellinus and the Lies of Metrodorus', in *The Classical Quarterly Review, New Series*, 31 (1981): pp. 464–8.

Watson, James A. F., 'Stop, Look, and Listen: Orientalism, Modernity, and the Shah's Quest for the West's Imagination', in *The UBC Journal of Political Studies*, 17 (2015): pp. 22–36.

Widengren, G., 'Sources for Parthian and Sasanian History', in Ehsan Yarshater (ed.), *The Cambridge History of Iran 3 (2): The Seleucid, Parthian and Sasanian Periods* (Cambridge, 1983): pp. 1261–83.

Wiesehöfer, J., 'Iranische Ansprüche an Rom auf ehemals achaimenidische Territorien', in *Archäologische Mitteilungen aus Iran*, 19 (1986): pp. 177–85.

——— *Das antike Persien. Von 550 v. Chr. bis 650 n. Chr.* (Munich/Zürich, 1994).

——— 'Augustus und die Parther', in R. Aßkamp and T. Esch (eds), *Imperium. Varus und seine Zeit* (Münster, 2010): pp. 187–95.

Wilcox, Peter, *Rome's Enemies (3): Parthians & Sassanid Persians* (Oxford, 1986).

Williamson, Clare, 'Safavid Persia Through the Eyes of French Travellers' in John Arnold and Susan Scollay (eds), *Persian Cultural Crossroads* (Melbourne, 2013): pp. 65–75.

Wolski, J., 'Les Achéménides et les Arsacides, Contribution à l'histoire de la formation des traditions iraniennes', in *Syria*, 43 (1966): pp. 65–89.

——— 'Arsakiden und Sasaniden', in R. Stiehl and H. E. Stier (eds), *Beiträge zur Alten Geschichte und deren Nachleben, Festschrift für Franz Altheim zum 6. 10. 1968* (Berlin, 1969): pp. 315–22.

——— 'L'heritage d'Alexandre le Grand et les Arsacides', in W. Will (ed.), *Zu Alexander d. Gr. Festschrift G. Wirth zum 60. Geburtstag am 9. 12. 86* (Amsterdam, 1988): pp. 991–1006.

——— 'Alexandre le Grand: légende et réalité. De l'avènement des Séleucides à la chute des Arsacides', in J.M. Croisille (ed.), *Neronia IV. Alejandro Magno, modelo de los emperadores romanos. Actes du IVe Colloque international de la SIEN, Collection Latomus 209* (Brussels, 1990): pp. 100–9.

——— 'L'Empire des Arsacides', *Acta Iranica 32* (Leuven, 1993): pp. 191–200.

Yarshater, Ehsan, 'Were the Sasanians Heirs to the Achaemenids?' in La Persia nel Medioevo (Rome, 1971): pp. 517–31.

——— 'Iranian National History', in Yarshater, Ehsan (ed.), *The Cambridge History of Iran: Volume 3 (1): The Seleucid, Parthian and Sasanian Periods* (Cambridge, 1983): pp. 359–477.

Yohannan, John D., *The Poet Sa'di – A Persian Humanist* (Lanham, 1987).

Young, David, 'Montesquieu's View of Despotism and His Use of Travel Literature', in *The Review of Politics*, 40 (1978): pp. 392–405.

Zahedi, Farshad, 'Diasporic Space and the Weight of Memory in Films Made by Exilic Iranian Female Directors' to-date unpublished paper, presented at the *Annual Conference of the Italian Society for Middle Eastern Studies (SesaMO)*, 17 March 2016 at the University of Catania.

Zandjani, Nina, 'Translator's Foreword', in Saadi: *Rosenhagen*, tr. Nina Zandjani (Oslo, 2006): pp. 7–10.

——— 'German Translations of Medieval Persian – The Rose Garden of Sa'di', in *Norm-Focused and Culture-related Inquiries in Translation Research*, *Gdansk Studies in Languages series* (Frankfurt am Main, 2016): pp. 63–99.

Zanjani, Ebrahim, Moghad'dameh '[Preface]' in Sanatiyadeh-ye Kermani, *Salahshur* (Tehran, 1933): p. aleph.

Zeller, Bernhard, 'Vorwort', in *Weltliteratur – Die Lust am Übersetzen im Jahrhundert Goethes* (Marbach, 1982): p. 5.

Zia-Ebrahimi, Reza, 'Self-Orientalization and Dislocation: The Uses and Abuses of the "Aryan" Discourse in Iran', in *Iranian Studies*, 44 (2011): pp. 445–72.

——— *The Emergence of Iranian Nationalism: Race and the Politics of Dislocation* (New York, 2016).

Ziegler K. H., Die *Beziehungen zwischen Rom und dem Partherreich. Ein Beitrag zur Geschichte des Völkerrechts* (Wiesbaden, 1964).

Zipoli, Riccardo, 'Poetic Imagery', in Bruijn (ed.), *A History of Persian Literature*, vol. I (London, 2009): pp. 172–232.

Zirinsky, Michael, 'Harbingers of Change: Presbyterian Women in Iran, 1883–1949,' in *American Presbyterians*, 70 (1992): pp. 173–86.

——— 'A Panacea for the Ills of the Country: American Presbyterian Education in Interwar Iran,' in *Iranian Studies*, 26 (1993): pp. 119–37.

——— 'A Presbyterian Vocation to Reform Gender Relations in Iran: The Career of Annie Stocking Boyce,' in Sarah Ansari and Vanessa Martin (eds), *Women, Religion and Culture in Iran* (Surrey, 2002).

Internet Sources

ABC Australia, *Rare Iran screening for controversial film 'Persepolis'* (16 February 2008) available at: http://www.abc.net.au/news/2008-02-16/rare-iran-screening-for-controversial-film/1044548. [Accessed 11 October, 2016].

Interview with the director for Vice Media: http://www.vice.com/video/talking-to-the-star-and-director-of-a-girl-walks-home-alone-at-night-000. [Accessed 26 July 2016].

The Qajar Women Archive: http://www.qajarwomen.org/en/items/1018A43.html to view the manuscript: http://iiif.lib.harvard.edu/manifests/view/drs:44579176$1. [Accessed 28 June 2017].

Quotes for Dilios (Snyder, *300*), *IMDb*, http://www.imdb.com/character/ch0002517/quotes. [Accessed 13 June 2017].

Afkhami, Mahnaz, '"Sunlight, Open Windows, and Fresh Air": The Struggle for Women's Rights in Iran', in *Shirin Neshat: Facing History, a major exhibit on the Iranian artist-in-exile's work*, The Hirshhorn Museum (Washington, DC: 2015). Online at: http://www.mahnazafkhami.net/wp-content/uploads/Proof.Afkhami.Essay_.2.5.15.pdf. [Accessed 5 August 2016].

Ahmadinejad, Mahmoud (2005): Address by H. E. Dr. Mahmood Ahmadinejad President of the Islamic Republic of Iran at the Sixtieth Session of the United Nations General Assembly, 9/14/2005. Available online at http://iran-un.org/en/2005/09/14/14-september-2005/. [Accessed 28 June 2017].

——— (2006): Address by His Excellency Dr. Mahmoud Ahmadinejad President of the Islamic Republic of Iran before the 61st Session of the General Assembly, 9/19/2006. Available online at http://iran-un.org/en/2006/09/19/19-september-2006/. [Accessed 28 June 2017].

——— (2007): Speech on a Missionary Conference in the Holy Month of Ramadhan (In Farsi), 9/6/2007. Available online at http://www.president.ir/fa/print.php?ArtID=10617. [Accessed 28 June 2017].

——— (2008): Address by His Excellency Dr. Mahmoud Ahmadi-Nejad President of the Islamic Republic of Iran before the 63rd Session of the UN General Assembly, 9/23/2008. Available online at http://iran-un.org/en/2008/09/23/23-september-2008/. [Accessed 28 June 2017].

Besant, Annie. *The Pedigree of Man* (1903). Available at www.anandgholap.net/Pedigree_Of_Man-AB.htm. [Accessed 15 June 2016].

Bush, George W. (2002): Address Before a Joint Session of the Congress on the State of the Union, 1/29/2002. Available online at http://www.presidency.ucsb.edu/ws/index.php?pid=29644. [Accessed 28 June 2017].

——— (2003): Address Before a Joint Session of the Congress on the State of the Union, 1/28/2003. Available online at http://www.presidency.ucsb.edu/ws/index.php?pid=29645. [Accessed 28 June 2017].

——— (2004): Address Before a Joint Session of the Congress on the State of the Union, 1/20/2004. Available online at http://www.presidency.ucsb.edu/ws/index.php?pid=29646. [Accessed 28 June 2017].

——— (2005): Address Before a Joint Session of the Congress on the State of the Union, 2/2/2005. Available online at http://www.presidency.ucsb.edu/ws/index.php?pid=58746. [Accessed 28 June 2017].

——— (2008): Address Before a Joint Session of the Congress on the State of the Union, 1/28/2008. Available online at http://www.presidency.ucsb.edu/ws/index.php?pid=76301. [Accessed 28 June 2017].

Dabashi, Hamid. 'Native Informers and the Making of the American Empire'. Al-Ahram Weekly Online, 2007. Available online at http://weekly.ahram.org.eg/Archive/2006/797/special.htm. [Accessed 28 June 2017].

Davar, Vahid, Sayeh-hash, Nahang va, Golestan, Sar-sokhan-e Goftegu ba Ibrahim, *Tuti Mag*, 2016. Available at: http://www.tootimag.com/%D9%85%D8%B7%

D9%84%D8%A8/2069/%DA%AF%D9%8F%D9%84%D9%90%D8%B3%D8%B3%D9%88%D9%86. [Accessed 27 November 2016].

Diba, Layla S., 'CLOTHING x. In the Safavid and Qajar periods', in *Encyclopaedia Iranica*, V/8, pp. 785–808, available online at http://www.iranicaonline.org/articles/clothing-x. [Accessed 28 June 2017].

Fulford, Robert. 'Reading Lolita at Columbia' in *National Post*, 2006. 1 November 2006. Available at: https://www.pressreader.com/canada/national-post-latest-edition/20061101/281913063609343. [Accessed 28 June 2017].

Fynes, R. C. C. 'Müller, Friedrich Max (1823–1900)' (*Oxford Dictionary of National Biography*, 2004). Available at www.oxforddnb.com/view/article/18394. [Accessed 20 April 2016].

Goethe, Johann W., *Noten und Abhandlungen zu besserem Verständnis des West-östlichen Divans* (1819). Available at http://www.wissen-im-netz.info/literatur/goethe/diwan/14.htm. [Accessed 24 September 2015].

Hillmann, Michael, *A Western Take on Jalal Al-e Ahmad (Jalal Al-e Ahmad az Chashme Gharbi), Second Part* (in Persian) available at: http://www.madomeh.com/site/news/news/3176.htm. [Accessed 24 July 2016].

Janmohamad, Shelina Zahra, 'A platform emerges for British Muslim Writers', in *Common Ground News Service: Constructive articles that foster dialogue*, 19 July (2011). Online at: http://www.commongroundnews.org/article.php?id=30086&lan=en&sp=0. [Accessed 4 August 2016].

Jensen, Paul M., 'Cooper, Merian Coldwell' in *American National Biography Online* (2000). Available at www.anb.org/articles/18/18-01970.html. [Accessed 28 June 2017].

Karimi, Meysam, *Naqd va barresi film-e dokhtari dar shab tanha be khane miravad*, available at: http://moviemag.ir/cinema/movie-reviews/world/10166-%D9%86%D9%82%D8%AF-%D9%88-%D8%A8%D8%B1%D8%B1%D8%B3%DB%8C-%D9%81%DB%8C%D9%84%D9%85-%D8%AF%D8%AE%D8%AA%D8%B1%DB%8C-%D8%AF%D8%B1-%D8%B4%D8%A8-%D8%AA%D9%86%D9%87%D8%A7-%D8%A8%D9%87-%D8%AE%D8%A7%D9%86%D9%87-%D9%85%DB%8C-%D8%B1%D9%88%D8%AF-(-A-Girl-Walks-Home-Alone-at-Night-). [Accessed 24 November 2016].

Khakpour, Porochista, 'What I saw at the Revolution', *The Daily Beast*, 2 November 2009, Available at www.thedailybeast.com/articles/2009/02/11/what-i-saw-at-the-revolution.html. [Accessed 28 June 2017].

Khamenei, Ali (2002): Leader's Address to Education Ministry Officials, 7/17/2002. Available online at http://english.khamenei.ir/news/159/Leader-s-Address-to-Education-Ministry-Officials. [Accessed on 27 June 2017].

——— (2003): Leader's Address on New Year's Day, 3/21/2003. Available online at http://english.khamenei.ir/news/133/Leader-s-Address-on-New-Year-s-Day. [Accessed 28 June 2017].

——— (2005a): Leader's Address to a Large Gathering in Mashhad, 3/21/2005. Available online at http://english.khamenei.ir/news/95/Leader-s-Address-to-a-Large-Gathering-in-Mashhad. [Accessed 28 June 2017].

——— (2005b): Leader's Address to Residents of Kerman, 5/1/2005. Available online at http://english.khamenei.ir/news/92/Leader-s-Address-to-Residents-of-Kerman. [Accessed 28 June 2017].

——— (2006): Leader's Speech at the Shrine of Imam Ridha (a.s.), 3/21/2006. Available online at http://english.khamenei.ir/news/1982/Leader-s-Speech-at-the-Shrine-of-Imam-Ridha-a-s. [Accessed 28 June 2017].

——— (2007): Leader's Speech at Imam Ridha's (a.s.) Shrine, 3/21/2007. Available online at http://english.khamenei.ir/news/1656/Leader-s-Speech-at-Imam-Ridha-s-a-s-Shrine. [Accessed 28 June 2017].

——— (2009): Leader's Speech in Mashhad, 3/21/2009. Available online at http://english.khamenei.ir/news/1076/Leader-s-Speech-in-Mashhad. [Accessed 28 June 2017].

——— (2012): Leader's Speech at Imam Ridha's (a.s.) Shrine, 3/20/2012. Available online at http://english.khamenei.ir/news/1620/Leader-s-Speech-at-Imam-Ridha-s-a-s-Shrine. [Accessed 28 June 2017].

——— (2013): Leader's Speech at Imam Ridha's (a.s.) Shrine, 3/21/2013. Available online at http://english.khamenei.ir/news/1760/Leader-s-Speech-at-Imam-Ridha-s-a-s-Shrine. [Accessed 28 June 2017].

——— (2015a): Leader's Speech at the Holy Shrine of Imam Ridha (a.s.), 3/21/2015. Available online at http://english.khamenei.ir/news/2025/Leader-s-Speech-at-the-Holy-Shrine-of-Imam-Ridha-a-s. [Accessed 28 June 2017].

——— (2015b): "Death to America" means death to American, 11/3/2015. Available online at http://english.khamenei.ir/news/2298/Death-to-America-means-death-to-American-policies-and-arrogance. [Accessed 28 June 2017].

Mail Online, '"Our lives aren't like Homeland or Argo!" Instagram's Rich Kids of Tehran claim to show off their £250,000 cars, £10m homes and opulent lifestyles . . . but are they fake?' http://www.dailymail.co.uk/news/article-2916388/Our-lives-aren-t-like-Homeland-Argo-Instagram-s-Rich-Kids-Tehran-250-000-cars-10m-homes-opulent-lifestyles-attack-view-think-ride-camels.html. [Accessed 25 July 2016].

Matin-Asgari, Afshin, 'Confederation of Iranian Students, National Union,' *Encyclopedia Iranica* online (2011). Available online here: http://www.iranicaonline.org/articles/confederation-of-iranian-students. [Accessed 28 June 2017].

Mottahedeh, Negar. 'Off the Grid: Reading Iranian Memoirs in Our Time of Total War' in *Middle East Research and Information Project* online (2004). Available at: http://www.merip.org/mero/interventions/grid. [Accessed 28 June 2017].

——— The Truth of Sex (12 January 2005). Available at: http://iranian.com/Najmabadi/2005/January/Sex/index.html. [Accessed 27 July 2016].

Nayeri, Dina, The Complicated Beauty of the Persian Nose (24 November 2014). Available at: http://www.vice.com/en_uk/read/shes-so-najoor-0000467-v21n10. [Accessed 27 July 2016].

New York Post, 'Meet the "Rich Kids of Tehran"'. http://nypost.com/2014/10/08/rich-kids-of-tehran-instagram-showcases-life-of-iranian-elite/. [Accessed 25 July 2016].

Obama, Barack (2010): Address Before a Joint Session of the Congress on the State of the Union, 1/27/2010. Available online at http://www.presidency.ucsb.edu/ws/index.php?pid=87433. [Accessed 13 June 2017].

——— (2011): Address Before a Joint Session of the Congress on the State of the Union, 1/25/2011. Available online at http://www.presidency.ucsb.edu/ws/index.php?pid=88928. [Accessed 13 June 2017].

——— (2012): Address Before a Joint Session of Congress on the State of the Union, 1/24/2012. Available online at http://www.presidency.ucsb.edu/ws/index.php?pid=99000. [Accessed 13 June 2017].

——— (2013): Address Before a Joint Session of Congress on the State of the Union, 2/12/2013. Available online at http://www.presidency.ucsb.edu/ws/index.php?pid=102826. [Accessed 13 June 2017].

Rachlin, Nahid, 'Interview with Nahid Rachlin', *Červená Barva Press* (2005–6), Available at http://www.cervenabarvapress.com/rachlininterview.htm. [Accessed 13 June 2017].

Rollinger, Robert, 'Xerxes according to Herodotus', Encyclopaedia Iranica, XII/3, pp. 270–6; available online at http://www.iranicaonline.org/articles/herodotus-vii. [Accessed 18 September 2015).

Rouhani, Hassan (2013): Statement by H.E. Dr. Hassan Rouhani President of the Islamic Republic of Iran at the Sixty-Eighth Session of the United Nations General Assembly, 9/24/2013. Available online at http://iran-un.org/en/2013/09/24/24-september-2013-2/. [Accessed 13 June 2017].

——— (2014): Statement by H. E. Dr. Hassan Rouhani, The President of the Islamic Republic of Iran Before the 69th Session of the UN General Assembly, 9/25/2014. Available online at http://iran-un.org/en/2014/09/25/25-september-2014/ [Accessed 13 June 2017].

Weiland, J., 14 March 2007, '*300* Post-Game: One-on-One With Zack Snyder', *Comic Book Resources*, http://www.comicbookresources.com/news/newsitem.cgi?id=9982. [Accessed 13 June 2017].

Filmography

Amini, Hassan, *Decadence and Downfall: The Shah of Iran's Ultimate Party* (2016), BBC4, 75 mins. https://learningonscreen.ac.uk/ondemand/index.php/prog/0C034B79 [Accessed 30 Nov 2016].

Cooper, Merian C. and Schoedsack, Ernest B., *Grass: A Nation's Battle for Life*, Famous Players-Lasky Corporation, Paramount Pictures, USA (1925).

——— *King Kong*, RKO Radio Pictures, USA (1933).

Flaherty, Robert, *Nanook of the North*, Les Freres Revillon, Pathe Exchange, USA/France (1922).

Golestan, Shahrokh, *Flames of Persia* (1971).

Lelouch, Claude, *Iran* (1971).

INDEX